Information Technology
Security & Risk Management

Jill Slay
Andy Koronios

WILEY

John Wiley & Sons Australia, Ltd

Third edition published 2006 by
John Wiley & Sons Australia, Ltd
42 McDougall Street, Milton Qld 4064

Offices also in Sydney and Melbourne

Typeset in 11.5/14 Minion

© Jill Slay, Andy Koronios 2006

National Library of Australia
Cataloguing-in-Publication data

Slay, Jill.
   Information technology security and risk management.

   Includes index.
   ISBN-13 9 78047080 5749.
   ISBN-10 0 470 80574 9.

   1. Computer security. I. Koronios, Andy. II. Title.

   005.8

Cover and internal design images: © Artville; © PhotoDisc, Inc.

Edited by Cathryn Game

Printed in Singapore by
Markono Print Media Pt Ltd

10 9 8 7 6 5 4 3 2 1

About the authors

Dr Jill Slay holds a degree in mechanical engineering, graduate diplomas in applied computing and further education, and a PhD from Curtin University of Technology. Jill spent several years working as an engineer in the UK before beginning a career in applied computing, and spent many years living and working in Asia. She is a member of the Australian Computer Society and the Institute of Electrical and Electronic Engineers and a Certified Information Systems Security Professional. She has extensive teaching experience in the tertiary sector at undergraduate and postgraduate levels and is currently teaching IT security and forensic computing courses in Australia and Asia.

She is a senior lecturer in the School of Computer and Information Science at the University of South Australia and leads the Enterprise Security Management Laboratory in the Advanced Computing Research Centre of the School of Computer and Information Science. She is also an affiliate faculty member at Idaho State University and is a board member of the newly formed Colloquium on Information Systems Security Education — Asia Pacific.

Jill has published five book chapters as well as numerous research papers in such areas as science education, multimedia and intelligent tutoring systems, complex systems and culture, information and electronic commerce security and forensic computing. She is also a member of several editorial boards and conference committees.

Currently, she carries out collaborative research in forensic computing and IT security with industry and government partners in Australia and the USA.

Professor Andy Koronios holds degrees in electrical engineering and education, a Master of Letters and a PhD from the University of Queensland. He has spent a number of years consulting in the IT industry and business management. Andy has extensive computing experience in the commercial environment, especially in small to medium-sized enterprises and was managing director of several enterprises.

He has extensive teaching experience both in the tertiary sector at undergraduate and postgraduate, MBA, DBA and PhD levels as well as in the provision of executive industry seminars. He has also provided professional seminars to IT executives in South-East Asia. In 1995 he was the USQ recipient of the Award of Excellence in Teaching.

He has served in a variety of university management posts, including coordinator of studies, head of program, head of department and head of division, and is currently the Head of School of Computer and Information Science at the University of South Australia.

Andy has published five books and one chapter as well as numerous research papers in such diverse areas as multimedia and online learning systems, information security and data quality, electronic commerce and Web requirements engineering.

Andy has regularly appeared on Australian radio (4QR and Radio National) and television commenting on a variety of issues pertaining to IT.

Currently, he is the research program leader of the Systems Integration and Information Technology Program in the CRC for Integrated Engineering Asset Management. Professor Koronios is the director of Strategic Information (SIM) Laboratory in the Advanced Computing Research Centre of the School of Computer and Information Science at the University of South Australia.

Brief contents

Contents

Preface

Modern society owes a lot to the Internet and related technology. This technology, on one hand, enriches the economic, political and social lives of the global population and on the other hand has rendered the security of communities, businesses and nation states vulnerable. Be it competition among businesses or a full-scale military conflict, new forms of intrusion into information systems and manipulation of information contained in them are being devised by businesses, communities, nation states and even individuals to impose their will on their adversaries.

Until recently, computer security was regarded as a non-productive activity. It was broadly accepted as 'support activity', where keeping back-ups of data was all that was deemed necessary, except for the military and the banking and aerospace industries. However, recent political developments have shown the corporate world that computer security is as important to it as ideological and physical security is to a sovereign country. Natural disaster, wars and terrorist attacks disrupted millions of computer operations and had a telling effect on business execution; in certain cases even on the survival of the business. Businesses have now realised that computer security actually maintains their lifeline and that they cannot afford any breach of computer security. Consequently, they are increasingly endorsing defensive measures to protect their information and information-related resources from breaches of security occurring inside and outside the organisation. However, a fundamental issue with information technology is that its security concerns are evolving alongside the development of technology; therefore it is difficult for a business manager to fully appreciate the scale of the problem at hand.

For this reason, this book provides a comprehensive approach to ensuring computer security. It serves the purpose of being a textbook as well as a reference book. Its intended audience is undergraduate and graduate students as well as practitioners. The layout of this book helps readers in understanding the way various security issues are identified in routine business activities, and it provides recommendations on the tried and tested security controls and safeguards. Although no background knowledge in computer security is necessary, we assume that readers are familiar with basic concepts, such as operating systems, and different communication and hardware architecture.

This book has four major goals. The first and foremost goal is to provide clear and precise understanding of the theory and practice of computer security in the emergent business paradigm. It is essential for business managers to recognise the theoretical underpinnings to computer security, such that they are able to apply best available controls to safeguard capture, exchange and storage of information and information-related resources. Computer security theory presented in the book equips readers to evaluate different security strategies, mechanisms and procedures according to business needs, thereby helping them to make informed decisions about security management. For example, the discussion on security models, such as the lattice and Clark-Wilson models, is followed by the tools and techniques available to implement these models. In this way, security designers not only have an understanding of the available security frameworks but also have an appreciation of the building blocks for their implementation.

The second goal is to provide insights into intranet- as well as extranet-based electronic commerce security issues and their defence, such as secured electronic payment systems, mobile commerce security issues, cryptography and its application to the electronic business environment. The book examines the foundations of network security and looks at system security issues, such as securing information flow by appropriate hardware and software controls, which include routers, firewalls, intrusion detection systems, network separation, operating systems and anti-virus software. Quite appropriately, the book also discusses security risks arising from the use of wireless networks and mobile and wireless devices. This discussion paves the way for understanding and implementing cryptography, under which the book discusses the popular types of cryptographic ciphers and provides comparisons of fundamental symmetric and asymmetric cryptography by looking at common algorithms.

The third goal is to reveal that computer security is not just a collection of technological controls; in fact it is strategic business activity and should be treated as such. The book clearly entails that a technological solution to computer security alone cannot insulate an organisation from security breaches, and therefore a comprehensive security plan must, in addition to technological controls, include security policies and procedures, policies or codes of conduct aimed at educating and enlightening employees on security assurance. These policies and procedures should reflect the business environment, such as elucidating how people within an organisation as well as from outside it gain access to the organisation's information resources. How can employees ensure that their information technology privileges are not abused by themselves or by other unauthorised third parties? What are the confidentiality requirements and provisions that an organisation demands from its employees?

The fourth goal is to provide an understanding of the issues that the public at large is facing from the masking of information semantics and forensics in Australia. Ever since the emergence of the Internet, the general public has been at the risk of being overwhelmed by the many ways in which information could be manipulated for unlawful and unethical purposes. Apart from discussing privacy and fraud issues on the Internet, the book particularly discusses the application of computer technology to the investigation of computer-based crime with a view to providing readers with an understanding of the field of forensic computing. Nevertheless, any discussion on security will be incomplete without touching on its future trends; therefore the book discusses emerging technology and related security issues.

Jill Slay
Andy Koronios
November 2005

Acknowledgements

As teachers, we have made use of ideas workshopped and tested in our undergraduate and postgraduate teaching in writing this book, and we are particularly grateful for the insights shared by many students over the past few years in the School of Computer and Information Science at the University of South Australia. As researchers, we have drawn on concepts developed as part of continuing research projects, particularly those centred in our labs in the Advanced Computing Research Centre. We are particularly grateful to Ben Turnbull, Phil Pudney and Tom Wilsdon, who allowed us to draw on their research, and to Eliud Kamau and Jing Gao, who both supported us in the preparation of this book. Abrar Haider has been of invaluable assistance to Andy.

The author and publisher would like to thank the following copyright holders, organisations and individuals for their permission to reproduce copyright material in this book.

Images

Pp. 8–9: 2004 Australian Computer Crime & Security Survey, page 17, reproduced with the permission of the copyright owner, The University of Queensland trading as AusCert; **p. 24:** 2004 Australian Computer Crime & Security Survey, page 7, reproduced with the permission of the copyright owner, The University of Queensland trading as AusCert; **p. 25:** 2004 Australian Computer Crime & Security Survey, page 8, reproduced with the permission of the copyright owner, The University of Queensland trading as AusCert; **p. 14:** *Business Continuity Management Better Practice, A Guide to Effective Control — January 2000*. Australian National Audit Office, © Commonwealth of Australia reproduced by permission; **p. 147:** Microsoft Corporation; **p. 112:** Symantec, http://securityresponse.symanted.com/avcenter/venc/data/pf/w32.mimail.s@mm.html; **p. 285:** © 2002 World Wide Web Consortium, (Massachusetts Institute of Technology, European Research Consortium for Informatics and Mathematics, Keio University). All rights Reserved http://www.w3org/Consortium/Legal/2002/copyright-documents-20021231.

Text

Pp. 107–9: 2004 Australian Computer Crime & Security Survey, page 21, reproduced with the permission of the copyright owner, The University of Queensland trading as AusCert; **p. 70:** appears on Link: http://www.acs.org.au/about_acs/acsregs.htm#nr4, © 2003 Australian Computer Society Inc. reproduced with permission; **p. 80:** Reproduced by kind permission of The Australian Copyright Council. Appears on link http://www.copyright.org.au/publications/G056.pdf; **p. 81:** Reproduced with kind permission of The Australian Copyright Council, www.copyright.org.au; **p. 77:** Guidelines for companies about avoiding spam/Department of Communications, Information Technology and the Arts and Australian Communications Authority 2004. available at: www.acma.go.au, © Commonwealth of Australia reproduced by permission; **pp. 218–19:** Bill Goodwin, Computer Weekly.com, 22 March, 2005. Appears on link: www.computerweekly.com/Articla137434.htm#; **p. 293:** by Bill Goodwin, Computer Weekly.com, 21 September 2004. Appears on Link: www.computerweekly.com/Articles/2004/09/20/205302/Webserviceslooksettobethenextbigrisk.htm; **p. 110:** Craig Valli © 2002; **p. 71:** (ISC)_, http://www.isc2.org/cgi/content.cgi?page=31; **pp. 33–5:** Johnson & Johnson tackles security pain, by Ellen Messmer, Network World, 03/14/05; **pp. 302–4:** Web services you can bank on, by Beth Schultz, Network World, 12/27/04; **pp. 331–3:** Risks rise as factory nets go wireless, by Phill Hochmuth, Network World, 03/14/05; **pp. 207–8:** *Waikato Times*, October 21st, 2004. Appears on link: http://www.smh.com.au/articles/2004/10/21/1097951802576.htm.

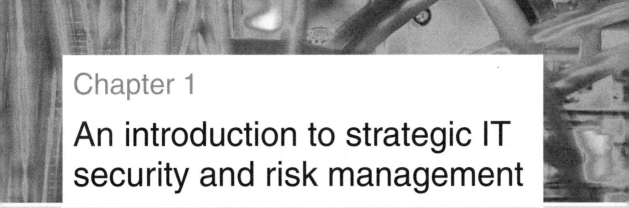

Chapter 1

An introduction to strategic IT security and risk management

Learning objectives

After studying this chapter, you should be able to:

- outline the risk management process

- explain business continuity management

- explain IT governance

- explain the importance of IT security and risk management

- discuss the role of IT in the business environment

- outline the types of risk that can threaten IT systems

- discuss the types of control that can be implemented to prevent
  or correct IT risk events

- explain the actions required to sustain the IT risk
  management strategy

- discuss the essential elements of an IT continuity plan

- explain how the business can ensure that its security
  and risk management strategy is followed.

Chapter overview

Modern information and communication technology has opened new opportunities for businesses in the areas of automation, interconnectivity and e-commerce as well as enabling the development of entirely new products and services. At the same time the adoption of this technology has exposed businesses to new risks — ranging from fires and floods to cyber criminals and cyber terrorists — that need to be managed. This chapter will look at the risk management process, which assesses the risks facing a business and designs steps to minimise those risks and to help the business recover should an adverse event occur. We will then look at business continuity management, which focuses on the business's plan to deal with those risks that have the potential to prevent it from achieving its key business objectives. Together, risk management and business continuity management form a complementary approach to protecting the business. An obligation under IT governance is to mitigate the IT risks facing the business. IT plays an integral part in today's businesses, and the risks affecting IT processes must be identified and managed to reduce the organisation's vulnerability. This is the core theme of this book. IT security and risk management are not ends in themselves; they are employed to support the overall business objectives.

Using a risk management framework, we will examine the IT risks, focusing particularly on the business context of IT, the types of risk that can threaten IT systems, the steps businesses can take to reduce their risks and the things that need to be done to maintain an IT security and risk management strategy. We will then look at the essential elements of an IT continuity plan.

Strategies and plans are useful only if they are implemented and adhered to. We will look at ways in which the business should go about ensuring that its IT security and risk management strategy is properly used. Finally, we will outline the key IT security issues that will be discussed throughout the rest of this book.

Risk management

Risk management is an ongoing process designed to assess the likelihood of an adverse event occurring, implement measures to reduce the risk that such an event will occur and ensure the organisation can respond in such a way as to minimise the consequences of the event (ANAO 2000). A risk is any event that has the potential to prevent the business achieving its objectives. In Australia and New Zealand, Australian Standard/New Zealand Standard 4360 'Risk Management' provides a framework to identify, analyse, assess, treat and monitor risks. HB 231 'Information security risk management guidelines' provides guidance specific to information security risk management.

An appropriate risk management process involves the following steps (AS/NZS 4360; HB 231; ANAO 2000):

- *Establish the organisational and risk management context.* This step defines the business objectives and the key business processes and resources that support those objectives.
- *Identify, analyse and evaluate significant business risks.* This step involves several actions:
  - It seeks first to *identify* the risks a business might face. Risks can be external or internal. External risks include: political, legal and administrative changes; economic and market changes; natural events and disasters; and technological factors, such as infrastructure failures or hacking. Internal risks can be strategic or operational in nature (ANAO 2000).
  - The risk *analysis* assesses the likelihood of each identified event occurring and the consequences given the current controls in place. It determines which risks are acceptable and which are not, on the basis of their effect on the business's outputs, resources, reputation, legal compliance and continuity.
  - The risk *evaluation* ranks the risks to establish the relative priority of managing each risk.
- *Design and implement preventive and corrective controls.* Responses to risks include accepting the risk, controlling the risk and transferring the risk. The controls could be aimed at stopping the risk from occurring (called preventive controls) or at minimising the consequences should the preventive controls fail and the event occurs (corrective controls). This step designs these controls and puts them in place. The business continuity plan, described on pp. 27–9, is one of the corrective controls.
- *Monitor and review the risks and controls.* Risk management is an iterative process. The business must regularly review the strategic and operational risks it faces and test and modify the controls to ensure that they effectively deal with changes to the risks.

Risk management requires the investment of resources (time, money and effort) to prepare the organisation for unforeseen circumstances. There will always be a trade-off between the resources invested against the risks faced and the probability that they will eventuate. Some risks threaten the continuity of the business's operations. Risks of this scale must be effectively managed. Hence business continuity management (discussed below) is an integral part of the risk management process. It prepares the business for when the preventive controls — implemented as part of the risk management process — have failed.

Business continuity management

Business strategies are based on the presumption that the business will continue to operate into the future. Any event that disrupts the continuation of business operations has significant consequences for the business and directly affects its ability to accomplish its objectives and those of its stakeholders. It can cost revenue, reputation, investor confidence and customer loyalty. Business continuity requires that the resources supporting the essential business activities are always available. Clearly, then, **business continuity management (BCM)** is a broad concept that covers the entire business and so it must encompass information technology. The concept of BCM is receiving increasing attention from the business world. BCM is part of risk management. In theory BCM:

- identifies those risks that have the potential to interrupt the normal course of business operations
- implements preventive controls to prevent the occurrence of such risks
- develops corrective controls for coping should the preventive controls fail and the risk eventuates (ANAO 2000).

The overlap with risk management is obvious, but whereas risk management is concerned with all of the potential risks that face a business and their likelihood of occurring, business continuity management is concerned just with those events that have the potential to interrupt the achievement of the business's objectives. The likelihood of their occurring is only relevant in determining the cost–benefit trade-off of controls. It prepares for all risks to business continuity, regardless of the likelihood of their eventuating. Any other approach leaves the business vulnerable should the unlikely occur (even if very unlikely). The scope of business continuity extends beyond the enterprise: it also considers external risks arising from political, economic and natural changes in the business environment, making use of such business tools as a SWOT (strengths, weaknesses, opportunities, threats) analysis.

The business continuity management process involves (ANAO 2000; Savage 2002):

- *Initiation.* This step establishes the objectives, personnel and responsibilities, budget and schedule. It recognises that the business is not in complete control of its environment and will in all likelihood one day face a threat to its continuity (Smith 2003).
- *Identification of key business processes.* This step identifies what resources and activities are essential to support the strategic, operational and support processes that produce the outputs that fulfil the key business objectives. It also ranks each business process according to its importance in achieving the business objectives.
- *Business impact analysis.* This step determines the impact on the business should a business process be disrupted. It establishes the maximum tolerable downtime for each business process and hence the priority for recovering those processes should an adverse event occur. Jordan and Musson (2003) report that 46 per cent of Australian government organisations believe they need to recover their critical services in less than eight hours in order to ensure that their business objectives are not threatened. A further 15 per cent believe they need to resume operations within 24 hours.

- *Planning and implementation of continuity controls.* This step designs controls
  to reduce the consequences should an adverse event occur and to help the
  business recover. This step involves the creation and implementation of
  the **business continuity plan**, which is a clearly defined and documented
  strategy and set of processes, designed to ensure the recovery of key business
  processes when an event threatens business continuity (Jordan & Musson
  2003). The plan should encompass alternative arrangements to cope with
  the loss of human resources (staff), physical facilities (such as buildings),
  telecommunications, information systems and of course business activities.
- *Testing and maintenance of the plan.* The plan should be regularly tested at the
  functional and business levels and amended as required to ensure it works.
  As far as possible, business partners, suppliers and distributors should
  be involved in this exercise. The business disruptions resulting from the
  terrorist attacks in the USA on 11 September 2001 taught businesses and
  other organisations that they must significantly expand the scope of their
  contingency plan testing to ensure that they can cope with the unforeseen
  (Vitiello & Kuhn 2002). Business managers must realise that a business
  continuity plan has to be a continuous project. Its cost is a premium the
  organisation must pay to protect itself (Swartz 2003).

Business continuity planning should not be confused with disaster recovery.
Often used in relation to IT, 'disaster recovery' refers to the recovery of the organisation after some unplanned and massive disruption (i.e. a disaster). Business
continuity, on the other hand, aims to maintain the availability of all business
resources and processes as well as their support resources and business activities (ANAO 2000). It builds resilience and the capacity for an effective response
(CMI 2003).

The business continuity plan is of course crucial, but the actual process of
creating the plan is also of immense value (Savage 2002). Each part of an organisation should 'own' and be accountable for its business risk, ensuring that its
part of the business continuity plan is up to the task (Smith 2003).

Business continuity and IT

The Chartered Institute of Management (CMI 2003) conducts a regular survey
to identify factors that managers believe could disrupt the operation of their
organisations. Loss of IT capacity consistently tops the list. It is an area of major
concern for business. In 2003, 82 per cent of the businesses surveyed that had a
business continuity plan included IT in their business continuity plan. However,
according to research for Meta Group (Greiner & Evans 2003), only one in five
of the world's top 2000 organisations (based on sales, assets, market value and
profits) has an effective business continuity plan.

IT governance

IT governance is concerned with two main tasks: delivering value to business through IT and mitigating the IT risks that could be faced (ITGI 2003). The second of these tasks will be the focus of much of this book. It must be remembered, however, that this second task is a necessary part of achieving the first — of delivering value.

As organisations increasingly derive value from intangibles, such as information, expertise and intellectual property, IT has become central to competitive advantage and business success. This same change, however, has made organisations more vulnerable than when businesses relied more on tangibles. Recent research suggests that sound IT governance can shield the organisation from such vulnerability, leading to enhanced security, better overall organisational outcomes and higher return on investment.

IT governance is part of the wider concept of corporate governance. **Corporate governance** principles are designed to ensure that the decisions made in an organisation align with the corporate vision, values and strategy. Such principles are a significant component of corporate accountability. A series of major corporate collapses since the late 1990s, combined with increasingly educated and assertive stakeholders, has made corporate governance an issue of major concern. Regulations establish board responsibilities and require that a board of directors exercise due diligence. Investors appear willing to pay a premium of more than 20 per cent for shares in businesses that have sound governance practices in place (McKinsey & Company 2000).

There is little doubt that senior management understands the influence that IT can have on organisational success (or failure). IT governance places responsibility on the board and executive management team to put the right mechanisms, systems, structures and standards in place to ensure that IT strategy operates in harmony with the vision and strategy of the wider organisation. In terms of security and risk management, it places the responsibility on senior management to ensure that effective control frameworks are in place and are followed. IT governance is not an isolated discipline; it is an integral part of overall corporate governance. The need for this integration is similar to the need for IT to be an integral part of the organisation rather than something practised in remote corners or separate from the rest of the business. Overall responsibility for IT governance rests with the board of directors, but in practice it takes place at multiple levels, from the board, to the chief information officer (CIO) and on to other IT executives. Localised aspects of corporate IT functions, such as customer relations and technical support, can still be decentralised to local IT managers. Those IT managers are still of course required to operate within the corporate IT strategic objectives and the overall requirements of sound corporate governance, and these responsibilities need to be specified and, in turn, their accomplishment appraised.

The organisation will need to establish the extent to which it centralises or decentralises security. In **centralised security**, an administrator provides access to information, software applications and the network. This policy could cause delays because one person or team has to process all requests. In **distributed security**, managers, team leaders or supervisors decide and grant access to information and applications. This model speeds up the process, but managers and supervisors need to have a clear understanding of secure practices.

IT governance should be effective, transparent and accountable. The IT Governance Institute (ITGI 2003) suggests the critical elements of IT governance are effectiveness in the following areas:
- alignment with the business strategy
- delivery of value
- management of risk
- management of resources
- measurement of performance.

The IT Governance Institute has developed a set of open standard IT governance guidelines: the *Control Objectives for Information and related Technology* (COBIT®), which it recommends businesses use to ensure that they implement effective IT governance. It is one of several IT governance documents produced by various organisations.

IT managers find that they have much more influence at the senior executive and board level as a result of implementing IT governance strategies. An IT governance study by PricewaterhouseCoopers found that 76 per cent of the 335 CEOs and CIOs surveyed were aware of IT problems that could be overcome if a formal IT governance committee was in place. However, 42 per cent said they had no plans to establish such a committee, owing to the costs involved and training that would be required (Hoffman 2004).

Strategic IT security and risk management

IT security is certainly a key area for risk management in modern organisations. IT has become a fundamental and integral part of most business processes, and so the reliance on businesses for IT systems has grown.

An **IT security risk** exists whenever there is a chance that an IT asset could be adversely affected by some event. The aim of IT security is to ensure that the IT system can deliver:
- *confidentiality:* information is available only to those authorised to view and use it
- *integrity:* the information and any changes to it are accurate and complete
- *availability:* the information can be accessed and used when needed.

The security of information and IT systems must be high on the strategic agenda of every business. As we will see, there are a multitude of security threats and concerns, both internal and external to an organisation. These range from hackers to 'professional' computer criminals, natural disasters such as floods, accidents, mistakes and strategic errors. All of these can cost the organisation significantly in terms of lost productivity and lost confidence. It is therefore extremely important for the business to have an integrated approach to the prevention, detection and management of IT risks from all possible threats and the exploitation of all vulnerability. IT Risk 1.1 reviews the scope of the IT security challenge facing businesses today.

IT risk 1.1

IT security incidents in Australia

A survey of Australian businesses (Jordan & Musson 2003) found that 54 per cent had experienced interruptions to their usual business owing to an IT incident. Twelve agencies in the survey reported stoppages of four hours or longer. The most common cause of the unscheduled stoppages was computer failure, followed by telecommunications failure. The 2004 Australian Computer Emergency Response Team (AusCERT) Computer Crime and Security Survey found that 49 per cent of respondents had experienced electronic attacks that affected data or system confidentiality, integrity or availability.

A number of studies (including AusCERT) have found that the number of attacks on businesses has increased in recent years. The 2001 CSI/FBI study (cited in Cooper 2002) found that as many as 85 per cent of businesses in the USA experience some kind of IT security breach each year and that many experience multiple breaches. According to a study by Exodus Communications, such breaches account for more than US$200 billion in annual losses.

Figure 1.1 shows the percentage of Australian organisations surveyed by AusCERT in 2004 that experienced electronic attacks or IT misuse.

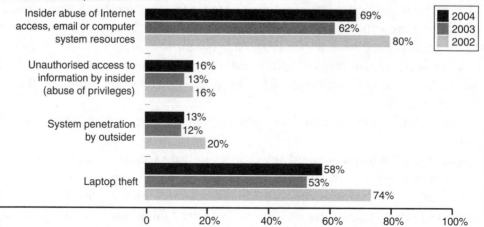

Information Technology Security & Risk Management

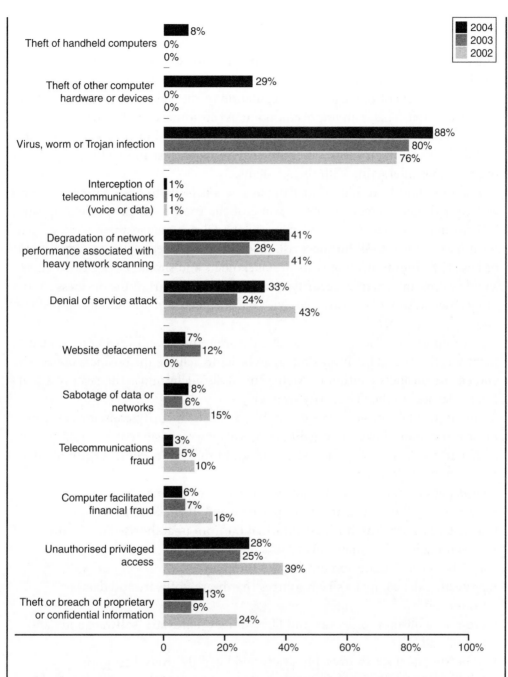

Figure 1.1   **Incidence of electronic attack or IT misuse**

Source: AusCERT 2004, p. 17.

It is reasonably easy to calculate the dollar cost of downtime caused by disruptions or security breaches. This might be a few dollars for a small business or millions of dollars for a bank or an airline. It is not so easy to estimate the legal liability when information is lost or compromised. Nor is it simple to quantify the important effects of damage to the reputation of the business and stakeholders' confidence in it. This is an important point. As customers and partners are asked increasingly to use IT in their dealings with businesses, businesses must ensure that their IT security measures are sufficient to create trust among the people and organisations interacting with their systems.

It is important to recognise that the business is likely to have a broader overarching risk management strategy. Some of the specific IT risks might already be controlled by that strategy. Conversely, the IT risk management strategy will form part of the overall business risk management strategy. The strategy should be based on communication with all stakeholders and should be documented. In simple words, information security strategy, which is a part of the business continuity strategy, should be consistent with the business direction and its immediate and long-term goals.

It is important to achieve management commitment and direction. Management sets the overall business strategy in order to achieve the business objectives and ensure business continuity. Management also determines the resources that can be devoted to the IT security strategy.

An effective IT security strategy requires a holistic security-conscious environment throughout the entire organisation, whereby management is committed to safeguarding the security of IT assets and the business as a whole is committed to achieving the following:
- ensuring stakeholders' confidence and trust in the business
- maintaining the confidentiality of personal and financial information
- safeguarding sensitive business information from unauthorised disclosure
- preventing illegal or malicious attacks on IT resources (hardware, software and data) from inside and outside the company
- protecting the company's IT resources (hardware, software and data) from misuse
- protecting business processes and IT resources (hardware, software and data) from fraud
- protecting the IT resources, physically and logically, from disruption
- fulfilling the legislative and regulatory requirements of the society in which the business operates
- creating a responsible work culture that promotes quality and security consciousness and curtails hostile and antagonistic employee behaviour.

Business managers needs to promote the risk management strategy and the preventive and corrective controls to all the stakeholders to ensure that the security strategy is implemented correctly. A plan, policy or strategy is not useful if it is ignored.

We will now look at the IT security and risk management process, using the risk management framework discussed earlier in the chapter.

IT security context

In exploring the IT security context, it is important to identify those parts of the IT system that support the key business activities, which in turn support the overall business strategy. This will generally include hardware, software and data, human resources, buildings and other facilities, and infrastructure, such as telecommunications and power.

Modern information and communication technology presents business organisations with new opportunities and challenges. Among other things, it provides for:

- new products and services based on information and knowledge
- better connectivity with business partners (e.g. suppliers and distributors)
- automation — and hence increased productivity and efficiency — of business processes (e.g. manufacturing, customer support and data capture)
- access to new markets through e-commerce.

As the level of business process automation is increasing, so is the dependence on information flows to realise business processes. Today, businesses increasingly rely on information to create value in what has been called the 'knowledge economy' or 'information economy'. Even businesses that do not produce explicit information as their output usually rely heavily on tacit information to conduct their business activities. Information should be seen as a fundamental building block of business operations. The confidentiality, integrity and availability of IT systems (including hardware, software, data and human resources) must be protected.

The interconnectivity of businesses has created a situation in which businesses come together — sometimes briefly, sometimes permanently — to interact to achieve their goals. This interconnectivity has reached a point where 'global networks of instrumental exchanges selectively switch on and off individuals, groups, regions and even countries, according to their relevance in fulfilling the goals processed in the network, in a relentless flow of strategic decisions' (Castells 2000, p. 3). In the current environment of intimate interconnections among different organisations in the supply chain, any disruption to one component is instantly felt by all the other components of the supply chain. It must be recognised, then, that a business cannot secure itself by looking only at its own systems. It is exposed to the vulnerability of the external systems with which it interacts. Hence it is only as secure as the weakest of its partners. It must ensure that all of its suppliers and other partners have adequate protection so that the business will continue to operate.

A modern business can have a large number of different systems, operating in different ways and having multiple points and modes of access. Such systems generate large amounts of data in often disparate repositories or 'pools'. Many businesses store their most valuable data electronically. This situation creates an extremely complex information infrastructure that must be carefully managed and controlled.

E-commerce has emerged as a major business model since the mid-1990s. It has brought many opportunities for businesses but also a number of risks that must be managed. IT Risk 1.2 discusses e-commerce and some of the risks — technological and otherwise — that it raises.

A business should assess its environment, including financial, operational, competitive, political, legal, social and cultural factors. It should assess the objectives of its stakeholders (employees, shareholders, customers, suppliers and so on). It is important, too, to recognise that IT systems and the business environment are constantly changing, so the business must continually monitor and revise its IT security context.

IT security risks

Once the IT security context is established, the IT security risks should be *identified*, *analysed* and *evaluated*. IT risks can take many forms. For example, the business's headquarters could be destroyed by fire or its customer database could be accessed and modified by a hacker. On the other hand, many risks are small in scale and relatively mundane, but still costly for the individual business affected. They could be a burst water pipe, a backhoe digging up a communications cable or simply a staff member dropping a hard disk drive and destroying its contents. Poor procedures for choosing and maintaining hardware and software are another risk.

Identification

The identification of IT security risks is crucial. The organisation should take a methodical approach to identifying all risks that can affect its IT assets owing to *vulnerability* in the IT system. It should include the risks under the organisation's control and those beyond the organisation's control. It should also examine how each risk might eventuate, which helps to inform the decision about how to control the risk. Any risk overlooked at this stage will be overlooked by the later steps in the risk management strategy. Any documented incidents of IT security breaches should of course be examined as part of this step.

IT risks can include among other things: corruption of data; employee error or deliberate sabotage; damage to physical facilities or infrastructure; industrial espionage or sabotage; terrorist activity; hacking; viruses, worms, Trojans; non-compliance with corporate governance, regulatory or legal obligations of the company; and natural disasters such as fire, floods and earthquakes. Figure 1.2 categorises the internal (strategic and operational) and external

IT security and e-commerce

Commerce in any form cannot take place unless there is mutual trust between the parties involved. In a simple, physical marketplace, people can use their intuition and their ability to read subtle and indirect cues to judge a potential business transaction. The customer can also rely on the reputation of the other party. In addition, a customer can expect that the vendor will act in such a way as to preserve their reputation. Beyond trust, traders rely on laws to enforce reasonable standards in transactions. Nevertheless, dishonest and disreputable business practices do still occur.

Consider some of the differences between the traditional bricks-and-mortar–based commerce models and the cyber-based e-commerce models. In engaging in e-commerce, the customer deals with a computer interface and cannot rely on making an intuitive judgement as to the integrity of the vendor, the vendor might be more or less anonymous, the customer might not easily refer to others about the vendor's reputation and the vendor is not necessarily operating in the same legal jurisdiction as the customer. In any case, pursuing a legal remedy can be complicated and expensive. Another characteristic of e-commerce is the need to provide personal details, such as credit card numbers and mailing addresses. This is not very different from traditional commerce, but combined with the anonymity of the vendor it does raise concerns about privacy and fraud for many people.

The consequence of these special characteristics of e-commerce is that vendors face a much more difficult task in establishing trust with customers. One way to do so is to have secure systems. Security is also important for protecting the business's assets. E-commerce, however, has some characteristics that make security more difficult.

Many businesses have chosen to use the Internet as the medium for exchanging crucial business information, both with other parts of the organisation and with external parties (e.g. customers and suppliers). Most large businesses and government agencies have a web presence, providing potential hackers with an obvious starting point for launching an attack against the organisation's wider IT systems: web servers, routers, switches, desktop computers and data. The Internet, although cheap, has significant security weaknesses. Further, many organisations use commercial software that is known to have security flaws and can be studied in detail by potential hackers. Many organisations and consumers are also quick to adopt new technology (such as web-enabled mobile phones), much of which has immature security. Computers are fast and tireless. Criminals can mount attacks from a single PC against an IT system anywhere in the world.

E-commerce security will be discussed in detail in chapter 8.

(political/regulatory, environmental/natural, economic/market and technological) risks a business can face. Risks can also be categorised according to whether they are naturally occurring or initiated by humans. *Naturally occurring* threats (so-called 'acts of God') include fire, floods, earthquakes and volcanic activity, tidal waves, cyclones and lightning strikes. Any of these can damage or destroy the IT assets of an organisation or the external infrastructure on which the organisation depends. *Human-initiated threats* may be inadvertent and accidental or may be intentional and deliberate. Accidental threats include mistakes made by employees that can affect hardware, software or data. Intentional threats include hacking, the acts of disgruntled employees, extortion, cyber crime and hoaxes.

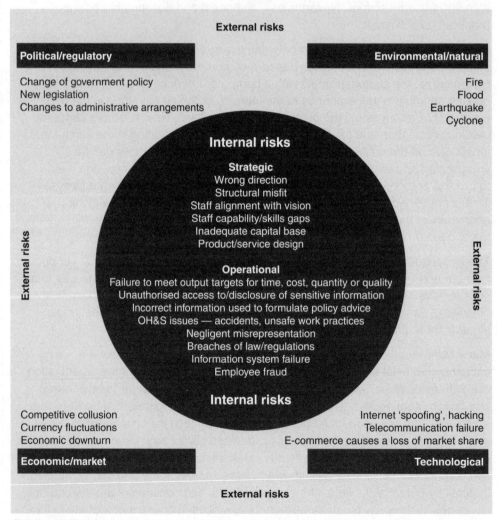

Risk may arise both from external sources and internally — emanating from within the organisation and arising from its strategic and operational processes.

| Figure 1.2 | IT risks |

Source: Australian National Audit Office (ANAO) 2000, p. 20.

Much of the focus in this book will be on more obviously technological risks, but it must be remembered that all risks should be managed. A firewall is of little use if the IT server room is flooded. A secure website for e-commerce will not succeed if the company is offering products the market does not want to buy. Therefore it is essential to consider all of the various types of risk identified in figure 1.2.

Analysis

Once identified, the risks can be analysed to determine which risks are acceptable and which are not. This also helps establish how to control risks. The analysis should examine the source of each risk, the consequences should the risk eventuate and the likelihood of the risk eventuating. In doing so, it examines the value of each asset in relation to achieving the business objectives and the effectiveness of controls already in place.

Evaluation

IT security risks should be evaluated on the basis of the *likelihood* of the risk eventuating and the *consequences* should it eventuate (i.e. what damage the event would do to the business). Combining these two factors will given an overall risk assessment that can be used to prioritise the management of the risks. Those risks that are relatively likely to occur and to have grave consequences would receive the highest priority; those unlikely to occur and with minor consequences would receive the lowest priority.

Once ranked, some risks might be considered acceptable. Others will need to be controlled. Some might be able to be transferred (e.g. through insurance or a joint venture).

Common IT security risks

We will briefly examines some examples of common IT risks. The discussion is by no means exhaustive. We will look at these and more in greater detail throughout the book. For now it will be useful to have an appreciation of the breadth of issues that must be considered.

Hacking

Hackers generally fall into one of two broad categories: *targeted attackers* or *attackers of opportunity*. Although targeted attackers represent only a small proportion of hackers, they are by far the more dangerous threat (Spitzner 2003, p. 25). Spitzner argues that targeted attackers attack only systems of high value. As Potter (2003) suggests, targeted attackers are most likely to attack a network or system that contains valuable information, such as financial information or trade secrets. The pay-off for breaking into the information resources of homes or small offices is too small to justify the effort. Attackers of opportunity operate differently.

Their goal is to intrude into as many systems as possible with the least effort (Spitzner 2003, p. 14).

Attackers can be motivated by any of numerous goals. The US Federal Bureau of Investigation describes the motives of criminals using the acronym MICE, which stands for Money, Ideology, Compromise and Ego (Spitzner 2003; Kilger, Ofir & Stutzman 2004). An adaptation of this acronym, MEECES, for Money, Ego, Entertainment, Cause, Entrance to a social group and Status, was conceived by Kilger, Ofir and Stutzman (2004) to explain the motives of criminals operating in the electronic sphere.

Edney and Arbaugh (2004, pp. 22–7) use a pyramid (see figure 1.3) to illustrate the motives of hackers. At the bottom of the pyramid are people with relatively weak tools. Higher up the pyramid are far fewer people, but they have much more sophisticated and powerful tools. At the bottom of the pyramid are people with too much time on their hands or 'script kiddies', who use tools sourced from others. In the middle of the pyramid are those motivated by profit or revenge. At the top are the attackers motivated by ego.

Attackers driven by ego are out to prove themselves and to gain status or social promotion within their peer group. They are motivated by the difficulty of the task. Ego attackers constitute the smallest number of attackers, but should be considered dangerous since they possess the expertise and sophisticated tools to breach a target's security successfully.

Attackers driven by profit or revenge aim to steal information, damage systems because of a grievance with the target organisation or alter data to acquire some tangible reward. For example, they might use blackmail to extort money from an organisation, they might steal financial information or they might be a disgruntled employee. Attackers motivated by these goals have specific motives and objectives and are prepared to spend time and money to achieve them. We will revisit this topic in chapter 4.

Finally, some people attack systems for entertainment or because they have too much time on their hands. They gamble their time and effort in the hope of a pay-off through a successful attack. Often, attackers of this sort have little understanding of IT security. Instead they download scripts to carry out their attacks; hence the term 'script kiddies'. Quite often, if any security is present, the attacker will move on. These people constitute the greatest percentage of attackers.

Honey pots are an effective way to study attackers to determine their motives. A honey pot is a system that appears to be an interesting target to hackers, but actually gathers data about them. In 2000 the Honeynet Project set up a honey pot to study the 'motivation and psychology of the black-hat community'. In a paper titled 'Know your enemy: Motives' (Honeynet Project 2000), they describe how a honey pot was compromised and the intruder installed an IRC (Internet Relay Chat) bot. (A 'bot', short for robot, is an automated client that monitors an IRC chatroom.) The intruder's compromise of the honey pot was logged, while two weeks worth of chats from the IRC bot were also captured. The full details of the intrusion and the captured chat logs can be read in their paper, which provides a fascinating insight into the motives of and methods used by attackers.

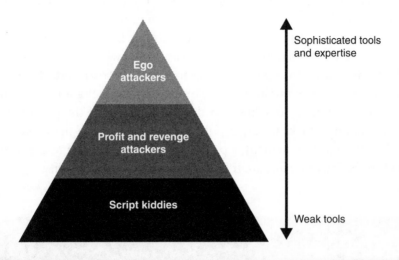

| Figure 1.3 | The hacker motivation pyramid |

Source: based on information from Edney & Arbaugh 2004, pp. 22–7.

Malicious code or malware

'Malicious code' or 'malware' is software written for some nefarious purpose. It is generally a virus, worm or Trojan. A virus replicates itself by attaching itself to other code. A worm propagates itself through penetration of networks and computers. A 'Trojan', as the name suggests, is software that appears to do something harmless but has some other hidden function. Viruses, worms and Trojans are the most common threat to corporate IT systems. Most businesses use virus shields (or antivirus software) to protect their systems. Despite this, viruses, worms and Trojans were responsible for 45 per cent of losses related to IT security among the respondents to the 2004 AusCERT survey. Ninety per cent of North American companies that responded to a survey by IDC reported that they had been considerably affected by viruses (Gorrio 2002). For example, in 2003, the Slammer worm caused severe problems in the performance of the Bank of America's network of automatic teller machines (PITAC 2005). The US Department of Defense took some of its network off the Internet to prevent infection from the Code Red worm. Unfortunately, the same system was used to control the locks on the Mississippi River, so they were disabled (PITAC 2005).

Because new viruses continually emerge, a virus shield will always be outdated and ultimately inadequate. Training staff to avoid exposing the business to viruses is another approach, but it is also open to failure. We will look at malware in some more detail in chapter 4.

Terrorism

The terrorist attacks on the USA on 11 September 2001 thrust the risk of business disruption owing to terrorist activity into the spotlight. It must be remembered, however, that terrorist activity has accounted for very few business disruptions. It is more often broken cables, fire and power outages that cause problems. In fact, a survey by a British newspaper found that London companies were 40 times more likely to suffer business interruptions owing to mistakes made by their plumbing contractor than they were to suffer a terrorist attack (BT 2003).

On the other hand, terrorism is not a threat that can be ignored. The incident in IT Risk 1.3 is cited around the world as an example of the potential for terrorist or malicious attacks to target public infrastructure via the IT systems that control it. Although the incident is probably better thought of as environmental vandalism rather than terrorism, it does demonstrate vulnerability.

IT risk 1.3
It's not just a theoretical risk

The Maroochy Shire Council on Queensland's Sunshine Coast was experiencing some problems with its new wastewater IT system. Communications sent by radio link between wastewater pumping stations were being lost, pumps were not working properly and the alarms installed to alert staff of the faults were not going off.

Initially it was thought there were teething problems with the new system. Eventually an engineer began to monitor every signal passing through the system and discovered that someone was hacking in and deliberately causing the problems. In time the perpetrator was located, arrested and jailed.

A former contractor used a laptop computer and a radio transmitter to take control of 150 sewage pumping stations. Over a three-month period, he released a million litres of untreated sewage into a stormwater drain, which in turn flowed to local waterways. The court commented that the attack on the system was motivated by revenge after the contractor failed to secure a job with the council.

This case is used widely around the world as a demonstration of the potential for damage should IT systems be insecure (e.g. it was cited in the US President's Information Technology Advisory Committee report on the efficiency of technical approaches to IT security). At the time it was the only known successful attack on a data control system linked to public infrastructure.

Sources: US President's Information Technology Advisory Committee (PITAC) 2005; Hughes 2003; 'Queensland cyber attack smells of vulnerability', *The World Today*, ABC Local Radio transcript, 2 November 2001.

Extortion

Extortion occurs when payment is demanded in return for not attacking a business. A poll of 100 US companies in 2004 found that 17 had been targeted by cyber extortionists (Carnegie Mellon University–Information Week in PITAC 2005).

Human resources

People often prove to be the weakest link in IT security. More and more, people interact with IT systems as employees, customers or business partners. An otherwise secure IT system can be easily compromised if those who interact with the system do not follow secure practices. Most of us know people who write their computer log-on passwords on a Post-It note stuck to their computer monitor or who carry their PIN in their wallet, a few millimetres from their bank card, or who leave their computer logged on and accessible while they go to lunch. Many people bypass security measures because they are inconvenient.

Another human resource threat relates to misuse of IT resources. Businesses don't like to publicise IT problems caused by employees, former employees, or (as in IT Risk 1.3) contractors, but damage from insiders' actions, whether deliberate or unintentional, is a significant problem. After viruses, worms and Trojans, laptop theft and misuse of IT resources at work are the most costly IT security problems for Australian businesses (AusCERT 2004).

Infrastructure failures

Businesses are heavily dependent on basic infrastructure, including the power supply, water supply, fuel supply, telecommunications, administrative buildings, transport network, rescue services and other commercial organisations, such as banks, stock exchanges and currency exchanges. Such infrastructure can be damaged or destroyed during war, as the result of terrorist activity or by natural disasters, such as earthquake or fire. The loss of critical infrastructure, such as telecommunications or power, for even a short time can result in crippling disruptions to businesses and the economy as a whole.

In 1999 severe hailstorms in Sydney, New South Wales, damaged many government and business buildings, requiring those organisations to relocate their operations. In the same year, an explosion at a Victorian gas plant left the state without a gas supply for several weeks, costing businesses and the government billions of dollars in lost revenue. Earlier in the 1990s a siege and fire in a government building in Canberra required the relocation of 400 staff and the department's infrastructure (ANAO 2000).

There is increasing recognition that the critical national information infrastructure must be protected. This infrastructure comprises the IT systems used by such crucial sectors as water supply, power supply, banking and telecommunications. Much of the critical national information infrastructure has been privatised, and the responsibility for its security is now largely in the hands of businesses. In

2004, 50 per cent of critical national information infrastructure organisations reported harmful electronic attacks (AusCERT 2004).

Non-compliance with corporate governance or ethical, legal or regulatory obligations

The risk of non-compliance with corporate governance or ethical, legal or regulatory obligations is a growing issue for many businesses.

In terms of *corporate governance*, company directors are increasingly being held personally responsible and liable for the actions of their companies. The collapse of major corporations, such as Enron in the USA and HIH in Australia, has brought corporate governance issues into the spotlight. Businesses have *legal* obligations to their customers and other stakeholders. For example, in Australia privacy laws oblige businesses to protect the data they hold about individuals. An example of a *regulatory* requirement is the need for all corporations to report their financial data to the Australian Securities and Investments Commission. *Ethical* issues must also be considered. Ethical, legal and regulatory obligations are explored in detail in chapter 3.

IT risk controls

IT risk controls (or treatments) could be aimed at preventing the risk from occurring (known as preventive controls) or at minimising the consequences should the event occur (corrective controls). Lying in between are *detective controls* that detect failed, in progress or successful security breaches and trigger the corrective controls. Detective controls are therefore closely linked to preventive and corrective controls. They will be discussed in more detail in chapter 2 and throughout the book. Generally all risks will be controlled by a combination of the approaches. Whenever a risk that threatens business continuity exists, an appropriate response should be built into the business's business continuity plan.

The appropriate controls to design and implement will depend on a judgement about the cost of implementing the control and the corresponding benefit (i.e. the reduction in the likelihood or consequence of the risk).

It is important to recognise that the controls are not exclusively technical in nature. The vulnerability of technology and the emergent nature of the technical security controls suggest that a technological control alone is insufficient; therefore these controls need to be supplemented by proper managerial and operational controls so that a robust defence can be maintained. It is also important to recognise that a layered approach is required, as shown in figure 1.4.

Consider for example the effect of fire. 'Preventive controls' refer to the way fire is prevented from taking place. For example it could be that the design of the building and its furnishings, such as carpets, are made of low-flammability material or that the administrative policies and procedures are put in place to minimise the effect of fire. However, even if these precautions are taken, fire can still occur.

A system will require the correct *detection* mechanisms, such as smoke and heat detectors, to ensure that the fire is detected at the earliest possible time and can therefore trigger *corrective controls*, such as a sprinkler system, to eliminate the fire and minimise the damage. Once this has occurred a process of *recovery* would be initiated, such as replacing damaged hardware and reloading data from back-up systems. It is then important to investigate why the preventive controls failed and, if possible, take steps to revise the controls to protect against a recurrence.

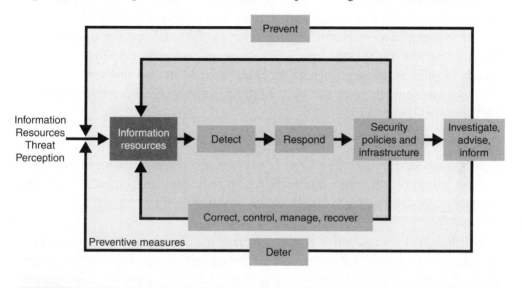

Figure 1.4   A layered approach to IT security

Preventive controls

Preventive controls aim to prevent the risk from occurring. We will look at these controls in detail in chapter 2 and throughout the book. For now, some examples are technical controls, management controls and operational controls, which are discussed below.

Technical controls

Technical controls include firewalls, virtual private networks (VPNs), intrusion detection systems, antivirus software and passwords. Firewalls are designed to prevent unauthorised access to a business's network. Unfortunately they also degrade network performance (Stevens 2002), and often virtual private networks provide a better way to secure access to a business's dispersed networks (Moore 2002). Antivirus software is designed to prevent malicious code entering the IT system.

Businesses often focus on protection from external attacks, but internal attacks are more common and often more damaging. Businesses need to have access controls that limit the extent to which a particular employee can access IT resources. Employees need access to only those resources required for performing their job.

Management controls

Management controls encompass the entire organisation and include security policies, security procedures and security guidelines. The information management policy, for example, illustrates the type of information that the organisation collects, holds and shares among its stakeholders. It describes the measures to control access to IT assets. Management controls also stipulate personnel security controls, such as workplace induction, separation of duties, security awareness initiatives and training in security-conscious practices. Such practices extend to using passwords and keeping them confidential and not opening suspicious attachments to emails. In practice, it appears that many employees regularly breach IT policies. Private Internet surfing and email use are just two examples. Management controls must not only establish policies but also ensure that they are translated into practice.

Operational controls

Operational controls include measures to physically protect IT assets from theft, fire and humidity and temperature hazards. Specific measures include employing security guards and fitting keypad locks to building doors.

It is important to recognise that information risk management requires a multifaceted approach and sometimes involves issues that are beyond the control of the business. Although the business might control its use of cryptography and the physical security of its facilities, it cannot directly control the laws of its society or the availability of secure software in the marketplace.

Corrective controls

Corrective controls aim to minimise the consequences of an adverse event once it occurs. The corrective controls will include the business continuity plan discussed earlier in the chapter. It is important to remember that corrective controls rely on the event being detected. Detective controls are discussed in more detail in chapter 2.

Ideally, modern businesses would have a mirror image of their critical aspects as a back-up strategy, ready to swing into action at any time. In reality, this is not feasible. Consequently, businesses focus on some key areas to develop an effective contingency plan to insulate them from the consequences of various threats. These key areas vary from business to business. Nonetheless, **recovery** is the term given to the process whereby the business restores its processes and operations. Recovery will include such things as replacing damaged hardware and restoring data from back-up copies. It is the process implemented by the corrective controls.

A number of corrective controls specific to managing IT risk will now be discussed: technical controls, management controls and operational controls.

Technical controls

Most IT systems generate activity logs from PCs and servers. (In the past, systems administrators had to check individual PC and server logs, and this might still be the case in some instances.) These logs record all activity on the PC or server and thus form an **audit trail**, which can be used to identify specific patterns and behaviour and to quickly trace the origin of a problem, be it internal or external (Cooper 2002). This will help the business recover quickly as well as identifying the cause of the problem so that it can be addressed to avoid it recurring (Cooper 2002). Audit trails ensure accountability. Awareness of their existence promotes compliance with security policies, so the existence of an audit trail also acts as a preventive control.

Data back-up allows the business's systems to be restored should data be lost or corrupted through deliberate actions, error or equipment failure. It is important that the business back up its data on a regular basis. The back-up should be stored in a different location from the primary data storage.

Management controls

Corrective management controls deal with providing the financial resources and physical infrastructure for recovery after a disaster has occurred.

Operational controls

Corrective operational controls include the creation and use of back-up data and activity logs to allow systems to be restored. These controls also include back-up equipment, such as a secondary power supply and the availability of an alternative operating site. This is easiest for businesses that have more than one office. The business could conduct its operations from the alternative site should its main site be damaged or destroyed or lose access to infrastructure (e.g. a power outage).

There are of course many corrective controls, and the appropriate ones to use will depend on the specific IT risk context of each business. Figures 1.5 (p. 24) and 1.6 (p. 25) show the use of security technology, policies and procedures by Australian organisations.

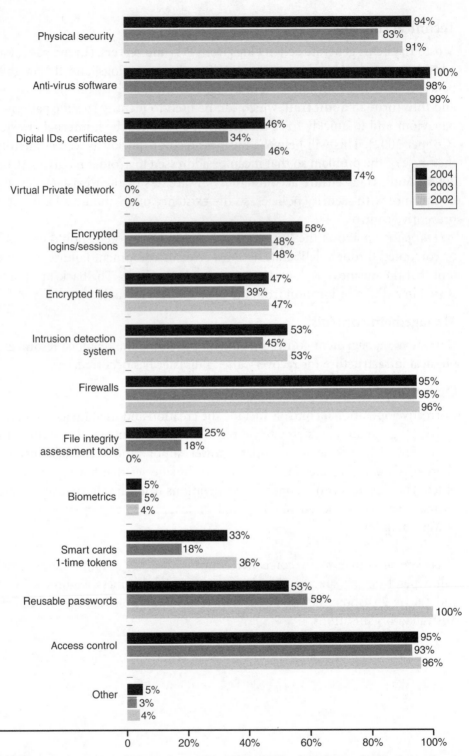

	2004	2003	2002
Physical security	94%	83%	91%
Anti-virus software	100%	98%	99%
Digital IDs, certificates	46%	34%	46%
Virtual Private Network	74%	0%	0%
Encrypted logins/sessions	58%	48%	48%
Encrypted files	47%	39%	47%
Intrusion detection system	53%	45%	53%
Firewalls	95%	95%	96%
File integrity assessment tools	25%	18%	0%
Biometrics	5%	5%	4%
Smart cards 1-time tokens	33%	18%	36%
Reusable passwords	53%	59%	100%
Access control	95%	93%	96%
Other	5%	3%	4%

Source: 2004 Australian Computer Crime and Security Survey
2004: 182 respondents/76%; 2003: 214 respondents/100%
2002: 92 respondents/97%

Note: In 2002 and 2003, respondents were asked if they had experienced
'file integrity assessment tools' and in 2002 and 2003, respondents were
not asked if they used 'Virtual Private Networks'.

Figure 1.5   **Use of security technology by Australian organisations**

Source: AusCERT 2004, p. 7.

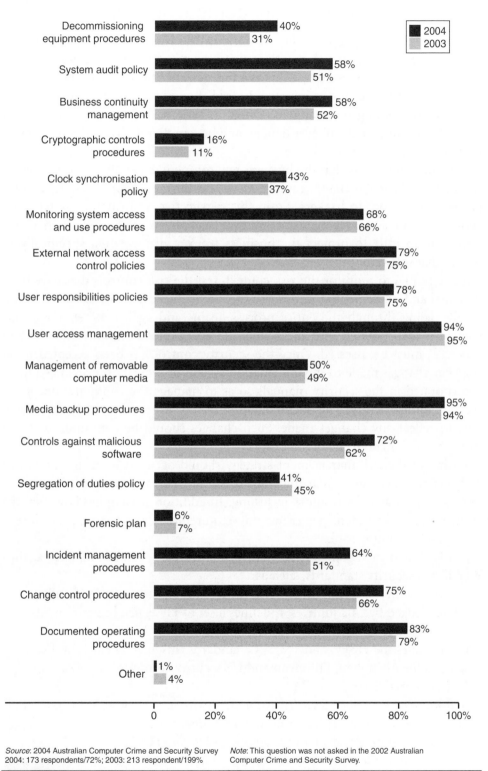

Decommissioning equipment procedures 40% 31%

System audit policy 58% 51%

Business continuity management 58% 52%

Cryptographic controls procedures 16% 11%

Clock synchronisation policy 43% 37%

Monitoring system access and use procedures 68% 66%

External network access control policies 79% 75%

User responsibilities policies 78% 75%

User access management 94% 95%

Management of removable computer media 50% 49%

Media backup procedures 95% 94%

Controls against malicious software 72% 62%

Segregation of duties policy 41% 45%

Forensic plan 6% 7%

Incident management procedures 64% 51%

Change control procedures 75% 66%

Documented operating procedures 83% 79%

Other 1% 4%

2004
2003

0   20%   40%   60%   80%   100%

Source: 2004 Australian Computer Crime and Security Survey
2004: 173 respondents/72%; 2003: 213 respondent/199%

Note: This question was not asked in the 2002 Australian
Computer Crime and Security Survey.

Figure 1.6 **Use of security policies and procedures by Australian organisations**

Source: AusCERT 2004, p. 8.

Maintaining the risk management strategy

In most areas of life, people and organisations who work hard and spend money expect something in return, but with security, the pay-off is that nothing happens. Human psychology does not see this as a true reward. It can be a challenge to see the benefits of the resources invested. Indeed, a good security manager oversees a site where nothing bad happens. Often, as time passes, people can begin to think that nothing bad will ever happen and be tempted to divert resources away from security.

A further problem is that the business environment generally and the IT environment in particular change rapidly. Just as the business adopts new, innovative IT systems, so too do hackers. From this perspective, information systems are about as secure as a hacking algorithm that hasn't been tried yet. Antivirus software will do little to protect the business from a virus written specifically to bypass that software.

It is essential to monitor the risk context, test the risk controls that have been designed and implemented, and revise them when necessary. In essence this will involve going through the entire process again (and again). Whenever a new control is incorporated into the system, its effect on other controls, risks and processes must be assessed. Once the security control has been accepted in all respects, changes made to the information system or security process need to be incorporated in the security manuals so as to manage the configuration of the security infrastructure. The documentation of the strategy should be kept up to date to reflect any changes made. Such changes should be communicated and promoted throughout the organisation.

Testing of the risk management strategy should occur at both the functional and business levels at regular intervals. It is important to involve business partners, suppliers and distributors in testing. In addition to gauging how well the strategy works and identifying changing requirements, the testing procedure is also a useful training tool.

In addition to testing, the IT risk management strategy can be evaluated against established security standards, such as:

- *Common Criteria*: Common Criteria (ISO 15408) is a standard officially acknowledged by 14 countries. It defines a set of IT security requirements for prospective products and systems. The Common Criteria standard incorporates the ITSEC and TSCSEC standards (discussed below) and so satisfies the Australian, European and US security communities (Common Criteria Portal 2005).
- *Information Technology Security Evaluation Criteria (ITSEC)*: ITSEC is a set of IT security criteria accepted in Europe and Australia.
- *Trusted Computing System and Evaluation Criteria (TCSEC)*:
  TCSEC is an earlier evaluation system used in the USA. It comprises multiple levels of assurance, ranging from simple testing through to formal evaluation and certification.

Essential parts of an IT continuity plan

Early in this chapter we explored the concept of business continuity management. Business continuity management is designed to prevent and control risks that threaten the ability of the business to meet its objectives. As such, business continuity planning is a broad concept that encompasses the entire business. IT continuity planning is one part of it. It has the same objective — to ensure the ongoing operation of the business — but is more limited in scope. It forms one part of the business's risk management strategy. It should cover those aspects of physical space, human resources and IT assets that are crucial to the continuation of the business.

Physical space

A business should have available an alternative site for carrying out its operations should its usual premises be damaged or destroyed. Businesses operating in areas with a history or risk of natural disasters (e.g. earthquakes), terrorist threats or activity or other calamities should consider a multicampus operation, so that operations can continue at another site should operations at one site be disrupted. This could involve facilities in separate parts of town, in different cities or even in different countries. This geographic diversity of operating units enhances recovery: the most successful relocation operations occur when there is a facility in running condition that performs the same functions as that of the group being moved (Vitiello & Kuhn 2002). This is especially important for complex plant and equipment that are difficult, laborious and expensive to set up. Geographic dispersion provides a particularly useful back-up for electrical and telecommunications infrastructure (McEachern 2002). It is useful to have different power and telecommunications suppliers at the business's primary and contingency business sites (Vitiello & Kuhn 2002).

Human resources

The employees are the most valuable asset affected when a disaster strikes a business. Employees hold the business intelligence — it is the knowledge and skills they have acquired on the job. That is why many large organisations in the USA have spread their managers among different locations in response to the perceived higher risk of terrorist activity (McEachern 2002).

Businesses are also increasingly recognising the importance of ensuring that corporate knowledge is captured and shared so that the business is not interrupted when an employee is absent or leaves the organisation. Knowledge management, knowledge sharing, employee multiskilling and the use of knowledge repositories are all responses to this need and are becoming increasingly common in business strategies, including business continuity plans.

IT assets

As we have seen, information and information technology have become crucial to business continuity. Traditionally, business continuity management has revolved around restoring key applications, but that model is of decreasing usefulness as contemporary IT-driven business operations are interconnected and interdependent (BT 2003). Back-up data storage is not of much use if it is not complemented by reliable network connectivity within the organisation and with its partners, suppliers, distributors and customers. Hence, it is imperative that the business's information infrastructure is well secured. This security must extend to physical security and logical security, which are discussed below.

Physical security

'Physical security' refers to the protection of IT infrastructure (servers, workstations, phones, cabling and so on) from natural disasters and from unauthorised intruders. Natural disasters include fire, floods, earthquakes, volcanic activity, tidal waves, cyclones, tornadoes, typhoons, snow storms, electrical storms and lightning strikes. Unauthorised intruders might intentionally cause physical damage to the information infrastructure or might use their physical access to the IT systems to compromise the logical security (discussed next) of the infrastructure.

Logical security

'Logical security' is concerned with the data held in the information infrastructure. The components of logical security are confidentiality, integrity and availability. Much of the rest of this book is dedicated to exploring logical security. We will briefly describe each component here.

Confidentiality must be protected to ensure that the information cannot be used against the interests of the business, its customers or its business partners. Confidentiality can be attacked by interception. This could be through direct observation of data (generally in an office environment), network interception (where data is read when it is being transmitted on a network) or electromagnetic interception (which is similar to network interception but is targeted at wireless networks).

Integrity of information refers to protecting the information from unauthorised modification. Modification can occur through direct access to the records or through gaining access to the data via the wired or wireless network. Integrity also relates to the authenticity or genuineness of data. The authenticity is compromised when data is modified or created so that it appears genuine but is not.

The **availability** of the information infrastructure is crucial to business operations. It can be compromised by software interruptions (e.g. bugs in the software, viruses or compromised data), hardware interruptions (e.g. physical damage to a computer) or staff interruptions (e.g. when a crucial employee is not at work). For example, in 2001, trading on the New York Stock Exchange was halted for more than an hour after a software upgrade went awry (BT 2003).

We will discuss logical security in detail in chapter 2.

Ensuring use of the IT security and risk management strategy

In the past, many organisations paid relatively little attention to the security of their information resources. Security was often seen as an afterthought rather than as a necessary and ongoing business cost. Recommendations to design and implement IT security plans were accepted with reluctance, and responsibility for them was often in the hands of technical staff well down the line of command.

It is only recently — and still mostly in larger organisations — that an appreciation has developed of the strategic value of protecting information and information systems. In many cases, this realisation has been forced by changing legal requirements and regulatory controls. Most recently, corporate governance issues have demanded a greater focus on IT security and risk management. Increasingly, chief executive officers and chief information officers are being held personally responsible for governance failings of their organisations, such as the failure to adequately protect data and computer systems from unauthorised access.

An organisation must have an integrated approach to the prevention, detection and management of attacks from all possible threats and the exploitation of all kinds of vulnerability. The 2004 Australian Computer Crime and Security Survey (AusCERT 2004) concluded that although organisations were making efforts to improve their IT security readiness by means of information security policies, practices and procedures, standards and guidelines, and engagement of qualified staff, the efforts were insufficient to cope with the ever-changing threats they face. In particular, IT system vulnerability is increasing in number and severity, and malicious code is becoming more common and spreading faster.

As we have seen in this chapter, the development of an IT security and risk management strategy is a crucial step. However, a plan or strategy is useful only if it is implemented, supported and used. Business managers are coming to recognise that IT security and risk management is not exclusively a technological problem and cannot be managed by means of security controls alone. Management needs to take a holistic approach to security planning and provide the necessary resources for a comprehensive security plan that involves technology, people and processes. It needs to ensure that IT security is a shared vision of the entire organisation. Figure 1.7 (p. 30) shows the components of a holistic approach to IT security.

Figure 1.7   A holistic approach to IT security

Management commitment is paramount in the protection of IT resources. Management must recognise the importance of IT to the overall business strategy. The management commitment is translated into a number of *business objectives* that define what the business's IT processes are intended to achieve. The main business objective is of course to continue operating to maximise profits in the short and long term. This business continuity is dependent on security policies. *Security policies* encompass the security infrastructure and security technology. Policy documents are often not given due importance by employees. Often, too, policies are difficult to understand. It is important to produce user-friendly policy documents and to promote their implementation to employees. Often this will mean constructing guidelines that show employees how to put the essence of the policy into practice.

It is important to recognise the difference between security infrastructure and security technology. *Security infrastructure* covers the broader range of risks that we have discussed in this chapter, including human resources. As mentioned earlier, people, not technology, are often the weakness in IT security. An otherwise secure IT system will fail if those who use the system do not follow the IT security strategy and plans. The security policies must be promoted to the organisation's personnel, they must be understood and commitment to implementing them must be achieved. Without this commitment throughout the organisation, *security technology*, such as antivirus software or cryptography, will not adequately protect the organisation.

Outline of this book

It has been our aim in this first chapter to provide an overview of how a business should approach IT security and risk management as a strategic issue. IT is integral to business operations, and it must be managed in a way that supports the overall business processes and objectives. In essence, it needs to deliver value to the organisation. To do so, risks must be managed to ensure that the systems and information within them exhibit the qualities of confidentiality, integrity and availability.

Chapter 2 will examine the building blocks of IT security. It will first examine physical and logical threats to IT security, building on the brief introduction we have provided in chapter 1. It will then look at the overall approaches to securing IT systems against those threats as well as specific technology, tools and methods that can be implemented by businesses as part of their IT security and risk management strategy.

Chapter 3 will look at the ethical, legal and regulatory framework in Australia. It must be remembered that IT security and risk management is not just about e-crime, hacking and computer crashes; businesses have significant obligations to the societies in which they operate. Non-compliance with these obligations must be treated as an important IT risk with potentially serious consequences for the business.

Chapter 4 examines the various types of electronic crime. It then moves on to the important issue of forensic computing and how businesses can ensure that they are prepared should their systems ever need to be forensically investigated.

Chapter 5 explains the use of cryptography (complex codes) to help achieve the central IT security requirements of confidentiality, integrity and availability, as well as authentication and non-repudiation, which are important qualities of secure electronic data exchanges.

Chapter 6 introduces network security. The increasing interconnectivity of businesses provides a multitude of access points for IT security risks. Protecting the network and its components is of crucial importance. This topic is carried through to chapter 7, which additionally discusses how to secure databases and applications.

Chapter 8 examines the security of e-commerce and the emerging area of m-commerce (mobile e-commerce). E-commerce security is one of the highest-profile areas of IT security, perhaps because it involves financial transactions or perhaps because it directly involves consumers. Establishing consumer trust in the security of e-commerce has been a major challenge for businesses in the first 10 years of this new business model.

Chapter 9 examines mobile and wireless security. More and more businesses are turning to wireless networking and taking advantage of the convenience of mobile and wireless devices, such as mobile phones and networks with wireless access points for laptops. Mobile e-commerce is also emerging as a feasible business offering. Compared to wired and cabled networks, wireless communications are easy to eavesdrop on or interfere with, but at the same time their potential has proved very appealing to businesses.

Chapter 10 discusses the security of web services. Web services are generic web-based applications that can be used in a modular fashion to perform various functions and to allow different systems to communicate with each other. When businesses take advantage of a web service, they need to be assured that the data they are exchanging is secure.

Finally, chapter 11 will examine some emerging issues in IT security. Throughout the book we discuss security themes and specific technology. Your study will provide you with a solid understanding of strategic IT security and risk management, but this study must be continued beyond this book. IT is one of the fastest changing areas in business. New innovations are adopted at a fast pace, bringing new associated risks with them. Any business reliant on IT systems to achieve its business objectives must adopt IT security and risk management as an ongoing, dynamic process.

Summary

A risk is any event that has the potential to prevent a business achieving its objectives. Risk management is an ongoing process for assessing the likelihood of an adverse event, implementing measures to reduce the risk that such an event will occur and ensuring that the organisation can respond in such a way as to minimise the consequences of the event should it in fact occur. The strategic risk management process involves (1) establishing the business context, (2) identifying, analysing and evaluating the risks the business faces, (3) designing and implementing preventive and corrective controls and (4) monitoring and reviewing the strategy to ensure that it is effective and that it responds to changes in the risk environment. Preventive controls are designed to prevent a risk from eventuating. Corrective controls are designed to minimise the consequences for the business should an adverse event occur. Particularly serious risks are those with the potential to threaten the continuity of the business; that is, the achievement of the business's main objectives. These risks should be managed using a business continuity management process.

IT governance is part of corporate governance. IT governance is concerned with two main tasks: delivering value to business through IT and mitigating the IT risks that could be faced. IT has become a fundamental and integral part of most business processes, and so the reliance of businesses on IT systems has grown. An IT security risk exists whenever there is a chance that an IT asset could be adversely affected by some event. The aim of IT security is to ensure that the IT system can deliver confidentiality, integrity and availability.

IT risks are not just technological in nature. In addition to technology, they also relate to political and regulatory matters, environmental and natural disasters, economic and market factors, strategic decisions and operational issues. A comprehensive IT continuity plan will go beyond the IT assets to also encompass the physical space and human resources necessary for the effective utilisation of the business's IT systems. The importance of personnel in achieving effective risk management cannot be overstated. Management must ensure that a security- and risk-conscious culture permeates the entire organisation. Technological controls will be useless if staff do not use secure practices.

Key terms

audit trail, p. 23	corporate governance, p. 6
availability, p. 28	distributed security, p. 7
business continuity management (BCM), p. 4	integrity, p. 28
	IT governance, p. 6
business continuity plan, p. 5	IT security risk, p. 7
centralised security, p. 7	recovery, p. 22
confidentiality, p. 28	risk management, p. 2

Questions

1. Briefly explain each of the steps in the risk management process.
2. What is the purpose of business continuity management?
3. IT governance requires that IT delivers value to the business and that IT risks are mitigated. Who is responsible for IT governance? Who is responsible for IT security and risk management?
4. Explain how IT represents both an opportunity and a source of vulnerability for business.
5. Choose an organisation that uses IT (e.g. your workplace or your university) and complete the following tasks:
   (a) Explain the role of IT in the organisation.
   (b) Identify, analyse and evaluate the IT risks that the organisation faces.
   (c) Suggest some controls that the organisation should, in your opinion, have in place to prevent and correct these risks. Be sure not to focus just on technological controls.
   (d) Try to think of a new risk the organisation might face in the future. What steps should the organisation take now and in the future to protect itself from this risk?
6. How would you create awareness about implementation of information security policy and controls in your organisation?

Case study

1: Johnson & Johnson tackles security pain

For Johnson & Johnson, the healthcare giant with more than 200 separate companies operating in 54 countries, one of the biggest problems encountered in e-commerce was finding a way to quickly get business partners access to the network but enforce security.

The problem vexed the Brunswick, NJ, maker of pharmaceuticals and medical equipment because e-commerce partners, once given access, sometimes introduced worms and viruses into J&J's network. In addition, the process of reviewing business requests for network access between a J&J unit and its intended partner had become burdensome, delaying e-commerce transactions.

However, IT staff at J&J said since new security procedures put in place a year ago altered the equation, it has been much faster to process network-access requests. Through the uniform monitoring and documentation processes, security has improved, with worm and virus outbreaks emanating from business partners reduced to nil.

'The documentation is still a bit cumbersome, but now it's a repeatable process,' says Thomas Bunt, director of worldwide information security at J&J, about the challenge of providing network access for business partners. 'We're facing an increased demand for external connections, and it wasn't easy to do this.'

When a business manager at J&J wants to have counterparts in outside firms gain access to internal applications for e-commerce, the IT department is summoned to assess risk.

First, the J&J unit and the outside firm have to fill out a detailed questionnaire about the nature of the connection request, says Denise Medd, information security senior analyst. In addition, J&J expects the intended e-commerce partner to submit to a security assessment and evaluation.

This vulnerability assessment may be done by a neutral third party, but the goal is to ensure that doing business via the network connection, which is typically opened up via a J&J firewall, presents no unnecessary risks. The J&J operating company, officially known as 'the sponsor', is held to the same standards, Medd emphasises.

Occasionally, a request for network access is turned down, especially if the J&J side has servers lacking proper patch-update mechanisms or other shortcomings. 'There is a final review, and we will not let an insecure connection go live,' Medd says.

The IT and security professionals at J&J worked with the legal department to craft standard procedures for requests and evaluations. J&J and its partner also must complete a contract or memo of understanding regarding the network connection to be established.

'We'll look closely at what the connectivity is, and typically a limited number of people could have access,' Bunt says, pointing out that J&J strives to accommodate requests for a range of VPN access methods.

J&J also includes an inspection process every six months to ascertain the security of the network connection. The risk management procedure has resulted in a dramatic drop in virus and worm outbreaks. Sometimes business project managers grumble about the assessment process, but management's solid backing of it has made it a uniformly enforced process that is in effect with hundreds of outside firms, Bunt says.

The IT department says it hopes to streamline the risk evaluation further by drawing up standardised interconnection security agreements and a uniform set of questions to ask outside firms wanting access to J&J's internal network.

'We also need to better explain to our partners why they need to do this and how they benefit by getting a good look at our security posture,' Bunt says.

Source: Messmer 2005.

Questions

1. Examine the process that Johnson & Johnson went through to balance its business and security needs. Has it achieved a fair balance in the policies and procedures described in this case study?
2. Describe how this case study illustrates the way Johnson & Johnson has implemented a holistic risk management and mitigation strategy.
3. Show how this case study can be used to illustrate Johnson & Johnson's commitment to good corporate governance.

Suggested reading

Australian Computer Emergency Response Team (AusCERT) 2004, *2004 Computer Crime and Security Survey*, AusCERT, University of Queensland, Brisbane. (Also see surveys of other years.)

Australian National Audit Office (ANAO) 2000, *Business Continuity Management*, Better Practice series, www.anao.gov.au.

HB 231, 2000, Information security risk management guidelines, Standards Australia, ISBN 0-7337-3360-3.

IT Governance Institute (ITGI) 2003, *Board Briefing on IT Governance*, 2nd edn, www.itgi.org.

National Institute of Standards and Technology (NIST) Computer Security Division, 'Security Guidelines (800 series)', NIST, Gaithersburg, MD, http://csrc.nist.gov.

Standards Australia 1999, *Risk Management*, AS/NZS 4360.

—— 2001, *Information Technology — Code of Practice for Information Security Management*, AS/NZS ISO/IEC 17799.

References

Australian Computer Emergency Response Team (AusCERT) 2004, *2004 Computer Crime and Security Survey*, AusCERT, University of Queensland, Brisbane.

Australian National Audit Office (ANAO) 2000, *Business Continuity Management*, Better Practice series, www.anao.gov.au.

BT 2003, 'Business continuity management: Exploiting agility in an uncertain world', White Paper, accessed 27 June 2005, www.downloads.bt.com/b4b/pdf/Bus_Continuity_WP.pdf.

Castells, M 2000, *The Rise of the Network Society*, Blackwell Publishers, Cambridge, MA.

Chartered Management Institute (CMI) 2003, *'Business continuity management'*, accessed 7 January 2004, www.thebci.org/BCM2003.pdf.

Common Criteria Portal 2005, accessed 15 April 2005, www.commoncriteriaportal.org/public/files/ccintroduction.pdf and www.commoncriteriaportal.org/public/consumer/index.php?menu=1.

Cooper, LF 2002, 'The authenticity imperative: Building trusted business processes in the digital marketplace', *The Business Continuity and Security Strategies Report*, vol. 1, Larstan Publishing, Inc., accessed 7 January 2004, www.larstan.net/Published_work/B2Bsecurity1%2002.pdf.

Edney, J & Arbaugh, WA 2004, *Real 802.11 security: Wi-Fi protected access and 802.11i*, Addison-Wesley, Boston.

Gorrio, F 2002, 'Real-time forensics: Closing the gap between incident and response', *The Business Continuity and Security Strategies Report*, vol. 1, Larstan Publishing, Inc., accessed 7 January 2004, www.larstan.net/Published_work/B2Bsecurity1%2002.pdf.

Greiner, C & Evans, R 2003, 'Few organizations have truly effective business continuity plans', Meta Group, *News Analysis,* no. 481, 29 January, accessed 7 January 2004, www.metagroup.com/cgi-bin/inetcgi/jsp/displayArticle.do?oid=37361.

Hoffman, T 2004, 'IT governance is on the hot seat: Committees of IT and business execs oversee spending at some companies, but survey finds lots of sceptics', *Computerworld,* vol. 38, no. 28, 12 July.

Honeynet Project 2000, 'Know your enemy: Motives', accessed 2 June 2005, www.honeynet.org/papers/motives/index.html.

Hughes, G 2003, 'The cyberspace invaders', the *Age,* 22 June.

IT Governance Institute (ITGI) 2003, *Board Briefing on IT Governance*, 2nd edn, www.itgi.org.

Jordan, E & Musson, D 2003, *Business Continuity Management: A Survey of Commonwealth Government Agencies*, Macquarie Graduate School of Management, Macquarie University, Sydney.

Kilger, M, Ofir, A & Stutzman, J 2004, 'Profiling' in Honeynet Project, *Know Your Enemy*, 2nd edn, Addison-Wesley Professional, Boston.

McEachern, C 2002, 'Is regulation right around the corner?', *Wall Street and Technology*, January, vol. 20, accessed 8 January 2004, www.wallstreetandtech.com/story/WST20011210S0014.

McKinsey & Company 2000, 'Global Investor Opinion Survey on Corporate Governance', June, www.mckinsey.com.

Messmer, E 2005, 'Johnson & Johnson tackles security pain', *Network World Fusion*, accessed 14 March 2005, www.nwfusion.com/news/2005/031405-johnson-johnson.html.

Moore, T 2002, 'Firewalls evolve to key on new business needs, new services and business continuity', *Business Continuity and Security Strategies Report*, vol. 1, Larstan Publishing, accessed 7 January 2004, www.larstan.net/Published_work/B2Bsecurity1%2002.pdf.

Potter, B 2003, 'Wireless security's future', *IEEE Security & Privacy*, vol. 1, no. 4, pp. 68–72.

President's Information Technology Advisory Committee (PITAC) (2005), 'Cybersecurity: A question of prioritization', National Coordination Office for Information Technology Research and Development, Arlington, VA.

Savage, M 2002, 'Business continuity planning', *Work Study*, vol. 51, no. 5, pp. 254–61.

Smith, D 2003, 'Business continuity and crisis management', *Management Quarterly*, January, pp. 27–33.

Spitzner, L 2003, *Honeypots: Tracking Hackers*, Addison-Wesley Professional, Boston.

Standards Australia 1999, *Risk Management*, AS/NZS 4360.

—— 2000, *Information Security Risk Management Guidelines*, HB 231:2000.

Stevens, G 2002, 'Virus recovery: Beyond a shield, a rapid path to business continuity', *Business Continuity and Security Strategies Report*, vol. 1, Larstan Publishing, accessed 7 January 2004, www.larstan.net/Published_work/B2Bsecurity1%2002.pdf.

Swartz, N 2003, 'Few organisations have effective continuity plans', *Information Management Journal*, May–June, vol. 37, no. 3, accessed 27 June 2005, www.findarticles.com/p/articles/mi_qa3937/is_200305/ai_n9260310.

Vitiello, C & Kuhn, J 2002, 'Business continuity planning', *AFP Exchange*, vol. 22, no. 5, September–October, pp. 56–60.

Chapter 2
Building blocks
of IT security

Learning objectives

After studying this chapter, you should be able to:

- explain the importance of physical security and logical security
- discuss a range of physical security risks
- discuss the four threats to logical security
- explain the purpose of access control
- outline the implementation of access controls using security models
- discuss technical, management and operational security controls.

Chapter overview

IT security deals with the prevention of unauthorised access, the prevention of intentional or unintentional manipulation or alteration of information, and the maintenance of availability. We refer to these characteristics as *confidentiality, integrity* and *availability.* The scope of security is not limited to information; it also includes the IT systems that produce, process and store such information. It involves technological and managerial procedures, and software and hardware tools. As we saw in chapter 1, information is a key business asset, crucial to achieving the business's objectives, so IT systems are one of the most precious assets of an organisation. Consequently business continuity strategies of contemporary organisations place extraordinary emphasis on the protection of their IT systems.

IT systems are vulnerable to numerous threats, both internal (strategic and operational) and external (political/regulatory, environmental/natural, economic/market and technological). In this chapter we will focus on the threats that directly target IT systems. Ironically, protecting an IT system requires much more effort and resources than are required to hack into that system. For a hacker, all it takes is a computer and the requisite intrusion skills. For an employee, it might just take a decision to abuse their access to the IT system. This paradox on the one hand exposes the vulnerability of technology and on the other hand accentuates the need for an all-encompassing IT security strategy.

First we will examine physical and logical security of the IT system. Physical security relates to ensuring that IT resources are safe from physical attack and harm, such as fire, lightning strikes and spilled coffee. Logical security entails protecting the IT system — its data and processes — from interception, modification, fabrication and interruption that could compromise the confidentiality, integrity or availability of the system.

The most basic step an organisation can take to secure its IT assets is to ensure that only genuine users are authorised to have access to information resources and that they can only perform actions and processes necessary for their role in the business process. This is known as *access control* and lies at the core of information systems security. Access controls are implemented through various *security models*. The access control matrix model applies an authorisation rule to each user, IT object and process. Together these control what the user can do. The security levels model controls the actions of users in accordance with the privileges of the organisational group they belong to. Each IT object is made available or unavailable to particular groups.

We looked at preventive and corrective controls in chapter 1. We will explore technical, management and operational security methods, tools and measures in more detail in this chapter.

Securing the components of the IT system

This section will explore the building blocks of a secure IT system. A secure system must be built on *physical security* and *logical security*. **Physical security** refers to protecting the IT assets from physical damage, such as fire or flood. **Logical security** refers to protecting the confidentiality, integrity and availability of the information. We introduced these concepts in chapter 1. We will now look at them in more detail as fundamental requirements of a secure IT system.

Physical security

'Physical security' refers to the protection of the IT system from physical damage by natural disasters or physical access from unauthorised people.

Natural disasters include fire, floods, earthquakes, volcanic eruptions, tidal waves, cyclones, lightning strikes and so on. As we saw in chapter 1, IT security requires a layered approach. The example given there of a fire shows that steps can be taken to prevent a fire (e.g. using non-flammable materials in the building), to detect a fire (smoke alarms) and to correct the problem (a sprinkler system and accessible fire extinguishers). Often, however, the prevention of such incidents is beyond the control of the business. A business cannot, for example, prevent a cyclone. In these instances, the corrective controls and the business's recovery process are central to ensuring business continuity.

Protection from unauthorised access by people takes place by means of building security, security personnel (guards) and sturdy locks on server rooms. Alarms and video surveillance also aid detection of a physical intrusion.

Although most of this book examines logical security, it is important to remember that physical security is as crucial as logical security. IT Risk 2.1 looks at a few examples in more detail before we move on to logical security.

Logical security

'Logical security' refers to the preservation of the confidentiality, integrity and availability of the IT system, particularly the information it contains. There are different categories of sources that threaten logical security, and these sources have different motivations. Further, they adopt a plethora of ways and means to achieve their objectives. IT Risk 2.2 examines the threats, motivations and sources. (Refer to IT Risk 1.1 on pp. 8–9 for the types of threat most commonly perpetrated on Australian organisations.)

Fire, flood and lightning

Fire is a serious physical security threat. Fires offer little time to react and can cause devastating damage. Consideration should therefore be given to the location of the business. Although many other considerations (such as proximity to customers) might outweigh the risk of fire, it is worth assessing the fire risk of choosing a building surrounded by gum trees or next to a paint factory. The flammability of the materials of the building and its furnishings should also be considered. It is important to ensure that the building is properly equipped with smoke detectors, alarms and fire extinguishing equipment. Minimum requirements will usually be stipulated by law and workplace health and safety regulations, but the business should conduct its own investigations to make sure that it is adequately equipped to survive a fire.

Fire risks can be controlled through the use of circuit breakers and by making periodic inspections of the building's wiring. Some thought should also be given to the type of extinguishing equipment. Some types of extinguisher will leave electrical equipment virtually unharmed; others will destroy it. Of most importance in the event of a fire is the health and safety of employees, and businesses must have procedures in place to protect them.

Floods are another potential physical threat. Floods can result from rising water, such as a flooding river or burst water main, or from falling water, such as rain or a leaking roof. Businesses should give consideration to where they locate their IT equipment. Locating the server room in the basement under ground level or in a room under overhead plumbing would be a poor choice that needlessly exposes the business to a heightened flood risk.

Lightning is a potent threat to IT systems because electrical circuits provide it with a path to flow to the ground. Direct lightning strikes on a building or power surges that result from strikes on power transmission lines, transformers and substations are disastrous for IT equipment. One possible defence is to switch off and unplug all equipment, but although this might be practicable for homes, it is not feasible for most businesses. Another defence is to use a surge suppressor, but this also is not necessarily effective protection. Other common measures include storing back-ups in grounded storage media or installing uninterruptible power supply units on all critical IT resources. Many types of lightning protection systems are available commercially, each designed to protect specific types of application. These systems work on the simple principle of having properly earthed surge protectors at several points on the IT infrastructure. Ideally, these protectors are installed to safeguard power lines and load cells used by the IT equipment.

Logical security threats

IT security threats are constantly evolving. Table 2.1 summarises the most common sources of threat and their motivations and actions. The constant changes in threats means that organisations need to develop robust security strategies that not only encompass the technical security aspects but also introduce management processes to ensure that security measures are in place at the operational levels.

Table 2.1   Source, motivation and actions of human threats

Source	Motivation	Action
Hacker, cracker	Challenge Ego Rebellion Publicity	• Hacking • Social engineering • System intrusion, break-ins • Unauthorised system access
Computer criminal	Destruction of information Illegal information disclosure Monetary gain Unauthorised data alteration	• Computer crime (e.g. cyber stalking) • Fraudulent act (e.g. replay, impersonation, interception) • Information bribery • Spoofing • System intrusion
Terrorist	Blackmail Destruction Exploitation Revenge	• Bomb/terrorism • Information warfare • System attack (e.g. distributed denial of service) • System penetration • System tampering
Industrial espionage (companies, foreign governments, other government interests)	Competitive advantage Economic espionage	• Economic exploitation • Information theft • Intrusion on personal privacy • Social engineering • System penetration • Unauthorised system access (access to classified, proprietary and/or technology-related information)

(*continued*)

Table 2.1	Source, motivation and actions of human threats. *(cont.)*	
Source	**Motivation**	**Action**
Insiders (poorly trained, disgruntled, malicious, negligent, dishonest or terminated employees)	Curiosity Ego Intelligence Monetary gain Revenge Unintentional errors and omissions (e.g. data entry error, programming error)	• Assault on employee • Blackmail • Browsing of proprietary information • Computer abuse • Fraud and theft • Information bribery • Input of falsified, corrupted data • Interception • Malicious code (e.g. virus, logic bomb, Trojan horse) • Sale of personal information • System bugs • System intrusion • System sabotage • Unauthorised system access

Source: National Institute of Standards and Technology (NIST) 2002, p. 19.

Attacks on information systems can be:

- local or via network connections (or, as shown in IT Risk 2.3, even wireless network connections)

- from a skilled and sophisticated or relatively unskilled and unsophisticated attacker

- perpetrated by someone inside or outside the organisation

- malicious or non-malicious in intent

- supported by varying levels of resources.

Although the sources, motivations and means of attackers vary, they can each be viewed as one of four types of threat to logical security: interception, modification, fabrication and interruption, which are discussed below.

Interception

Interception is an attack on the *confidentiality* of information and associated resources. It poses a major risk to an organisation as the intercepted information could be used for any purpose that could harm the business itself and its customers and business partners. IT Risk 2.3 later in the chapter provides an example of such interception. Nevertheless the risk of data interception largely depends on the type of data processed by the information systems, the mode of communication used for data transfer and the operating system.

Generally, interception is carried out by direct observation, network interception or electromagnetic interception, all of which are discussed further below.

Direct observation

Direct observation, as the name suggests, refers to the interception of data by simply looking at the source. It occurs within the physical setting of the office environment where unauthorised employees or visitors can watch the screens of other employees. In so doing they might be able to see confidential information to which they are otherwise not authorised to have access.

It is easy to control direct observation interception by simply locating screens in such a way as to provide maximum privacy to the user and restrict others' ability to view the screen. In addition, visitors to the site should usually be escorted and their activities controlled.

Network interception

Network interception refers to the interception of data by accessing and reading data as it moves through the data transmission channel. It usually occurs within the organisation, but it can occur from outside as well. IT Risk 2.3 later in the chapter provides an example of wireless network interception.

Ironically, the interceptor captures data from the data transmission channel by using the tools designed to monitor the network itself. The *promiscuous mode* in a network allows for any device within the network to catch and read every data packet. It is usually used for monitoring the network. For example, promiscuous mode in an ethernet-based local area network (common in business offices) will allow every data packet sent through the network to be read by any machine connected to the network. In *non-promiscuous mode* only the network device with the correct network address can accept the data packet.

Network interception can also occur through the use of spy programs that run in the background and feed data and perhaps screenshots to another computer inside or outside the organisation. This type of interception normally occurs only if the user accesses applications from the Internet. This type of interception can, for example, retrieve a user's bank password, PIN, credit card number and account number.

Some networks that broadcast messages are at particular risk as the interceptor can also send bogus data on the tapped line. This affects the integrity of the data, which will be discussed later.

Electromagnetic interception

Electromagnetic interception is similar to network interception, but relies on using a radio receiver to intercept electromagnetic energy radiated by the computer. It is a risk for wireless computing environments, which are often used in engineering industries. The interceptor needs to be nearby. Nevertheless, this type of interception can have disastrous consequences if the captured signal relates to the health of the plant and equipment in a manufacturing or production facility.

Modification

Modification means changing the nature of data. This attack is aimed at the *integrity* of the IT system. The ways and means of modification are the same as have been described in the discussion of interception. Modifications are either *reversible* or *irreversible*, which are discussed below.

Reversible modification

A **reversible modification** occurs where the changes made to the information or data can be undone — the data can be restored to its original condition — if the modification is detected. The restoration process requires adequate back-up strategies, including images of the workstations and servers. A back-up strategy will allow modifications of databases and data files, registry changes, configuration file changes and so on to be undone.

Irreversible modification

Irreversible modification occurs where the changes made to the information or data cannot be undone. The data is either destroyed along with its back-up or it is changed beyond recovery. Apart from direct human intrusion, viruses and Trojans are the major causes of such modification.

Fabrication

Fabrication also affects the *integrity* of the IT system. **Fabrication** occurs when the information and information resources are created or manipulated so that the information appears to be correct but is not. This attack is aimed at the *authenticity* of information. It is done in such a way that the changes are difficult to identify, but sometimes the application of the false information will make it obvious. Fabrication can also occur owing to the malfunctioning of hardware components, through deliberate introduction of a faulty hardware component, through software bugs and through human intrusion or hacking into the system. For intentional fabrication by intrusion, the intruder needs to know the processes so as to conceal the manipulation of information beyond easy recognition.

Interruption

Interruption attacks are aimed at the *availability* of the IT system. **Interruption** refers to stopping the flow of information or IT services that realise the flow of such information. It can occur in three ways, which are discussed below: software interruptions, hardware interruptions and staff interruptions.

Software interruptions

Software interruptions occur owing to modification and fabrication of data, bugs in application software, illegal copies of software, programming code alteration, Trojans, viruses and the destruction of original and back-up data.

Hardware interruptions

Hardware interruptions occur owing to natural disasters, advertent or inadvertent misuse of equipment, crashed servers, misconfigured hardware, unwarranted additions to computer equipment and theft. These all result in the breakdown or the malfunctioning of hardware that interrupts normal operation.

Staff interruptions

Staff interruptions occur where employees cause some interruption to the business processes. Staff interruptions can occur when an employee with unique skills or knowledge leaves the business or is unavailable for a long period owing to illness, accident or some other reason. If other employees lack the training and experience, those business activities performed by the absent employee are affected. A preventive control over staff interruptions is knowledge management that encourages the sharing of skills, knowledge and practices.

Another type of staff interruption is the disclosure of sensitive information to competitors or unauthorised personnel by disgruntled or laid-off employees.

Basic frameworks of IT security

IT security revolves around the concepts of deterence, detection, protection, reaction and recovery. It means having security procedures that not only protect the information resources in an organisation but also work as a deterrent and, if a breach occurs, detect the problem as soon as possible. The security should therefore include the follow-up actions or reactions necessary to enable the organisation to recover from the damage inflicted by interruption.

Organisations use various security frameworks to safeguard their information resources, depending on their requirements. IT security policies consist of clearly defined rules that outline various issues, such as how information is accessed and by whom, the level of security required and the steps to be taken when these requirements are not met. In simpler terms, it refers to the measures taken to limit the probable actions of the user, so that the organisation ensures that only genuine users are authorised to have access to information resources and they can perform only permissible actions and processes. This is known as *access control* and lies at the core of information systems security. Access controls are implemented through various *security models*.

Access control

Access control limits the user to accessing and using only those IT resources that are necessary for performing their tasks. For example, there is no need for most employees to access the accounting software of the business they work in, so they should not be able to access the software or indeed most of the data the software uses. More obviously, an online banking customer does not need and should not have access beyond their personal account details.

Access control is achieved through hardware, software applications and protocols, logical and physical policies, and supervision by system administrators. This access supervision is done by identifying user requests for access, recording attempts made to gain access (which form part of an audit trail) and granting or denying access on the basis of predetermined rules.

To this point, we have talked about secure IT systems being characterised by confidentiality, integrity and availability. We will now look at the taxonomy of access control, which adds two more principles: authentication and identification. **Authentication** is the process of establishing procedures that guarantee correctness and verification of information. **Identification** is the process of establishing the identity of users and other entities involved in the operation and maintenance of IT systems.

Recall that *confidentiality* involves measures taken to protect exclusive information from unauthorised viewing; *integrity* involves processes to maintain the authenticity of data so that it is not corrupted or manipulated in an unauthorised way; and *availability* involves ensuring that the IT systems are available and usable. In summary, access control is based on the principles of authentication, identification, confidentiality, integrity and availability.

Just as every organisation has unique information needs, security arrangements are also exclusive to business size, structure and location. However, the underlying philosophy of enforcing security is based on following access control policies: discretionary access control, mandatory access control and role-based access control, all of which are discussed below.

Discretionary access control

Discretionary access control (DAC) limits access to information and information systems by restricting a user's access to an information source, such as a file, server or a workstation. The owner of the information source controls the access. They stipulate who should have access and what type of access they should have (e.g. to read, write or delete the data).

DAC is flexible, as it provides for *centralised security* as well as *distributed security*. In centralised security, an administrator provides access to information, software applications and the network. In large businesses this policy can cause delays because one person or one team has to decide and act on granting access. In distributed security, managers, team leaders or supervisors decide and grant access to information and applications. This model speeds up the process and avoids delays, but managers and supervisors need to have a clear understanding of the data sources and IT security generally. Centralised security usually results in the consistency of access rights among those with similar job descriptions; distributed security can result in inconsistencies. Both models have their own advantages and disadvantages, and the organisation must decide which model is most suitable to its settings and size.

DAC is used by the Unix, Windows, NetWare, Linux and Vines operating systems. For example, Novell NetWare's workgroup manager provides for the creation and modification of accounts and access rights. The Windows operating system allows users to be related to an administrators group, which provides for creation of user accounts and granting access on workstations or on servers.

Mandatory access control

Mandatory access control (MAC) imposes universal security conditions that apply to all users, information systems and information resources. MAC is employed when an organisation decides that information security decisions must not be taken by the owner of the information or information resource. The security conditions are hard-coded into software, such as application programs or operating systems. MAC is most suited to military environments and other such organisations where there is considerable standardisation of processes and procedures. Common practice in this regard is to classify information on the basis of its sensitivity, secrecy and confidentiality.

Role-based access control

Role-based access control (RBAC) controls access to information systems and information resources on the basis of the individual's role in the organisation. The approach is based on the idea that in an organisation stakeholders change roles and, with changing roles, their information access needs also change. RBAC is an effective means for developing and enforcing security policies exclusive to the enterprise. It aids in rationalising security management processes.

RBAC draws on the characteristics of both DAC and MAC, such that the privileges are predefined and applied according to role. It caters for the hierarchies as well as for business constraints. *Hierarchies* help to define the level of responsibilities and their related job functions, whereas *constraints* provide for the boundary of the job assignment. For example, only one individual can be assigned to a specific role, or only a senior manager can take strategic decisions. In simpler terms, constraints provide for the regulation of the hierarchal structure.

Security models

Security models are based on the approaches to access control discussed above. Access controls are implemented through the access control matrix model or the security levels model.

Access control matrix

An **access control matrix** (ACM) defines a set of subjects (S) or requesting entities (e.g. users), a set of objects (O) or requested entities (e.g. data, programs or devices) and a set of access types (T) (e.g. read, write, append, execute) that are used to control access. For example, in a database context, subjects are the users of the database, objects are the items in the database and the access type could be insert, delete, retrieve, append or update. A combination of subject, object and access type defines an *authorisation rule*.

An extensive ACM might include a predicate, condition, flag and an authoriser. The *predicate* specifies constraints on access that depend on the context, whereas the *condition* has to be true in order for the rule to be applied. This operates as the guard against unauthorised access. The *flag* has to be in an 'on' state to allow the subject of the rule to permit access to other subjects. The *authoriser* designates who can carry out the authorisation.

The access control matrix allocates one row and one column per subject. The entry for a row and column reflects the mode of access between the corresponding subject and object. For example in figure 2.1, user Adam has read-only access to the object 2. Using this method, read–write access and execution of certain programs is bestowed on different employees according to their level of involvement in a process and their job description.

Subjects (S)	Objects (O)			
	1	2	ABC	XYZ
Adam		Read	Own Read Write	Read
Bruce		Write	Read Write	
Charlie	Read Write		Read	

Figure 2.1   An access control matrix

Although figure 2.1 is useful for conceptualising an ACM, in practice an ACM is an entirely logical mechanism. It is categorised into subdivided portions, and there are two ways of doing so:

1. *Capability lists* divide the matrix into rows, such that the access rights of one subject or user are defined. This approach is shown in figure 2.2.
2. *Access control lists (ACLs)* divide the matrix into columns and thus the access rights of a particular object are defined. An example of ACL is LDAP (Lightweight Directory Access Protocol) in the Microsoft Windows operating system. LDAP entries are related to each other in a hierarchical structure, and each entry contains the name of the object and the associated access attributes and values, such as read or write. This approach is shown in figure 2.3.

ACM is primarily used for operating systems security, but it can be applied to any system. It controls both the confidentiality and integrity of information.

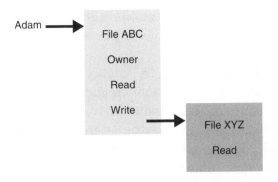

Figure 2.2   A capability list

Figure 2.3   An access control list

Security levels

The **security levels** model applies different levels of security to groups of people and data objects rather than controlling access at the individual subject or object level. There are a number of approaches to implementing a security levels model, including the multilevel, multilateral, lattice and accountability models.

Multilevel models

In a **multilevel model**, also referred to as the **data flow model**, information is categorised by sensitivity and users are provided with access on the basis of their level of responsibility. This approach is suitable for a hierarchical organisation, and most military security frameworks are based on a multilevel model. These models provide a framework for handling data of different classifications levels, such as unclassified, confidential, secret and top secret. Multilevel models are based on two rules: (1) a subject with a lower classification cannot read data at a higher classification, and (2) a subject with a higher classification cannot write data to a lower classification. Examples of such models are the Bell–La Padula model and the Biba model.

The **Bell–La Padula model** (Bell & La Padula 1975) ensures the confidentiality of information resources. It classifies subjects and data into precise sets according to confidentiality levels (e.g. secret and top secret). Categories are also specified for groups, departments and divisions of an organisation. In this model users need to have security clearance to have access to information corresponding to each level, which prevents information flow from higher security levels to lower security levels and vice versa. For example, if a user with only a secret security clearance requests access to data with a top-secret classification, this model will deny the request. These two properties are known as 'simple security property' and 'confidentiality *-property'. Simple security property means subject A (user A) can read object B (file or data B) only if subject A's classification is higher than object B's classification. This property means that the subject cannot read anything pertaining to a higher level of sensitivity. Confidentiality *-property means that subject A, who can read object B, can only write to object C if the classification of C is higher than B. This means that the subject cannot write anything pertaining to a lower level of sensitivity. However, this model also includes such subjects that could be termed as trusted subjects. These trusted subjects perform systems and information administration activities.

The **Biba model** (Biba 1977) complements the Bell–La Padula model and ensures information integrity. It works the same way as the Bell–La Padula model, except that it classifies data into levels of integrity rather than confidentiality. The two properties of this model are known as 'simple integrity property' and 'integrity *-property'. Simple integrity property means that subject A is allowed to modify object B only if the clearance level of subject A is higher than that of object B. Integrity *-property means that subject A, who can modify object B, can modify object C only if the classification of B is higher than the classification of C.

Multilevel models are secure, and it is possible to build database management systems (DBMS) and operating systems that follow multilevel approaches. However, they are most suited to hierarchical organisations, such as the military. In addition they require every piece of information to be classified. In fluid business structures, this would obviously not work.

Multilateral models

Multilateral models provide for the security requirements of all the parties involved in information exchange and information systems usage. In a way, it regards all the parties involved in the process as potential invaders of information systems security. This aspect is essential for open communication to take place. These models take into consideration four principles of information and information systems security:

- *Confidentiality.* The confidentiality of the message and its contents should be maintained, such that all the parties remain anonymous and no party should be able to identify the parties (such as sender, receiver or the systems) involved in the communication of information.
- *Availability.* The network should ensure the availability of the communication medium for all the parties involved in the communication and at the same time should prevent access by parties who are not involved in the process.
- *Integrity.* The network should be able to determine if and when a message is manipulated.
- *Accountability.* The sender and the receiver of the information should be able to confirm that the respective party sent and received the message, that the message is authentic and that it was actually sent by the sender and was received by the receiver.

In multilateral security models, information does not follow a hierarchical structure; rather it is categorised into several classes on the basis of the usage pattern of the information. This model could be viewed as balancing the needs of the stakeholders. For example, the users of a network system need their usage to be protected from hackers, unauthorised employees and competitors. At the same time the organisation needs to protect its information resources from pilferage, manipulation and destruction. Within the organisation, network operators need to protect these resources from viruses, Trojans and intentional or unintentional modification and manipulation of information resources. Network operators need protection from sabotage that could endanger the use of their systems.

The Chinese wall model (Brewer & Nash 1989) is an example of multilateral security. The objective of the Chinese wall model is to prevent information flow that would cause a conflict of interest. Users are not allowed to access, communicate or process information that has a conflict with the interest of a department, another user or a system within the organisation. Therefore users are allowed to possess and process only information already held within their computer systems or previously processed by the user. For example, someone from a marketing team would be allowed to access only information within the workgroup formed for that team. The user would not be allowed to access information of another team within the same department. If there is no conflict of interest between the two teams, the user would be allowed to access information of the other team. However, the user will not be allowed to access information from another department. This model is common among consultancy and financial service organisations where several clients might operate in the same market. Clearly it would not be appropriate for those working with one client to have access to information about a competitor.

This Chinese wall model has two properties. The 'simple security policy' means that a subject can access an object only if such a subject has or had access to such a type of object. The '* property' means a subject could write to an object or database within company A or department B only if a subject does not have read access to information in the company or department that has a conflict of interest with company A or department B unless such objects or information need sanitisation creaming.

Lattice model

Security models are aimed at securing information flows, which means that no unauthorised user is allowed to access information or even participate in the process of information flow. However, *multilevel* models are intended for hierarchical organisations, such as government or the military, where users cannot access or process information from a higher security classification to a lower classification and vice versa. *Multilateral* models are intended to control access to information without taking into consideration the information flow and the trail that information follows.

A **lattice model** (Denning 1982) combines the properties of the multilevel models and the multilateral models. This model works on the need-to-know basis, such that the information is classified into certain levels of security and the user must have security clearance in the form of a codeword to access information. In this model, the flow and relation of information form a lattice. The lattice consists of subjects, objects and security classes, and their relation defines the authorised flow of information. This flow can be reflexive and occur between subjects and objects among the class to which they belong. The relation could be *anti-symmetric*, such that if subject A has access to object ABC and object ABC has a relation with object XYZ, then subject A can access object XYZ. The relation could be *transitive*, such that if subject A has access to object ABC, object ABC has a relation with object XYZ and object XYZ has a relation with LMN, then subject A also has access to object LMN.

Accountability model

Information systems consist of people, processes (including the information communication process) and computer systems; therefore a security model must take all these aspects into consideration. An **accountability model**, as the name suggests, is aimed at the prevention of fraud and losses by employing the principle of separation of duties and clear documentation of all the activities associated with a transaction. This model actually forms an association between the subject and object through the procedures applied to the object that are intended at fulfilling a specific business process.

The Clark–Wilson accountability model (Clark & Wilson 1987) addresses the security requirements of commercial applications. It aims at enforcing information integrity on the basis of well-formed transactions and separation of duty. The model stipulates the integrity requirements of a transaction as internal and external consistency, whereby internal consistency is enforced by the computer system and external consistency is enforced through auditing. The model stipulates that users may have access to applications that manipulate data rather than having direct access to data items themselves. At the same time, *static separation of duty* is achieved by the security administrator assigning the user to membership of a workgroup, and *dynamic separation of duty* is achieved by providing for the way permissions will be used at the time of access of information. For access control the model takes into consideration the following principles:

- Subjects must be identifiable and legitimate.
- Only a restricted set of applications and programs are permissible to manipulate information.
- Subjects have execution rights of a specific set of applications and programs.
- All activities are logged.
- The system's proper operation is certified.

Protecting information and information systems

Security controls for containing and managing risks and threats posed to information resources are employed at different levels in an organisation. Consequently these controls range from simple measures on the machine level, such as password protection, through to a comprehensive information systems policy at the business level. All such measures work towards the same objective: to provide secure information systems so that business processes continue to operate smoothly. In the following sections we will discuss technical, management and operational security methods, tools and measures. Technical controls include identification, authentication, access control, audit, accountability, and system and communications protection. Management controls include risk assessment, planning, acquisitions and certification. Operational controls include personnel security, physical protection, contingency planning, maintenance, media protection and incident response (NIST 2003, p. 6).

As discussed in chapter 1, controls can be preventive, detective or corrective in nature. Given that detective controls usually trigger a corrective action, we will consider those together.

Technical controls

Technical controls are those controls that are employed at the machine level or network level. They include software and hardware controls aimed at preventing a risk event, detecting an attempted security breach or detecting an event that has occurred. These controls are supported by operational guidelines that correspond to organisational policies. Technical controls can be grouped into support, preventive, and detection and recovery controls.

Preventive controls are focused on the prevention of a security breach, for example, by limiting access to information resources. *Detection and recovery controls* are designed (a) to detect any attempts made to intrude on or affect the system and its information resources, (b) to detect a disaster or a security breach that has already occurred, and (c) to identify recovery options.

Figure 2.4 presents an overview of the controls and the relationship they strike with other security measures to ensure the technical security of the information resources of an organisation. This figure will be explained in detail in the following sections.

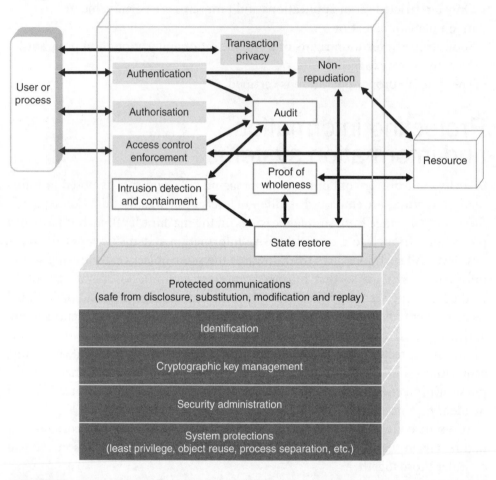

Figure 2.4   Technical security control architecture

Source: National Institute of Standards and Technology (NIST) 2002, p. 33.

Support technical controls

Support controls are derived from the security policy, information systems policy or IT policy of a business. These policies lay down the type of hardware and the software the business will procure, the mode of their procurement, the mode of software development (whether in-house or commercially developed), storage and back-up procedures and information communication procedures. These controls are at the base of the technical security control architecture shown in figure 2.4 (dark shading) and should achieve:

- *Identification.* Identification of the subjects (users) and objects (information resources and processes) provides a basis for the implementation of other security controls, such as access control policies (see discussion on pages 47–9).
- *Cryptographic key management.* Cryptography (see chapter 5) means encoding of information for transmission such that only the intended recipient is able to decode and read the actual information. The cryptographic key is the mechanism used in combination with the algorithm to validate, authenticate, cipher and decipher the information. Private keys must be safeguarded from unauthorised disclosure, alteration and replacement, and public keys must be guarded against illegal modification and substitution.
- *Security administration.* Security administration reflects the security privileges of a user within the operational environment, for example the right to install an application and the protection of user profiles and security of the workgroup.
- *System protections.* The system should ensure that groups can access the information resources they need, but not have access to information resources that should be protected from them. This represents both the physical implementation of the systems, for example in a network, and the implementation of the access to information, for example separation of access on the basis of process, department or duties.

Preventive technical controls

Preventive controls (light shading in figure 2.4) are intended to limit the violation of information resources security policy. One of the key preventive controls is *protected communications*, shown at the top of the base in figure 2.4. Critical and sensitive data, such as financial information, when communicated over a network is at the mercy of interception by means of eavesdropping and packet sniffing techniques. Protected communications ensure that the confidentiality, integrity and availability of information and related resources are maintained throughout the communication process. Common examples of this control are Virtual Private Network (VPN), Internet Protocol Security (IPSEC) protocol and cryptographic technology. Preventive control is based on five principles:

1. *Authentication.* Authentication proves the identity of the subject and makes sure that the subject is the actual receiver of particular information.
   Examples of this control include personal identification numbers, passwords, smart cards and digital certificates.
2. *Authorisation.* Authorisation controls the ability to perform certain actions on data. For example, a database administrator allows users with modification access authorisation to modify data in a database.
3. *Access control.* Access control enforces data integrity and confidentiality. It is derived from the access policy of an organisation, such as discretionary and mandatory access control (see the discussion on pp. 48–9). Access control is implemented through the hardware and software provisions, particularly through the operating system. However, the strength of this control depends

on how the access mechanism has been devised and the robustness of the application software.

4. *Non-repudiation.* In simple terms non-repudiation is the process by which the identity of the sender is known to the receiver and the sender is acknowledged on the delivery of information at the receiver's end. It works as an accountability mechanism, so that the identity of the imitator of a message could be established or the sender would know that a message intended for a particular user has not been delivered. This preventive control ensures denial of information to unauthorised users and is generally applied at the sender and receiver end. A digital certificate is an example of this control. A digital certificate uses encryption technology and works as a digital stamp.

5. *Transaction privacy.* Transaction privacy ensures confidentiality of information. Suppliers, businesses and customers are increasingly using the Internet for transactions, which requires that data (e.g. credit card details) is kept confidential in transit. This control uses such tools as Secure Sockets Layer (SSL).

Detective and corrective (recovery) technical controls

Detective controls are the whistle-blowing tools that warn an organisation of any wrongdoings, security violations or attempts made to breach the security of their information resources. These controls normally use such tools and methods as logs, audit trails and intrusion detection software to discover violations. After a security incident has occurred, corrective controls also aid recovery and prevent a recurrence. Detective and corrective controls are closely linked, as the detection of a security incident should trigger corrective action. The detective and corrective tools are shown unshaded in figure 2.4.

Audit

Audit controls deal with the analysis of security breaches. Server logs on a network server and event logging are common examples of finding out how, where and when a disaster occurred. Once the exact nature and location of the problem are found, it is easier to recover and to recommend follow-up actions to prevent the same sort of incident from happening again. In this sense audit controls are both a detective and a corrective control.

Intrusion detection and containment

Consistent monitoring of the traffic on the organisational network provides for the early detection of security breaches so that the threat can be managed at an early stage. Intrusion detection software and firewalls are common examples of detective controls.

Proof of wholeness

This control examines system integrity and the integrity of the data contained in the system and detects offences, which aids in identifying potential risks posed to information resources within an organisation.

Restore secure state

Restoring a secure state is a corrective control that enables an organisation to restore its information systems and other information resources to working condition after a security breach has occurred. This includes back-up of information and critical applications on a regular basis and having back-up hardware to complement the recovery process.

IT Risk 2.3 provides an example of how a technical corrective control led to the first conviction for wireless hacking.

Management controls

Management controls are implemented organisation-wide and are mostly in the form of policies. These controls not only manage the information resources but are also aimed at controlling the way business is conducted and the way employees contribute to the business processes. Therefore these controls are generic in nature and cover the social, economic, environmental and cultural aspects of organisational behaviour. Management security controls are enforced through information security policies and guidelines that are followed to carry out the business processes and procedures towards attaining business goals and missions. IT Risk 2.4 (p. 61) outlines how a business with centralised security management can ensure that management controls are implemented throughout the organisation.

Preventive management controls

Preventive management security controls encompass the entire organisation. These controls include the development of security policies as well as plans to ensure that an information security policy's guidelines are followed. However, it is also management's responsibility to provide for adequate security infrastructure to safeguard mission-critical applications and systems. It includes assessment of processes and the security effect of any changes on procedures and infrastructure. As a continuous measure to enforce the security of information resources, this control also stipulates personnel security controls, such as computer user access and termination, separation of duties and security awareness initiatives, and to provide training for ensuring the security of information resources.

Detective and corrective (recovery) management controls

Detective controls are aimed at continuous risk assessment. Management must continue to assess and reassess its risk environment so it becomes aware of any changes to the context in which it operates. An example of a specific detective management control is to have a policy in place to ensure that a background check is conducted on each potential new employee.

Corrective management controls deals with providing the financial resources and physical infrastructure for recovery after a disaster has occurred. This category of controls describes the follow-up actions if a major disaster occurs, so that business continuity (see chapter 1) is maintained.

IT risk 2.3

The first documented case of wireless hacking

In 2003, patients of Wake Internal Medicine in North Carolina, USA, received copies of their confidential patient records in the mail, signed by a 'Dr.StrANg3L0v3'. Several media organisations also received copies of the records. Patients who received the letters contacted Wake Internal Medicine, which in turn contacted the local police.

The medical company had recently installed a wireless network to augment its existing wired network. Unfortunately, the wireless network was insecure and had no authentication or encryption systems, thus providing a hacker with an access point to the network. However, Wake's wired network was equipped with auditing and logging software. An examination of the logs revealed that the intruding computer's name was 'conquerer.454homenet.com' and recorded the MAC address.

Network administrators at Wake searched for the term '454homenet' on the Internet and found numerous postings from a 'Clay Dillard', associated with computer security firm Securespeed. Securespeed had sent a brochure to Wake advertising its network security consulting services several weeks before the intrusion. Police found that the address for Clayton Dillard corresponded to the business address of Securespeed. The address was consistent with the postmarks of the envelopes sent to Wake patients and the media. On the basis of this, a search warrant was drawn and the FBI High-Tech Task Force investigated. Sufficient evidence of intrusion into Wake's system was recovered, and Dillard eventually confessed to the intrusion in which he accessed more than 2000 confidential patient records.

Dillard was charged with the (US) offences of unlawful access of a computer and computer trespass. He was sentenced to 18 months supervision, $9200 in restitution to Wake, 24 hours community service and forfeiture of his laptop for police department training.

The most remarkable facts of this case relate to the way Dillard was traced and eventually arrested. The major clues — the intruder's MAC address and computer name — came from Wake's internal auditing system, which was implemented on the wired network. However, these could have been manually altered before the attack, had Dillard thought to do so. Many commercial networks would not have the robust auditing that is usually found in the medical industry. Without this audit trail, or if Dillard had edited his MAC address and computer name, there would have been no way of tracking the offender. In this sense, it was only through the intruder's own carelessness that an arrest was made.

Sources: Villani 2003; Whitmire 2003; Anderson 2004.

Centralised security management

It is important that all departments in a business are represented when security polices are formulated and procedures are enacted. If each department has representation on a centralised IT security team, the needs of all departments can be covered and the existing security situation can be easily assessed. These representatives need not be IT experts: diversity allows a better insight into the issues by providing different perspectives. At the same time, it helps to formulate standardised security policies that are workable across the entire organisation. Four major activities help in managing security centrally:

1. *Formulate an organisation-wide team.* This ensures that the interests of all departments are represented, allows for appropriate resource allocation and identification of training needs, ensures that management is quickly apprised of the security situation in each department (as it provides a formalised passage of communication from lower levels to the top level) and ensures consistency of policy and practice throughout the organisation.

2. *Give the team independent access to senior executives.* Generally, information security initiatives fail or are compromised because they are formulated at the top level but enforced at the functional level. If the security team has direct access to senior management, issues at the functional level can feed back into the formulation of the policy.

3. *Allocate adequate resources.* Information security is a trade-off between costs and benefits. Like any other activity in a business, it is subject to budgetary constraints, but the business must consider the importance of IT to its operations and provide commensurate funding and other resources.

4. *Undertake staff training.* Information producers, processors, custodians and users should be well versed in security needs and controls. Training is an ongoing process, and it provides the best form of defence against the emergent threats and vulnerability of information security. Security awareness provides a second line of defence after the conventional defence provided by system administrators. Such issues as integrity of information can be detected and revealed only by those using or processing the information. Those employees who have direct responsibility for ensuring security should have some industry-accredited education, such as Certified Information Systems Security Professional (CISSP).

Operational controls

Operational security controls are the process-level measures that an organisation has to enforce in order to ensure that technical and management controls work properly. These controls should be derived from the business strategy so that they contribute to achieving the objectives of the business. Senior management commitment plays an important role in the proper administration and implementation of control policies. Operational controls not only ease the financial burden and effort involved in maintaining the security of information resources but also at the same time reduce inconsistencies among processes and their outcomes. A well-documented description of these controls with a step-by-step methodology for their implementation is necessary.

Preventive operational controls

Preventive operational security controls include such measures as preventing physical access to hard drives to restrict theft and destruction and ensuring that the media are protected from fire, magnetic, humidity and temperature hazards. These measures can be implemented by enacting such polices as having security guards, protocols for visitors, PIN requirements for access to buildings, management of locks and keys, erecting fences and having secure wiring, hubs and cables.

Detective and corrective (recovery) operational controls

Detective controls include the equipment and practices necessary to detect security breaches, such as video surveillance, alarms and smoke and fire detectors.

Corrective operational security controls include the creation and use of back-up data and activity logs to allow systems to be restored. These controls also include back-up and safety equipment, such as uninterruptible power supplies, fire extinguishers, sprinkler systems and the availability of a contingency building where the operation could be transferred in case of a major catastrophe.

Summary

IT security threats are ever-changing. At the same time, businesses are becoming increasingly reliant on information to perform their core activities. It is therefore crucial that businesses assess and continually reassess the threats posed to their information resources. Businesses must implement physical and logical security controls. Physical security relates to ensuring that IT resources are safe from physical attack and harm caused by such things as natural disasters. Logical security entails protecting the IT system from interception, modification, fabrication and interruption that could compromise the confidentiality, integrity or availability of the system. Interception occurs when an unauthorised party gains access to data through direct observation, network interception or electromagnetic interception. Modification occurs when data is changed without authorisation. Modification can be either reversible or irreversible. Fabrication occurs when data is created or manipulated but still appears to be correct.

Interruption occurs when the IT system or information becomes unavailable owing to a problem with software, hardware or staff.

Organisations should secure their IT assets by ensuring that only genuine users can access information resources and that they can perform only those actions and processes necessary to fulfil their role in the business process. This is known as access control. Discretionary access control limits access to information and information systems by restricting a user's access to the information source. The owner of the information source controls the access. Mandatory access control imposes universal security conditions that apply to all the users, information systems and information resources. The security conditions are hard-coded into software. Role-based access control controls access on the basis of the individual's role in the organisation. The approach is based on the idea that the role of the individual determines their information access needs.

Access controls are implemented through security models. The access control matrix model applies an authorisation rule to each user, IT object and process. The security levels model controls the actions of users on the basis of which organisational group they belong to; each IT object is made available or unavailable to particular groups.

The IT security plan will include a number of controls. These can be categorised as preventive, detective and corrective (or recovery) controls. Preventive controls are designed to prevent IT risks from eventuating. Detective controls are designed to detect an attempted, in-progress or successful security breach. Detective controls trigger corrective controls, which are designed to contain the problem, minimise the consequences and help the business restore its systems. The controls can be technical, management or operational in nature. Technical controls are applied to the IT system by means of hardware and software. Management controls are mostly in the forms of policies and guidelines. Operational controls work at the process level and are designed to ensure that the technical and management controls work properly. A comprehensive solution for implementation of a security infrastructure includes control measures at the technical, management and operational levels.

Questions

1. Compile a list of physical security risks.
2. Define the four types of logical security risk, providing an example of each.
3. Define access control and explain the five principles on which it operates.
4. Explain the three major access control policies and how each one differs from the others.
5. What are the main differences in approach between an 'access control matrix' and a 'security levels' model of access control?
6. Explain the purpose of (a) preventive, (b) detective and (c) corrective controls.
7. Explain at what level of the organisation technical, management and operational controls operate. Provide an example of each.

Case study
2: Secure collaboration

A small research organisation that dealt largely in research into terrorism experienced a surge in demand for its services and grew very large, very quickly in the period following the terrorist attacks on the USA on 11 September 2001. It began to take on research of a classified nature for its own government and for its government's allies.

Its research staff represented a wide range of disciplines. There were anthropologists, criminologists, economists, lawyers, security experts and several others. Some of the research staff maintained only adjunct positions; their full-time work was in universities situated around the country. They needed to carry out their work remotely as well as having secure reliable access to information.

As is the case in many situations, the information within the organisation of a classified nature could not be connected to the Internet, although the Internet was widely used for non-classified work. The staff work together on a range of projects, but not all projects require the involvement of all staff.

Questions

1. Analyse and classify the potential threats to the security of the organisation's IT infrastructure and information.
2. Describe the most useful access control mechanism that needs to be implemented in the organisation.
3. Is the Bell–La Padula security model an appropriate choice for this organisation? Describe both the human and technical issues that must be considered if it were to be implemented.

Suggested reading

National Institute of Standards and Technology (NIST) 1995, *An Introduction to Computer Security: The NIST Handbook*, SP800–12, US Department of Commerce, Washington.

—— 2002, *Risk Management Guide for Information Technology Systems*, SP800–30, US Department of Commerce, Washington.

—— 2003, *Recommended Security Controls for Federal Information Systems*, SP800–53, US Department of Commerce, Washington.

References

Anderson, H 2004, *One Year to Go — Getting Started with Your HIPAA Security Self-assessment and Planning*, North Carolina Healthcare Information and Communications Alliance (NHCICA), www.nchica.org.

Bell, DE & La Padula, LJ 1975, 'Secure computer system: Unified exposition and multics interpretation', MTR-2977, Mitre Corp., Bedford, MA, July.

Biba, KJ 1977, 'Integrity consideration for secure computer system', EDS-TR-76-372-USA, Election System Division, Bedford, MA, April.

Brewer, DFC & Nash, MJ 1989, 'The Chinese wall security policy', *IEEE Symposium on Research in Security and Privacy*, 1–3 May, Oakland, CA, pp. 206–14.

Clark, DR & Wilson, PR 1987, 'A comparison of commercial and military computer security policies', *IEEE Symposium on Research in Security and Privacy*, 1–3 May, Oakland, CA, pp. 184–94.

Denning, DE 1982, *Cryptography and Data Security*, Addison-Wesley, Reading, MA.

National Institute of Standards and Technology (NIST) 2002, *Risk Management Guide for Information Technology Systems*, SP800–30, US Department of Commerce, Washington.

—— 2003, *Recommended Security Controls for Federal Information Systems*, SP800–53, US Department of Commerce, Washington.

Villani, G 2003, 'Landmark conviction handed down', www.fuquay-varinaindependent.com.

Whitmire, T 2003, 'Three indicted for hacking Lowe's computer system', www.usatoday.com.

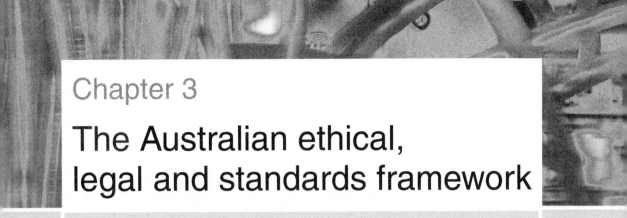

Chapter 3

The Australian ethical, legal and standards framework

Learning objectives

After studying this chapter, you should be able to:

- discuss the ethical issues in IT security and the role of professional codes of conduct

- understand the Australian legal system

- discuss Australian legislation that affects IT management, including telecommunications, cyber crime, spam, privacy and intellectual property laws

- list the key guidelines and codes of practice relating to IT security.

Chapter overview

In this chapter we review the ethical and legal principles that govern the behaviour of computing professionals, IT security managers and their employers. We examine the professional codes of conduct and Australian legislation that applies to IT security and computer crime.

Australian governments have legislated to deal with some of the major areas related to IT. These include intellectual property laws, such as privacy, copyright and patent, software piracy, telecommunications, spam and cyber crime. We investigate the way the Australian legislative framework guides and protects us in the risk management of IT security.

We conclude with an overview of Australian and international guidelines and codes of practice on IT security and risk management, security evaluation and the handling of evidence. This allows us to appreciate the frameworks that support and guide Australian IT security managers towards best practice in their management of risk.

Ethics

In order to examine the ethical and legal issues pertaining to IT security and risk management, we need to understand the difference between ethics and law. A set of **ethics** comprises impartially defined principles and values that pertain to an individual or group in society. The **law** that expresses particular behaviour that is deemed acceptable to a given society or culture and then seeks to enforce this behaviour.

In Australia, we are all governed by Australian law, but we are a multiracial and multicultural nation and we draw, individually and collectively, on principles and values that might have been established by, for example, our religious or political belief systems. These will obviously differ from faith to faith, ideology to ideology and individual to individual.

It is therefore important, when working in such a sensitive area as IT security, for us to understand that ethics are not only crucial but also that they can differ widely from individual to individual within an organisation. We need to make 'good' decisions, and we need to know that others in the organisation will make 'good' decisions so that the IT infrastructure is protected from risk. However, there are no absolutes by which we can define 'good'; what is 'good' to you is not necessarily 'good' to me. Morality will differ between individuals according to their nature, background, temperament and upbringing. Such differences must be taken into account when managing IT security risk. Examples of ethical differences involved in the work life of IT security professionals include attitudes to:

- downloading pirated software, music and video files
- non-business use of the Internet while at work

- using the organisation's software, hardware and other resources for personal work or entertainment.

Different ethical positions that might be encountered in the administration of systems and risk management include:

- the attitude of hackers to breaching systems: we might not expect hackers to be as bold as they sometimes are in their attempts to use our resources or bandwidth
- the attitude of staff to protecting the IT system from risk: managing the risk to the organisation's IT system is a time-consuming struggle, and different individuals will have different attitudes about the worth of devoting time and effort to dealing with risks that have a high degree of uncertainty.

Professional bodies, such as the **Australian Computer Society** (ACS) and the US Institute of Electrical and Electronic Engineers (IEEE), have tried to deal with this issue by establishing general **codes of ethics** for computing professionals. By doing so, they are declaring that if an individual intends to be an IT professional then the rest of the profession and its 'elders' have professional expectations of morality, conduct and an ethical rationale behind professional decision-making. Membership of these organisations imposes an obligation to uphold the codes. An extract of the code of the Australian Computer Society is shown in figure 3.1 (p. 70). This code describes the moral principles to which members commits themselves as general computing professionals. A company that employed an IT security manager who was able to demonstrate the integrity encapsulated in this code of ethics could expect a trustworthy employee and have a set of values and principles against which to hold the IT employee accountable.

The professional bodies seek to enforce compliance with the codes through a range of penalties. The penalties have true power only when there is a link between professional membership and employability. In some contexts and professions, it is difficult or impossible to get an expert position unless one is a member of the relevant professional body. Generally speaking, however, Australian IT professionals can gain employment without membership of the Australian Computer Society. Therefore the society is limited in its ability to enforce the code. (This situation is quite different from that of professional engineers in Australia, who cannot be employed in positions of authority without membership of the Institution of Engineers Australia. Hence the Institution of Engineers is in a stronger position to enforce its code.)

Organisations that employ computing professionals who belong to such organisations as ACS and IEEE can be assured that members will have both studied ethics as they pertain to computing and committed themselves to work according to these ethical principles and values.

Other bodies have also devised codes of ethics. For example, the **International Informations Systems Security Certification Consortium ((ISC)²)**, a non-profit organisation that oversees such professional certifications as Certified Information Systems Security Professional (CISSP), has devised a code. The CISSP certification is becoming more desirable and essential for IT and information systems security practitioners in Australia and the Asia–Pacific. The ethical principles on which such bodies as (ISC)² are founded extend the general ethical values of ACS and apply them specifically to IT security and risk management. The (ISC)² Code of Ethics is based on four basic principles, referred to as canons (see figure 3.2). The canons have been designed to give direction to IT security professionals as they go about their work. They have a particular focus on protecting individuals, IT infrastructures and society.

4.3 Values and Ideals

I must act with professional responsibility and integrity in my dealings with the community and clients, employers, employees and students. I acknowledge:

4.3.1 Priorities

I must place the interests of the community above those of personal or sectional interests.

4.3.2 Competence

I must work competently and diligently for my clients and employers.

4.3.3 Honesty

I must be honest in my representations of skills, knowledge, services and products.

4.3.4 Social Implications

I must strive to enhance the quality of life of those affected by my work.

4.3.5 Professional Development

I must enhance my own professional development, and that of my colleagues, employees and students.

4.3.6 Information Technology Profession

I must enhance the integrity of the information technology profession and the respect of its members for each other.

Figure 3.1	Australian Computer Society Code of Ethics, extract

Source: extracted from ACS 2004.

Australian law

Computer crime is a significant risk to individuals and companies. Australian federal and state laws have had to be adapted to deal with the growth in magnitude and sophistication of computer crime. Each state has its own legislation, and both major similarities and some differences can be found between the legislation of the states. It must be remembered that in many cases existing legislation is applicable to new crimes. For example, the growth of e-commerce and trading has given rise to a range of common offences, such as items being paid for via Internet auctions but not being delivered. This type of offence can be dealt with by existing criminal legislation since it is still an issue of fraud, albeit perpetrated electronically. Similarly the theft of a computer does not need to be covered by its own 'cyber' law.

Protect society, the commonwealth, and the infrastructure

- Promote and preserve public trust and confidence in information and systems.
- Promote the understanding and acceptance of prudent information security measures.
- Preserve and strengthen the integrity of the public infrastructure.
- Discourage unsafe practice.

Act honourably, honestly, justly, responsibly, and legally

- Tell the truth; make all stakeholders aware of your actions on a timely basis.
- Observe all contracts and agreements, express or implied.
- Treat all constituents fairly. In resolving conflicts, consider public safety and duties to principals, individuals, and the profession in that order.
- Give prudent advice; avoid raising unnecessary alarm or giving unwarranted comfort. Take care to be truthful, objective, cautious, and within your competence.
- When resolving differing laws in different jurisdictions, give preference to the laws of the jurisdiction in which you render your service.

Provide diligent and competent service to principals

- Preserve the value of their systems, applications, and information.
- Respect their trust and the privileges that they grant you.
- Avoid conflicts of interest or the appearance thereof.
- Render only those services for which you are fully competent and qualified.

Advance and protect the profession

- Sponsor for professional advancement those best qualified. All other things equal, prefer those who are certified and who adhere to these canons. Avoid professional association with those whose practices or reputation might diminish the profession.
- Take care not to injure the reputation of other professionals through malice or indifference.
- Maintain your competence; keep your skills and knowledge current. Give generously of your time and knowledge in training others.

| **Figure 3.2** | **(ISC)² Code of Ethics, extract** |

Source: extract from (ISC)² Code of Ethics, www.isc2.org/cgi-bin/contact.cgi.

It is important to consider that the law not only protects the business, providing a deterrent and an avenue of redress; it also imposes significant obligations on the business. As discussed in chapter 1, non-compliance with legal obligations is a significant IT risk that must be managed.

The Australian legal system

Australia's legal system is based on English law. Australians are subject to two legal systems: the federal system and the system of their state. There are two sources of law: **statute law**, which is the legislation enacted by parliaments, and **common law**, which is judge-made law derived from court judgements handed down throughout the history of the legal system. Common law relies on the doctrine of precedent and is based on the idea that the law should evolve gradually and logically and that cases similar to earlier cases should be treated in the same way (Quirk & Forder 2003).

There are also two types of law: criminal law and civil law. **Criminal law** applies to those actions that the state considers significant enough to warrant taking action against. **Civil law** refers to legal matters between individuals or organisations (Quirk & Forder 2003).

International law is a special area in that it is generally not enforceable. Many countries agree to observe international laws by entering into international treaties or conventions, but an international law only becomes applicable within a country once its parliament enacts legislation to give the law force (Quirk & Forder 2003). International law is of increasing importance in the context of e-commerce, in which transactions and information exchange regularly and easily occur across national borders. Which laws would apply, for example, if an Australia-based employee of a Japanese company uses the Internet to purchase software from a US company that has its e-commerce servers in its European office?

A discussion of the laws affecting business and IT could (and do) fill many books. Here we will focus on the key legislation that governs IT in Australia.

Telecommunications legislation

In Australia, the primary federal networking and communications legislation is the *Telecommunications Act 1997*. This legislation provides protection for personal and corporate risk by prohibiting breaches of privacy in telecommunication traffic. It includes clauses presuming that personal communications will be kept private and forbids all outside or illegal access to wired telecommunications networks. It does allow for exceptions where police and intelligence agencies need to tap phone calls or request electronic data to investigate crime or terrorism. Section 282 of the Telecommunications Act allows police and other intelligence agencies to request that Internet service providers (ISPs) provide telecommunications records if the disclosure is reasonably necessary for the enforcement of the criminal law. If an enterprise is operating as an ISP it is obliged to store the required files, then to release them to the police or other intelligence agencies on request. It will be seen later that the Australian privacy legislation allows release of data to a range of agencies in the case of legal action and life-threatening circumstances.

The security of wireless networks and the ability for insecure networks to be used for the launching of attacks on the Australian national (or international) IT infrastructure is a matter of national concern. Wireless networks are a relatively new innovation, and in Australia there is no legislation that prevents listening in to wireless networks. As we will see in chapter 9, wireless networks are relatively easy targets for attackers. An offence is committed only after an unauthorised individual connects their computer to a wireless network resource (a very simple task using Windows XP and family operating environments.)

The Cybercrime Act (see below) does not specifically mention the monitoring of wireless networks and becomes relevant only in the event that the communication medium is deliberately made unusable or intentionally impaired. This law was written for wired networks, and further legal issues would arise if it was enforced over an unregulated radio frequency.

However, state laws differ. For example the South Australian Summary Offences Act dictates that a 'person who, without proper authorization, operates a restricted-access computer system is guilty of an offence'. This law would be violated if one entered a network, wired or wireless, without specific approval to do so.

The *Cybercrime Act* 2001

In January 2001, the Model Criminal Code Damage and Computer Offences Report was produced for the Australian Government as a result of consultation between the various Commonwealth and state justice and law enforcement agencies so as to determine the need for new computer legislation to deal with the risk to the Australian national IT infrastructure. This report was commissioned to examine the conflict between the development of new computer crimes and older criminal legislation. One of the results of this process was the *Cybercrime Act* 2001. This Commonwealth Act inserts new material into the Criminal Code, producing a number of new computer offences, such as denial of service and virus propagation, and provides legislative powers to aid law enforcement agencies in the investigation of these crimes. The offences are broadly consistent with international approaches.

The offences are contained within sections 477 and 478 of the *Criminal Code Act 1995*. Offences under section 477 include:
- 'Unauthorised access, modification or impairment with intent to commit a serious offence' (s. 477.1)
- 'Unauthorised modification of data to cause impairment' (s. 477.2)
- 'Unauthorised impairment of electronic communication' (s. 477.3).

Offences under section 478 include:
- 'Unauthorised access to, or modification of, restricted data' (s. 478.1)
- 'Unauthorised impairment of data held on a computer disk etc.' (s. 478.2)
- 'Possession or control of data with intent to commit a computer offence' (s. 478.3)
- 'Producing, supplying or obtaining data with intent to commit a computer offence' (s. 478.4).

The offences place an emphasis on the degradation or damage of IT systems and their interactions. Specific offences deal with the possession of data (e.g. malware code) with the intent to commit a crime. The application of the laws will depend on judicial interpretation, which will be established over time (Quirk & Forder 2003).

It is beyond the scope of this book to examine state legislation in a comprehensive way, but by way of comparison, IT Risk 3.1 outlines South Australia's approach to dealing with computer offences.

IT risk 3.1

South Australian computer offence legislation

In many cases older legislation cannot be adapted to deal with new, technically mediated crime. In January 2000 the Model Criminal Code Officers Committee released a discussion paper on Criminal Damage and Computer Offences (quoted in SAPOL 2003). On 30 May 2004 amendments to the South Australian *Criminal Law Consolidation Act 1935* (CLCA) and the South Australian *Summary Offences Act 1953* (SOA) were established to deal with computer offences.

South Australian legislation includes the offences of:

- 'unauthorised access to or modification of computer data' (s. 86C, CLCA)

- 'unauthorised impairment of electronic communication' (s. 86D, CLCA)

- 'Use of a computer with intention to commit, or facilitate the commission of, an offence' (ss. 86E–86F, CLCA)

- 'Unauthorised modification of computer data' (s. 86G, CLCA)

- 'Unauthorised impairment of electronic communication' (s. 86H, CLCA)

- 'Possession of computer viruses etc with intent to commit a serious offence' (s. 86I, CLCA)

- 'unlawful operation of computer system' (s. 44, SOA)

- 'unauthorised impairment of data held in credit card or on computer disk or other device' (s. 44A, SOA).

In its entirety, the South Australian legislation deals with unauthorised modification of data (without permission of the owner of the data), impairment of communication within a network, use of a computer to modify data (i.e. hacking) or to commit another offence inside or outside the state, and all types of denial of service. Sentences can be up to 10 years in length if offenders are found guilty. The act of supplying data so that this type of crime can be carried out also carries a sentence of three years imprisonment, as does the supplying of a computer virus or a document to allow such a crime to be carried out.

An offender who accesses a system but does no harm to it has still committed an offence that makes them liable to a fine of $2500 or imprisonment for six months. Similarly, it is an offence to damage data stored on a computer disk, credit card or other kind of device used to store data by electronic means (although this act must have been carried out intentionally or irresponsibly). A penalty of up to two years imprisonment accompanies this offence.

Other South Australian legislation relevant to the issue of computer-enabled crime includes:

- 'dishonest manipulation of machines' (s. 141, CLCA), such as breaking into automatic teller machines, hacking, and accessing bank and other kinds of electronic account. This kind of crime can draw a sentence of up to 10 years.

- 'unlawful stalking' (s. 19AA, CLCA). The unlawful stalking legislation was extended in 2001 to include 'cyber stalking'. This can involve offences committed by the use of email, chatrooms, newsgroups and offensive websites. The offence, or suspected illegal action, has to be carried out at least twice to be considered stalking.

- 'interference with approved system or equipment' (s. 41, Casino Act). This legislation deals with computer-enabled crimes in casinos (e.g. using software to cheat at cards or roulette).

- 'making available or supplying objectionable matter on an on-line service' (s. 75C, Classification (Publication, Films and Computer Games) Act)

- 'making available or supplying matter unsuitable for minors on an on-line service' (s. 75D, Classification (Publication, Films & Computer Games) Act).

The last two offences relate to the online supply of Internet content consisting of a film that is classified X or that would, if classified, be classified X; or a film or computer game that is classified RC (refused classification) or that would, if classified, be classified RC.

Spam legislation

Spam is unsolicited email. Generally it advertises a range of legal and not-so-legal or moral services. It has become a major problem in recent years. It is an IT risk for companies for three reasons:
1. It uses up human and IT resources in the maintenance of mail servers and mail boxes and the establishment of filters and rules to try to keep spam off corporate and ISP servers.
2. Spammers might use corporate servers to send their spam.
3. Small to medium-sized enterprises that wish to use email as a legitimate marketing tool might inadvertently breach spam rules. IT managers and system administrators need a clear understanding of the nature of spam from the perspectives of both sender and receiver.

As mentioned in IT Risk 3.2, the *Spam Act 2003* was developed to deal with the large amount of unwanted email that clogs and even literally blocks email boxes. The legislation prohibits unsolicited commercial electronic messages but seeks to allow legitimate business communication activities.

Privacy laws

The risk to privacy is an issue of great concern in many parts of Australian society, particularly to some subcultures. Although some have no qualms about giving personal data for surveys and market research (for example), other individuals protect their personal information fiercely and will not allow it to be disclosed unless they have strict control over the manner and scope of this activity.

The *Privacy Act 1988* deals with the manner in which government, businesses and health providers collect information from individuals and what they can do with it. It is built around 10 privacy principles that deal with:
- Principle 1: Collection
- Principle 2: Use and disclosure
- Principle 3: Data quality
- Principle 4: Data security
- Principle 5: Openness
- Principle 6: Access and correction
- Principle 7: Identifiers
- Principle 8: Anonymity
- Principle 9: Transborder data flows
- Principle 10: Sensitive information.

The IT security manager has to deal wisely with issues of privacy of data since this legislation provides for a high level of privacy for individuals. General principles that apply include that of openness and fairness in the collection of data. Besides the legal risk, the organisation's reputation could be seriously damaged by a breach of privacy obligations. We will now look at the application of the 10 privacy principles.

Collection

When data is collected the individual to whom it relates must be aware of the name and nature of the organisation collecting the data and the use to which the data will be put. They must be able to contact the organisation to access the data and know any legal implications of withholding the data. This means that to protect against risk of breaching this legislation, the organisation collecting the data must make sure that, for example, any web forms used for data collection are properly headed and labelled and that clear warnings, disclaimers and instructions are included.

IT risk 3.2

Is my company inadvertently sending spam?

The Australian Government has devised guidelines (DCITA and ACA 2004) for industry to consider when deciding whether they are complying with the *Spam Act 2003*. Two major points raised are those of 'consent' (you must have the recipient's consent before you send your message) and 'identity' (you must identify yourself). Other issues include providing a method whereby a consenting subscriber or recipient is able to 'unsubscribe'. The guidelines include the advice given in figure 3.3.

Step 1 — Consent

Your commercial messages should only be sent when you have **consent**.

This may be **express consent** from the person you wish to contact — a direct indication that it is okay to send the message, or messages of that nature.

It is also possible to **infer consent** based on a business or other relationship with the person, and their conduct.

Step 2 — Identify

Your commercial messages should always contain clear and accurate **identification** of who is responsible for sending the message, and how they can be contacted.

It is important for people to know who is contacting them, and how they can get in touch in return. This will generally be the organisation that authorises the sending of the message, rather than the name of the person who actually hits the 'send' button.

Identification details that are provided must be reasonably likely to be accurate for a period of 30 days after the message is sent. This would be a consideration if the business was about to change address.

Step 3 — Unsubscribe

Your commercial messages should contain an **unsubscribe facility**, allowing people to indicate that such messages should not be sent to them in future. This could be as simple as a line in your message saying 'If you wish to opt out from future messages, send a reply with the subject UNSUBSCRIBE'.

After a person indicates that they wish to unsubscribe, you have five working days to honour their request.

Similar to the identification of the message's sender (step 2, above) the unsubscribe facility must be reasonably likely to remain accurate and functional for a 30-day period. It need not be an automated process, but should be reliable.

Figure 3.3	Guidelines for companies about avoiding spam

Source: DCITA and ACA 2004.

Use and disclosure

This principle relates to disclosure: allowing another party access to the collected data for secondary purposes other than those stated when the data was collected. Although there are some exceptions to this principle for extreme or 'life and death' issues, individuals needs to give permission before their data is used for alternative reasons. From an IT risk management perspective, this means that database security management assumes a high level of importance. Database management systems must be configured correctly, and special attention must be focused on authentication and access control so that information cannot be accessed, without authority, from a user within an organisation or from an external breach to the system.

Data quality and data security

Organisations are obliged to deal with issues of confidentiality, availability and integrity as described throughout this book so as to ensure that all data is kept safe and secure. If a user's data is disclosed to a third party, once again the greatest potential risk is to the reputation of the organisation collecting the data and of public and corporate trust in the organisation.

Openness, access and correction

An organisation must have open policies describing how it manages the privacy of collected information and then has to make this information accessible to the individuals from whom the data has been collected so that they can correct any errors in it.

Identifiers

If an organisation collects information on an individual it is not allowed to use the **identifier**, such as a membership number or other number by which the individual supplying the information may be identified, for indexing the data. This principle means that, for example, an individual's tax file number may not be used by an organisation other than the Australian Taxation Office for indexing an individual's personal information.

Anonymity

Where possible, an individual should be allowed to supply information anonymously. This action is one that will drastically reduce risk should there be a breach of confidentiality of data.

Transborder data flow

This principle describes several important conditions under which data may be transferred overseas. This has to be done either with the permission or in the interests of the individual who has given the data, and where the data will be handled in a manner similar to that specified within the 10 privacy principles and where there is little or no risk of disclosure of information.

Sensitive information

This kind of information, such as medical history or bank account details, may not be collected without permission unless legally required, or without regard to the benefit of the individual owning the data.

Intellectual property law

Intellectual property refers to literary, artistic and scientific works, performances, inventions, scientific works, performances, inventions, scientific discoveries, industrial designs, trade marks and protection against unfair competition and all other rights resulting from intellectual activity in the scientific, literary and artistic fields (Quirk & Forder 2003, p. 180). Intellectual property is protected by law under the principle that the creator has the right to control and profit from their creation, but the laws vary considerably around the world. There is considerable risk when computers are used to store intellectual property and when websites, files and other networked resources are considered as intellectual property. This also impinges on the development of software, hardware and computer peripherals, the copying of files, websites and other Internet-mediated resources and any other matter where computers and new products or ideas may be linked.

Legislation related to intellectual property governs topics such as: patents, trade marks, designs and circuit layouts and diagrams, copyright, confidentiality and trade secrets. Increasingly, businesses rely on intellectual property for competitive advantage. The protection of intellectual property, then, might well impinge on issues of IT security risk management. Issues of particular importance in the IT arena include copyright, software piracy, trademarking and patenting, all of which are discussed below.

Copyright

In Australia, **copyright** is governed by the *Copyright Act 1968*. This Act protects the expression of ideas in all forms of artistic media, such as music, literature and art, as well as computer programs. The *idea* itself is not subject to copyright but the *expression* of the idea is. This is an important distinction. I might want to express an artistic concept: 'A portrait of a systems administrator installing a firewall'. I can paint a picture and sell a portrait of the systems administrator. You can also paint a portrait of a systems administrator and sell it. I do not 'own' the idea for that painting. However, you cannot copy my painting or use my illustration. You cannot scan it or do anything else to replicate it. In Australia, copyright protection is free and automatic for the person expressing their ideas. Under the Copyright Act, there are a number of exceptions that allow some copying. These include fair dealing for research, study, criticism or review.

An understanding of the IT risks accompanying copyright protection is important in the IT world for those who develop and use software and for those who develop websites or wish to download online information or files of many formats available via the Internet.

The Australian Copyright Council, a non-profit organisation set up to educate copyright owners and the public on the rights of copyright owners and the legal responsibility of the public, states:

> Generally, you will infringe copyright if you use copyright material in one of the ways that copyright owners control, without permission, in circumstances to which no exception applies. For example, you might infringe copyright if you do any of the following:
>
> - print material from a website or a bulletin board without express or implied permission;
> - download a pirated version of a movie (that is, a movie posted to the Net or made available by P2P software or over P2P networks without permission);
> - save material from a website or a bulletin board onto your hard drive without express or implied permission;
> - download pirated copies of a song or software; or
> - email material from a website or a bulletin board to other people without express or implied permission. (ACC 2004)

These regulations are very stringent. If the copyright owner of a resource, such as a website, has not explicitly given permission for its download, then permission must be sought before any of the following is carried out: downloading files, copying information or forwarding material.

Systems administrators and those who manage other IT resources could consider both implementing policies that ban the downloading of particular files to their intranets (e.g. mp3 files) so as to comply with the Copyright Act and limiting the risk to the organisation of the deliberate downloading of pornographic images and large music files, all of which waste the organisation's resources.

Business organisations should also consider a range of methods to protect their own intellectual property. Publishing materials on the web makes it quite easy for people to copy or repurpose that material. One relatively easy method can be to post all web documents that need to be available to customers (e.g. white papers or fact sheets) in portable document format (.pdf) rather than in the application in which they were created and then to copy-protect the pdf document.

Computer software and software piracy

The Australian Copyright Council makes it clear that creators of computer software have some very distinct rights under Australian law:

> Owners of copyright in computer programs have a number of exclusive rights, including the right to:
>
> - reproduce the program in a material form (this includes copying the program to the hard disk of a computer, and writing or typing the source code of the program);
> - publish the program (this means to make the program public for the first time in Australia);
> - make an 'adaptation' of the program (this means making a version of the program in either the same or a different language, code or notation: for example, a program in object code may be an adaptation of its source code version); and
> - communicate the program to the public (by making it available online, or by electronically transmitting it, using any type of cable or wireless technology including the Internet). (ACC 2003b)

Anyone else who wishes to have any of the same rights of reproducing, editing or publishing the software must purchase a licence to do so from the original creator. The licence will specify what the licensee may do. There are some problems with the creation of applications; a licensed owner of, for example, a spreadsheet application, might develop a spreadsheet for very specific purposes. The copyright of the new application, as with the copyright of every piece of code, will rest with the developer unless it was developed under a contract between a client and the programmer's employer.

Software piracy involves the copying of software, usually by a licence holder, for distribution and resale to others who do not hold licences for the product. This is a widespread offence, and many products are made available, often for very short periods, through illicit websites, hosted in many parts of the world and most commonly in China.

The Business Software Alliance 2003 Survey noted that, of the US$85 billion of software installed worldwide in 2003, only US$51 billion of it was installed legally (BSA 2003). The Australian piracy rate in 2003 was 31 per cent compared with 32 per cent in 2002. The Australian rate is much higher than that of its peers and neighbours; New Zealand shows a piracy rate of 23 per cent, the USA 22 per cent and the UK 29 per cent. This study showed a total loss of US$341 million in Australia in 2003 through software piracy.

Organisations should ensure that all of the software on their IT systems is properly licensed and that policies and controls to deter or prevent unauthorised employees from installing software are in place.

Patent

A patent (IP Australia 2004d) is an acknowledgement that a newly invented piece of equipment, compound, technique or procedure is original. In the IT world, patents apply to hardware and devices, and copyright is used to protect software and its underlying mathematical models, algorithms and coding.

Patents are received by application to Intellectual Property Australia (IP Australia; an Australian Government organisation). All applications and claims are thoroughly examined and then, if an applicant can prove they have a novel idea, a patent, granting exclusive rights to all commercial income from the technology, is issued.

Standards and guidelines

If we move our focus from the law, which we have seen is intended to establish correct and acceptable behaviour, we then turn to standards and guidelines. International bodies and national government establish such standards and guidelines to help their members and citizens, in this context, to run businesses and control enterprises that have safe and secure IT infrastructures. **Standards** and **guidelines** of this kind cannot then be enforced by law (and neither would governments intend this to be the case). Rather they serve as models and templates to ensure efficient and protected networks and systems for Australian government, industry and commercial enterprises.

A series of national and international standards guide the establishment and maintenance of secure systems, and others deal with risk management in this IT security environment. We referred to some of these in chapter 1 when we first explored the concept of risk management. Here we look in detail at several different guidelines and standards:

- *OECD Guidelines for the Security of Information Systems and Networks: Towards a Culture of Security*
- AS/NZS ISO/IEC 17799:2001, *Code of Practice for Information Security Management*
- HB 231:2000, *Information Security Risk Management Guidelines*
- HB 171: 2003, *Guidelines for the Management of IT Evidence*
- COBIT
- ITIL
- the US Federal Chief Information Officers Council risk management guidelines (CIO 2004).

OECD *Guidelines for the Security of Information Systems and Networks*

The *OECD Guidelines for the Security of Information Systems and Networks* (OECD 2002) are subtitled 'Towards a culture of security', and the theme of an

IT security culture (and even the effect of culture on IT security) is one that the authors have explored in their research. The guidelines establish principles for the creation of an environment in which information systems (IS) security is valued and encouraged. In this context, the use of the word 'culture' implies that IS security has to be so embedded in work practice that it is a feature which does not have to be considered separately. As the OECD guidelines state, security of systems used to be an afterthought, something to be considered when a system had been designed, developed and implemented, but, given the risks that arise globally with the interconnection of systems, the perspective of system security as an 'add-on' can no longer be allowed to linger.

The OECD guidelines present nine basic principles on which a culture of IS security can be founded. These are:
1. awareness
2. responsibility
3. response
4. ethics
5. democracy
6. risk assessment
7. security design and implementation
8. security management
9. reassessment (OECD 2002, pp. 10–12).

These IS security principles draw a rich picture in which every enterprise, large or small, is aware of the need for security within their own organisation and the measures they, as individuals or companies, need to take to ensure the security of their organisation's information systems (**awareness**). They are also cognisant of the fact that they personally are accountable for system security (**responsibility**) and that they need to take action if their computer or network is breached (**response**).

They will react, in circumstances where IS security is at risk, putting the legitimate interest of others first (ethics) and negotiate, where there is any dissension or disagreement, in a consultative fashion (**democracy**).

They will regularly assess their own systems to ascertain whether there are new security risks to be understood and dealt with (**risk assessment**). To aid in the process of risk management they will embed security controls and processes at initial the system design and implementation stage (**security design and implementation**).

They will implement a well-thought-out security management plan (**security management**) and regularly reassess it as their organisation and its systems change or grow (**reassessment**).

AS/NZS ISO/IEC 17799:2001 *Code of Practice for Information Security Management*

Having established some basic principles for system security and the minimisation of risk to systems within the OECD guidelines, the AS/NZS ISO/IEC

17799:2001 *Code of Practice for Information Security Management* (AS/NZS 2001) then provides a basis for fleshing them out and supplies a detailed code of practice for establishing good information security management in an organisation. The code of practice establishes that an enterprise needs to deal with the following issues:

1. security policy
2. organisational security management
3. asset classification and control
4. personnel security
5. physical and environmental security
6. organisational communication and operations management
7. access control
8. systems development and maintenance
9. business continuity management
10. compliance.

The International Organization for Standardization (ISO) and the International Electrotechnical Commission (IEC) are bodies set up to establish worldwide technical standards. The Australian implementation of this standard is AS/NZS 7799:2:2003 *Specification for Information Security Management Systems*. It provides the evaluation criteria that can be applied to achieve a formal certification. This certification thus declares that a specified information system can meet the established **evaluation criteria** (a set of predetermined features that can be used as metrics to determine system security).

More guidance on setting up a secure system can be found in AS/NZS 13335:2000, *Guidelines for IT Security*. The information included in this standard is useful for a small organisation that does not require a formal security evaluation but nevertheless wishes to implement a secure system.

Security policy

A **corporate security policy** (discussed briefly in chapter 1) is a set of rules, regulations and practices that comprise the ways in which the IT assets, including data, within the organisation are to be protected. The policy must address all forms of data and all aspects of control. The rules in the policy are high level and of a general nature. Specific techniques and processes are not detailed in this document, but it should define a range of countermeasures that management intends to be used and the manner in which and the extent to which the countermeasures will be utilised.

There will then be a set of **subsidiary security policies** for each major system or network within the company. Each policy will bear a resemblance to the corporate IT policy but will be tailored to each subsystem and describe specific countermeasures that will be used.

Within a very sensitive environment it might also be necessary to produce a **technical security policy** that specifies the hardware and software security aspects in more detail. It is also necessary to produce a **personnel security policy** so that all staff who operate IT equipment operate in such a way that data safety and security are ensured. If staff are not trained in a systematic manner, it is highly unlikely that they will be able to meet management objectives and so will carry out this kind of work in their own way. It will be very difficult to hold them accountable if something goes wrong.

Security **operating procedures** must detail security arrangements, staff responsibilities and staff duties. These operating procedures must be easy to understand, promoted throughout the organisation and enforced.

Operating procedures need to include all those aspects of IT security detailed in the IT security policy statement. They will need to be system specific and be clear, concise, relevant and understandable. This documentation needs to be prepared as part of the cycle of procurement, development and commissioning (or developed by a new manager for an existing system if there is not one in existence). They need to be approved by senior managers to ensure they receive appropriate support.

Refer to chapters 1 and 2 for more discussion on the development of security policies.

Organisational security management

The AS/NZS ISO/IEC 17799:2001 *Code of Practice for Information Security Management* (ISO 2001) suggests that the management of any organisation should establish a cross-disciplinary framework for coordinating information and systems security within the enterprise. This establishes how policy should be set and controlled, who by and in what manner information security is monitored throughout the organisation and how to establish mechanisms for gaining external advice and developing cooperation with other organisations. It also establishes methods of dealing with information security issues that arise in the employment of contractors and in outsourcing information processing and other IT services.

Asset classification and control

In this section of the AS/NZS ISO/IEC 17799:2001 standard (ISO 2001, p. 8) recommendations are given on the need for the inventory and classification of all hardware, software and information owned by an organisation. The standard emphasises also that processes must be developed for the appropriate labelling and handling of data.

Personnel security

Personnel security, as described in the AS/NZS ISO/IEC 17799:2001 standard (ISO 2001, p. 11), involves mapping the role of IT or system security in a given position description and the particular responsibilities that accompany a given role in the organisation.

Concerns that need to be considered include: clearances and confidentiality agreements, training and incident reporting, and the establishment of disciplinary processes to enforce security policies.

Physical and environmental security

This section of the standard (ISO 2001, p. 13) encourages enterprises to determine the level of sensitivity of information that will be handled within an organisation and then to establish physical security measures of an appropriate level to handle the perceived risks to the information.

Topics that need to be considered include: the nature of the security perimeter (e.g. a fence, a manned reception desk) and the physical entry controls; how offices and other facilities might be secured; how secure areas are to be managed; and the security and maintenance of equipment, cabling, power supply and their protection against fire, flood and a variety of other natural and human disasters.

Communication and operations management

This section of the standard (ISO 2001, p. 19) deals with the operation of information processing facilities. It requires managers of enterprises to consider how they are going to document and manage change in all the procedures that govern information systems management within the organisation. They all need to consider how the reporting of security breaches and any other suspected security incident might be handled. They need to take into account how to protect an organisation through 'segregation of duties', so that 'no single person can perpetrate fraud in areas of single responsibility without being detected. The initiation of an event should be separated from its authorization.' (ISO 2001, p. 21)

Other issues of concern in this section involve: how new systems might be implemented; how an organisation could protect itself against viruses and malware; the backing-up of data, network management and handling of computer media software licensing; and email and e-commerce security. Many of these issues are dealt with in detail in other chapters of this book.

Access control and authorisation

In this part of the standard (ISO 2001, p. 33) the major recommendations include:
- advising companies to set up business rules and then technical controls to determine which users need access to specific information
- recommending the strict management of all users and the granting of appropriate rights and privileges
- proposing procedures to protect access to networks, operating systems and applications (including mobile ones)
- advocating proper monitoring and logging
- urging that security is built in to all systems and that cryptographic controls are used where appropriate.

Systems development and maintenance

IT infrastructure, hardware, software and data systems should be planned, developed and maintained in such a way that security is built into the organisation's information systems. This requires security requirements to be identified and evaluated early.

Business continuity management

Organisations are urged to plan how they will continue operating in the event of any kind of system breach or natural or human disaster that shuts down their system or in the event that critical network infrastructure becomes unavailable to them. They are urged to develop, test and maintain continuity plans that deal with all aspects of their enterprise. This issue was discussed in depth in chapter 1.

Compliance

An organisation needs to comply with all legislation (as illustrated earlier in this chapter), technical guidelines and any government regulations on such technical issues as cryptographic control and security audit.

HB 231:2000 *Information Security Risk Management Guidelines*

When we begin to consider IT security risk management in a deeper fashion, we assume we have set up an organisational information system in a manner that conforms to both the *OECD Guidelines for the Security of Information Systems and Networks* and the AS/NZS ISO/IEC 17799:2001 *Code of Practice for Information Security Management*. In this idealistic situation, we would then have engendered a culture of IT security and established a comprehensive framework of policies and procedures that implemented sound security work practices, approaches and techniques.

After this was in place, the next task would be to establish an overarching IT security risk management program to sit inside the organisation's overall risk management plan and to focus on controlling the special risk to IT hardware and software and to information and data processing security. We need to do so in a systematic fashion so that we consider any kind of risk to our organisation (physical, natural, electronic or human) and then put controls in place to deal with the potential risk.

HB 231:2000 (p. 5) assumes that a company already has an efficient generic **risk management framework** in place and that a security management process such as that recommended in AS/NZS ISO/IEC 17799:2001 has already been implemented.

HB 231:2000 (p. 16) provides an exhaustive examination of the risk management process and in so doing establishes the 'strategic context', 'organisational context' and 'risk management context' within which an enterprise will carry out the risk management process. Facets of the context include:

- an 'organization's overall risk management philosophy, culture and structure'
- 'the financial, operational, competitive, political (public perceptions/image), social, client, cultural and legal aspects of the organization's functions'
- 'the organization and its capabilities, as well as its goals and objectives and the strategies that are in place to achieve them' (HB 231:2000, p. 17).

This means that diverse organisations will need to treat risk in a dissimilar manner; for one organisation (such as a bank) damage to reputation or public perception of its IT security infrastructure might be far more injurious than it would be to another (such as a garage).

Risk management criteria against which information security risk can be assessed must therefore be determined on an organisation-by-organisation basis, taking into consideration their varying operational, technical, financial, legal and social situations. The criteria may be associated with:

- how a breach of *confidentiality* would affect customer perceptions and what regulatory or legal issues it might trigger
- what effect the *unavailability* of systems or data would have on the business
- what effect a loss of *confidentiality* of business intelligence would have
- how a loss of *integrity* of data would affect the business's operations (HB 231:2000, p. 18).

An outline of the risk management process was given in chapter 1. A more specific risk management process for IT security is carried out by:

1. *Defining all information assets that make up the company's information IT infrastructure.* These include (HB 231:2000, p. 19): cabling and network components; hardware; software; communications; documents; personnel; confidence, trust, image and reputation.
2. *Determining which risks might affect each component of the infrastructure and the probability of the risk occurring and its significance.* HB231:2000 (p. 43) lists a range of 'possible threats' that need to be considered as part of the risk management process. These include those caused by: weather and natural disaster; crime; terrorism; power or other utility outages; human error; poor judgement; deliberate or accidental interference.
3. *Determining existing mechanisms for managing the risk.* Every organisation, except one that is at start-up stage, has some provision for risk management. This might only be antivirus software and a poorly configured firewall, but both of these controls can play a part in a risk management process. In managing risk, the effectiveness of existing controls should be reviewed. Areas of vulnerability or gaps in the existing controls should be identified.
4. *Carrying out vulnerability and threat assessment.* There are various means of assessment. One possibility is:
   (a) *Describe the effect of threat outcomes for all critical assets.* Such descriptions might be conceptualised around such terms as disclosure, modification, loss, destruction or interruption. For example, if 'lightning strikes the company HQ' is a threat, then a potential risk

might be 'power supply is cut off for 24 hours while this is fixed', and the effect might be 'loss of all unsaved data'.

(b) *Create evaluation criteria to prioritise the threats to critical assets.* The combination of a threat and the resulting effect on the organisation's critical assets defines the risk to the organisation. Each risk is assigned an effect value on a scale such as 'high, medium, low' or 'major, minor, insignificant'. Evaluation criteria might depend on such issues as legislation or insurance regulations. The possibility of occurrence of the threat is affected by the location of assets, the motive, means and opportunity of potential attackers, any historical evidence on threats and their frequency of occurrence, and sociopolitical and business reasons for a particular threat to a specific asset.

5. *Establishing cost-effective means of controlling risk* (HB 231:2000, p. 28). The cost of measures to manage risk must be weighed against the evaluation of the risk. Where possible, controls should be implemented. This process is discussed at length in subsequent chapters of this book.

6. *Documenting the risk management process.* After carrying out the risk management process, a table that looks like table 3.1 will be produced.

Table 3.1	Example of a risk management table					
Asset	**Access**	**Means**	**Motive**	**Outcome**	**Effect**	**Probability**
Web server	Internal/ external	Human	Accidental/ deliberate	Disclosure	High	High

HB 171:2003 *Guidelines for the Management of IT Evidence*

As mentioned in IT Risk 3.3, a growing need for some guidelines on the management of IT evidence was met at the end of 2003 with the production of HB 171:2003, which provides guidance on how to manage electronic records that might be used in legal proceedings and/or that might be investigated following suspected criminal activity.

The guidelines point out (HB 171:2003, p. 5) that IT evidence needs to be managed in the same way as any other evidence is managed and that this management affects every part of the system development and system security process. The greatest risk we are managing in an IT security sense is twofold:

1. If we do not ensure that appropriate record-keeping systems are designed and developed (and we need to consider a range of issues, including system design, data storage and 'volatility' of data) we will have no evidence for any kind of judicial or administrative investigation.

2. If we do not take full cognisance of legal and forensic computing requirements (see chapter 4), our records, however technically accurate, might not be legally admissible in court.

Are Australian companies using IT security standards and guidelines?

As detailed in this section, a range of national and international IT security standards and guidelines are available to Australian companies. However, there has always been some interest or even concern that Australian industry and commerce were not taking IT security risk management standards seriously enough.

The Australian Computer Emergency Response Team survey (AusCERT 2004, p. 43) shows a marked increase in users of IT security standards; an improvement from 37 per cent in 2003 to a more healthy 58 per cent in 2004. There is a marked increase in the use of AS 17799 (from 63 per cent to 71 per cent of those surveyed) and in the use of a range of other standards, including state government, industry-based and vendor-specific standards.

The same survey (AusCERT 2004, p. 43) also notes that companies are beginning to use HB 171:2003 *Guidelines for the Management of IT Evidence*, which is discussed here. The survey shows that in 2004, 6 per cent of those surveyed had begun to use this standard and presumably had also begun to develop a forensic management plan for their organisation. Previously there was no common awareness in industry or commerce that one possible ending to the management of IT security risk might be an appearance in court in a criminal action and that, as a victim of crime, there is some need to be able to provide IT evidence to police or other judicial agencies. This question could not be asked in previous surveys since the standard was published in late 2003; this is indicative too of the Australian Government's recognition of the growing effect of computer crime and the accompanying need for proper processes for the collection, handling and management of IT evidence.

In these guidelines, basic principles for the management of IT evidence are presented (HB 171:2003, p. 9). These include:

- *The 'obligation to provide records'.* Organisations should be aware of the circumstances in which they will be obliged to provide records, the nature of such records and the laws surrounding the issue of record-keeping and record disclosure. Records must exhibit confidentiality, integrity and availability. All files must be identified and labelled, and the authors must be known. Version control of documentation must be very strict, and a change log must be kept. All software used must be validated and reliable.
- *The need to 'design for evidence'.* The organisation must ensure that its IT systems supply good-quality records in a timely fashion and that auditing and logging have been carried out in a secure manner.

- *Responsibility for 'evidence collection' and 'custody of records'.* All evidence must be collected and stored in such a manner that the evidence will be admissible in court (e.g. logs must be kept). Original and copy records must be kept separate, and any analysis must be carried out on a copy. The original must not be changed.

The guidelines give a full picture of how investigations must be carried out and information on principles for recovery of digital evidence (HB171:2003, p. 27), principles for evidence collection, and the role and duties of expert witnesses in this context. Forensic computing is discussed in detail in chapter 4.

COBIT

Other international IT management standards followed in Australia include Control Objectives for Information and related Technology (COBIT), issued by the IT Governance Institute. COBIT is a comprehensive set of standards and procedures that establish good practice for senior management in governing the information infrastructure in their organisation. COBIT also contains control objectives for establishing a security baseline or minimum standard for IT security as part of the IT governance of an organisation (ISACA 2004).

ITIL

The UK Government has established the IT Infrastructure Library (ITIL; www. itil.co.uk) as a set of standards for best practice in service support and delivery, service management planning, information and communications technology infrastructure, and applications management and business planning. These too are being rapidly adopted worldwide and having an influence on Australian businesses as the standard for best practice in the provision of IT service. Incorporated in ITIL is the explicit need to establish security policies and how to properly manage security and risk in an organisation.

The US Federal Chief Information Officers Council risk management guidelines

The US Federal Chief Information Officers Council (CIO 2004) proposes a set of five principles, which are further divided into various guidelines for risk management associated with information and information systems security (see figure 3.4 on p. 92). These principles are based on the principle of continuity and, if followed, will ensure smooth business operations in an automated and interconnected environment. These principles, all of which are discussed below, are:

- assessment of risk and business needs
- centralised security management
- implementation of policies and controls
- creating awareness
- monitoring and evaluation of policies and controls.

These guidelines provide a cyclical activity which ensures that the information security policies and controls are addressed on a continuing basis. You will recognise that these broadly align with the risk management process described in chapter 1.

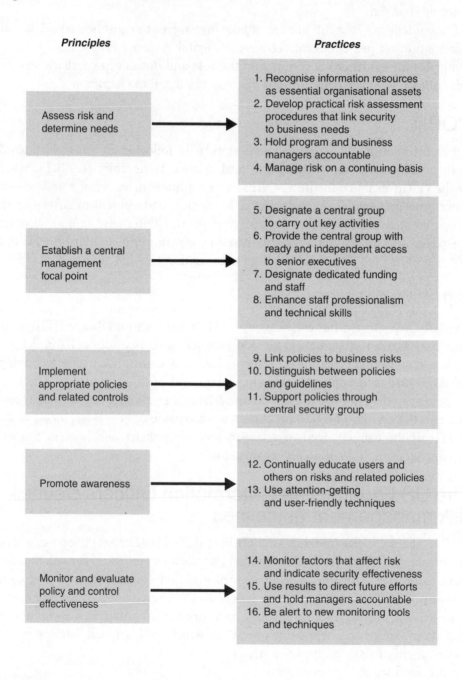

Figure 3.4   **Risk management principles and practices**

Source: US Federal Chief Information Officers Council 2004.

Assessment of risks and business need

Risk identification and assessment needs to be directly linked with the needs of the business, which means identifying the critical information assets and business processes of an organisation and what are the potential threats posed to it. This assessment and analysis provides management with a series of alternatives concerning controlling and managing risks posed to information resources.

Centralised security management

As mentioned earlier, it is important for all departments to have representation in formulating security polices and enacting procedures to provide continuous input for these policies and their enforcement. If the business manager or a senior employee within the department is given this responsibility and the department follows the reporting procedures as described in earlier sections, this kind of representation provides requisite coverage of all the departments of a business as well as providing a comprehensive picture of existing information security situation in the organisation. These measures could further be consolidated by having a centralised security team that consists of representatives from all the departments.

These representatives need not be and must not be technology experts, for diversity at this stage provides a comprehensive insight into information security from different angles, such as business process execution, inter- and intra-organisational information exchange and information management. At the same time, it helps in formulating standardised security policies and implementation of them throughout the organisation.

Policies and control implementation

Generally, policy documents are not given due importance by employees. They consider them yet more pieces of paper that tell them how to do their job. Apart from other factors, an important reason for not giving policy documents due importance is the fact that they are difficult to understand and basically present an order to employees. Information system security policies ought to be written in such a way that they are easy to understand and each employee in the organisation understands what their responsibilities are in fulfilling the demands of the policy document. Furthermore, the controls and countermeasures prescribed by these policies should be user friendly and easily implemented.

Creating awareness

While implementing information security policy, the most important factor is the awareness of the employees, for it is the employees who will implement the controls as enunciated in the policy document. If they do not understand the criticality of these controls, they are not going to take them seriously and breaches will keep occurring. At the same time, if the employees do not understand the risks and threats posed to the organisation's information resources, they will not necessarily abide by the policies designed to reduce these risks. However, in order for the employees to understand what is written in the policy document and to comply with the instructions given in it, businesses need to educate employees on risks and related policies and to include user-friendly implementation techniques in the policy and guidelines document.

Monitoring and evaluation of policies and controls

Monitoring and evaluation of policies and controls is the most important aspect of computer or information security risk management. It involves a series of activities which ensures that the controls and measures put in place for security are working well, considers whether they need to be updated or whether they are redundant and need replacement, and so on.

Summary

In this chapter we have begun to develop an understanding of the role of ethics, laws, standards and guidelines in IT security and risk management. Ethics comprises impartially defined principles and values that pertain to an individual or group in society. Laws seek to enforce behaviour that is deemed acceptable to a given society or culture. The IT professional bodies have professional codes of ethics that impose ethical obligations on their members, but these are not always enforceable. Ethics works with the law and standards to regulate 'good' IT security risk management.

Australia's legal system includes federal and state legislation and criminal and civil law. Federal legislation covers such matters as privacy, intellectual property, spam, telecommunications and cyber crime or e-crime. The law provides protection for businesses in the form of a deterrent and avenue of redress against attacks on their IT assets. It also imposes obligations on the business to respect the legal rights of others in their dealings with them, including the management of data. In chapter 4 we will examine the effect and risk of e-crime and the issues surrounding computer forensics in more depth.

Finally, there are a number of international and Australian standards, guidelines and codes of practice that relate to IT security risk management. These can be used as the basis of an efficient security policy.

Key terms

Australian Computer Society, p. 69
awareness, p. 83
civil law, p. 72
code of ethics, p. 69
common law, p. 71
copyright, p. 79
corporate security policy, p. 84
criminal law, p. 72
democracy, p. 83
ethics, p. 68
evaluation criteria, p. 84
guidelines, p. 82
identifier, p. 78
intellectual property, p. 79
International Information
    Systems Security Certification
    Consortium (ISC)², p. 69
international law, p. 72

law, p. 68
operating procedures, p. 85
personnel security policy, p. 84
reassessment, p. 83
response, p. 83
responsibility, p. 83
risk assessment, p. 83
risk management framework, p. 87
security design
    and implementation, p. 83
security management, p. 83
software piracy, p. 81
spam, p. 75
standards, p. 82
statute law, p. 71
subsidiary security policies, p. 84
technical security policy, p. 84

Questions

1. Obtain a copy of the code of ethics of the Institute of Electrical and Electronic Engineers. Compare it with the Australian Computer Society code. Can you see any cultural bias in these two codes?
2. This chapter has focused on federal legislation. Research the computer crime legislation in your own state and one other state.
    (a) Compare and contrast the two. Give possible reasons for any differences that you can discover.
    (b) Give possible reasons for any overlap or discrepancies with federal legislation.
3. Assume you work for a company that uses email to send regular newsletters to its customers. Develop a 300-word briefing for your non-technical manager on how your company could protect itself from accusations of sending spam.
4. Develop a brief privacy disclaimer to be attached to your company website to indicate to your customers that all company record-keeping is being carried out in accordance with Australian privacy legislation.
5. Draw up a 300-word document to be supplied to new members of your company as part of their induction explaining:
    (a) the nature of software piracy
    (b) the constraints of the *Copyright Act 1968* on the downloading of files and information from the Internet.
6. Develop a list of 40 information assets that a small to medium-sized enterprise (SME) engaged in software development might possess.

7. If the software development company in question 6 was located in a multistorey building on the bank of a river in semi-rural Queensland, outline 25 possible threats to the security of its information assets.

Internal Audit Report

Improper operating procedures used by employees:

- Lack of security awareness and general security laziness.
- Nil acceptance of security responsibility.
- Inadequate standard operating procedures.
- Unattended machines.
- Failure to take care of media.
- Printing sensitive material.
- Failure to turn off computers at the end of the working day.
- Failure to back up information.

Hardware problems:

- Failure to secure the hardware adequately (e.g. laptops unsecured).
- Effects from the physical environment causing damage.

Software concerns:

- Some application software is of inferior quality and untested in the field and therefore not able to be trusted in the office environment.
- Nil audit logs.
- Lack of access control.
- Lack of secure identification and authentication techniques.
- Limited antivirus software.
- Information exposed to the Internet.
- Lack of restrictions to specific files when certain applications are operating.

Figure 3.5   **Internal Audit report**

Case study

3: A big task ahead

New management has taken over the operation of a small software development company in South Australia. This particular company is now endeavouring to secure defence contracts and to expand in the current South Australian economy. With the impending assessment from an external auditor to determine viability as a defence contractor, the management is concerned that IT security measures are not sufficient and that company information assets are at great risk. Small amounts of proprietary and outdated antivirus software are the only existing security measures.

The chief executive officer has asked for help and has just had you (the IT security manager) complete an internal audit. You now need to understand the current risks and how they can be managed. Your shocking results are listed in figure 3.5.

In your report you identified the greatest risks as:
- lack of security awareness and general security laziness
- information exposed to outsiders such as the Internet and each employee being separately connected to the Internet via a web server
- lack of file access control.

Figure 3.6 is also an extract from your report.

The following risk management procedures are a minimum standard if your company wishes to be a defence contractor:

- All personnel accessing classified computer systems must read the relevant policy sections every six months, signing their understanding and acceptance.

- Classified processing is not done on computers forming part of the business domain. These computers display a warning sticker informing users that the computer terminal is not secured.

- Only those people with a justifiable need to know and a security clearance at least equal to the system's security rating are given the authority to access the classified computer systems.

- The computer systems are left unattended only in certain circumstances, for example, an evacuation of the area, temporarily for periods less than one hour, provided no user is logged on and the door is secured.

- Password control is implemented. Passwords are not divulged to anyone and not written down except for root passwords. A determined length of password is given as with the required number of alpha characters, numeric and symbols. Passwords are changed at intervals no longer than that specified.

- The security officer controls any changes of system configuration, including hardware and software upgrades.

- Information is encrypted before transmission via a modem.

- Virus checking is installed to run each time any computer is powered on using Norton's Corporate edition. This edition regularly provides live updates, thus maintaining the latest antivirus protection.

- Volatile and non-volatile media are classified or declassified accordingly.

- A log is kept of all maintenance and the relevant maintenance precautions taken.

- Archiving is performed on a regular basis to remove obsolete data stored on hard disks.

- The security officer holds a security violations log to assist in resolving security problems.

- Classified material is stored accordingly, and classified work area doors are locked.

- Random security checks are carried out, and the assistant secretary security (ASSEC) conducts accreditation checks.

- There is a requirement to encrypt information paths, and firewalls are also put in place.

Figure 3.6 Minimum risk management procedures

Questions

1. Using AS/NZS ISO/IEC 17799:2001, *Code of Practice for Information Security Management*, devise an IT security management plan for your CEO to mitigate for the risks identified in your report.

2. Establish an IT security risk management program using the HB 231:2003 guidelines for your company to deal with the risks identified above (for brevity, you do not need to go beyond the scope of your audit report).

3. Discuss the applicability of the HB 171:2003 guidelines to your company and how, if they are to be followed, your company practices might need to be modified to conform with them.

Suggested reading

Intellectual Property Australia (IP Australia) 2004a, *What is Intellectual Property: Copyright,* accessed 4 October 2004, www.ipaustralia.gov.au/ip/copyright.htm.

—— 2004b, *What is Intellectual Property: Introduction,* accessed 4 October 2004, ww.ipaustralia.gov.au/ip/introduction.htm.

—— 2004c, *What is Intellectual Property: Confidentiality,* accessed 4 October 2004, www.ipaustralia.gov.au/ip/confidentiality.htm.

—— 2004d, *What is Intellectual Property: Patents,* accessed 4 October 2004, www.ipaustralia.gov.au/ip/patents.htm.

International Standards Organization 2001, ISO/IEC 17799:2001 *Code of Practice for Information Security Management.*

Organisation for Economic Co-operation and Development (OECD) 2002, *OECD Guidelines for the Security of Information Systems and Networks: Towards a Culture of Security,* OECD Publications, Paris.

Standards Australia 2000, HB 231:2000 *Information Security Risk Management Guidelines.*

—— 2003, HB 171:2003, *Guidelines for the Management of IT Evidence.*

References

Australian Computer Emergency Response Team (AusCERT) 2004, *2004 Computer Crime and Security Survey,* AusCERT, University of Queensland, Brisbane.

Australian Computer Society (ACS) 2004, *Australian Computer Society Code of Ethics,* accessed 18 April 2005, www.acs.org.au/about_acs/acsregs.htm.

Australian Copyright Council (ACC) 2003a, *Information Sheet G57: Websites: Creating and Publishing on the Internet,* accessed 4 October 2004, www.copyright.org.au.

—— 2003b, *Information Sheet G50: Computer Software and Copyright,* accessed 19 April 2005, www.copyright.org.au.

—— 2004, *Information Sheet G56: Internet: Copying From,* accessed 19 April 2005, www.copyright.org.au.

Business Software Alliance 2003, 'Key finding', *First Annual Business Software Alliance and IDC Global Software Piracy Study,* www.bas.org/globalstudy.

Chief Information Officers (CIO) Council 2004, www.fcw.com/fcw/articles/2004/0830/web-fea-09-03-04.asp.

Department of Communications, Information Technology and the Arts (DCITA) and Australian Communications Authority (ACA) 2004, *Spam Act 2003: An Overview for Business,* http://internet.aca.gov.au/acainterwr/consumer_info/spam/spam_overview_for%20_business.pdf.

Information Privacy Principles under the Privacy Act 1988 (IPP), 1988, accessed 4 October 2004, www.privacy.gov.au/Information Privacy Principles under the Privacy Act 1988.htm.

Information System Audit and Control Association (ISACA) 2004, www.isaca.org.

National Office for the Information Economy (NOIE) 2003, *Spam Act: A Practical Guide for Business*, Canberra.

Organisation for Economic Co-operation and Development (OCED) 2002, *OECD Guidelines for the Security of Information Systems and Networks: Towards a Culture of Security*, OECD Publications, Paris.

Quirk, P & Forder, J 2003, *Electronic Commerce and the Law*, 2nd edn, John Wiley & Sons Australia, Brisbane.

South Australian Police (SAPOL) 2003, *Contemporary Policing Issues Module: Electronic Crime*, Professional Development Section, South Australia Police Academy, Adelaide, SA.

Spam Act 2003, accessed 4 October 2004, www.austlii.edu.au/au/legis/cth/consol_act/sa200366.txt.

Standards Australia 2000, HB 231:2000, *Information Security Risk Management Guidelines*, accessed 4 October 2004, www.standards.gov.au/catalogue.

—— 2001, ISO/IEC 17799:2001, *Code of Practice for Information Security Management*.

—— 2003, HB 171:2003, *Guidelines for the Management of IT Evidence*, 4 October 2004, www.standards.gov.au/catalogue.

Chapter 4

Electronic crime and forensic computing

Learning objectives

After studying this chapter, you should be able to:

- describe current trends in electronic crime

- define the common types of electronic crime

- understand foundation issues in forensic computing

- explain the difference between computer forensics and network forensics

- outline the four rules of forensic methodology

- outline the three phases of a forensic investigation

- discuss the main elements of forensic readiness.

Chapter overview

This chapter reviews current trends in electronic crime in Australia, providing an insight into the challenging IT risk context and the daily threats that businesses face. We also briefly look at the emergence of organised e-crime and cyber terrorism.

We examine various kinds of computer crime perpetrated in Australia and internationally, and discuss the risks involved and possible protection mechanisms and controls that might be put into place to provide safeguards.

Should a business be the target of a computer crime, it is important for it to be prepared. This issue of forensic readiness relates to the way businesses can gather the evidence they would need should they have to go to court in a criminal or civil action against a cyber criminal. We will review forensic computing tools and techniques and discover how forensic computing investigations are carried out.

E-crime

Since the mid-1990s, and as commerce and industry have increasingly adopted IT solutions for their everyday business needs (ABS 1997), there has been an escalation of computer misuse and e-crime (McKemmish 1999; ACPR 2000, 2001; Broucek & Turner 2001).

The Australian Bureau of Statistics' Internet Activity Survey (ABS 2004) provides the following information on Internet activity carried out via the Internet service provider (ISP) industry in Australia. In the period between December 2003 and March 2004 there were, in Australia:

- 694 Internet service providers supplying Internet access services
- more than 5.2 million Internet users, an increase of 135 000 (3 per cent) in the previous year
- 834 000 subscribers with permanent connections, an increase of more than 27 per cent in the previous six months.

It is very difficult to obtain comprehensive data on the incidence of e-crime within Australia other than those observations made by the Australian Computer Emergency Response Team in their annual surveys (e.g. AusCERT 2004). Their 2003 survey showed that financial losses owing to computer attacks that harmed the confidentiality, integrity or availability of network data or systems had doubled in that year, standing at $12 million in 2003, compared with $6 million in 2002 (AusCERT 2003). The AusCERT 2004 survey reported an increase in this figure of approximately 33 per cent to $16 million in 2004.

The figures indicate an upward trend in reported crime and financial loss. Data reported by Australian police researchers indicates that the above statistics could be considered artificially low. Their accuracy is compromised by a significant degree of non-reporting and non-detection of computer misuse and e-crime (ACPR 2000, Etter 2001).

Electronic crime or **e-crime** can be defined as: 'Offences where a computer or other electronic device is used as a tool in the commission of an offence, or as a target of an offence, or used as a storage device in the commission of an offence.' (SAPOL 2003) This definition helps us to identify three categories of electronic crime. The first type, such as perhaps in a drug-related offence, is that in which the computer is used as a tool in committing the offence. This could involve sending emails relating to a proposed crime or carrying out research into bomb-making using the Internet. The second type involves cases in which the computer is the target of an offence, such as the hacking of networks and systems, so as to commit an offence such as fraud. The third type, which is also very common, is when a computer is used as a storage device for illegal materials (e.g. child pornography) or for letters and other files or documents relating to crime.

When we try to ascertain the extent of electronic crime by reading statistics, we have to take into account the fact that very few offences fall into the category of 'pure' electronic crime *per se*. Some can, for example, be categorised and reported as fraud. In this way, true statistics on electronic crime might be understated and producing a biased picture of the reality of electronic crime.

E-crime has also become very sophisticated. It has become commonly linked with **cyber terrorism** and **information warfare (IW)** since the terror attacks on the USA on 11 September 2001. It is also commonly linked with **organised crime**. Examples of this include Chinese triad gangs' employment of computer programmers since 1998 (Galeotti 2001) and Colombian drug cartels' utilisation of cutting-edge IT to assist them in their operations (Kaihla 2002). IT Risk 4.1 (p. 104) discusses a number of organised crime groups' use of IT in the commission of crimes. Within issues raised in the 'war on terrorism', post 9/11, there has also been increasing international concern over the potential for cyber terrorism or a cyber dimension to the next terrorist attack (Vatis 2001).

Cyber terrorism

Considerable questions hang over the definition — and even the existence — of cyber terrorism. We will explore it in IT Risk 4.2 (p. 105). However, the definition given by Dorothy Denning, professor of computer science at Georgetown University, is worthy of consideration:

> Cyberterrorism is the convergence of terrorism and cyberspace. It is generally understood to mean unlawful attacks and threats of attack against computers, networks and the information stored therein when done to intimidate or coerce a government or its people in furtherance of political or social objectives. Further, to qualify as cyberterrorism, an attack should result in violence against persons or property, or at least cause enough harm to generate fear. Attacks that lead to death or bodily injury, explosions, plane crashes, water contamination, or severe economic loss would be examples. Serious attacks against critical infrastructure could be acts of cyberterrorism, depending on their impact. Attacks that disrupt nonessential services or that are mainly a costly nuisance would not. (Denning 2000)

It can be somewhat difficult to differentiate between cyber terrorism (which Denning sees as an act designed to cause fear and try to affect government agendas) and organised crime that could, in some cases, also cause the same amount of fear and societal damage and economic loss.

IT risk 4.1

Organised e-crime

The Russian Mafia is made up of a large number of warring factions. It is thought that thousands of crime groups actually exist in Russia but that only a few pose any real threat. These groups were mainly formed for economic reasons (basically to avoid poverty) after the dissolution of the Soviet Union. Computers are a very important tool for the Russian Mafia for a number of reasons. Such crimes as money laundering and extortion are just a few of the activities they are involved in. It is also thought that many of the current viruses have been created by Russian Mafia groups so that they can compromise computers and launch denial of service attacks on those businesses and organisations that have failed to pay protection money (Lyman 2004). The Russian Mafia has also been linked with such sinister crimes as the sale of weapons of mass destruction (Nemets & Torda 2001).

Movies have often glorified the Sicilian Mafia. It is a large criminal organisation that has on occasion the potential to threaten the stability of governments. Extortion is one of the largest crimes committed by this organisation, and it has been made easier with the use of computers and the Internet. As an example, it is thought that such groups as the Mafia are behind extortion rackets that are threatening sports, gambling and financial websites. Owners of these sites have been threatened with denial of service attacks if they do not pay a large amount of money to a specified account. In a more conventional use of information warfare, one example shows how the Mafia was found to have diverted $115 million from Italian banks with help from telecommunications insiders (ProtectedComputer.com n.d).

Categories of electronic crime

Although it can sometimes be difficult to differentiate between pure cyber terrorism and electronic crime, the AusCERT survey (AusCERT 2004) highlights some interesting general trends in electronic crime in Australia. This survey shows not only that computer security incidents are growing rapidly in number but also that the source and nature of attacks in Australia are changing. An increase in electronic attacks caused an average rise in financial loss of 20 per cent over the preceding year, bringing the average sum lost to approximately $116 000 per

Information Technology Security & Risk Management

IT risk 4.2

What is cyber terrorism?

> If you ask 10 people what 'cyberterrorism' is, you will get at least nine different answers! When those 10 people are computer security experts, whose task it is to create various forms of protection against 'cyber terrorism', this discrepancy moves from comedic to rather worrisome. When these 10 people represent varied factions of the governmental agencies tasked with protecting our national infrastructure and assets, it becomes a critical issue. However, given the lack of documented scientific support to incorporate various aspects of computer-related crime into the genre 'cyberterrorism', this situation should not be surprising. (Gordon & Ford 2004)

This quote from the Symantec research and development team in the USA summarises some of the widely held views about cyber terrorism in Australia, too. The terrorist attack on the World Trade Center in New York on 11 September 2001 heightened international awareness of terrorism, and there has been much conjecture since this time on the types of cyber terrorist attack that might be carried out in Australia. However, it is very difficult for us as IT security managers, or potential managers, to guard against the risk of cyber terrorism if the term is still undefined.

Nevertheless we can be sure that an insecure network will provide an opportunistic or unstructured attacker with the opportunity to search our network and allow them potentially to use our bandwidth and servers for their own purposes. It might just be that the attack was a purposeful and structured one and that our system intruder was going to launch an attack from our network rather than steal our resources. The attacker might just carry out a cyber terrorist attack of the (electronic) magnitude of 9/11 — we will just not know in advance and therefore, for the sake of our own national IT infrastructure and that of our allies, we need to discover all potential threats to our information assets before such an attack can be launched.

company surveyed. The survey also revealed that organisations that make up part of Australia's critical national information infrastructure (CNII) reported more loss — 50 per cent compared to 42 per cent — than those organisations that are not part of Australia's CNII.

Other key findings in this survey showed that more organisations experienced electronic attacks that harmed the confidentiality, availability and integrity of network data or systems in 2004 than in 2003. The increase reported was from 42 per cent of organisations surveyed in 2003 to 49 per cent in 2004. Most attacks were sourced externally (88 per cent), but fewer organisations experienced external attack than in 2003 (91 per cent). For the third consecutive year, infections from viruses, worms or Trojans were the most common form of attack reported, accounting for 45 per cent of total losses in 2004. Other prevalent forms of electronic crime were laptop theft, followed by abuse and misuse of computer network access or resources (AusCERT 2004). Table 4.1 on pp. 107–9 shows the cost of computer crime identified in the AusCERT survey.

In South Australia (SAPOL 2003) and following a general Australian trend, some of the more prevalent crimes include paedophilia and other sex-related crimes, fraud and hacking so as to transmit viruses and other malware. Other inappropriate or criminal behaviour investigated includes identity theft, denial of service attacks, spamming and phishing. We will examine these in the following sections.

Paedophilia and sex crimes

Although it is not appropriate to examine this issue in depth here, it is important to note that paedophilia and sex crimes are growing in prevalence and magnitude. Statistics (SAPOL 2003) show that while South Australian Police's first offender prosecuted for this kind of crime — the use of the Internet to display and exchange child pornography — had only three images on his computer, one offender in 2001 had at least 21 000 graphics stored on his hard disk and other storage media.

Companies must have established policies for Internet usage for their employees, yet there is always a risk that even so employees will abuse or misuse company-supplied Internet access and will download and store pornographic images in work time on company IT storage media. Such misuse of corporate IT assets can be deterred, identified and addressed through the use of such controls as Internet usage policies, limiting employee access to the Internet and auditing web logs. IT Risk 4.3 on p. 110 explores this issue further.

Table 4.1 The cost of computer crime

How losses were incurred	Number of respondents with quantified losses			Lowest reported ($)			Highest reported ($)			Average loss ($)			Total annual loss ($)		
	2002	2003	2004	2002	2003	2004	2002	2003	2004	2002	2003	2004	2002	2003	2004
Theft/breach of proprietary or confidential information	4	7	8	10 000	3 000	10 000	150 000	150 000	500 000	72 500	36 857	167 500	290 000	258 000	1 340 000
Unauthorised privileged access	8	10	7	1 000	1 000	1 000	50 000	200 000	50 000	13 275	32 200	9 714	106 200	322 000	68 000
Computer-facilitated financial fraud	7	8	8	500	10 000	2 000	600 000	1 400 000	1 500 000	115 288	440 625	307 125	807 000	3 525 000	2 457 000
Telecommunications fraud	2	6	6	1 000	200	1 000	100 000	250 000	130 000	50 500	69 200	36 370	101 000	415 200	218 220
Sabotage of data or networks	5	3	3	1 000	5 000	4 000	1 000 000	100 000	80 000	204 600	41 667	44 667	1 023 000	125 000	134 000
Website defacement	—	8	2	—	500	1 000	—	30 000	2 000	—	7 313	1 500	—	58 500	3 000
Denial of service attack	8	16	15	1 500	300	1 000	100 000	200 000	100 000	22 688	24 831	25 200	181 500	397 300	378 000

(continued)

Table 4.1 The cost of computer crime (cont.)

How losses were incurred	Number of respondents with quantified losses			Lowest reported ($)			Highest reported ($)			Average loss ($)			Total annual loss ($)		
	2002	2003	2004	2002	2003	2004	2002	2003	2004	2002	2003	2004	2002	2003	2004
Degradation of network performance associated with heavy scanning	7	14	24	1 500	1 000	500	100 000	200 000	700 000	23 071	37 729	71 208	161 500	528 200	1 709 000
Interception of telecommunications (voice or data)	2	1	1	1 000	4 000	5 000	10 000	4 000	5 000	5 500	4 000	5 000	11 000	4 000	5 000
Virus, worm, Trojan infection	23	66	93	100	200	100	100 000	400 000	2 000 000	38 743	33 695	76 313	891 100	2 223 900	7 097 100
Laptop theft	48	82	84	2 000	1 999	1 000	100 000	350 000	200 000	26 331	27 539	17 670	1 263 900	2 258 183	1 484 244
Theft of hand-held computers	—	—	12	—	—	1 000	—	—	10 000	—	—	4 708	—	—	56 500
System penetration by outsider	7	7	6	1 000	2 000	1 000	40 000	50 000	250 000	26 143	21 571	51 833	183 000	151 000	311 000

How losses were incurred	Number of respondents with quantified losses			Lowest reported ($)			Highest reported ($)			Average loss ($)			Total annual loss ($)		
	2002	2003	2004	2002	2003	2004	2002	2003	2004	2002	2003	2004	2002	2003	2004
Unauthorised access to information by insider	5	3	3	5 000	2 000	5 000	100 000	250 000	200 000	29 000	87 333	70 000	145 000	262 000	210 000
Insider abuse of Internet access, email or internal computer resources	17	30	1	100	500	20 000	200 000	400 000	20 000	36 300	42 417	20 000	617 100	1 272 500	20 000
TOTAL ANNUAL LOSSES													$5 781 300	$11 800 783	$15 921 064

2004: 137 respondents/57% response rate; 2003: 126 respondents/58% response rate; 2002: 75 respondents/80% response rate.

Source: AusCERT 2004, p. 21.

Just how much unacceptable material is being downloaded at work?

In a study carried out between 2001 and 2004, Craig Valli (Valli 2002) analysed the Internet usage of 13 top abusive users of an Australian university departmental web server. He comments on the online behaviour of a university staff member:

> Staff3 has what appears to be a modest 1623Mbytes of bandwidth of which 1200MB was downloading of patches for their systems all legitimate traffic[;] however, this is where it ends.
>
> The remaining bandwidth, while only 423MB, is very problematic. MP3 and movie traffic accounted for 190Mbytes of this 423MB, which is against policy and some of the traffic was in breach of copyright.
>
> Of the remaining non-legitimate traffic, pornographic traffic accounted for 45MB of this activity. What made this case even more problematic was that Staff3 had paid memberships to several hardcore pornographic sites that they were accessing from this connection providing a further audit trail for this activity.

He goes on:

> The downloading of pornographic material, although not large in volume when compared to other traffic, does however represent quite a significant problem for the University. The students who were accessing this sort of material were doing so at times where [*sic*] detection of this activity would be highly unlikely except in case of an audit of log files. The volume of material that the students downloaded, coupled with the fact that they requested some of these files more than once from the system, would indicate possible problem behaviours on their part.
>
> Staff3 who is accessing pornographic material is not doing so in an ad hoc or opportunistic fashion as the students are. Staff3 is actually a paid member [of] several hardcore pornographic sites and is deliberately accessing these sites during their working day in breach of existing University policy and potentially jeopardising their employment.

It can be seen that the IT security manager has to be very vigilant to ensure that policy is well written and that measures are taken to ensure staff do not abuse or misuse their Internet privileges and commit this kind of crime in the workplace.

Source: Valli 2002, p. 5.

Fraud and phishing

Fraud committed by means of the Internet is a very serious crime and one that is growing (SAPOL 2003, p. 5). The major IT security risk for an individual or company is that they might be tricked into parting with money in an online transaction for non-existent goods or they might be deceived into giving details of bank accounts and credit cards to an online entity claiming to be their own bank. Other types of fraud are carried out by those who claim to have unclaimed money that the receiver of the email will be able to claim (with their assistance); as we see in IT Risk 4.4, these fraud attempts often originate in Nigeria and are thus known as the Nigerian letter fraud.

IT risk 4.4
The Nigerian letter fraud

There are many variations on the Nigerian letter fraud. This warning story from the US Internet Fraud Complaint Center gives details of how one version of this type of crime is committed.

> The scheme targets individuals that use Internet classified ads to sell merchandise. Typically, an interested party located outside the United States contacts a seller. The seller is told that the buyer has an associate in the United States that owes him money. As such, he will have the associate send the seller a cashier's check for the amount owed to the buyer. This amount will be thousands of dollars more than the price of the merchandise and the seller is told the excess amount will be used to pay the shipping costs associated with getting the merchandise to his location. The seller is instructed to deposit the check and as soon as it clears, to wire (Western Union) the excess funds back to the buyer, or to another associate identified as a shipping agent. In most instances, the money is sent to locations in West Africa (Nigeria). Because a cashier's check is used, a bank will typically release the funds immediately, or after a one or two day hold. Falsely believing the check has cleared, the seller wires the money as instructed. In some cases, the buyer is able to convince the seller that some circumstance has arisen that necessitates the cancellation of the sale and is successful in conning the victim into sending the remainder of the money. Shortly thereafter, their bank notifies the victim that the check was fraudulent and the bank is holding the victim responsible for the full amount of the check.

Source: Internet Fraud Complaint Center (IFCC) 2003.

Levy (2004) reports that 300 000 Internet-related fraud complaints in the USA were reported in 2003 and accounted for losses of US$200 000 000. He also states that although more of the general public are aware of common fraudulent offences and thus less likely to be tricked into giving details of bank accounts or allowing criminals access to funds, there is a prevalence of phishing. **Phishing** occurs when criminals try to find out personal information through all kinds of social engineering and technical means so as to obtain sensitive personal information about an intended victim. Levy (2004) notes that offenders are continually trying to find methods by which they can gain access to victims' credit card details, and they create intricate mechanisms by which this can be achieved. They have created Trojans (malicious code) that imitate organisations' websites (in the case quoted by Levy, that of the American Red Cross) and attempt to trick individuals into giving their credit card details in response to a request or an appeal by the organisation. According to Symantec (2004), the W32.Mimail.S@mm worm was used to display a message purporting itself to be a notice from Microsoft detecting that the user's version of Microsoft Windows had expired and requiring the user to enter personal details, including credit card number and PIN number (see figure 4.1).

Most Australian banks have warned their online banking customers not to respond to emails purportedly from the bank that request the customer to respond with personal details. Often these emails include a link to a website that mimics the bank's real website and asks customers to enter their account details and passwords. This is usually the first step in an identity crime (discussed next).

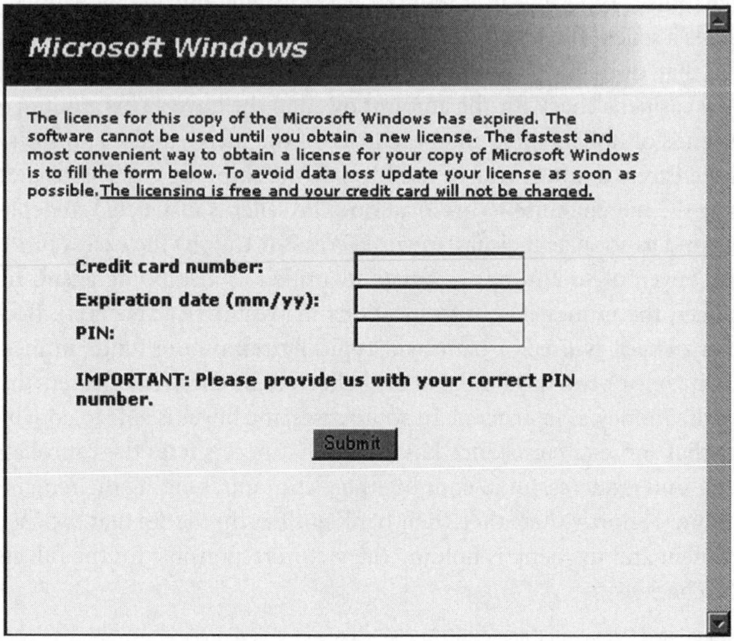

Figure 4.1   Screen shot of W32.Mimail.S@mm dialog box

Source: Symantec Security Response.

Identity theft

The Australasian Centre for Policing Research (ACPR 2003b) defines **identity crime** as follows:

> [Identity crime is] a broad term used to describe offences in which a perpetrator uses a false identity, or a real identity other than their own identity ('identity theft'), in order to facilitate the commission of a crime. Identity crime can underpin and facilitate a range of crimes including people smuggling, drug trafficking, money laundering, paedophilia, terrorism and murder, but is most commonly typified by 'identity fraud'.

From this definition, it can be seen that **identity theft** involves using someone else's identity in order to commit a crime. **Identity fraud** involves the use of a false identity to gain illegal benefit. An example is the use of stolen credit cards (or credit card details). Apart from direct loss, victims of identity theft might suffer damage to their reputation owing to the actions of the individual who assumed their identity.

Fear of credit card details being stolen has been one of the major impediments to widespread adoption of e-commerce by consumers. It is obvious, then, that businesses must take steps to protect data they hold about individuals and organisations. They must also protect data while it is in transit in the context of e-commerce. If the confidentiality of such data is compromised, there is potential for identity theft. Further, controls (such as audits) must be in place to ensure that those with authorised access to confidential data (such as bank officers) do not misuse it. Some new security technology also offers protection against identity theft, including biometrics whereby identity is proved through the individual's voice, fingerprints or other unique characteristic.

Viruses, worms, Trojans and other malicious code

We have already seen in figure 4.1 how a worm was used to carry out Internet-mediated fraud. A worm is one of a number of types of malicious code (malware).

A **virus** is a program that attempts to find other programs and 'infect' them by attaching a copy of itself to them. When it has done this, it then seeks other programs to attach itself to and thus it spreads. There are many different kinds of virus; some are inserted into Microsoft Office applications as **macro viruses** (visible within Office macros), some are in the boot sector of hard disks (**boot sector viruses**), and there are many other types, too. For the sake of proper IT security risk management, consistent use should be made of modern antivirus software and automatic updates used to detect the signatures of new viruses. Only when an update for a specific virus is installed will the antivirus software provide the business with protection. Another effective control is to train users not to open emails or email attachments from suspicious or unknown sources and not to install software. Another potential risk related to malware is that the business will unwittingly infect a supplier, distributor or other partner's system, causing damage to the business's reputation.

Worms differ from viruses as they can multiply and spread without becoming attached to a piece of existing code, and there are many examples of this. A **Trojan** is a piece of code that pretends to offer a necessary function but that contains hidden malware, viruses or links designed to trick users or to damage their systems or both. Businesses can protect themselves from worms and Trojans in the same way as they protect themselves from viruses.

Denial of service

A **denial of service (DOS) attack** (which is illegal in Australia) is one that sends so many requests for service to a given server that it becomes overloaded and thus unavailable. A **distributed denial of service (DDOS) attack** is one in which many different computers are used to launch the attack simultaneously. St George Bank's online banking service was subject to a denial of service attack in 2000, preventing many genuine customers from using the service.

Businesses generally must rely on technical controls to prevent denial of service attacks. Depending on the particular business, a denial of service attack can be a significant threat to business continuity.

Forensic computing

Forensic computing is a varied discipline that involves the preservation, identification, extraction, documentation and interpretation of computer data with a view to reconstructing a sequence of events that occurred on the system in the past (Marcella & Greenfield 2002).

McKemmish, an Australian ex-police officer turned forensic consultant and researcher, offers a definition that has been widely accepted in the forensic computing field in Australia, classifying **forensic computing** as 'the process of identifying, preserving, analysing and presenting digital evidence in a manner that is legally acceptable' (McKemmish 1999, p. 1). McKemmish's definition encompasses both the technical and non-technical aspects of forensic computing. It is one of the first definitions to state explicitly that the result of forensic computing must be presented in a legally acceptable manner.

There are two practical applications for forensic computing: the discovery of criminal evidence and the determination of failure within a computing environment (Kruse II & Heiser 2002).

Development of forensic computing

Just as forensic medicine evolved from the study of anatomy, criminal forensics has evolved in parallel from the study of fingerprints and other individualised forms of identification. Fingerprints are thought to be unique, as the chances of two humans having the same fingerprints are extremely small. Fingerprints are accepted in courts as proof of identity, and criminal forensics is based on fingerprint collection and identification methods. In the late 1980s and early 1990s computer-based recognition systems began superseding traditional paper fingerprint records and offering searching and comparison tools. This move towards the use of computing by police was one factor that led to forensic computing.

However, as computers became an integrated component of global society, they also began to be used as tools in crime or to become the target of crime. Computers also became repositories of criminal evidence, or more simply a place where evidence of the existence of crimes could be detected, but there was no standard method of searching for or protecting this data. As a science, forensic computing is a relatively new classification; it was not until 1996 that forensic computing was first mentioned by any relevant academic journal (Betts 2000). Until this point, this type of investigation was conducted by law enforcement officers on a case-by-case basis; it had no standards or known methodology; and there existed no communication channel for disparate law enforcement officers to discuss advances in the field. By far the largest hindrance to forensic computing was the lack of acceptance by other scientific fields of study, as this lack of support meant that computer evidence was rarely given as evidence in a court of law. Instead, forensic computing became a method of searching for other admissible evidence, rather than comprising evidence itself (Betts 2000).

Forensic computing is made up of two distinct areas: **computer forensics** and **network forensics** (also called **Internet forensics**). This coincides with the two major types of computer crime, the first involving the use of computers to commit a crime and the second in which the computer itself is the victim of crime (Berghel 2003).

There are a number of reasons why forensic computing is necessary. Typically a forensic investigation might be carried out in the case of intellectual property infractions, theft of information, inappropriate Internet or email usage, electronic tampering and unauthorised intrusion. This type of investigation also occurs when the computer has been used as a tool in a crime and when evidence of financial transactions, program installation and malicious network activity might be required not only to convict perpetrators of a crime but also to understand the sequence of events that have occurred over the period in which the crime has been carried out.

Computer forensics

In the case of computer forensics, the goal is to capture a representation of the system(s) that is as accurate and free from distortion and bias as possible (Farmer & Venema 1999). In this respect, computer forensics was born out of necessity; computers found at crime scenes contained clues, but methods were required to extract them. 'Computer forensics' generally refers to the search and analysis of stand-alone computers or single hard disk drives. The actual task of computer forensics is to examine what has occurred on a machine in the past as a method of determining what the machine has been used for and what the machine has done.

Network forensics

Network or Internet forensics was developed alongside the phenomenal growth of networked computing, and it serves as a tool for post-incident analysis of computers victimised by intrusion or malicious code (Berghel 2003). Although the techniques and aims of computer forensics and network forensics overlap, they are quite distinct from an operational perspective. However, both forms of forensic computing must be accurate to a demonstrable degree to be considered as evidence in a criminal court (Morris 2002).

Network forensics relies on analysis of network traffic, knowledge of operating systems and areas of vulnerability, as well as those of forensic toolkits. Often the methodology is less clear than in computer forensics, as it involves computer forensics among other skills. Whereas computer forensics examines computers as individual entities and is aimed at finding the contents and history of a single machine, network forensics is aimed at the larger picture and examining an entire sequence or intrusion.

The skills required by network forensics engineers are often similar to those who perpetrate computer crime or become hackers, and it should also be noted that the tool sets are similar to an extent. Network traffic analysers can be used to identify unusual network activity or to search for plaintext network passwords. Port scanners are used by both network administrators and potential intruders to test the security of firewalls. 'In Internet forensics it is customarily the case that the forensics specialist undergoes the same level of education and training as the hacker he or she seeks to thwart. The difference is one of ethics, not skill.' (Berghel 2003)

The majority of network forensics involves passive examination and comparison of network and Internet usage, as a method of discovering network intrusions and suspicious network activity that could be evidence of a computer intrusion or crime. Unaccountable network usage spikes, data transfer or open ports might indicate unauthorised network intrusion or computer crime being perpetrated by a user known to the system. In the event of a virus entering the network, network forensics cannot stop it or prevent it from infecting computers, but post-incident, it can examine how the virus entered the system and take countermeasures to prevent a recurrence of the attack.

Not all forensic computing is passive; there is a branch known as 'Tiger Teaming', named after US military security analysts, which analyses network security and potential breaches as a pre-emptive method to patch software vulnerability before it is exploited. Often this is done by a third party or as part of a security analysis. The benefits of this are obvious: it exposes network and computer vulnerability to system administrators rather than to potential intruders.

With the growth in wireless networking, some concern has been raised over the criminal use of wireless networking and the lack of availability of forensic tools for wireless network forensics. *Seizing Computers and Other Electronic Evidence: Best Practice Guide,* a guide for police officers without forensic computing experience on seizing electronic evidence, makes no mention of wireless networks and how to approach a case with electronic devices running them (ACPR 2003a). The only applicable component of the guide states: 'Do not seize any networked computer without forensic computing advice. (Business computers are often networked as are some home systems).'

When this is brought into a wireless networking context, the serious issue is that officers cannot detect easily whether a wireless network is present at the scene of an investigation. It cannot be determined whether a computer is connected to a wireless network, and the result might be that several other pieces of potential electronic evidence are not seized as they are not easily locatable. A suspect might have a wirelessly networked computer hidden in a place that would escape a basic police investigation but would still be accessible. As there are no other applicable steps suggested in *Seizing Computers and Other Electronic Evidence* (ACPR 2003a) that relate to wireless networking, it can be assumed that the presence of a wireless network is not specifically searched for.

A number of tools are available to assist in network security on wireless networks, but these make no claim at being applicable to a forensic investigation; nor do they provide an output that would be acceptable in a forensic investigation. So although these programs are useful in a network management framework, they might not meet the strict requirements of a program applicable in a forensic computing investigation. The strict series of requirements might preclude its use. Also, the analysis tools that exist are not designed with forensic computing in mind, so although they are used within network management, there might be functions that would be of assistance in a forensic computing context that are not suitable for network management, which is where these tools originate from.

Forensic investigations

The primary goal of a forensic computing investigation is to construct a timeline of events that can interpret the sequence of events that have occurred on that computer. If this is post-incident, it allows an unbiased view of what caused the incident (including how a potential intruder was granted access to the system), the damage to the system and lasting effects of the intrusion. If the aim is to search for evidence to investigate a crime, then a timeline sequence can produce legally admissible evidence on what exactly occurred on the computer system.

Methodology in forensic computing is the process that governs technology, skills and competence, and determines whether an investigation is successful. Methodology governs the correct procedure and protocols as well as rights and responsibilities in the field. Methodology in forensic computing ties the technological and the humanistic as each cannot operate independently. Forensic computing has strict guidelines that are based on the acceptable creation of and analysis of evidence. It is only when people, equipment and protocols work together that a forensic investigation produces verifiable results (Yasinac et al. 2003). A flaw in any of these three constitutes a flaw in the entire process, which might result in a potential loss of evidence or tainting of evidence in a way such that it would not be admissible. This is particularly true of the methodology: strict procedures are in place in the Best Practice Guide to ensure data integrity during an investigation. This is where McKemmish's (1999) four rules come into play:

- *Rule 1: Minimise handling of the original.* All work done within the course of a forensic investigation must be unable to damage original evidence. To prevent such damage, original evidence is handled only to clone. For computer hard disks, which represent the majority of forensic computing analysis , an exact duplicate is created of the original hard disk and a hash made from it (a hash is a number generated from a text string to allow information access). After this has been done, the original evidence is then securely stored, and the duplicate is then stored and hashed. This hash comparison ensures that the cloned drives are exact duplicates of the original drive. Any analysis work is then done from the second duplicated drive. In the event that files are accidentally edited on a drive in progress, it can be replaced from the first clone drive without disturbing the original drive that contains the original evidence. Using this rule of minimal handling, it is all but impossible to tamper with digital evidence (McKemmish 1999).

- *Rule 2: Account for any change.* Some situations might require the editing of files or the copying of them from their original location. An example of a change to file types might be to decrypt encrypted files to discover their contents. The decryption process would obviously change the files from their original state, and this type of change would need to be documented, as although the evidence was gained from the original drive, it has been explained only through a change in state. This indicates rule 2: accounting for any change (McKemmish 1999).

- *Rule 3: Comply with the rules of evidence.* McKemmish's third rule is intentionally broad and refers to the rules of handling evidence, which can vary internationally. As forensic computing was originally based on (and is still heavily involved with) police investigation, and the final product of a forensic investigation could be used in a legal context, the process by which evidence is obtained is extremely important. In a forensic computing investigation, all evidence must be accounted for at all times and logs kept of its movements. In this respect, it is no different from physical investigative evidence, for any movement or analysis of evidence must be accounted for. This is referred to as 'chain of evidence'. McKemmish's rule stipulates that evidentiary rules must be abided by.

- *Rule 4: Do not exceed knowledge.* The final of McKemmish's rules is that forensic computing investigators should not exceed their own knowledge and should refer an investigation to a more knowledgeable investigator rather than attempt to continue an investigation alone (McKemmish 1999).

These rules are not legal requirements, but represent good forensic computing investigative practice. However, as guidelines, the four rules given by McKemmish are followed within commercial and law enforcement situations.

Phases of forensic investigation

A forensic computing investigation has three phases: the acquisition, authentication and analysis of data (Kruse II & Heiser 2002; Marcella & Greenfield 2002); these are described in further detail below.

Acquisition of data

Acquisition of data from a live machine poses problems. Traditionally, the first step is to switch off the target machine. Using a 'soft' shutdown procedure edits a number of system files, including timestamps, so often shutdown will require physically unplugging the machine while it is running (Kruse II & Heiser 2002). Although this saves temporary files such as cache and virtual memory, it can lead to data corruption, and often the only evidence of attack or previous history on a computer is found in RAM, which is lost when the machine is powered off (Farmer & Venema 1999). Hostile code can be added to logon scripts also, which could potentially remove data when a user next logs in (Farmer & Venema 1999). Furthermore, a machine might not be shut off for non-technical reasons, especially if it is a critical networking or commercial component (Kruse II & Heiser 2002).

However, shutting down the machine allows the duplication of the hard drive contents, which can perfectly duplicate a machine at a given time. This allows technicians to operate from any one of a number of duplicates without fear of destroying the original. Also, the isolation of a machine can prevent further problems, such as the spreading of backdoor viruses or similar programs that could compound the problem, as well as leaving the original intact for possible entry into evidence if the situation becomes a police matter.

Authentication of data

Gathering evidence of crime committed by electronic means is a difficult process, especially as there are few systems that provide true non-repudiation in electronic formats, which makes prosecution difficult. However, if computer forensics is to be of value, rules of evidence must be followed as with paper-based records (AGLIECEI 2003). Authentication is the process of ensuring that data is collected in accordance with law and that, if a duplicate is made, it is an exact copy of the original.

In Australia, the rules of evidence are governed individually by state and, although there is a movement to base all state legislation on a common Commonwealth model, only New South Wales has adopted it (AGLIECEI 2003).

In South Australia, for example, rules of evidence are defined by the Evidence Act of 1929, which states that electronic data can be entered as evidence as long as a correct chain of evidence occurs and that it can be linked to the original author or owner. Also, the use of the Telecommunications (Interception) Act of 1988 can aid in the collection of data for prosecution.

At a technical level, the process of ensuring that a duplicate made of a target hard disk is an exact replica of the original is done with hashing programs, such as MD5 hash (Deering 2000). Typically, this functionality is built into a forensic toolkit, and it will hash the entire contents of both the original and duplicate hard disks and operating systems, and compare the hashes (Farmer & Venema 1999). Only an exact match will produce the same result.

Analysis of data

There are many techniques for analysing data, depending on the object of the search. At a basic level, operating system utilities such as recent documents, Internet bookmarks, Internet history, cache, cookies and username/password combinations for a proxy server can determine who accessed the Internet and for how long, and can report on what documents have recently been opened (Marcella & Greenfield 2002). If the computer network being investigated uses centralised login procedures, this also can indicate when a user was using a specific computer. At a more advanced level, registry information, timestamping and analysis of Microsoft Windows security logging tools can yield results on what programs have been installed, what programs have been run and whether any unsuccessful attempts to access a system have been made.

Analysis is the final step to the production of known facts, and it is the analysis of data that determines the value of the forensic evaluation. Digital evidence processing is the area that requires the greatest skill as it determines from a number of small clues what actually occurred in a method that cannot be disagreed with and is fully documented (Anderson 1998).

Forensic tools

Encase, from Guidance Software, is one of the most widely used forensic software suites. This suite allows the imaging and examination of hard disk drives and removable media. Encase is a component of a suite of tools used by the FBI and the US Department of Defense (Morris 2002). It is one of the most highly recommended suites as it utilises its own scripting language to fully customise searches (Guidance Software 2002).

The latest Encase solution is experimenting with a new technique aimed at capturing the contents of RAM on a live computer. This technique, if successful, will alleviate the difficulties associated with capturing data from an operating machine (Guidance Software 2003). This, combined with Encase's methods for duplicating the contents of hard disk drives while they are operating, could prove to be a great technical advance for data collection (Guidance Software 2003).

Vogon International produces a number of forensic suites and utilities, and is also recognised internationally. Its flagship product, Vogon International Laboratory Based Forensic Workstation, is built on imaging and non-repudiation of target hard drives. The software creates an MD5 hash of both the original and the duplicated drive as a form of validation. The system also introduces automatic write-protection, allowing read-access only to the original target drive. This system is able to duplicate only static drives and is unable to save volatile computing information, such as RAM. The analysis tools are largely automatic and require no in-depth knowledge of the system. Vogon's Laboratory Based Forensic Workstation can analyse a number of different operating systems and file formats, including Windows, Macintosh, Linux and Unix (Vogon International 2003).

Many authorities write that there are tools beyond the predefined software suites and that the best sources for software are 'hacker' sites themselves. Among these, Astalavista (www.astalavista.com) is one of the better known and has a myriad of tools available that could potentially be used to aid network security, perform computer or network forensics or, conversely, to exploit network insecurities.

Nmap (www.insecure.org) is a well-known port-scanning utility that also gives specific information regarding what programs are operating on which open ports. Used in combination with Nessus (www.insecure.org), a program that documents flaws and vulnerability in particular versions of operating systems or programs, Nmap gives detailed information on potential ways to exploit a given system.

Forensic readiness

The exponential growth in e-crime and the need for forensic computing investigations results in the requirement to link good IT management, particularly security management, with forensic readiness. IT managers need to plan for the day when they need to present forensic evidence in court and so need to be able to draw on standards to help instigate processes for developing systems that are capable of producing legally admissible evidence; this is essentially a major feature of the forensic readiness process.

Rowlingson (2004) defines **forensic readiness** as preparing in such a way as to maximise the potential to use digital evidence and minimise the cost of a forensic investigation. In his review of current research and practice of forensic readiness techniques, Rowlingson produced '10 steps' that he believes must be followed to enable a forensic readiness process to be undertaken:

1. Identify which business scenarios might require digital evidence.
2. Identify the various sources and types of potential evidence.
3. Determine what is required to collect the evidence.
4. On the basis of step 3, establish the capability to gather legally admissible evidence.

5. Establish a policy to ensure that potential evidence is securely stored and handled.
6. Establish monitoring procedures to both deter and detect incidents.
7. Determine those circumstances that should trigger a full formal investigation (which might use the digital evidence).
8. Train staff to understand their role and responsibilities in the forensic process and the handling of digital evidence.
9. Document any incident and its effect on the basis of the evidence.
10. Ensure that the incident is reviewed by a legal authority (Rowlingson 2004).

These 10 steps indicate a need for major involvement by both senior management and IT managers in devising strategies whereby forensic readiness concepts will be embraced in an enterprise. One major obstacle to the acceptance of forensic readiness as part of the IT management process could be senior management's lack of awareness of the current focus on forensic readiness as a major corporate responsibility.

One technical project that exists to support and prepare small and medium-sized enterprises in the forensics readiness process is Cyber Tools On-Line Search for Evidence (CTOSE), a project funded by the European Union (EU) (Hannan et al. 2003). CTOSE has developed a methodology that aims to provide a consistent approach for identifying, preserving, analysing and presenting digital evidence. The focus of the CTOSE model is on the acquisition of digital evidence and on the way it is to be collected, conserved and analysed so that it will be legally admissible should court proceedings be instigated. However, its context is primarily that of IT security management for network administrators rather than a forensic computing tool *per se*.

A major motivation for the establishment of the CTOSE project was the recognition that in most companies IT security management still often consists of purely technical measures in the area of prevention and detection of IT incidents. In these circumstances, the first priority is always the prevention of further incidents and the elimination of the vulnerability of the technology, whereas little attention is usually given to forensic investigation to find out what happened or trace the perpetrators. Even where investigations occur there is often a problem of a lack of experience or knowledge of how to proceed correctly from a technical and/or legal perspective.

To address these issues and improve the ability of companies to respond to computer misuse incidents the CTOSE project began by developing a reference process resembling organisational, technical and legal guidelines on how a company should proceed when computer misuse occurs. The focus of the model is on the acquisition of digital evidence and on how it is to be collected, conserved and analysed. This reference model is linked with a detailed examination of technical, legal and presentational requirements, which in turn are linked to a project software demonstrator.

The reference process model consists of five phases: preparation, running, assessment, investigation and learning. It articulates the flow of actions and decisions that have to be considered or executed in the case of an investigation of computer misuse. Moreover, additional information (including roles and their necessary skills, checklists, references to documents and tools, and legal advice) is provided to support the action or decision in each step. In this way, before reporting an IT incident a user can, for example, consult a checklist that covers what technical information about the incident law enforcement agencies might require from the person involved.

In their discussion Hannan et al. (2003) concluded that the CTOSE project has made a very significant contribution to developing a methodology for a standardised approach to computer misuse. They comment on the critical role of the 'forensic readiness' phase and the need for proactive monitoring and analysis of digital evidence.

Summary

E-crime and its costs are growing rapidly in Australia and internationally. There are many sources of e-crime, and e-criminals have a variety of motives. Some organised crime groups now use e-crime approaches in their operations. Cyber terrorism has gained prominence following the terror attacks on the USA on 11 September 2001. However, many people argue that cyber terrorism *per se* does not exist. Nevertheless, IT security managers, and particularly those with responsibility for IT systems that operate the critical national infrastructure, need to protect systems against possible cyber terrorist attacks.

More common IT security risks relate to fraud, identity theft, phishing, denial of service attacks and malicious code, such as viruses, worms and Trojans. There are a range of technical, operational and management controls that should be implemented to secure an organisation against each threat.

Forensic computing is the process by which digital evidence is identified, preserved, analysed and presented in a legally acceptable manner. 'Computer forensics' generally refers to the forensic investigation of a single computer or hard disk. Network forensics is the investigation of a sequence of events on a network. The four rules of forensic investigation are: minimise handling of the original, account for any change, comply with the rules of evidence and do not act beyond your own knowledge. The steps in a forensic investigation are: acquisition of data, authentication of data and analysis of data. The tools and techniques of forensic investigation are similar to, if not the same as, the tools and techniques of hacking. Indeed an investigator and a hacker have the same skills. It is important that businesses prepare themselves for the possibility that a forensic investigation might be required. A forensic readiness program should be put in place to ensure that digital evidence is captured and handled in such a way as to be legally admissible.

Key terms

boot sector viruses, p. 113
computer forensics, p. 115
cyber terrorism, p. 103
denial of service (DOS) attack, p. 114
distributed denial of service (DDOS)
  attack, p. 114
electronic crime (e-crime), p. 103
forensic computing, p. 114
forensic readiness, p. 121
fraud, p. 111
identity crime, p. 113

identity fraud, p. 113
identity theft, p. 113
information warfare (IW), p. 103
Internet forensics, p. 115
macro viruses, p. 113
network forensics, p. 115
organised crime, p. 103
phishing, p. 112
Trojan, p. 114
virus, p. 113
worm, p. 114

Questions

1. Choose an organisation and prepare a brief report on how much of a target
   you think it would be for e-criminals.
2. By reference to the information in this chapter and your own research beyond
   the chapter, explain how the following attacks may be carried out and what
   kind of IT security controls could be put in place to manage the risk of this
   kind of attack:
   (a) a denial of service attack
   (b) a distributed denial of service attack
   (c) Internet auction fraud
   (d) a Nigerian letter scam
   (e) credit card fraud
   (f) a worm
   (g) a phishing attack.
3. Describe the main difference between computer forensics and network
   forensics.
4. Explain the purpose of each of the rules of forensic methodology.
5. Choose an organisation. Assume you have responsibility for IT security
   for that organisation. Prepare a report that explains the organisation's need
   for forensic readiness. Try to identify issues specific to that organisation's
   business needs.

Case study
4: A forensic evidence plan

Elisabeth Chan is the CEO of a two-year-old electronics company. The company
designs, develops and manufactures the micro midget widget, which is Elisabeth's own invention. It is a small but important component in a wide range of

complex video and other specialised hardware. Elisabeth is an engineer, but she has no modern technical understanding of IT security issues.

Elisabeth has had no problems with IT security until very recently when the company's network was subject to a series of attacks. In three days, the company's website was defaced, a serious virus infected the company's email and large quantities of data were corrupted.

Elisabeth's IT security risk management concerns are wide-ranging. She needs to determine whether the same hackers are likely to hack the company again. She believes the recent attacks suggest that the hackers were interested in proprietary theft of sensitive information for personal and/or financial gain or disrupting the company in such a way as to give competitors an edge. There is no evidence of any previous disgruntled employees, so revenge has been discounted as a motive. Common industry knowledge of a range of micro midget widgets as a new defence product reinforces this conclusion.

Elisabeth has become very worried about cyber terrorism and is concerned that she might inadvertently allow her unprotected system to be the launch pad for a major denial of service attack on the Australian national information infrastructure. She is also very concerned about becoming a victim of e-crime.

She believes that her company ought to develop a forensic readiness plan so as to be prepared for possible action against the hackers who have been attacking her company.

Questions

1. By reference to HB 171:2003, *Guidelines for the Management of IT Evidence* and the 10 steps to forensic evidence (Rowlingson 2004) prepare the outline of a forensic evidence plan for Elisabeth.
2. Indicate how this plan could deal with possible litigation arising from the current attacks.
3. Suggest some other human resource or technical controls that Elisabeth might put in place to help with her current problems.

Suggested reading

Marcella, A & Greenfield, R 2002, *Cyber Forensics: A Field Manual for Collecting, Examining and Preserving Evidence of Computer Crimes*, Auerbach Publications, London.

McKemmish, R 1999, *What is Forensic Computing?* Australian Institute of Criminology, Trends and Issues in Crime and Criminal Justice, no. 118, 1–6, Canberra.

References

Action Group into the Law Enforcement Implications of Electronic Commerce, *Evidence and the Internet* (AGLIECEI) 2003, Evidence and the Internet, accessed 26 October 2003 www.austrac.gov.au/publications/agec/evidence_and_the_internet.pdf.

Anderson, M 1998, *Computer Evidence Processing: Good Documentation is Essential,* New Technologies Inc., accessed 29 October 2003, www.forensics-intl.com/art10.html.

Australasian Centre for Policing Research (ACPR) 2000, *The Virtual Horizon: Meeting the Law Enforcement Challenges — Developing an Australasian Law Enforcement Strategy for Dealing with Electronic Crime,* Australasian Centre for Policing Research, Adelaide, SA, pp. 1–132.

—— 2001, *Electronic Crime Strategy of the Police Commissioners' Conference,* Australasian Centre for Policing Research, Adelaide, SA.

—— 2003a, *Seizing Computers and Other Electronic Evidence: Best Practice Guide,* Australasian Centre for Policing Research, Adelaide, SA.

—— 2003b, *Australasian Identity Crime Policing Strategy 2003–2005,* Australasian Centre for Policing Research, Adelaide, SA.

Australian Bureau of Statistics (ABS) 1997, 'Take-up rate for modem and Internet use low' ABS, Canberra.

—— 2004, *Internet Activity Survey,* ABS, Canberra.

Australian Computer Emergency Response Team (AusCERT) 2003, *2003 Australian Computer Crime and Security Survey,* accessed 20 July 2004, www.auscert.org.au/crimesurvey.

—— 2004, *2004 Computer Crime Survey,* accessed 19 April 2005, www.auscert.org.

Berghel, H 2003, 'The discipline of Internet forensics', *Communications of the ACM* [Association of Computing Machinery], vol. 46, no. 8, pp. 15–20.

Betts, B 2000, 'Digital forensics: Crime seen', *Information Security Magazine,* accessed 22 October 2003, http://infosecuritymag.techtarget.com/articles/march00/cover.shtml.

Broucek, V & Turner, P 2001, 'Forensic computing: Developing a conceptual approach in the era of information warfare', *Journal of Information Warfare,* vol. 1, no. 2, pp. 95–108.

Deering, B 2000, *Data Validation using the MD5 Hash,* New Technologies Inc., accessed 29 October 2003, www.forensics-intl.com/art12.html.

Denning, DE 2000, 'Cyberterrorism', Testimony before the Special Oversight Panel on Terrorism Committee on Armed Services, US House of Representatives, accessed 19 October 2005, www.cs.georgetown.edu/~denning/infosec/cyberterror.html.

Etter, B 2001, *The Forensic Challenges of e-Crime,* Australasian Centre for Policing Research, Adelaide, SA, pp. 1–8.

Farmer, D & Venema, W 1999, *Computer Forensic Analysis Class,* accessed 13 September 2003, www.porcupine.org/forensics/handouts.html.

Galeotti, M 2001, 'Criminalisation of the DPRK', *Jane's Intelligence Review,* June 2001, pp. 10–12.

Gordon, S & Ford, R 2004, *Symantec White Paper: Cyberterrorism?* accessed 5 October 2004, www.symantec.com.

Guidance Software 2002, *Encase Enscript,* accessed 28 October 2003, www.guidancesoftware.com/support/enscript/index.shtm.

Hannan, M, Broucek, V, Frings, S & Turner, P 2003, 'Forensic computing theory and practice: Towards developing a methodology for a standardised approach to computer misuse', *Proceedings of First Australian Computer Network, Information and Forensics Conference*, Perth, WA.

Internet Fraud Complaint Center 2003, Intelligence Note 11/04/2003, accessed 18 August 2005, www.ifccfbi.gov/strategy/11403NigerianWarning.pdf

Kaihla, P 2002, 'The technology secrets of Cocaine Inc.', *Business 2.0*, July 2002, accessed 23 June 2005, www.business2.com/b2/web/articles/0,17863,514820,00.html.

Kruse II, W & Heiser, J 2002, *Computer Forensics: Incident Response Essentials*, Addison-Wesley Professional, Boston.

Levy, E 2004, 'Criminals become tech savvy', *IEEE Security & Privacy*, March–April, pp. 65–8.

Lyman, J 2004, 'Worm variants part of Russian Mafia extortion scheme', accessed 5 October 2004, www.technewsworld.com/story/33127.htm.

Marcella, A & Greenfield, R 2002, *Cyber Forensics: A Field Manual for Collecting, Examining and Preserving Evidence of Computer Crimes*, Auerbach Publications, London.

McKemmish, R 1999, *What is Forensic Computing?* Australian Institute of Criminology, Trends and Issues in Crime and Criminal Justice, no. 118, pp. 1–6, Canberra.

Morris, R 2002, 'An introduction to computer forensic tools', *Security Focus*, accessed 25 September 2003, www.securityfocus.com/guest/16691.

Nemets, A & Torda, T 2001, 'Finding the real source of Sept. 11', accessed 5 October 2004, www.newsmax.com/archives/articles/2001/10/16/15905.shtml.

Rowlingson, R 2004, 'A ten-step process for forensic readiness', *International Journal of Digital Evidence*, Winter, vol. 2, no. 3, pp. 1–28.

South Australian Police (SAPOL) 2003, *Contemporary Policing Issues Module: Electronic Crime*, Professional Development Section, South Australia Police Academy, Adelaide, SA.

Valli, C 2002, 'The proxy baker's dirty dozen: An analysis of abusive users of a WWW proxy cache', www.collecter.org/coll02/papers/valli.pdf.

Vatis, MA 2001, *Cyber Attacks During the War on Terrorism: A Predictive Analysis*, Institute for Security Technology Studies at Dartmouth College, accessed 23 June 2005, www.ists.dartmouth.edu/analysis/cyber_a1.pdf.

Vogon International 2003, *Evolution of Forensic Computing*, accessed 26 March 2004, www.vogon-international.com.

Yasinsac, A, Erbacher, R, Marks, D, Pollitt, M & Sommer P 2003, 'Computer forensics education', *IEEE Security and Privacy Magazine*, July–August 2003, pp. 15–23.

Chapter 5

Basic cryptography and Public Key Infastructure

Learning objectives

After studying this chapter, you should be able to:

- use cryptographic terminology

- define the different types of cryptographic attack

- differentiate between types of cipher in common use

- discriminate between symmetric and asymmetric encryption

- explain why hashing is used alongside cryptography

- describe the use of cryptographic standards and protocols

- describe the ways cryptographic techniques are applied and integrated

- discuss Public Key Infrastructure.

Chapter overview

Cryptology, the study of codes and secret messages, has existed from as far back as the Egyptian and Mesopotamian eras. Within this area of study, cryptography, the science of writing secret codes, has been used throughout history and has proved a practical means by which we can hide messages so that our enemies or competitors cannot understand our plans. A more modern usage of the term cryptography includes the concept of helping to achieve our security goals of confidentiality, integrity, availability, authentication and non-repudiation and thus avoiding serious IT security risks, such as unwanted disclosure of information or denial of service.

This chapter introduces the specialised terminology developed to explain the features of cryptography. It uses this vocabulary to explain the foundations of cryptography and expand on common cryptographic definitions.

We then examine the mechanism of basic types of cryptographic cipher that are, or have been, used and compare fundamental symmetric and asymmetric cryptography by looking at some common algorithms. We begin to scrutinise some of the issues that cause risk within cryptography, including the problem of key management and the choice of the use of block and stream ciphers.

We continue by looking at two contrasting but complementary issues that both include risks we need to contend with. First, we examine how cryptography can be attacked by competitors or hackers, then we examine some common applications of cryptography, including both software and hardware applications.

The chapter concludes by demonstrating how cryptographic applications can be integrated to provide a secure Public Key Infrastructure (PKI) so as to protect a complete enterprise system and by looking at Australian government specifications and government and commercial applications of PKI in Australia.

Foundations of cryptography

Before we can begin to investigate the way cryptography can be used to mitigate IT risk in an enterprise, it is necessary to have a sound understanding of the terminology of the field and to have a basic grasp of the underpinning mathematical issues on which it is based. The self-titled 'non-mathematical' student or manager has nothing to fear in this discipline; although cryptographers and cryptanalysts are often post-graduate mathematicians, those of us who use or apply cryptographic techniques need only to use sound common sense and to comprehend high school mathematics.

Terminology

If we take a top-down perspective to our understanding of this field, we need to start with **cryptology**, which is the study of both writing and deciphering hidden messages or codes. **Cryptography** really just refers to the writing of codes —

secret writing — whereas **cryptanalysis** is the deciphering of hidden messages or codes. A cryptographer can take a simple message, **plaintext**, which is readable in their own language, and disguise it. This process of disguising the text is to **encipher**, **encrypt** or **encode** it. This means that no-one else can understand it unless they have been given the **secret key**, a number that depends on an **algorithm**, a mathematical formula or set of functions, by which the **code**, the secret text, can be broken. On the other hand, a cryptanalyst, most likely a mathematician or experienced linguist, using statistical techniques and charts can combine these with high-level computational power and take some of the code, which is also known as **cipher text** (or **encoded text**), and **decipher**, **decrypt** or **decode** it so that it is now readable in the language in which it was written.

When we combine our algorithm, our keys and our cryptographic standards and protocols, the agreed technical methods by which encryption and decryption can be carried out and implemented in a particular context, then we have a complete **cryptosystem**. Within cryptology therefore a major goal for cryptographers is the design of strong cryptosystems, ones that will stand many types of attack and hence reduce risk.

Strong cryptosystems, algorithms and keys

When learning cryptographic principles it is easy to be confused by the use of examples based on the encoding of simple words. For example, it is easy to guess this code, and you will quickly be able to decipher that 'nffu nf bu uif pme hvo usff bu njemjhiu' is a very simple transformation of 'meet me at the old gum tree at midnight'.

We can accomplish this by replacing each letter with the one that follows in the English alphabet (a simple substitution, which is explained more fully below). If we express this 'algorithm' in simple English we can say 'take each letter within your message and replace it with the one that follows it in the English alphabet'. More mathematically we might express this as '+1' or a simple right shift. We can thus see that, in this case, +1 is the **key** — the secret number — and without this secret we cannot break the code. This fact lies at the heart of a good understanding of cryptography.

The problem with this example is that it is a very weak cryptosystem based on a simple algorithm. Even if we change the key and make it any other number between 1 and 25, this algorithm, which was used by Julius Caesar and thus is always known as the Caesar cipher, would not protect us in the real world.

In real life, cryptography, our plaintext, keys and cipher text are handled in digital form, in bits and bytes, and our mathematical algorithms are highly complex, ranging from modular arithmetic and the factoring of large prime numbers through to mathematics of elliptical curves to the random behaviour expressed in quantum physics. Currently, except in a few special cases where US national or foreign policy forbids it, algorithms are not kept secret so we cannot depend on mathematical complexity or obscurity alone to protect our data.

Strong cryptosystems nowadays depend on the use of algorithms consisting of a series of formulae. The key determines the order in which the formulae within the algorithm will be used; it is also used within the process as part of the calculation. A key is not a fixed value, as in the example above where we have chosen '+1' as the secret value, but is a large set of random values from which one is chosen. Neither is it a small number since it can be seen that, with a small number as the key, a code is very easy to break; common keys may be 40-bit, 56-bit or 128-bit in length. This means that they are impossible to guess and very difficult to break by systematically trying every combination of the digits within the key (this is known as a brute force attack). The major issue, then, is that, for every algorithm, the mathematical basis of the algorithm must be one which produces a very large key space. The **key space** is a range of numbers from which the algorithm can choose the key in any given act of encoding a message.

Two situations of risk that need to be avoided are **key clustering** and making keys unnecessarily long. Key clustering occurs when two different values of the key produce the same cipher text from the plain text; this would be a fault within the algorithm. It might be tempting to believe that the use of a long key would produce a greater level of defence against attack, but the consequence of a long key is a longer computation time in the cryptographic process, which thus raises the cost of computation and processing.

Cryptographic attacks

A cryptographic attack is one where a deliberate attempt is made to break cryptography. Given enough time and data, a cryptanalyst (hacker) can determine and break an algorithm. Advances in technology aid these processes, which might include attempts to break a simple message, efforts to recognise patterns in cipher text and attempts to find other weaknesses in algorithms. Other techniques include: guessing, frequency charts (e.g. in a JAVA source code book we expect to see the word 'Java' many times), frequency analysis for 'finger printing', and always having some clues to context, author and so on.

Attacks can be carried out in one or more of the following ways.

- *Cipher text-only attack.* A **cipher text-only attack** is one in which the cryptanalyst is able to identify a portion of cipher text but has no access to the associated plaintext. Generally speaking, a cryptanalyst who has only cipher text to work with will have to rely on statistical tables or public knowledge and information gained from hacker websites to decipher the cipher text. By reference to figure 5.1, if a simple substitution code had been used, then cipher text would be much easier to attack since probabilities of particular character combinations in the English language are well known and easily obtainable.
- *Plaintext attack.* There are two kinds of **plaintext attack**. A known-plaintext attack is one in which the cryptanalyst acquires a section of cipher text and the equivalent plaintext as well. In a chosen-plaintext attack the cryptanalyst is

able to select an amount of plaintext and then get hold of the parallel encoded cipher text.

- *Brute force attack.* A **brute force attack** is one where an exhaustive search is made using every known key combination. This kind of attack is made easier with the increasing development of computational and processing power. Longer keys and more efficient algorithms strengthen users against this kind of attack.

Types of cipher

When we come to examine some of the encryption algorithms in common use we will become aware that there as two major types of cipher, the **substitution cipher** and the **transposition cipher**. In substitution ciphers one character is replaced in a logical manner with another (e.g. as we discussed above, we can replace every letter with the letter that follows it in the English alphabet) and in a transposition cipher (see figure 5.3) the characters in the message are forced into swapping places by writing the lines in the message over a specified number of columns and then writing each column of letters as a row. We will also discover that some ciphers encrypt data one bit at a time, a **stream cipher**, while others, **block ciphers**, process bits in blocks of predetermined size. Product ciphers use a combination of substitution and transposition to produce cipher text and other non-mathematical means such as **one-time pads**, **running key ciphers** and even **steganography** are used to protect data. These three methods of hiding data are explained below.

Substitution ciphers

A substitution cipher is one where an individual character or bit within a word is replaced with another in a prearranged manner. The Caesar cipher described earlier is a simple substitution. Figure 5.1 shows the effect of different kinds of simple substitutions with a shift of +5 as the key values.

Plaintext	a b c d e f g h i j k l m n o p q r s t u v w x y z
Key	Shift 5
Cipher text	f g h i j k l m n o p q r s t u v w x y z a b c d e
Plaintext message	Come quickly enemy is approaching
Cipher text message	htrj vzsnqd jsjrd nx fuuwtfhmnsl

Figure 5.1 **Simple substitution cipher**

It might appear that a simple substitution cipher is very vulnerable, even to an untutored observer, since characters remain in the same order after substitution. However, the principle of simple substitution is often used in current cryptographic algorithms; strength is produced when the substitution process is iterated many times within the algorithm.

Extensions to simple substitution ciphers include **polyalphabetic ciphers**. These ciphers use two, or more, simple alphabetical substitutions. We might decide that odd characters within a plaintext message might be substituted with a 'shift 5', as shown in figure 5.1. We might, however, use a 'shift –1' to encode the even characters. The plaintext would then be affected, as shown in figure 5.2. 'C' is an odd character, so it becomes 'H' (shift 5); 'O' is an even character so it becomes 'N' (shift –1); and so on.

Plaintext	a b c d e f g h i j k l m n o p q r s t u v w x y z
Key (odd characters)	Shift 5
Cipher text (odd characters)	f g h i j k l m n o p q r s t u v w x y z a b c d e
Key (even characters)	Shift 1
Cipher text (even characters)	b c d e f g h i j k l m n o p q r s t u v w x y a z
Plaintext message	Come quickly enemy is approaching
Cipher text	hnrd vtnbpkd drdrx nr fouqtzhgnml

Figure 5.2   Polyalphabetic substitution cipher

Transposition ciphers

A transposition cipher is one that is accomplished in three steps and in which a plaintext message is taken and written across a predetermined number of columns, then reconstructed as shown in figure 5.3. In most normal cases the length of the text is unknown in advance. The characters within the message are numbered to help you see the effect of transposition.

Presume we have already agreed a protocol whereby we will write the plaintext across four columns, as shown in panel A of figure 5.3. Since the number of characters in the message is not divisible by four, we will use three more blanks as **padding**; this data has no meaning here but will hide the real length of the message.

The text is transposed by writing vertical columns horizontally, then reconstructed to produce the cipher text shown in panel B of figure 5.3. Characters have changed places when compared to original plaintext.

Panel A

1	c	2	o	3	m	4	e
5		6	q	7	u	8	i
9	c	10	k	11	l	12	y
13		14	e	15	n	16	e
17	m	18	y	19		20	i
21	s	22		23	a	24	p
25	p	26	r	27	o	28	a
29	c	30	h	31	i	32	n
33	g	34		35		36	

Panel B

1	5	9	13	17	21	25	29	33	2	6	10	14	18	22	26	30	34	3	7	11	15	19	23	27	31	35
c	c		m	s	p	c	g	o	q	k	e	y			r	h		m	u	l	n		a	o	i	

4	8	12	16	20	24	28	32	36
e	i	y	e	i	p	a	n	

Plaintext message: Come quickly enemy is approaching
Cipher text: c c mspcgoqkey rh muln aoi eiyeipan

Figure 5.3 Transposed cipher text

The cipher text from a transposition cipher is not as easy to decipher as that produced in a simple substitution. Word length and spacing do not resemble that of the original English and therefore special techniques would be necessary for decryption. Once again it must be observed that the example here is a trivial one developed to illustrate the principle of transposition; real algorithms are much more complex and use both substitution and transposition iteratively and in combination to produce product ciphers.

Product ciphers

Product ciphers are strong ciphers formed by combining two other kinds of cipher. An example of a product cipher based on the simple substitution illustrated in figure 5.1, with the transposition method illustrated in figure 5.3, is shown in figure 5.4 on p. 136.

This is a far stronger cipher than either of those illustrated above since word lengths are not the same as those of the original plaintext message and characters have changed places. Therefore the original message cannot be simply reconstructed.

Panel A: Substitution

Plaintext	a b c d e f g h i j k l m n o p q r s t u v w x y z
Key	Shift 5
Cipher text	f g h i j k l m n o p q r s t u v w x y z a b c d e
Plaintext message	Come quickly enemy is approaching
Cipher text	htrj vznhpqd jsjrd nx fuuwtfhmnsl

Panel B: Transposition

Write cipher text over 4 columns	h	t	r	t
		v	z	n
	h	p	q	d
		j	s	j
	r	d		n
	x		f	u
	u	w	t	f
	h	m	n	s
	l			
Construct new product cipher text by transposing columns and rows	h h rxuhltvpjd wm rzqs ftn jndjnufs			

Figure 5.4   Product cipher

One-time pad

The examples shown above use mathematical relationships to produce code, and we can see how increasing mathematical complexity produces stronger cryptosystems. A very strong cryptosystem, maybe even an unbreakable cryptosystem, can also be built on a one-time pad.

The one-time pad simply consists of a stream of bits (you could think of this as a stream of random letters if this helps with conceptualisation). The value of the first bit of the plaintext is added to the value of the first bit of the plaintext message and this value is recorded (this is an X-OR operation). The length of the one-time pad is the same as the length of the message and provides strength because it is never used again. The receiver of the message is the only person to own a copy of the pad. There is no algorithm and no key, and hence no brute force attack can be successful against it. Weaknesses do exist, and we examine these below when we consider how cryptography can be attacked.

Running key ciphers

Running key ciphers are also non-mathematical in nature and based on books or texts in a prearranged fashion. They might be based on putting an advert in the Personals column of the *Australian* newspaper on a prearranged day, signed with a name known only to the sender and receiver of a message. The ad contains some numbers that indicate pages in a book, which once again are known only to the sender and receiver of a message. These numbers identify words and phrases in the book that together detail the message the sender wished to transmit. This kind of cipher is *never* used in real life but occurred frequently in the spy movies of the 1950s.

Steganography

Steganography is another method of hiding data, but it does not depend on algorithms and keys as detailed above. Steganography involves hiding information inside a 'container' file and using the least significant bits (LSB) to transport data. Common containers included .mp3, .gif and .jpeg graphic files and so are actually messages hidden in pictures. If we use a 24-bit colour image as a container and use two bits to store hidden data, the result is a 22-bit colour image nearly identical to the original and, unless an opponent is aware of the possibility of the use of steganography, this becomes a very secure (but complex) method of transmitting data. This means we are literally hiding our message in a picture and, with some basic IT skills, can hide it in such a way that it cannot be seen. It does not even affect the quality of the picture to the naked eye.

Block and stream ciphers

In our thinking so far we have imagined substituting or transposing text on a character-by-character basis. The simple substitution ciphers that we have examined are examples of stream ciphers. They are not strong because they do not cause *confusion*; an attacker can easily determine the relationship between our plaintext, algorithm, key and cipher text because the length of the original words, the position of short words, double letters and spaces have not changed from the original message. When we used a polyalphabetic cipher in figure 5.2 we were able to cause a little confusion, but not enough to begin to deter a real attacker.

When we considered transposition we dealt with blocks of four characters. When we used both substitution and transposition on a block of characters in figure 5.4 we reduced the risk of an attacker breaking our code by using *diffusion*. The blocks have moved around and are not in their original places in the message.

Encryption algorithms often use block ciphers. Although these are slower to process than stream ciphers, since we have to wait for a block of text to arrive before we can encode it, they are stronger because they produce diffusion and can withstand insertion attacks (see below) since they are of predetermined size. Their major weakness is that errors can be propagated very easily, damaging the whole message to such an extent that it is unreadable, when compared with a stream cipher. If we make an error in one character of a bit stream, this will influence just that one character and a message will still generally be understood. If we make an error in a block cipher, this will affect all the other characters in the block and might obscure the meaning of the message.

Symmetric and asymmetric cryptography

There are two basic forms of cryptography: symmetric and asymmetric cryptography, also known as secret key and public key systems. In the examples we have been examining so far we have been thinking in terms of an individual encryption and sending a message using an encryption algorithm and a key. We might have assumed that the receiver of the message will be able to decrypt the message using the same secret key. This is in fact an example of symmetric or secret key cryptography.

This kind of encryption is very basic since it assumes that key management is not a problem and that we have developed secure techniques for sharing keys over long distances. It also assumes that the size of our enterprise is small and that we do not wish to expand to develop a network of trusted partners with whom we will share our data, since there is a second-order relationship between the number of individuals sharing secret keys and the number of keys required. We study this so as to understand the foundations of cryptography, remembering, as shown in IT Risk 5.1, that cryptographic techniques are rather under-used by Australian businesses. If the basic techniques were more fully comprehended by industry and commerce, perhaps there might be broader adoption of this IT security solution.

Asymmetric encryption or public key (PK) cryptography is based on the use of two different keys; one key is used for encryption and another for decryption. Although the mathematics of public key cryptography is complex and the processing time up to a thousand times slower than that of symmetric cryptography, the major advantages include improved key management processes, better scalability and the ability to use this form of cryptography to develop PK cryptographic applications and a Public Key Infrastructure (PKI) to provide authentication and non-repudiation as well as confidentiality.

Each type of cryptography is shown in figure 5.5 on p. 140.

How many Australian companies use encryption techniques?

Each year, AusCERT (Australia's national computer emergency response team) and a variety of national and federal law enforcement agencies survey a large number of companies, both small and large, from various sectors to identify risks and trends in IT security management. In their 2004 analysis, AusCERT surveyed more than 200 companies to discover what kind of security technology they were using. The responses are shown in table 5.1.

Table 5.1 Comparison of use of IT security technology, 2002–04

Security technology	2002 (%)	2003 (%)	2004 (%)
Physical security	91	83	94
Firewalls	96	95	95
Antivirus software	99	98	100
Reusable passwords	100	59	53
Intrusion detection systems	53	45	53
Cryptographic techniques:			
— PKI (digital IDs, certificates)	46	34	46
— Encrypted files	47	39	47
— Encrypted logins/sessions	48	48	58

Source: data from AusCERT 2004, p. 7.

These results indicate that although almost all companies have become convinced about the effectiveness of physical security, access control and firewalls as security techniques, only between 46 per cent and 58 per cent used any kind of cryptographic protection or a PKI infrastructure in 2004.

The survey also reveals an alarming increase in financial losses owing to computer crime; in 2002 the losses were of the order of $5.8 million with an increase to $11.8 million in 2003 and $16 million in 2004 (see table 4.1, pp. 107–9).

Symmetric cryptography

As has been described, **symmetric encryption** is a simple form of encryption whose major advantage is its speed. To a certain extent, symmetric encryption can be used to ensure authentication and thus to reduce the risk of sharing secret data with a non-trusted other. If there is only one secret key and if this key has been shared with only one trusted other, then it can be assumed that any response in an encrypted transaction has actually originated with the individual with whom the key has been shared.

The basic issues of risk with symmetric encryption, if we wish to compare its security to that afforded by PK encryption, are: the longer the key and the more difficult the mathematical function is to crack, the higher the level of protection. The longer the key and the more difficult the mathematical function is to crack, the higher the decryption effort becomes, so this can lead to huge performance problems! The secure transmission of keys requires a secure communication channel, and hence key management (particularly key distribution) is an important issue.

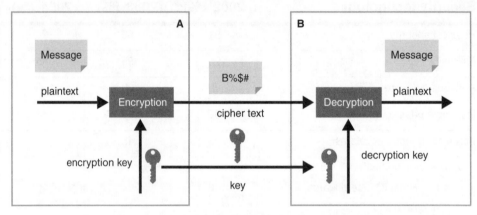

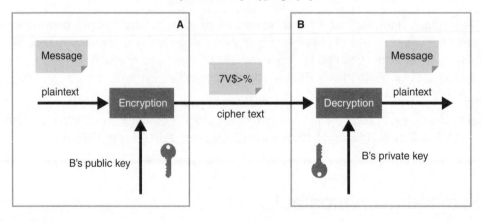

Figure 5.5 Encryption

Symmetric encryption and key management

The best method of key management and distribution is via a trusted third party who holds copies of all keys, in the way that a bank is entrusted with money and accounts.

If two individuals wish to communicate in this way they have no common keys, but the trusted third party has a copy of each key. When the sender needs to communicate with the receiver, they send an open request to the trusted third party along with an official identifier.

The trusted third party sends a response encrypted with the sender's key that contains a temporary key for communication between the sender and receiver, the official identifier sent by the sender and the temporary key encrypted using the receiver's key.

The sender decodes the message from the trusted third party and passes the information, encoded with the receiver's key, to the receiver. A major disadvantage is that the trusted third party must be available 24/7 if this kind of cryptographic methodology is to have (or was to have had) widespread adoption. This kind of problem possibly hastened the development of widescale PKI.

Common symmetric algorithms

Many symmetric cryptographic algorithms have been developed over the past 40 years, but none is quite so well known, or has been so well written about, as the Data Encryption Standard (DES). As DES has become older and its relatively short key length has made it more vulnerable, attempts have been made to replace it with Double DES and Triple DES. DES has been replaced with the Advanced Encryption Standard (AES), but applications of DES are still found in common use.

Data Encryption Standard

Burr (2003, p. 43) writes:

> DES has proven itself over the years. It has become the standard to which all block ciphers are compared. However, by the mid 1990s, it was clear that the DES's 56-bit key was no longer big enough to prevent attacks mounted on contemporary computers, which were thousands of times more powerful than those available when the DES was standardized. During the original DES selection, there was discussion of using DES more than once with different keys to extend its effective key size and a standard for Triple DES (TDES) that encrypts each block three times with DES, using two or three different keys, was introduced with FIPS 46-3 in 1999.

DES has definitely become an international standard and was developed as the result of international desire to set standards for both hardware and software encryption devices; a major need at the time was a need to be able to work across different manufacturers' platforms and products. This was achieved by the design

Chapter 5 Basic cryptography and Public Key Infrastructure

141

of a secret key cryptographic algorithm based on the principles of substitution and transposition illustrated in figures 5.2 and 5.3.

When DES is employed for enciphering data exchanges, both sender and receiver must know the secret key, which can be used to encrypt and decrypt the message, or to generate and verify a message authentication code (MAC). DES can also be used for single-user encryption, for example in the case of single-user or personal encrypted data storage. In a multi-user environment, secure key distribution becomes problematic.

The algorithm works by iterating 16 cycles of transposition and substitution. We illustrate just one cycle of substitution and transposition on our plaintext in figure 5.4. We can see in our example that in this first cycle the message has become both confused and diffused, and it is not possible to recognise the plaintext from the cipher text or to work out how to decipher this text (without some specialised software). After 16 cycles, diffusion and confusion would be very thoroughly accomplished. The algorithm works with 64-bit blocks of texts and a 64-bit key, which is reduced mathematically to a length of 56 bits (for reasons that we don't need to understand here).

As Burr (2003) states above, there was always some intention to extend the key length of the DES algorithm, but this never occurred and so it was implemented with a 56-bit key. As we have already stated, the strength of a symmetric algorithm is largely dependent on its key length, so the downfall of DES has come about with increased computing power, which can use a brute force attack to break DES. Many researchers have felt perturbed by this, so double DES and triple DES were implemented to deal with the problem of the short DES key length.

Double DES is an attempt to implement the DES algorithm twice, one application after the other, with the use of two separate keys. However, Merkle and Hellman (1981) showed that in fact this provided only twice the amount of protection afforded by DES.

Triple DES

Triple DES can also be implemented in different modes. In this case there are three modes, and each provides a 112-bit effective key length with 48 rounds of substitution and transposition iterated within the algorithm. It has proved to be a very strong algorithm. The modes differ in as much as either of three different keys can be used for encryption; the second mode allows for encryption, decryption and re-encryption should an application developer consider this necessary; and the third mode uses the same key for the first and third parts of the encryption process.

Advanced Encryption Standard (AES)

As Burr (2003, p. 45) states: 'A strong symmetric key encryption algorithm such as the AES has one basic security goal — that the best attack against it should be key exhaustion (trying every possible key until you find one that works).'

The AES is built on the Rijndael algorithm. It has variable key lengths of 128, 192 and 256 bits and is a 128-bit block cipher. As with DES, it is based on substitution and row transposition, which produce confusion, then column transposition, which causes diffusion. A small part of the key is also incorporated at the transposition phase of the iteration.

The AES is predicted to have a long life since it is mathematically very sound, and it does not have a limited key length (it can be extended beyond 256 bits) or a limited number of iterative cycles (in this algorithm they are known as rounds). It is therefore predicted that risk to those who might use the standard in costly implementations is thus reduced.

Asymmetric cryptography

In asymmetric cryptography, both sender and receiver control a public key and a private key. The public key can be made widely known and distributed to everyone with whom electronic transactions might be made, whereas the private key must be kept secret and does not have to be distributed. **Asymmetric encryption** is always performed with each user's public key whereas decryption is always carried out with the private key. It is impossible to decipher an asymmetric encryption algorithm with the private key if it has been encrypted with the private key, and the same also applies for the public key. The two keys are mathematically related, but, although each can be used both to encode and decode plaintext, they are not able to be deduced or inferred from each other.

Asymmetric encryption, key management and trust

The major benefit within public-key cryptography is that security and convenience is provided since private keys never need to be transmitted or shared with anyone. Therefore the risks that arise within key management of secret key cryptography can be totally avoided.

The existence of public and private keys within PK cryptography means that PK cryptography can be used to ensure non-repudiation and authentication of users. Authentication via secret-key systems requires the sharing of some secret and sometimes the use of a trusted third party, as detailed above. If the secret is not kept or if this trust is breached, the sender can repudiate a previously authenticated message by claiming that the shared secret was somehow compromised by one of the parties who were party to the secret. Public-key authentication averts this type of repudiation; each user alone is solely accountable for protecting their private key.

The major drawback to public key cryptography is its lack of processing speed. There are many secret-key encryption methods that are significantly faster (between 100 and 1000 times) than any currently available public-key encryption method.

In some situations, public-key cryptography is not necessary, and secret-key cryptography alone is sufficient. These include environments where secure secret key distribution can take place, or where a single authority manages all the keys, or in a single-user environment where only personal files and records need encryption.

Common asymmetric algorithms

Generally a public key algorithm has to fulfil the following conditions:
- the generation of a key pair (public key; private key) has to be easy
- encryption and decryption have to be straightforward operations, and
- it should be hard to compute the public key from the corresponding secret key.

Rivest-Shamir-Adleman (RSA) encryption

RSA is a public key asymmetric algorithm. It is based mathematically on the fact that it is hard to determine the factors of large prime numbers. The following steps are taken:

1. Take two large primes, p and q, and find their product $n = pq$; n is called the modulus.
2. Choose a number, e, less than n and relatively prime to $(p-1)(q-1)$, which means that e and $(p-1)(q-1)$ have no common factors except 1.
3. Find another number d such that $(ed-1)$ is divisible by $(p-1)(q-1)$. The values e and d are called the public and private exponents, respectively.
4. The public key is the pair (n, e); the private key is (n, d).

It is difficult to obtain the private key d from the public key e. If one could factor n into p and q, however, then one could obtain the private key d. Thus the security of RSA is related to the assumption that factoring is difficult. An easy factoring method or some other feasible attack would 'break' RSA.

If a sender wants to transmit a message m to a receiver, the sender generates the cipher text c by exponentiating: $c = me$ mod n, where e and n are the receiver's public key. The sender transmits c to the receiver. To decipher, the receiver also exponentiates: $m = cd$ mod n; the relationship between e and d ensures that the receiver correctly recovers m. Since only the receiver knows d, only the receiver can decipher the cipher text c.

Elliptical curve cryptography

Elliptical curve cryptography (ECC) is a public key encryption technique based on elliptic curve theory that can be used to create faster, smaller and more efficient cryptographic keys. ECC generates keys through the properties of the elliptic curve equation instead of the traditional method of generation as the product of very large prime numbers. The technology can be used in conjunction with most public key encryption methods, such as RSA and Diffie-Hellman.

According to some researchers, ECC can yield a level of security with a 164-bit key that other systems require a 1024-bit key to achieve. Because ECC helps to establish equivalent security with lower computing power and battery resource usage, it is becoming widely used for mobile applications.

Their use within cryptography was first proposed in 1985 (separately) by Neal Koblitz from the University of Washington and Victor Miller at IBM.

An elliptic curve is not an *ellipse* (oval shape), but is represented as a looping line intersecting two axes (lines on a graph used to indicate the position of a point).

ECC is based on properties of a particular type of equation created from the mathematical group (a set of values for which operations can be performed on any two members of the group to produce a third member) derived from points where the line intersects the axes. Multiplying a point on the curve by a number will produce another point on the curve, but it is very difficult to find what number was used, even if you know the original point and the result. Equations based on elliptic curves have a characteristic that is very valuable for cryptography purposes: they are relatively easy to perform and extremely difficult to reverse. This can lead to smaller key sizes and better performance in certain public-key operations for the same level of security. Since there is currently a large amount of research in this particular mathematical problem, it is likely that advances in this area will be very rapid.

Hashing

Hashing is used, with or without cryptography, to supply assurance that a message has not been altered or modified in transmission, and this can determine for us whether the number of bits of text received are the same in length and nature as those transmitted. Hashing is an important method of ensuring that the risk to **message integrity** is reduced.

This means we first write a message that we wish to send secretly. In a business context this might be our personnel records or our credit card details. We count the number of text characters in the message and send this value (i.e. the number of characters) along with the message. Then the receiver of the message can check and make sure the whole message has arrived.

Hash algorithms

A **hash algorithm** is a mathematical expression containing one or more hash functions. Typically a **hash function** is a mathematical function that is easy to calculate but difficult to reverse engineer so as to obtain the inverse. An example of this kind of function is the cube of a number. Although it is possible to simply calculate the cube of x, it is not so simple to calculate the cube root of a large number $x3$. A hash function might simply direct that we cue the number of characters in the text of our message or that the sum (X-OR) of all the bits in a message should be calculated; this number, the result of applying a hash function, is the **hash value**.

Message authentication code or digest

If hashing is combined with cryptography, a cryptographic algorithm can be applied to a document's hash value, such as that produced above, to produce a guarantee of message integrity.

If the sender attaches a message digest to the message, the receiver first has to cryptographically decipher the message digest sent by the sender, then put the message through the same function used by the sender and compare the two values. If they are the same, the message has not been modified. It is not necessary, in all circumstances, to divulge the contents of a document to prove its integrity.

Digital signatures

Digital signatures are produced in a similar fashion to that described above. **Digital signature** standards combine hash functions with PK cryptography to verify identity.

The purpose of a digital signature is to provide authentication so that the sender of a message can be sure that it has been sent to the correct person.

How does digital signing work?

Suppose the CEO of a small company wants to send a signed message to a potential business partner assuring him of cooperation in some mutual business transaction. The CEO generates a message digest by using a hash function on the message. The message digest acts as a guarantee of authenticity of the message; if any part of the message were to be changed in transmission, the hash function would produce a different value. The CEO then encrypts the message digest with his private encryption key. This encrypted message digest becomes the digital signature for the message.

The CEO transmits both the message and the digital signature to his business partner. On the arrival of the message, the partner deciphers the signature using the CEO's public key (which she already possessed), thus displaying the message digest. To ensure the authenticity of the message, she then hashes the message with the same hash function that the CEO used and compares her result with the one that accompanied the message she received from the CEO (remember she is just comparing two numerical values here).

If they prove to be identical, the business partner can be assured that the message did originate with the CEO and has not been modified since he first signed it. If the message digests do not prove to be the same, the message might have either originated elsewhere or been tampered with after it was signed.

IT risk 5.2

Checking Windows system files for digital signing

Even if you have never created a digital signature of your own, you can see how Microsoft uses this technology to guarantee the integrity of the system files on your own Windows PC. If you just choose Help from the Windows Start menu and search on the term 'digital signature' you will find the article shown in figure 5.6, which helps you to test your own system files for digital signatures. If you run this program you would expect to find that your system files are signed, which proves that they originated with Microsoft. This application also allows you to check your PC to identify whether other files are signed, too.

If your system files are not signed, we might well assume that they did not originate with Microsoft or that they have been tampered with in some way!

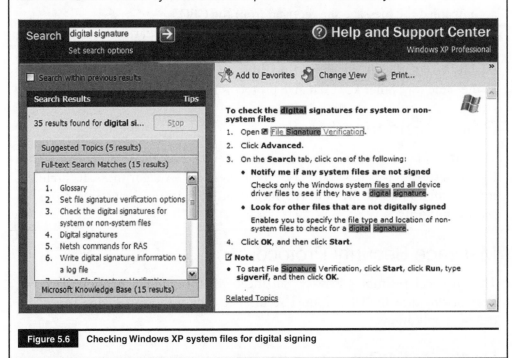

Figure 5.6   Checking Windows XP system files for digital signing

Key exchange protocols

One other issue we need to consider is that of establishing methods: protocols by which cryptographic keys can be exchanged. Before we can, for example, decide that a topic is so confidential that we must encrypt all email dialogue on this issue, we need to have a pre-established method for exchanging cryptographic keys so that we can decipher each other's email messages.

We have seen in the previous section that we can calculate a message digest and digitally sign a message. For further protection we can then use a combination of symmetric and asymmetric encryption.

Suppose our CEO of a small company wants to send an encrypted email message to a potential business partner discussing secret financial details of a mutual business transaction. The CEO generates a message digest by using a hash function on the message. The CEO encrypts the message digest with a temporary session key (a secret symmetric key). He encrypts the message digest with his private encryption key (his digital signature for the message). He then encrypts the temporary secret key with his partner's public key.

The CEO transmits both the message and the digital signature to his business partner. On the arrival of the message, the partner deciphers the temporary session key with her private key and decrypts the message digest with the CEO's public key. She then deciphers the message with the temporary secret session key. To ensure the authenticity of the message, she hashes the message with the same hash function that the CEO used and compares her result with the one that accompanied the message she received from the CEO.

This protocol — a pre-established method between two parties for determining how encryption and decryption can be carried out — builds on the precepts established for digital signatures and adds an extra cryptographic component. In the same way, other key exchange protocols have also been established.

Privacy Enhanced Mail

This protocol was established to allow secure email over the Internet and within large enterprises. It is based on both the DES and RSA algorithms. Its architecture resembles that of PKI and is a hierarchical trust model clustered around a central authority.

Message Security Protocol

This protocol resembles Privacy Enhanced Mail, but its algorithms have not been disclosed by the US National Security Agency since it is used in secret and defence applications.

Pretty Good Privacy

This protocol was implemented within freeware and allows users to develop 'key rings'. Each user develops trust with others and collects their public keys. Its model is not hierarchical but resembles a web. The model presumes that if you trust me and I trust you, then you will trust my friends (or business partners) and I can trust yours. We can also establish degrees of trust with different groups of users.

Cryptographic authentication techniques

Cryptographic techniques can be used for user authentication. Two common approaches are challenge and response protocols and digital signatures.

We have seen that identification and authentication are separate issues. Anyone can claim to be an authorised user. Identification is the process whereby a user *asserts* their identity. When a user authenticates onto a system they are being asked to *prove* their identity. This proof may be provided by: asking a user to provide ID (identification), then supply a password (user authentication); use of magnetic cards; and recall of shared secret and PIN number.

A cryptographic form of authentication can be used in a challenge response mechanism; we would expect to see this in use in a highly secure environment. The user is presented with a login dialogue or screen that has a series of numbers displayed. The user encrypts these numbers in some type of cryptographic device and types them in as a response to the logon string. The login mechanism has the same key (be it public or secret key cryptography). A user who does not know the key cannot respond to the challenge and is locked out of the system.

Cryptographic applications and a Public Key Infrastructure

At this stage we have examined some of the components that might be assembled to produce a complete cryptographic framework to protect an enterprise's data and electronic transactions. These components include software, hardware, algorithms, standards and protocols. This complete framework is known as a **Public Key Infrastructure (PKI)**. The reason we have spent time understanding the basics is so that we can understand how and why we might use them in an integrated fashion to provide authentication, confidentiality, integrity and non-repudiation throughout wide and local area networks and on the Internet.

Certificates

In a PKI, the major item required by an individual is a **certificate**. The reason this certificate is important is that it contains the public key linked to the personal ID of the certificate holder, and it could include other details, such as a validity period. These details must then be endorsed by the certification authority by appending a digital signature. The signed combination of personal data and public key becomes the certificate.

It is not essential that there should be a one-to-one relationship between individuals and public keys. A certificate exists to link a discrete public key and a specific identity. These keys and identities do not need be unique to that certificate. A single person or company could possess many keys and use them for different reasons and at varying times. It would be possible to assign one public key to several individuals, but this would seem to defeat the purpose of PK cryptography.

Certificate authorities

Certificates have to be controlled by a trusted third party who issues and manages them. This is known as a **certificate authority** (CA). An organisation has the choice of implementing a complete PKI internally or using the services of an external provider, such as VeriSign. Certificates do not have to be kept secure or confidential since the CA is a trusted third party and can be proved genuine and reliable via its own public key.

Many issues are not guaranteed or assured by the use of a certificate or a certificate authority. A certificate can really only assure a party to a confidential transaction of the link between the ID of the certificate's holder and the ID of the public key's holder. It does not offer any guarantee that the individual maintains high professional standards, is financially secure or even that they are honest. The only assurance available appears to be that of a guarantee of the ID of the individual holding the public key. There is no assurance that the public key has not been transferred to another who is using it on behalf of the true owner. There is also no protection is the case of breach of confidentiality once the secret message has been transmitted or in a dispute over ownership of IP of the data, messages or files transmitted. There can be no guarantee that either party will honour any commitments made in the encrypted transaction.

Registration authorities

A registration authority (RA) is a subsection of a certification authority. The purpose of the RA is to check the ID of a certificate holder and manage the data in this part of the transaction. It also provides secure communication pathways between the individual, itself and the CA. It cannot, however, issue the certificate.

The RA might be an integral part of the same organisation as the CA or it might be a totally separate business entity.

How the Australian Government uses PKI to manage IT security risk

In late 1997 the [Australian] Government decided to take the lead in the development of a national framework for the authentication of users of electronic online services. The Office of Government Information Technology (OGIT) was charged with ensuring that there is an agreed strategy in place so that the Commonwealth Government can make optimal use of Public Key Technologies (PKT) for electronic transactions. (AGIMO 1998, p. 4)

The Gatekeeper strategy report explains: 'Key requirements included, interoperability, addressing the privacy issues, confidentiality, non-repudiation, integrity, ease of use, marketability and archiving.' The report also explains:

Specific standards have been identified for:

• asymmetric key exchange;

• symmetric keys;

• key generation;

• proof of identity (POI);

• key storage; and

• protective security. (AGIMO 1998, pp. 4–5)

The purpose of this has been:

1. To establish a rational voluntary mechanism for the implementation of PKT by government agencies;

2. To facilitate interoperability and allow users to choose from a panel of service providers whose products and methods of delivery have been evaluated and accredited to meet prescribed government standards for integrity and trust;

3. To provide an operational mechanism to manage the Commonwealth's activities and interests in the area of PKT. (AGIMO 1998, p. 5)

Current activity of Gatekeeper includes the accreditation of organisations and the recognition of PKI domains. It also deals with cross-recognition of PKI schemes, compliance audit and legal and physical security evaluation of organisations seeking Gatekeeper accreditation (AGIMO 1998).

Source: http://www.agimo.gov.au/infrastructure/gatekeeper and AGIMO 1998.

Who sets the standards for PKI?

Several internationally recognised standards bodies have expressed interest in promoting the use of PKI. Among these are the International Organization for Standardization (ISO), the European Committee for Standardisation (CEN) and the American National Standards Institute (ANSI). Some other groups have an interest in promoting the use of particular PKI technology (Palmer & Buck 2003)

We saw in IT Risk 5.1 (p.139) that cryptographic protection mechanisms have not had as wide adoption as, for example, firewalls and antivirus software. Perhaps a solution to this issue is given by Palmer and Buck (2003), who see a conflict between the various parties involved in setting the standards for PKI. Some come with a technical agenda and some with particular business or commercial software and hardware agendas. These all provide a confusing context for the small business that wishes to reduce IT security risk.

Palmer and Buck (2003) comment that the PKI tools available today are suitable for implementation only by technical experts with the expertise to understand certificates and other technology underlying PKI. In reality, users want to know that the messages they send and receive can be trusted. This has been a stumbling block for PKI. Its application is not transparent for the user. The problem is compounded by the different perspectives and arguments presented by groups promoting their own agendas (e.g. their own proprietary PKI solutions) and by groups or people without the necessary expertise.

Source: information from Palmer & Buck 2003, pp. 6–13.

The PKI process

Our CEO has finally understood the power of cryptography and now feels happy that he can hide all his confidential transactions. He now wants to implement PKI for himself.

He first needs to obtain a private and public key pair; he will keep one totally secret, and he will share the other with everyone whom he wants to send encrypted data. Either he can generate the key pair himself and give the public key to the CA as he registers with them, or the CA will have to have some mechanism of secretly transferring the private key to the CEO.

Our CEO applies to the RA for a certificate. He needs to supply a certain amount of documentation, to triangulate and prove his ID from public documents, such as his driving licence and birth certificate. When the RA is able to verify the CEO's identity it sends a request to the CA for a certificate for the CEO. This certificate is issued and bound to the CEO's public key and ID.

The certificate lists such details as:
- version
- certificate serial number (unique identifier)
- signature and algorithm ID used to produce it
- name of CA
- validity period
- username
- public key
- CA's ID
- user ID.

If our CEO now wants to communicate with his business partner, he requests the partner's certificate and public key from a public certificate directory. When he gets the certificate he uses the CA's public key to decipher the message digest of the certificate; now he can assure himself it is genuine and it is validated. He can create a temporary session key and encrypt it with his partner's public key and send it to the partner with his own certificate and public key.

His partner can use software to check whether it trusts the CA, the trusted third party we have mentioned before; this software will also check whether the CEO's certificate is still current or whether he has carried out some suspicious transactions and whether it might have been revoked. If the CA is trusted, then the pair can trust each other within this business interaction (and to the extent described previously — PKI does not carry any kind of attached moral or ethical judgements).

Summary

Many modern cryptographic techniques used to protect the confidentiality and integrity of data are founded historically in the writing of secret codes. Cryptography allows text to be disguised, transmitted so that no-one else can read it, then read only by the owner of a secret key. There are two major types of cryptography: symmetric and asymmetric cryptography, and two specific types of ciphers: block and stream ciphers. These are used within fairly complex mathematical algorithms to provide some of the building blocks of cryptography. Hashing and other mathematical techniques provide a method by which digital signatures can be produced, guaranteeing the integrity of transmitted data. If an opponent wants to attack our cryptography then they will, given enough time and processing power, probably be able to break our code; some algorithms are stronger than others, but we have to pay for strong algorithms in increased routine data-processing times.

Cryptography has well-established international standards and protocols; these define the way specific electronic transactions will be carried out. These, when integrated with the software, hardware and algorithms, provide the foundation of cryptographic applications that will help achieve our security goals of *confidentiality, availability, integrity* and *non-repudiation*. A Public Key Infrastructure is an authentication framework; it is not a product or a protocol but specifies how products and protocols should be used with government and commercial electronic transactions.

Key terms

algorithm, p. 131
asymmetric encryption, p. 143
block ciphers, p. 133
brute force attack, p. 133
certificate, p. 149
certificate authority, p. 150
cipher text, p. 131
cipher text-only attack, p. 132
code, p. 131
cryptanalysis, p. 131
cryptography, p. 130
cryptology, p. 130
cryptosystem, p. 131
decipher, p. 131
decode, p. 131
decrypt, p. 131
digital signature, p. 146
elliptical curve cryptography, p. 144
encipher, p. 131
encode, p. 131
encoded text, p. 131
encrypt, p. 131

hash algorithm, p. 145
hash function, p. 145
hash value, p. 145
hashing, p. 145
key, p. 131
key clustering, p. 132
key space, p. 132
message integrity, p. 145
one-time pads, p. 133
padding, p. 134
plaintext, p. 131
plaintext attack, p. 132
polyalphabetic ciphers, p. 134
product ciphers, p. 135
Public Key Infrastructure (PKI), p. 149
running key ciphers, p. 133
secret key, p. 131
steganography, p. 133
stream cipher, p. 133
substitution cipher, p. 133
symmetric encryption, p. 139
transposition cipher, p. 133

Questions

1. Describe what a good cryptographic system for a start-up small to medium-sized enterprise (SME) would need to achieve in terms of confidentiality, availability and integrity. How would you express this risk within your company security policy?
2. Explain how you would begin to define acceptable risk in the context of an SME and its cryptographic system.
3. Cryptographic protocols have an increasing tendency to come under attack. Research this issue, report on the accuracy of this statement and investigate how protocols have been extended and strengthened to deal with the risk of attack.
4. The sharing of secret keys has been aided by the development of threshold cryptography. Investigate current trends in threshold cryptography to determine its role in the reduction of risk or enhancement of trust in the encryption process.

5. The Australian Government has had long-term interest in the development of a national authentication framework achieved through PKI. Examine the recent history of the development of this kind of PKI framework in Australia, identifying its strengths and weaknesses and any developmental trends.
6. Imagine you are developing a new hardware encryption device that will be inserted into every new desktop or laptop computer on the market. What kind of cryptosystem will you implement and why? What features will your new device contain to reduce the IT security risks faced by home or small business PC users?
7. Research quantum cryptography and see whether it is going to provide any short-term solution to the provision of asymmetric algorithms.

Case study ~~~~~~
5: Cryptography

We met Elisabeth Chan in chapter 4 when she was considering how to protect her company when its website was defaced. Here is part of her story again.

Elisabeth realises her organisational skills have been poor and that, as CEO, she has an obligation to ensure that security measures are adequately implemented, enforced and fully operational. Since the company has recently experienced these network attacks, Elisabeth questions whether the attacks resulted from the company's development of novel and defence-related products.

She knows as CEO that preventive measures are required to restrict or eliminate potential threats and possibly expose the parties responsible and that an additional level of security and high level of integrity are required with military standards. Not only are the company's security interests at hand but also, more importantly, lack of care in this regard can influence the nation's defence considerations. This is even more heightened in today's international defence climate.

Elisabeth realises that an emerging international awareness of the interrelationships between defence electronic applications and company IT security measures makes it imperative that all employees within the hierarchy chart, from the CEO down (see figure 5.7 on p. 156), have a fundamental understanding of security measures. As she knows, all defence-standard IT security operating procedures and policies are undergoing major reform. Governments, large companies, small businesses and the general public now recognise that the economic wellbeing of our country largely depends on a greater IT security awareness.

With the impending assessment from an external auditor determining her viability as a defence contractor, Elisabeth is concerned that her company's security measures are not adequate. Small amounts of proprietary and outdated antivirus software are the only existing measures she has in place.

Elisabeth's IT security risk management concerns are wide-ranging. She needs to determine whether the same hackers are likely to hack the company again.

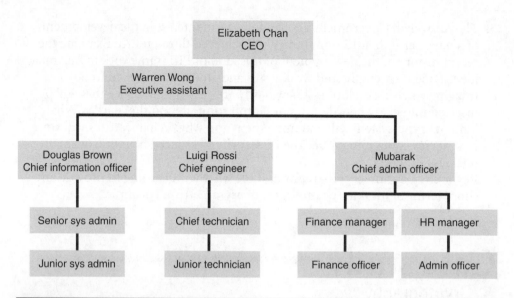

| **Figure 5.7** | **Elisabeth's company organisation chart** |

She believes the recent attacks suggest that the hackers were interested in either proprietary theft of sensitive information for personal and/or financial gain or to disrupt the company in such a way as to give competitors an edge. There is no evidence of any previous disgruntled employees; therefore revenge is discounted. Common industry knowledge of a range of micro midget widgets as a new defence product reinforces this conclusion.

Currently she is concerned with her cryptographic requirements and the cryptographic methods that she might use to defend herself against hackers and to ensure the confidentiality and integrity of all data transmitted. She knows that Defence Security Policy (Department of Defence n.d.) minimum standards require:

- *Authentication:* verification of the identity of users with some credentials, such as passwords, smart cards and signatures, to access all resources, such as secure hard drives, printers, registry keys and so on.
- *Confidentiality:* all information that unauthorised parties might view must be hidden by using encryption techniques.
- *Integrity:* all information must be protected from intentional or accidental modifications or deletions.
- *Availability:* authorised employees must not be denied access to resources at any time.

Elisabeth believes she requires cryptography because of the recent occurrences of data corruption. She has heard that cryptography ensures confidentiality, verifies authenticity and ensures integrity; that is, that data is not modified or corrupted. She needs some advice on this issue.

Elisabeth is also trying to create a vision for her company and is wondering how she can begin to use e-commerce and other kinds of electronic transaction

Information Technology Security & Risk Management

to improve her business processes. She wonders whether she can begin to deal with these more visionary aspects of business development as she also deals with the risk of further breaches to her systems. She has many different kinds of transaction, which she carries out on a regular basis with the Australian Government. She works with a range of departments including the Department of Defence, the Australian Taxation Office and the Australian Customs Service.

Questions

1. Should Elisabeth now implement some cryptographic protection to secure her company? Which part of her business transactions should be encrypted?
2. Does she need:
   (a) a digital signature?
   (b) a digital certificate?
3. Refer to her company's organisational chart (figure 5.7). How many other departments will need to be involved in the process of embedding encryption into their business processes? Which specific daily or weekly transactions would need to be encrypted? (Remember that cryptography costs money, which Elisabeth cannot really afford to waste while she is still in start-up mode.)

Suggested reading

Kahn, D 1996, *The Codebreakers,* Scribners, New York.

Mel, HX & Baker, D 2001, *Cryptography Decrypted*, Addison-Wesley Professional, Boston.

Stallings, W 1998, *Cryptography and Network Security*, Prentice Hall, Upper Saddle River, NJ.

References

Australian Computer Emergency Response Team (AusCERT) 2004, *2004 Computer Crime & Security Survey*, accessed 21 April 2005, www.aucert.org.

Australian Government Information Management Office (AGIMO) 1998, 'Gatekeeper Strategy', www.agimo.gov.au/_data/assets/file/18894/Gatekeeper_Strategy.pdf.

Burr, WE 2003, 'Setting the Advanced Encryption Standard', *IEEE Security & Privacy*, March–April, pp. 43–52.

Department of Defence, *Information System Security SECMAN 3*, 5th edn, Department of Defence, Canberra.

Merkle, R & Hellman, M 1981, 'On the security of multiple encryption', *Comm. of the ACM*, July, vol. 24, no. 7, pp. 465–7.

Palmer, T & Buck, SP 2003, 'PKI needs good standards?', *Information Security Technical Report*, 9 July, vol. 8, no. 3, pp. 6–13.

Chapter 6

Securing the network

Learning objectives

After studying this chapter, you should be able to:

- describe the basic features of a network and the risks they face
- explain the operation of firewalls
- outline the use of intrusion detection systems to defend networks
- describe the operation of virtual private networks
- discuss the approaches to inter-network security
- discuss the security issues relating to system software
- explain the use of antivirus software.

Chapter overview

In this chapter we examine the foundations of network security and look at system security issues, such as securing information flow by appropriate hardware, and software controls. These include routers, firewalls, intrusion detection systems, network separation, operating systems and antivirus software.

We study a range of network security controls, including firewalls, intrusion detection systems and virtual private networks, and compare and contrast types and configuration methods.

We also make the link between the desire for network security in an organisation and the need to write, implement and monitor sound network security policies, and we give an example of a possible network security policy for a medium-sized company.

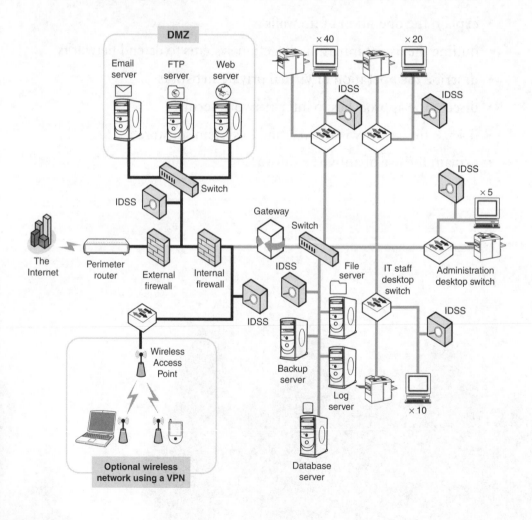

Figure 6.1   **Company network topology**

Introduction to network security

In any business computing environment, security is a key issue that needs to be taken into consideration as early as the design of the network. In this section, we will describe security methodologies currently available, both as hardware and as software.

Computer hardware is the physical components of computing, which are designed to process streams of 'bits' (1's and 0's). Hence, hardware security devices are generally considered to be more resistant to electronic attack, as they are designed in such a way that incoming and outgoing 1's and 0's physically cannot modify their operation. When designing a network, hardware security obviously has to be considered, as insecure hardware, or hardware designed for a different purpose, can ultimately lead to a compromised network.

Let us assume that figure 6.1 shows the design of a network for a new enterprise. This network was designed with a **defence in depth** strategy, which allows for overlapping layers of control. The importance of such a design is that if one security vulnerability has been exploited, features and controls within the other layers will compensate for it and thus help to keep the company's internal network secure (ISSA 2004).

Since networks are created from a range of different and interchangeable devices and pieces of hardware, including workstations, servers, hubs, bridges, routers and wireless access points, they will provide a range of security challenges, depending on the system architecture. Each device and every component of infrastructure, down to the smallest piece of cable, will need to be managed from a security perspective. Due consideration will need to be given to transmission media, communication devices, storage media and all kinds of documentation.

The first security mechanism, or control, is an **external firewall** that determines which internal services can be accessed from the outside and vice versa. This is used to protect the system from hackers and malicious code (3Com 2000).

The next layer of security is an **intrusion detection system (IDS)**. If a hacker manages to get past the firewall, the IDS will act as a 'burglar alarm' and alert the network administrator to the fact that someone has breached the system (Rozenblum 2001). As a result, an IDS is set off just like an alarm in a house, but the alarm will be triggered only if the **signature database**, which is a collection of patterns and definitions of known suspicious or malicious activity, is reported (Conklin et al. 2004, p. 312). Unfortunately, in high bandwidth network environments there are physical limits to an IDS system's capacity and, as a result, throughout the network diagram added **intrusion detection system sensors (IDSS)** have been added (Oxenhandler 2003). These act to monitor only the most sensitive areas of the network.

Another layer of security is a **demilitarised zone** (DMZ), which is an intermediate network placed between the protected **internal network** and any untrusted part of the network, such as the Internet. The importance of the DMZ is that external sources can access permitted information, such as company web pages, while not having access to its internal network. As a result, this further protects the company's internal network (ISSA 2004).

The next security layer is an **internal firewall**, which is used to protect the internal network from the DMZ. If a hacker has been able to breach the external firewall and detection by the IDS, the internal firewall will further help to keep the internal network secure (Ford 2003). Also placed within this network design is a wireless network, which will have access to various parts of the internal network via a virtual private network (VPN).

Finally, the last security layer is the **segmentation** of all departmental networks. This is a big concern as a Gartner Group report estimates that 70 per cent of security incidents were committed by insiders (Koenig 2002), although this statistic is often challenged. Therefore, it is very important to segment the network as there is no rationale for allowing various internal departments to have free access to other departmental information assets. As a result, by properly segmenting the network, the potential for insider abuse will be reduced, and this will limit the potential damage caused by an intruder who does gain illegal entry to the network (Ford 2003).

Network segmentation depends on a company's structure and operating context, but a common deployment of network segments might be:
- *user:* contains user workstations
- *servers:* maintains the corporate production servers for a specific locale (email, file and application servers)
- *vendor:* provides access for visiting vendors and is restricted to the Internet only
- *remote access:* provides an entrance point for employees to gain access remotely and would contain VPN and remote access server (RAS)
- *storage:* network attached storage maintained on isolated networks.

Although we can see segmentation as a last formal way of securing a network, we do need to add that even computer housings provide protection and physical support to hardware, such as desktop computers. In some environments, however, more secure housings are required, especially for servers. In a medium-sized to large business, servers are generally kept in lockable cabinets and in some cases bolted or locked to a wall. This is, of course, in addition to the server residing in a locked room.

Cases are also available for standard PCs that incorporate physical security, particularly the ability to lock the case, preventing unauthorised access to the hardware inside. Some cases also have lockable doors at the front, preventing access to disk drives and even the power and reset switches. (The concept of 'diskless workstations' also prevents use of removable media.) In an environment in which computer theft poses a moderate to high risk, such as a school or university, chassis intrusion modules and security systems can be installed in the case to prevent unauthorised access to the case, as well as theft of the system itself.

Network fundamentals

There are two basic types of **network architecture**: **local area networks** (LANs) and **wide area networks** (WANs). By definition these vary from each other just in size and scope. Obviously a larger network will present more IT security threats, risks and challenges.

In the case of computer networks, there are three main topologies: token ring (every computer connects to a physical network cable ring with two connections), linear bus (every computer connects to some point in a backbone, which is terminated at each end) and star (every computer connects to a central point, e.g. hub or switch). Token ring and linear bus networks are rarely used in business today because there are too many possibilities for failure, as well as being inconvenient in many situations. The star network is most common; however, the security issue is whether the network is broadcasted or switched. (See figure 6.2.)

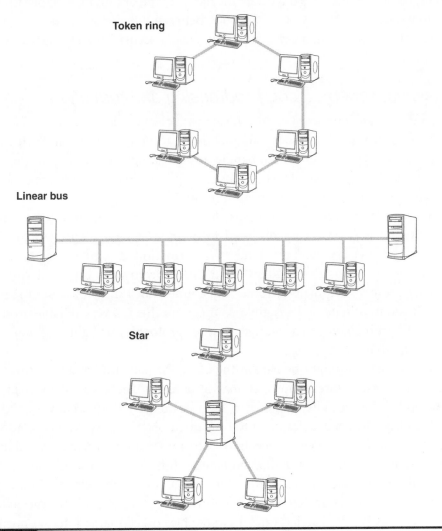

| Figure 6.2 | Three main network topologies: token ring, linear bus and star |

Use of a hub creates a broadcast network, in which packets sent from one computer to another are 'broadcast' across each port until the receiving computer accepts them. A computer with a packet sniffing program connected to the hub can then 'listen in' to network traffic and grab information, which might contain usernames and passwords. Use of a switch creates a switched network, which, apart from providing a much faster connection to all connected computers, renders packet sniffers useless. This is because in a switched network, a direct connection is created between the sending and receiving computers. In figure 6.1 we can see how each of these network topologies is incorporated into a company LAN.

Devices on a network can be connected by cable, optical fibre, microwave or satellite. Each of these will bring with it its own security risk, which will need to be dealt with at the network design stage. Fibre optic cabling is the safest cabling to use because it is physically the hardest type of cabling to 'tap'. This type of cabling is typically used as a backbone between hubs or switches, or as a link between two separate networks, providing greater security than standard twisted pair cable.

Basic network protocols, addressing and routing

When devices on a network communicate with each other to exchange data they have to use **protocols**. These are an established technical format (involving such factors as file type, compression, bandwidth and range, depending on the technical context) for exchanging or transmitting data between systems, enabling computers and other devices to communicate.

When data is broadcast over a network, it is usually broken up into smaller pieces called **packets**. Protocols need to define the kind of packets that will be sent and received and the kind of information contained in an area of the packet known as the **header**. The **TCP/IP** protocol is the most common Internet protocol requiring a three-way connection (known as the three-way handshake) to initiate and sustain a connection; this is a very reliable protocol. The **UDP** protocol is an alternative Internet protocol; it is lightweight and less reliable than TCP/IP.

Every device that might be part of the company network has an exclusive and specific hardware address known as an **MAC address**. Packets are delivered to the MAC address of an individual device. Devices are also given a network address, an IP address, which enables them to be located on the network; this **IP address** is a 32-bit number, which is then translated into a domain name by a domain name server (DNS). A typical domain name is http://www.unisa.edu.au.

The route by which packets are transported from one network location to another is known as **routing**. Devices, known as **routers**, provide the mechanism by which this can be carried out. It is possible to keep large internal portions of a company network and its IP addresses private and non-routable and use a method called **Network Address Translation** (NAT) to determine the route of a packet created externally to the company network. This provides good security to a company LAN or WAN.

Firewall types and techniques

A *firewall* is a hardware device or software that filters packets as they are sent between networks, and it is a necessity for a business network today. This is one particular case where hardware can do a better job than software, but there is software that can perform the task adequately, depending on the situation. In the case of the Linux operating system, the software firewall (part of the Linux system) could be complemented by a hardware firewall for additional security. There are three types of firewall: packet filters, circuit level gateways and application gateways, which are discussed below.

Packet filters

Packet filters are constructed so as to examine the header in a TCP/IP packet and examine the routing information, such as the packet source and destination address. If a system administrator wants to ban packets travelling to or from specific source or destination addresses prohibited by the firewall **access list**, the packet is discarded. Routers can serve as packet filters in a network.

Advantages of using packet-filtering routers are that they are easier to construct than most other types of firewall configuration. They also use simple equipment that provides reasonable security at a low price for a small or start-up company. Their rules provide basic functionality and a fair degree of flexibility, since they allow access to be accepted or denied from and/or to a particular host or network.

The disadvantages of packet filters are that they are vulnerable since they have a very simple traffic logging mechanism and have several security-related design weaknesses. Attackers can use 'IP spoofing' attacks to fool packet filters by forging IP headers. If the security of a packet filter is compromised, an attacker has access to the entire network.

Gateways

There are two styles of gateway firewall: circuit-level gateways and application gateways.

Circuit-level gateways transmit requests for Internet connections. Outbound connections from an internal network intended for the Internet travel to a relay gateway, which reads the destination address of the request and creates a link to the target. The gateway then passes information between the internal connection request and the external target link. The internal connection request never communicates directly with the external destination, and the external destination believes it is just communicating with the relay gateway. Everything behind the relay gateway is hidden from the rest of the Internet.

Network Address Translation, as described above, is used to hide details about hosts on the internal network, behind the gateway, from the outside world. NAT can hide an entire intranet behind one Internet address (this is also known as masquerading), or it can use a range of Internet addresses assigned to the organisation running the gateway.

A circuit-level gateway's chief shortcoming is that it depends on static rules to determine whether a connection should be relayed. Applications that rely on random destination addresses for services, such as FTP and ICQ, are not supported in a circuit-level gateway's predefined access control list.

Application gateways use specially written code for each specific application. They are able to examine and interpret the data within the packet, not just the packet header, as in the case of a circuit-level gateway. A physical application gateway uses **proxy servers**, code that represents both clients and servers.

Since application gateways filter at the application layer, they have strong control of incoming and outgoing traffic. They can also hide host names and IP address, enabling outsiders to see only the gateway. The routing and filtering rules are simplified since traffic needs only to be sent to the gateway and the rest is rejected. One drawback of using proxy servers is that they require specific code for each service. Applications can also require modified clients since they might need to connect first to the gateway and then access the host.

Firewall configurations

Packet filters, applications gateways and circuit-level gateways can be configured in several different ways to meet the security needs of an organisation. Depending on the configuration, a firewall could be implemented on a single machine or could include multiple machines and routers. There are five firewall configurations: packet filtering, stateful inspection, screened host, screened subnet and multi-homed host.

Packet filtering

A packet filtering firewall simply filters packets. Based on the packet header information, including the source and destination addresses and port numbers, the packet filter can pass some packets while blocking others. A packet filter is often implemented using a screening router that can be programmed, for example, to block all packets from a particular untrusted system or to block all incoming connections except those for email and FTP. Packet filtering is available on all routers, and a variation can be implemented on hosts running UNIX, WinNT/2000/XP and MacOS X.

Stateful inspection packet filtering

An alternative to simple packet filtering is stateful inspection. This method also filters on packet header information. Stateful inspection looks at the packet to see whether it is the beginning of a session, a continuation of a session or the termination of a session. It builds up a table containing information about the current status of each Internet session. On the basis of the current state of a session, the packet might or might not be allowed to pass. Because of the table, stateful inspection prevents IP spoofing. Stateful inspection is usually implemented as an add-on product of most routers.

Screened-host

A screened-host firewall allows only trusted services to bypass the gateway. A screening router or firewall appliance is used to ensure that a host on an external network can communicate only with a bastion host that is attached to an internal network. The bastion host can communicate with other computers on the Internet network. The screened-host configuration allows only certain types of connection. Using the screened-host architecture, for example, direct connections between internal hosts and external hosts can be disallowed, or direct connections may be allowed but only for select services. The advantages of the screened-host configuration are that it provides strong security, as long as it is working. The problem is that there is a single point of failure. Since the bastion host is on an internal network, if the host or the router is compromised, all the internal hosts can be directly attacked.

Screened-subnet or demilitarised zone

The screened-subnet firewall has the advantages of a screened host but is more secure. Instead of connecting to an internal network, the bastion host is connected to a perimeter network or demilitarised zone (DMZ). This DMZ is connected to the internal network and to an external network through screening routers or a firewall appliance. The main advantage with this configuration is that there is no single point of failure. If the bastion host fails, an attacker must still get through the screening routers or firewall appliance in order to access internal hosts.

With the availability of firewall systems that support NAT, many screened subnets use private network numbers to further enhance security. Since private network numbers are never to be routed around the Internet, most Internet service providers discard those packets. Companies that employ private network numbers use NAT to translate the private source address to a public source address assigned to the company. Internet resource servers can communicate only with the public source address. Therefore connections from the Internet can never directly access the private hosts of the company since the private addresses are never revealed.

Multi-homed host

A **multi-homed host** firewall provides the highest-level of security because it allows absolutely no access to internal systems. A dual-homed host firewall is a single computer with at least two interface cards. A host on the internal network can communicate with the firewall, as can a host on an external network; however, hosts inside and outside the firewall cannot directly communicate with each other. The multi-homed hosts do not route packets directly from one network to another, although they could be configured to do so. Packets can go from one network to another only after being inspected, authenticated, authorised and proxied. Most modern firewall systems use the multi-homed host configuration.

Intrusion detection systems

In addition to firewalls, security can be taken further by employing intrusion detection systems to further help identify attempts to break into a computer system or to misuse it. An intrusion detection system (IDS) reads and interprets log files from routers, firewalls, servers and other network devices (Shimonski et al. 2003) to deter, detect and deflect unauthorised use or attacks on a system.

IDSs can be host-based or network-based, depending on the activities that need to be monitored (Cisco Technologies 2004). Network-based IDSs can be placed between a router and a firewall to act as another defence layer (Conklin et al. 2004, p. 45). They can be used to combat unauthorised intrusions and malicious Internet worms along with bandwidth and e-business application attacks (Cisco Technologies 2004). Host-based IDSs solely deal with the machine on which they are installed and can help prevent insider hacking via incorrectly configured firewalls, and can catch intrusion attempts that fail (Graham 2004).

Because attacks can span packets, IDS examines packets in two different ways. It scans each packet individually looking for patterns (signatures) that are typical of an attack, and it monitors the packets as a stream of information, thus identifying attacks spread across multiple packets.

A major feature of an IDS is its ability to detect and deal with insider attacks as well as external ones, and a company would be well advised to install both network-based (to monitor network backbones) and distributed IDS (to function as remote sensors and report to a central station).

An **anomaly-based IDS** contains a database of 'normal' patterns of network behaviour and looks for behaviour or activity that does not match this collection of signatures. Alternatively, a **misuse-based IDS** contains a database of suspicious or malicious patterns that it matches to current network behaviour. Some IDSs include mechanisms to disable suspected packets or block them from reaching their proposed destination. However, this leads to the problem of 'false negatives' and 'false positives' where an IDS either fails to recognise a rogue packet or alternatively labels an innocent packet as suspect and drops it.

Virtual private networks

A **virtual private network (VPN)** operates on the public telecommunication infrastructure, using a tunnelling protocol and security procedures to maintain its privacy (VPNC 2003). VPNs were developed to allow private networks to be spread over a large geographic area without the high expense of leasing private lines. The VPN allows multiple private networks to be connected over a public infrastructure.

When a VPN is implemented between two locations it works in a very similar manner to the way encrypted data is sent over a wide area network. To communicate using a VPN, the packets are encrypted using a point-to-point protocol (PPP), then are sent over the public network encapsulated with an authorised protocol (IPSec, PPTP or L2TP; see IT Risk 6.1 on pp. 170–1). When the packet is received at the destination, data is decrypted allowing the receiver to access the plaintext.

An important part of VPN security is the authentication of users; users need the appropriate credentials (information) before a VPN session can be established, which can be accomplished through password authentication and cryptography. This stops unauthorised users from gaining access to the network, even if they are aware of the VPN.

VPNs have been implemented globally to secure inter-network communications. There are multiple implementations of virtual private networks: hardware controlled, software controlled and a combination of both. Virtual private networks can be configured with combinations of authorisation and encryption protocols, allowing adequate authorisation to achieve the level of security required.

Product vendors are releasing products that try to make it easier for business to implement a VPN. Companies such as Netgear are producing hardware products that provide a VPN solution. One such product is the Netgear FVS318, which is a combination firewall and VPN router that uses the IPSec authorisation protocol and DES, Triple DES encryption, plus many others. This is an example of a hardware solution that can be implemented to allow secure encrypted communication between two of these devices over an open network. An example of software VPN solutions is the Linux S/WAN, which is free downloadable software that runs on a Linux system. It uses the IPSec tunnelling protocol, and the current version of the software supports only Triple DES Encryption. These two solutions are only a small example of what can be used when implementing a VPN. The most common set-up for a VPN is the implementation of a firewall or VPN to the network, as this provides adequate security. Installation of these devices can range from being as simple as a plug-and-play device to being very complex, depending what is required from the VPN.

Currently most products available for implementing a VPN are for communication over the Internet between two networks and have become common solutions for securing wireless networks. When implementing a VPN over a

VPNs and protocols

For those who need a little more information on VPN protocols some basic information follows.

Internet protocol security

Internet protocol security (IPSec) was developed by the Internet Engineering Task Force (IETF) because the TCP/IP protocol did not have any security features, thus providing authentication and encryption to TCP/IP networking. Some of the main features of IPSec are authentication, integrity and replay protection. IPSec integrity protection checks to make sure that, when the receiver receives the data, it has not been altered or tampered with. Replay protection is where the protocol prevents packets from being resent, therefore not allowing unauthorised users to resend packets and capture information (Al-Muhtadi & Feng 2002).

Some advantages of IPSec are that, because it functions on the network layer, whatever applications or protocols it runs do not affect performance; it is also compatible with any application. In addition it is an international standard for many product vendors for use in their products.

Some disadvantages of IPSec are that it has many features and is very complex to implement, therefore needing highly trained staff. Poor implementation could allow holes, thus giving unauthorised users access to private information.

Point-to-point tunnelling protocol

Point-to-point tunnelling protocol (PPTP) was developed by a group called the PPTP Forum (consisting of 3Com, Microsoft, Ascend Communications, US Robotics and ECI Telematics) to provide remote users with access to a private network. Point-to-point protocol (PPP) is used to provide users with dial-up access to the Internet, and PPTP builds on this protocol to provide access to remote locations via authorised connections through the public infrastructure (Kent & Atkinson 1998).

User authorisation is handled using the PPP encryption protocols, PAP and CHAP; it also uses Microsoft's point-to-point encryption (MPPE). PPTP can also handle other protocols, such as IPX and so on, instead of just IP.

Layer2 tunnelling protocol

Layer2 tunnelling protocol (L2TP) was developed by the IETF and combines the PPTP and layer2 forwarding (L2F) protocols. L2F was developed by Cisco Systems at the same time as PPTP and is similar to PPTP except that it is not dependent on IP communications (Townsley et al. 1999).

The developers of both protocols (PPTP and L2F) worked together to develop L2TP, a better authorisation protocol. L2TP works similarly to PPTP by establishing the dial-up access using PPP, then choosing its own authorisation protocol. It also uses the PPP encryption protocols, PAP and CHAP, for its user authorisation.

L2TP also supports the use of the IPSec encryption protocol; therefore L2TP is used for encapsulation of packets and IPSec is used for the encryption. This is known as L2TP/IPSec. The main advantages of using IPSec encryption with L2TP is that it provides better security features, such as certificate authentication, before connections can be established instead of just using password-based authentication when using PPP.

wireless network, a software solution is the best choice. An alternative is having a combined hardware/software solution, whereby the hardware device is at the network side and the software is at the wireless device side.

The major benefit of using a VPN is the cost saving: communicating securely through the Internet eliminating vast cable installations. Virtual private networks are also very scalable, compared to leased line counterparts, as using the Internet allows connections on a global scale. The initial cost of implementing a wireless network might be expensive, but future extensions to this medium will be quick, easy and inexpensive.

Another major benefit — and the most important reason for using a VPN over public infrastructures — is security. VPNs provide strong security using high-level authorisation and encryption techniques. The level of security can be customised to the needs of the user, making it very flexible.

There are many benefits to using VPNs to secure communications, but there are also a few drawbacks that must be considered. Virtual private networks require additional resources for the communication, and hence will decrease available bandwidth; resources are used for encryption and so on. As discussed in the earlier section, the major benefit of using a VPN is the cost saving, but there can be many unexpected costs. VPNs are technically complex, and the cost of implementation and maintaining the VPN in the future could become expensive. Although VPN standards are developed, different vendors' technology might not be compatible. This is a drawback of VPN, but good research and preparation before implementation will help overcome these configuration issues and incom-patibilities will be minimised (Kosiur 1998).

Inter-network security and network separation

Increasingly, modern enterprises need to integrate networks that have differing levels of security (Froscher et al. 1994). Inter-network security is the process of linking two or more networks to give functionality but also maintain the integrity of such networks. It is a difficult balance to achieve, as often one is a trade-off against the other.

Inter-network security has the precondition that each network is already secure independently. The level of security also largely relies on the users of the networks, but inter-network protection exists to limit and define the boundaries of its users.

At any given time, there are three commonly used methods of maintaining security in an environment that has one or more independent networks: network isolation, firewalls and perimeter guards, and multilevel security networks.

Network isolation

Network isolation is one of the most commonly used practices in the military and defence. Network isolation is the practice of keeping two or more networks entirely separated, and no connections are allowed between the two. This keeps each network of computers entirely distinct from the other, with no knowledge of each other's existence. This means that it is physically impossible for data to transfer between networks.

The problem with this solution is that network isolation pays a high price for the security. Isolated networks have no physical method of transferring data, which limits the use of both networks. At the price of limiting movement of unauthorised data between networks, the system stops all movement, even that of required data. Where an isolated network excels in security, it lacks in functionality (Tenix Datagate 2002).

An isolated network is also expensive in initial outlay and maintenance. To maintain isolated networking successfully, those with access to two or more of these networks require a distinct terminal or computer system for each of the networks they wish to access. This could be considered a waste of resources, as for every two terminals that need to be activated, only one would be in use at any one time.

By far the greatest disadvantage of an isolated network situation is the belief that it stops data leaks between networks. Although it is a solution to stopping data flow between two or more networks, users who have rights for multiple network logins can access all networks at once and hence copy data manually between two or more. This involves manual typing, but it is not prevented by the system. It has long since been proven that humans are the weakness in any information security system (Mitnick & Simon 2002).

Firewalls and perimeter guards

The use of firewalls and monitoring software to separate two or more networks is even more flawed as a system of maintaining data integrity than isolating networks (Connolly 1997). There are two types of firewall: proxy and filtering. Firewalls are primarily used to block certain types of traffic, or to allow traffic only to move into a network as a response, which makes them ideal as a network perimeter defence. Firewalls are considered standard as a form of defence on a computing network, but their use is not considered appropriate as a barrier within an internal network.

Firewalls are an inappropriate guard against traffic moving between networks that has not been authorised, as although it might stop people on a less secure network attempting to access data on a more secure network, there is nothing to stop individuals on a more secure network moving data into a less secured network. Firewalls work only in a single direction.

Another failure of firewall units is that they cannot differentiate data. Monitoring software cannot, in real time, find hidden data, analyse potential threats and block data well. Although monitoring software and firewalling are critical tools in managing networks, they are not enough on their own. A firewall alone is simply not a strong enough tool to manage and monitor file transfer across a network as it simply is not designed to do so.

Multilevel secure networks

Multilevel secure networks are a modern idea that aims to maintain the security that an isolated network achieves while allowing a larger degree of flexibility. It is designed for environments that have two or more networks, a high-level (or more secure) network and a low-level one (less secure). Within a multilevel secure network, data may be transmitted from the low-level network to the high-level network but may not travel from the high-level network to the low-level one, not even for acknowledgement of data, which prevents any form of data being leaked from a more secure computing environment into a less secure one. This environment of high-level and low-level networks is common in military or defence environments when there are several levels of data classification (*Journal of Aerospace and Defence Industry News* 1999). In particular, users on the high-level network might require data or services available to the low-level network, and this method allows these to be utilised without compromising security (Landwehr & Froscher 1997; Froscher et al. 1994).

Multilevel secure networks rely on unidirectional network bridges to operate. A unidirectional network bridge is either a software application or a combination of software and hardware that allows data to travel in only a single direction. The use of a unidirectional bridge does require some technical challenges to be overcome; the largest being that TCP, a common networking protocol, requires two-way communication in the form of handshaking and acknowledgements. In networking environments such as the Internet or, to lesser extent, internal networks, acknowledgements and packet numbering are required owing to the lossy nature of the network and the fact that different packets might take different paths and hence arrive out of order.

The network challenges required for unidirectional data movement are different from that of the Internet as they are not as stringent. Data would rarely arrive out of order, and packet loss would be minimal. This points towards UDP, a connectionless protocol often used for streaming data over the Internet. It is assumed that the UDP protocol has been modified for retransmission and possibly encryption.

The disadvantage of using the unidirectional network bridge is that it still relies on sneaker nets to provide information flow from the more secure network to the less secure one. This does not remove the security concerns with sneaker nets as one of the primary dangers with sneaker nets is the unauthorised transfer of information from high-security networks to low-security networks. Several companies are producing or developing unidirectional data bridges to provide multilevel secure networks.

Network separation

Network separation is a security technique used primarily in military and defence networks as a method of ensuring that those without authorisation do not access classified data. In the use of separated networks, there is often one 'insecure' network: a network that is often connected to the Internet or acts as an internal intranet. There exists a second network: the 'secure' network, which might contain a repository of classified data or processes (Tenix Datagate 2002). It is the data on the secure network that must be protected. The basis of network separation is that the secure and insecure networks are maintained separately and are never connected in any form. With this solution, all data on the secure network is never at risk from activity on the insecure network. Although the user base of the insecure network could be large, especially if connected to the Internet or large intranet, the secure network is monitored and the user base is kept to a minimum. The use of multiple networks poses operational constraints, as users often require access to two or more separated networks. Users typically must use separate computers or use keyboard or monitor switches to access each network. The other major constraint that separated networks impose is in part the functionality that the system provides; no data can be transferred between networks.

Although network separation has historically been a military solution, it is of growing interest to the business and e-commerce world (Slay & Turnbull 2004). Although separated network infrastructures add to the complexity of a network topology and restrict functionality, they have a potential to protect critical and core computer systems from the threat of electronic attack. The restriction of functionality that this entails can be partially countered with the use of a unidirectional network bridge between the two networks. Unidirectional bridges are still not commonly built and pose problems that much cutting-edge technology has contended with during development, but they do have uses outside military domains. The defence of a unidirectional bridge exists at a physical level, making it impervious to changes in technology, new techniques, operating system vulnerability and network threats. However, unidirectional bridges have limitations; they cannot defend against everything.

System software security

Although much security is provided through hardware and devices, system software plays an important role in securing networks.

BIOS and boot loader

The system's BIOS essentially controls the behaviour of all system hardware before booting the operating system, when control of most hardware is delegated to the operating system. Securing the system's BIOS can be done by creating a BIOS password and specifying several other options. As well as protecting the BIOS settings, security can also be extended to protecting the actual booting on the system, requiring a password for booting to proceed. The first step in securing a system's BIOS, however, is to make sure it is recent, as older BIOSs contained default and backdoor passwords, which are now well known.

The system's BIOS also includes the following options to strengthen security:

- *Boot sequence.* This contains the list of data storage devices that the system can boot from, which gives a systems administrator the option of preventing booting from external media, such as CDs and floppy disks.
- *Virus warning.* If set to 'enabled', this will cause the BIOS to prevent or warn when a piece of software attempts to modify the disk boot sector of a hard drive.
- *Security option.* Many BIOSs will have this option, in which either 'System' or 'Setup' can be selected. 'Setup' instructs the BIOS to require a password before allowing a user into the BIOS settings screen to make changes. 'System' instructs the system to require a password before booting the system, as well as accessing the BIOS settings.

These options could be worded differently in some BIOSs, as all BIOSs are different. It is also important to note that the security of the system's BIOS depends on the CMOS RAM, which is maintained by a battery on the system's motherboard. It is therefore important to have appropriate physical security in place to prevent access to the system's motherboard, as the BIOS security can be switched off with jumper settings or by removing the CMOS battery.

The operating system's boot loader should also be secured to prevent any changes to the system before booting and to prevent unauthorised users gaining access to single-user mode and command consoles. Under Microsoft's Windows NT-based systems, this can be done by assigning access control lists to the boot files. Additionally, all alternative modes that can be selected at start-up still require user authentication and the administrator password is required to access the recovery console. Under Linux, the boot loader (GRUB or LILO) can be password protected.

The operating system

By far the most important software on a computer is the operating system. In a multi-user computer network, it is essential for the network's security that an operating system with appropriate security controls is deployed on both the servers and the client computers. Hardware security alone is ineffective in a network if, for example, Microsoft Windows 95 were to be used as the operating system on all machines. The Microsoft Windows operating system versions 95, 98 and ME were designed for home use and should never have been used in a business network owing to their lack of stability, reliability and, above all in this case, security. The majority of businesses use Microsoft-based and UNIX-based systems, but for illustration purposes here, the two multi-user operating systems we will examine security-wise are Microsoft's Windows 2000 and Linux.

Microsoft Windows 2000

Operating systems in general and versions of Microsoft Windows specifically are continually under review. Here we have reviewed Windows 2000 as an operating system for networks as an example of the type of security feature that can be found in this and any modern Windows-based operating system.

File system security

One of the first steps in establishing network security in a Windows 2000 environment is to make sure the file systems on all computers are secure. Windows 2000 provides the option of using the FAT32 or NTFS file systems. FAT32 (32-bit file allocation table) is the file system used by Windows 98 and ME. It has no features to control user access to data and as such is not recommended by Microsoft as a file system for use in business. NTFS (New Technology file system) is the file system used by Windows NT-based operating systems and is the recommended file system in all business situations, not only for its support for file and folder access permissions but also because it is required by Windows 2000 Server if Active Directory is to be installed. NTFS is also required for EFS (Encrypting File System), which is available in Windows 2000 and later (Todd & Johnson 2001).

The Encrypting File System, as the name suggests, allows any part (or all, if desired) of the file system to be encrypted on demand. NTFS controls access to a volume when it is in use by a system, but is not effective when the volume is removed and placed into another computer. The EFS is a particularly important security measure in this case because if physical security into the computer system is breached, the files are encrypted, making discovery of the actual data extremely difficult.

User accounts

Being a multi-user operating system, Windows 2000 gives administrators the ability to give every user in the organisation their own user account so that users can access computer systems with their own credentials and everyone from outside is virtually locked out. A user's 'account' contains information about the user, particularly three important things:

- the account 'username', which is used by the user to tell the system who they are
- the account 'password', which is the access key that the user uses to prove their identity to the system
- a 37-character security ID (SID), which starts with the character 'S' and is followed by 36 digits, arranged in groups and separated by hyphens. The SID is unique to a particular user account.

Password security

In all of the Windows NT operating systems (including Windows 2000), user authentication has required the use of a username and password; the password essentially being the key to the user's account. Unencrypted passwords are never sent over the network when logging on to a Windows 2000 system (except for inherently insecure services like FTP and Telnet, unless using NTLM authentication). All password information is stored as password hashes in Windows 2000 SAM file, which cannot be accessed by any user (including the administrator) when the system is running. Using Kerberos authentication makes security even stronger, because no password hashes are sent over the network.

In a secure business network running a Windows 2000-based network, it is vital that all user passwords remain secure, regardless of the user's access rights. Windows 2000's security policy controls provide the following options to help ensure that a user's password is secure:

- 'Enforce password history.' This option allows administrators to specify the number of passwords that the system remembers so that passwords cannot be reused.
- 'Maximum password age.' The maximum number of days before the system forces the user to change the password.
- 'Minimum password length.' The required minimum number of characters in a user's password.
- 'Password must meet complexity requirements.' If this policy is on, the password must meet the following requirements: not contain all or part of the user's account name; be at least six characters in length; and contain characters from at least three of the following four categories:
  — English uppercase characters (A to Z)
  — English lowercase characters (a to z)
  — base 10 digits (0 through to 9)
  — non-alphanumeric characters (e.g. *, !, $, #, %).

Account lockout policy

Just as an automatic teller machine captures a card after three incorrect PIN entry attempts, Windows 2000 can deactivate a user's account after a specified number of incorrect password entry attempts.

- 'Account lockout duration.' The length of time an account is locked out after the number of incorrect password entry attempts reaches the threshold. If this is set to 0, then the account remains locked out indefinitely until an administrator unlocks it.
- 'Account lockout threshold.' The number of invalid password attempts before the account is locked out.
- 'Reset account lockout counter after …' The length of time before the recorded number of invalid password entry attempts is reset to zero.

Security audits

Security audits are essentially logs of every action that the user performs and actions that the computer itself can automatically perform. By default, the systems logs can be accessed only by administrators. Windows 2000 allows administrators to audit the following activities:

- *account logon events:* when a user logs on or off, in which the computer maintaining the audit is the computer that validates the username and password
- *account management:* when a user accounts are modified
- *directory service access:* any object accessed in Windows 2000's Active Directory
- *account logon events:* when a user logs on or off, or makes a network connection
- *object access:* when a user accesses an 'object' on the system (e.g. requiring the use of services)
- *policy change:* when the audit policy is modified
- *privilege use:* when a user makes use of any special privileges
- *process tracking:* when a user interacts with a process
- *system events:* when the system performs an activity that would normally be placed in the event log. Auditing system events can also be used in conjunction with the security option 'Shut down the system immediately if unable to write an event to the security log' to prevent DOS attacks, which would normally fill up the security log rather quickly.

Access to files and folders can also be audited by changing a file or folder's security information. This requires that the system is using the NTFS file system.

User rights assignment policy

The user rights assignment policy options allow administrators to specify which users have the rights to perform more specific actions, other than those allowed by the group to which a particular user belongs. Changes made to these options control whether any particular user can:

- access the system over the network using their username and password
- act as part of the operating system, giving the user the ability to perform almost any action on the system, as if they were using a Windows 95-based system
- locally log on to the system
- shut down or restart the system (locally or remotely)

- perform maintenance on hard drive volumes
- install, uninstall and update device drivers
- adjust memory usage
- change the system clock
- take ownership of files.

Some options in this section (e.g. 'log on locally' or 'access this computer from the network') also have a corresponding 'deny' option. If a user is placed in both the 'allow' and 'deny' options, then the 'deny' takes precedence.

Additional security options

The security policy controls also provide a set of security options not covered elsewhere. These options include:
- renaming the administrator or guest accounts (which can also be done from within the 'Local users and groups' controls for stand-alone servers and workstations or from within 'Active Directory users and computers' for domain controllers and domain members). Renaming the administrator account provides the opportunity to create a 'dummy' account called 'administrator' (with no access rights), which can then be monitored for any suspicious activity.
- preventing users from accessing the system over the network
- forcing the user's log off or disconnection when their permitted logon hours expire
- preventing the system from being shut down without having to log on
- preventing the username of the last user on the system being displayed in the 'username' box when the next user logs on
- whether the 'Everyone' access permission applies to anonymous users
- preventing the installation of drivers that have not been digitally signed.

Active Directory

Since the focus here is on security, we will not dwell on what Active Directory is but rather on some of the security benefits it provides. Briefly, Active Directory is the name given to the directory service in Windows 2000 that is installed when the server is 'promoted' to a domain controller. Like Windows NT domain controllers, it provides centralised security so that local user accounts on each client computer (which could pose as a security risk) are unnecessary and can be disabled. Active Directory also allows the creation of separate 'organisational units' for the grouping of Active Directory objects, including user accounts, shared folders and printers.

Active Directory contains a feature called 'operations masters'. This feature allows a Windows 2000 server running the directory service to delegate roles to other. Using this feature, it is possible to create several domain controllers, each responsible for performing different tasks. This means that if one server is the victim of an attack, the others can continue to perform their roles and support the business. The victim server's role can be replaced immediately if it has a corresponding back-up operations master. Typically, this sort of environment would be hard to manage; however, the Active Directory administrative tools allow every operations master to be administered from one console.

Additional security features of Active Directory include the Kerberos authentication protocol and the ability to run the directory services protocol (LDAP) over Secure Sockets Layer (SSL) so that directory transactions can be carried out over a secure channel (e.g. for use over an extranet or for e-commerce purposes). Switching the directory services to 'native mode' (which is available only when all domain controllers are Windows 2000 servers) strengthens security to Windows 2000 level across the entire domain. One benefit of this is that anonymous users cannot read information on the domain.

Linux

Linux is an open-source operating system, so its source code is freely available in the public domain. This has two major benefits in a secure organisation:
- Patches for any problems can be created by the organisation, rather than waiting for someone else to discover bugs and release patches.
- As the source code is publicly available, the operating system can be put through a common criteria security evaluation by the organisation itself, rather than having to wait for a group of individuals outside the company to perform this evaluation.

Linux is also a multi-user operating system that, like Windows 2000, supports file and folder access permissions. However, since Linux is an entirely different operating system, these security principles work slightly differently; furthermore, there are different areas in which security can be adjusted.

We will now examine a number of areas in which Linux allows security to be strengthened.

Boot loader

Password protecting the Linux boot loader prevents unauthorised access to single-user mode (whereby the user becomes the 'root' user) and prevents the loading of any other operating system (if running a dual-boot system), which might be less secure. Also, if GRUB is the boot loader, password protection prevents unauthorised access to the GRUB console, where configuration options can be changed. Securing each of these boot loaders requires root access.

Passwords

For best password security, Linux will automatically select MD5 and shadow passwords during installation. MD5 is a more secure encryption method, which also allows non-alphanumeric characters in passwords. If this option is deselected, Linux uses DES encryption, which allows only alpha-numeric characters and 56-bit encryption. Password shadowing is important for security; otherwise password hashes are left in the password file, which is readable to everyone and susceptible to a brute force attack off-site. If password shadowing is enabled, the password hashes are kept in the password shadow file, which can be read only by the root user.

The PAM (Pluggable Authentication Module) works in a similar way to Windows 2000 password policies and is customisable so that administrators can specify password requirements. When a user changes their password using the passwd command, passwd checks PAM to see whether the password conforms to the specified requirements. Linux also has a password ageing policy, which allows administrators to specify the maximum amount of time a password can remain in use on an account.

Limiting use of the 'root' account

By default, the user 'root' can only access a Linux system locally. The file/etc/securetty controls that computers the root account can be used on. If this file is empty, the root user cannot log on at all (except through SSH). If this file does not exist, the root user can log on from anywhere, which is potentially unsafe. Further options exist that are designed to limit the use of the root account, such as changing the root shell and preventing SSH logins.

Services

For security, most network services in Linux are turned off by default. Some exceptions include 'lpd' (print server), 'portmap' (required), 'xinetd', 'sendmail' and 'sshd' (secure shell — replacement for telnet). All services that pass sensitive information over the network, especially username and password combinations, should be used with caution, if not avoided altogether. The two major inherently insecure services that fall into this category are FTP and telnet.

Security can be strengthened for telnet and FTP by using the 'sshd' service and the secure client programs 'ssh' (secure shell) and 'sftp' (secure FTP). The services 'telnet', 'rlogin', 'rsh', 'vsftpd' and 'wu-ftp' (which are all inherently insecure secure services) can then be switched off. Alternatively, all user access to the FTP server can be denied. It should also be noted that although SSHD is an inherently secure service, it must be kept up to date to help prevent any security threats.

Security of services can also be strengthened using a Linux feature called a 'TCP wrapper'. As well as denying access to services, TCP wrappers can be used to extend logging capabilities, ban connections and send warnings. Preventing denial of service (DOS) attacks can be achieved by using the 'xinetd' command, which can block access to a service for a certain period, as well as restrict the load on a particular service.

Sendmail is an inherently insecure message transfer agent and can be susceptible to a number of attacks. However, there are some options that can be used to secure it:

- The sendmail configuration can be modified to specify a limited number of concurrent connections, child services, and header and message size. These are not set by default and leave the sendmail service open to a DOS attack.

- The mail spool directory can be stored on a non-NFS volume to protect privacy and security of email messages from other users.
- If the sendmail service is running on a machine that does not require users to access a shell, then shell access can be denied.
- Use of the third-party port scanner tool 'nmap' can be used to monitor open ports, and any suspicious open ports can then be investigated. An open port running a service indicated as 'unknown', although not always sinister, still deserves some attention.

Firewall

Linux includes tools for creating a simple firewall. The security level configuration tool and the GNOME Lokkit are GUI-based tools that create 'iptables' rules. 'iptables' is the interface for the 'netfilter' subsystem of Linux, which provides packet filtering options. Command line use of 'iptables' provides access to such functions as IP masquerading, NAT and IP bans, and can also be used to control network access to specified services. This can be used to secure the 'portmap' service and other RPC services with weak security mechanisms.

The GUI tools provide a general-purpose configuration typically recommended for home use, but the best set-up for a business is to use the command line tools. Although they are more complex, they provide the greatest functionality.

Antivirus software

Although hardware can provide security in the form of a firewall, it does not have any technical possibility of providing protection against viruses. Viruses are malicious (or just annoying) pieces of software that append themselves to legitimate files, programs or emails, waiting to be activated by an unsuspecting user. Once a malignant virus is activated, its goal is usually to destroy as much data as it can in a short space of time. Hardware fails here mainly because new viruses are discovered every day. Although hardware can be designed to pick up existing viruses, in a few days the hardware device will long be out of date. Making hardware 'updatable' also presents a problem, as a virus could be designed to attack the programmable circuits and render the unit useless.

Viruses are far from likely to be totally eradicated, so software has been designed to scan files, programs, emails and so on for viruses before they become active. Two well-known companies that develop antivirus software are Symantec and McAfee. Each of these companies has produced antivirus solutions for enterprise, including separate products designed for client and server systems. Antivirus companies are continuously being alerted to new viruses and regularly release updates for their antivirus packages. These updates need to be obtained regularly (ideally as soon as they are released) and installed so that the company's antivirus software guards against new viruses.

Summary

Networks can be secured by hardware, software or mixed technical security controls. The range of network security controls includes firewalls, intrusion detection systems and virtual private networks, all of which have relative strengths and weaknesses. A defence in depth approach provides overlapping layers of control so that if one is breached, the other layers are still in place to maintain security. Network security is an area of constant development. So is network hacking.

External firewalls control which parts of the network can be accessed from the outside. An intrusion detection system detects suspicious activity and alerts the network administrator. Intrusion detection system sensors add a second level of intruder detection. The demilitarised zone separates publicly accessible parts of the network (such as the company's website) from the internal network. Internal firewalls prevent network access through the demilitarised zone. A virtual private network is the establishment of private connections using a public infrastructure. Segmentation separates the departmental networks within the organisation, reducing the risk of internal misuse and limiting the scope of a successful intrusion from outside.

Increasingly, businesses' networks are interconnected with other networks. It is important to ensure that each network is secured independently and that the connection between them is secured, without impeding the necessary flow of information.

System software, particularly the operating system, is also crucial to network security. All operating systems have security features, but all also have some vulnerability.

Antivirus software provides an important protection against malicious codes. The advantage of antivirus software is that it can be updated to cope with new threats, whereas hardware cannot be so easily upgraded. A weakness, however, is that the upgrades occur only after the virus has been detected by the software companies. Security depends on the upgrade being available before the virus gets to the company's network.

In chapter 7 we examine some more aspects of network security and some application and database security issues that also affect overall system security and can be controlled by effective policy development as well as efficient use of human resources and technical controls.

access list, p. 165	MAC address, p. 164
anomaly-based IDS, p. 168	misuse-based IDS, p. 168
application gateways, p. 166	multi-homed host, p. 168
circuit-level gateways, p. 165	Network Address Translation, p. 165
defence in depth, p. 161	network architecture, p. 163
demilitarised zone, p. 161	packets, p. 164
external firewall, p. 161	protocols, p. 164
header, p. 164	proxy servers, p. 166
internal firewall, p. 162	router, p. 164
internal network, p. 161	routing, p. 164
intrusion detection system (IDS), p. 161	segmentation, p. 162
	signature database, p. 161
intrusion detection system sensors, p. 161	TCP/IP, p. 164
	UDP, p. 164
IP address, p. 164	virtual private network (VPN), p. 169
local area network, p. 163	wide area networks, p. 163

Questions

1. What is a protocol?
2. Identify three protocols defined in this chapter and explain their purpose.
3. Compare and contrast the differing types of firewall discussed in this chapter and identify the most sophisticated one, giving reasons why you believe it is the most sophisticated.
4. Assuming you are an IT security manager, briefly discuss the security features of Windows 2000 and Linux operating systems, and propose a sound argument to a non-technical manager for the adoption of Windows 2000.
5. Write a checklist documenting the process you would go through as a systems administrator in instructing a new user of a Windows 2000 network on system security features.
6. Identify for your new user some good methods of password choice.

Case study
6: A secure network

We met Elisabeth Chan in chapter 4 and again in chapter 5 when she was considering how she might be able to use encryption to protect her data. Her story continues here.

Elisabeth has improved her organisational and technical skills, and her company is growing. She has gained a new awareness of the IT security environment in which she is trading and has decided to go back to basics and have a look at her network architecture and its security.

Elisabeth now also has a good understanding that a secure network is founded on a sound security policy. She is using e-commerce effectively, and her network has grown and resembles figure 6.1 (p. 160).

Questions

1. Prepare a report for Elizabeth on her current network architecture. Describe the current topology in non-technical terms.
2. Using the details of HB 231 identified in chapter 4, carry out a vulnerability and risk analysis for the network described.
3. Identify possible areas of technical or procedural insecurity, and offer possible remedies.

Suggested reading

Thomas, T 2004, *Network Security First-Step*, Cisco Press, Indianapolis, IN.

References

3Com 2000, 'Network security: A simple guide to firewalls', accessed 10 September 2004, http://support.3com.com/software/fw/503090-001_firewall.pdf.

Al-Muhtadi, J & Feng, W 2002,
'A general security infrastructure for wireless communication', IEEE International Conference on Networks (ICN 2002), August, Atlanta, GA.

Cisco Technologies 2004, 'Intrusion detection', accessed 15 September 2004, www.cisco.com/warp/public/cc/pd/sqsw/sqidsz.

Conklin, WA, White, GB, Cothren, C, Williams, D & Davis, RL 2004, *Principles of Computer Security: Security+ and Beyond*, McGraw-Hill, Boston.

Connolly, J 1997, 'Does your network need a firewall? The Mitre Advanced Computing Newsletter', accessed 12 September 2004, www.mitre.org/pubs/edge/july_97/third.htm.

Ford, D 2003, '8 simple rules for securing your internal network', SANS, accessed 18 September 2004, www.sans.org/rr/papers/index.php?id=1254.

Froscher, J, Kang, M, McDermott, J, Costitch, O & Landwehr, C 1994, *A Practical Approach to High Assurance Multilevel Secure Computing Service*, Proc. Tenth Annual Computer Security Applications Conference, December, Orlando, FL.

Graham, R 2004, *Intrusion Detection Systems*, accessed 12 September 2004, www.robertgraham.com/pubs/network-intrusion-detection.html.

Information Systems Security Association (ISSA) 2004, 'Network security basics', accessed 16 October 2004, www.issa-ne.org/documents/NetSecBasics.pdf

Journal of Aerospace and Defence Industry News 1999, 'Australian ministry accepts first multi-level information product', accessed 12 September 2004, www.aerotechnews.com/starc/1999/112399/Australia_Comm.html.

Kent, S & Atkinson, R 1998, 'Security architecture for the Internet protocol', RFC 2401, http://rfc.sunsite.dk/rfc/rfc240.html.

Koenig, R 2002, 'Beware of insider threats to your security', *CyberDefence*, accessed 23 October 2004, http://cyberdefensemag.com/aug2004/ciconfidential.php.

Kosiur, D 1998, *Building and Managing Virtual Private Networks*, Wiley Computer Publishing, New York.

Landwehr, C & Froscher, J 1997, *Architecture and Components for Data Management Security: NRL Perspective*, Naval Research Laboratory Center for High Assurance Computer Systems, accessed 10 September 2004, http://csrc.nist.gov/nissc/1997/proceedings/722.pdf.

Mitnick, K & Simon, W 2002, *The Art of Deception: Controlling the Human Element of Security*, Wiley Publishing, Indianapolis, IN.

Oxenhandler, D 2003, 'Designing a secure local area network', SANS, accessed 20 September 2004, www.sans.org/rr/papers/index.php?id=853.

Rozenblum, D 2001, 'Understanding intrusion detection systems', SANS, accessed 11 September 2004, www.sans.org/rr/papers/index.php?id=337.

Shimonski, RJ, Shinder, DL & Shinder, TW 2003, *Best Damn Firewall Book Period*, Syngress Publishing, Rockland, MA.

Slay, J & Turnbull, B 2004, 'The uses and limitations of unidirectional network bridges in a secure electronic commerce environment', INC2004, 8 July, Plymouth, UK.

Tenix Datagate Pty Ltd 2002, 'Veto uni-directional network bridge and data pump applications white paper', accessed 16 October 2004, www.tenix.com/PDFLibrary/78.pdf.

Todd, C & Johnson, NL Jr 2001, *Hackproofing Windows 2000 Server*, Syngress Publishing, Rockland, MA.

Townsley, W et al. 1999, *Layer Two Tunnelling Protocol (L2TP)*, IETF RFC 2661.

Virtual Private Network Consortium (VPNC) 2003, 'VPN technologies: Definitions and requirements', accessed 10 September 2004, www.vpnc.org/vpn-technologies.html.

Chapter 7

Securing network operations, databases and applications

Learning objectives

After studying this chapter, you should be able to:

- describe the methods used to attack networks, including hacking, probing and scanning

- discuss some of the basic motivations for hacking

- make a cross-cultural comparison of the controls used to secure networks

- draft a network security policy

- explain the major issues in database security

- discuss the major factors faced in the design of secure software.

Chapter overview

Chapter 6 introduced the operation of networks in business organisations. This chapter will examine the basic methods by which networks are attacked and look at hackers and their motives. An understanding of the motives of those who try to breach systems will help in the management of risk.

We also examine the practical trends in computer, network and system security and make a cross-cultural comparison of the nature of the threats and the types of control used to defend such systems from attack.

We also make the link between the desire for network security in an organisation and the need to write, implement and monitor sound network security policies, and give an example of a possible network security policy for a medium-sized company.

Finally we examine both database and software security to determine how these two factors affect the security of an organisation's complete network and system.

Network attack and defence

We saw in chapter 4 how a worm, a malicious piece of software, can be used to carry out Internet-mediated fraud and that we have to protect our networks from viruses (since they can multiply and spread) and Trojans (pieces of software that pretend to offer a necessary function but contain hidden malware or viruses, or links designed to trick users or to damage their systems, or both).

We have recognised that we need to be aware of the threat of a denial of service (DOS) attack in which a perpetrator might send so many requests for service to our server that it becomes overloaded and hence unavailable to carry out the work that we intend. This kind of attack could extend to become a distributed denial of service (DDOS) attack, whereby many different insecure computers are used to launch a simultaneous targeted attack on an organisation's network.

It is therefore easy to conclude that there is a potentially enormous problem, which might have a major financial effect on a company, from unstructured threats to networks, such as viruses, Trojans, worms and other malware, and the possibility of targeted and structured attacks on an enterprise network in the form of distributed or localised denial of service attacks.

Trends and motivation in hacker attacks

Hacker is the term broadly used to describe any person with the desire and technical knowledge needed to attempt to gain unauthorised access to a computer system. Motives of hackers can vary greatly and often include the desire to steal information for personal gain, to change details within a system in order to defraud the system operators and simply to cause malicious damage or frustration to system users — digital vandalism, in effect (Foltz 2004).

Hacker codes of ethics have traditionally revolved around the belief that all information should be free and that authority should be mistrusted. There is a perceived 'romance' in hacking into a computer, freeing its information and not having the owner of the network ever know it has been violated. As we have seen in earlier chapters, hackers are no longer rebellious teenagers looking for a challenge. Hacking can come from highly structured and organised groups who seek to steal intellectual property or destabilise a company by causing network failure (Cyberpunk 2004).

Sniffers or wiretapping can enable the hacker to gather information being sent throughout the network cabling to cables external to the network. The advent of wireless technology lends itself to eavesdropping as the information is transmitted within a radius that could extend beyond the building that houses the network. Hackers can now travel around in their cars listening for wireless transmissions to eavesdrop on or utilise the company's Internet bandwidth for free (see more on this in chapter 9).

As we have seen, organised crime has now entered the domain of hacking in order to commit cyber theft from banks or other financial institutions. These are highly organised groups that hire professionals to attack predetermined sites. Many organisations believe they are victims of indiscriminant attack and therefore rarely report the crime. However, there is always the chance that the company was not a target of opportunity and was attacked for specific reasons.

Computers have become such an essential part of society that most government documents, emails between parties and other data can be found on a local computer or network server. A hacker can be used to gain access to that information and, without the recommended controls and safeguards we discussed in chapter 6, the owners of the data might never know they have been hit.

The motivation of hackers is one of the most difficult aspects of risk management to anticipate. It is an easy step of logic to assume that a user who desires financial gain through fraud will target systems that contain financial records, such as credit card details; however, it is more difficult to anticipate such threats as industrial espionage, which could occur through accessing unexpected streams of information, or malicious damage as quite often these potential threats will occur completely unexpectedly through surprising points of entry for apparently no reason other than vandalism. It is therefore necessary to implement strong systems to prevent unauthorised access at all levels of the computer network, not merely the areas that seem most vulnerable. Hackers do not necessarily fit a given mould, and to assume that a system is safe owing to its being of little financial or industrial significance is an extreme hazard. Hacking is a threat that cannot be overlooked for the sake of financial considerations.

As can be seen from the AusCERT survey (2004), hacking is still a very frequent occurrence, and network access misuse and abuse by insiders make up a large proportion of this type of electronic attack or computer crime. The main targets of hackers are databases, operating systems, hardware, software, networks, network boundaries, communication channels and people from the targeted organisation. The main risks of hacking are theft or interception of information and assets, interruption of network services, modification of network components, including data and access controls, and the fabrication of counterfeit objects or unauthorised programs. Hackers can also use the hacked system to launch an attack on other computer systems or networks, thus obfuscating the actual source of the hacking to these systems.

Motivation for hacking and network attack

The main motivations for hacking are:

- *satisfaction:* whereby individual or a small group of hackers randomly pick a target network or organisation to hack to prove their skills or for entertainment purposes
- *profit:* whereby professional hackers, organised crime or terrorists target a network or organisation to steal data to sell to third parties or extort money
- *dissatisfaction:* where disgruntled employees or members of the public hack an organisation's computer network to get revenge or to pursue social or political issues
- *business competition:* where business competitors employ professional hackers, or spies, to hack an organisation or computer networks, for the purposes of decision-making, competitive advantage, profit and intellectual property theft
- *policy-making and price-setting:* where organisations and possibly governments use professional hackers, or spies, to hack computer networks or other organisations for policy-making, decision support and profit-making purposes
- *information warfare and terrorism:* whereby hostile governments or terrorists attack networks or organisations for strategic, political or conventional warfare reasons using highly motivated and skilled professional and/or amateur hackers.

Other network attacks

Network attacks can be categorised according to the components of the attack and the order in which a hacker uses tools and techniques to attempt to access a system. It is hypothesised that, if large-scale and long-term data is kept, profiles of hacker behaviour online could be obtained. This data might point to certain types of perpetrators' *modus operandi* or even tie crimes to specific individuals if their method of attacking an insecure system was similar every time.

Attack events that can be recognised within a complex distributed denial of service attack, for example, might include probing and scanning to find vulnerability, ways of compromising a user account to gain access to the root account, packet sniffing to identify packet destinations, potential use of malware or viruses to compromise a target's system and possibly much broader Internet or organisation-wide breaches and distributed denial of service. These events are described in more detail below.

When attacking a system, hackers need to gain as much information as possible about a system. They are most likely trying to get hold of '**root**' (a term in Unix systems that now has a wider usage). This means that they will then have all the system privileges of the administrator and access to all user accounts and system resources.

The first step in the hacking process is therefore **probing** so as to try to find simple system weaknesses or perhaps some information about the system that can then be used to gain access to the system. This is an attempt to find the weakest link, which is the first goal of every hacker. Probing can be carried out semi-innocently by a naïve would-be perpetrator or the first step in a targeted attack.

The second step in a would-be attack is **scanning**; this is carried out by automating the probing process most likely after a manual inspection has already yielded some evidence of weakness to the intruder.

Another part of the attack process could be the **compromise** of a user account. This kind of attack can be carried out by several means. An obvious means is by social engineering whereby an attacker phones or emails the user pretending to be an individual of authority in the organisation demanding to know the employee's username and password. Another alternative means is by a software **key logger**, which is installed without the employee's knowledge and simply records all their keystrokes, thus allowing the attacker to retrieve this data remotely, then hack into the system with the employee's credentials.

As explained above, every attacker wants to control 'root' and thus have the privileges of administrator and control all the system resources of an organisation. This might be done to commit a major crime, but it can also be a means whereby a hacker in another country accesses storage media for graphics (for innocent or criminal means) or music files. A clever hacker can change system privileges so that the real root has problems accessing the system, and can also hide all traces of their activity, which is a good reason why intrusion detection systems, honey pots and forensic readiness techniques are essential for a modern organisation.

The next step in a complex attack is most likely the use of a packet sniffing program. As we saw in chapter 6, using the TCP/IP protocol, data is transmitted in packets of specified size and with strategic and important information about the nature of the information, its source and destination hidden in the header. This might be transmitted in an unencrypted form, so a hacker needs to 'capture' packets to find the information. This is an intermediate step before perhaps carrying out a man-in-the-middle or denial of service attack. The packet sniffer is able to extract the header information for the hacker's use.

A common attack against networks is to use a packet sniffer such as *tcpdump* on a network host that has already been compromised. The sniffer is a program that listens on the ethernet port for packets that contain useful data. When it detects a packet containing words like 'passwd', 'login' or 'su' (superuser), it logs the following traffic, which probably contains the relevant passwords and/or usernames in clear text. A packet sniffer doesn't even have to be run on a compromised host — it can be run on a laptop brought into a building or on traffic intercepted from a wireless or microwave LAN or WAN (although the latter's multiplexing makes packet sniffing much harder.) This kind of attack can be defeated by using the Secure Shell (ssh) client/server to provide authentication and encryption services.

Depending on whether an attack is focused and targeted or is just an attack of opportunity, the next step might be a denial of service attack whereby the hacker, who now controls root and has access to all the resources of a corporate network, can now use automatic software to send as many packets as desired and 'flood' a target server. In this way, for example, a hacker could close Australian Government websites for political reasons or any other purpose. In flooding the server of their choice it would be possible for the hacker then to block all other network connections to it or use up the processing capacity of the target system.

Once an organisation's root was accessed, and with the hacker in control of all the system resources, it would then also be possible to access all other networks that were linked in 'trust' relationships with the first system and access their resources, too.

With root access a hacker could then infect the system they now controlled with Trojan horses, viruses and worms if desired. In this way (and in fact in many other ways, too) the hacker could perhaps infect the email server and spread a virus internationally if the system belonged to a large multinational company. The hacker could, however, cause major disruption, deleting or altering files and covering all traces of their activity, changing user privileges and access rights, hiding and installing software that would give them access to the system at any time in the future.

If the hacker allowed themselves the right to access the system again, allowing a '**back door**', they could then move on, hiding all evidence of the breach, hack into another system and thus control more resources. If a large amount of system resource was amassed in this way the hacker could construct wide-scale distributed denial of service attacks or even try to damage the Internet infrastructure.

Current trends in securing organisational IT security

In chapter 6 we reviewed the kind of security control and technology used by organisations to defend their corporate networks. It is useful here to review the current trends in Australia, and for comparison Hong Kong and the USA, to find some indication of the developments in modern IT security practice.

As can be seen in figure 7.1, the practice of most Australian organisations in the use of security controls and technology to manage risk compares favourably with that of their counterparts in the USA. However, only 40 to 50 per cent of

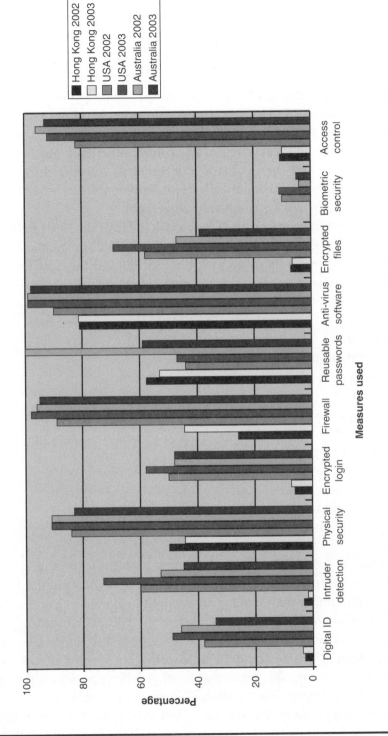

Figure 7.1 Trend in use of security controls and technology: Australia, Hong Kong and the USA, 2002–03

Source: data from HKCERT 2003; AusCERT 2003 and 2004; CSI/FBI 2003.

Australian organisations use encryption, and this figure compares unfavourably to the 60 to 70 per cent of US companies that use this kind of control. In the case of reusable passwords there was a significant drop in their usage from 2002 to 2003, with Australian usage falling from 100 per cent to 59 per cent compared to the US figures of 40 and 47 per cent in the same period (AusCERT 2003; Computer Security Institute/FBI 2003). It is difficult to explain this trend.

Hong Kong statistics seem to indicate that companies are either slow to implement many of the available security controls and techniques or perhaps they place little value on the effectiveness of any control other than physical security, reusable passwords and the installation of antivirus software. In these cases the number of companies using these measures approaches or exceeds half the number of Australian and US companies using them.

The types of computer attack listed in HKCERT (HKCERT 2003) fall into only four categories, namely virus, denial of service, theft of information and hacking. So that comparison may be made with the CIS/FBI and the AusCERT Survey (AusCERT 2003; Computer Security Institute 2003), their more detailed list of attacks is grouped into the following categories:

- virus
- denial of service
- theft of information
- active wiretapping
- telecom fraud
- financial fraud
- telecom eavesdropping
- theft of proprietary information
- hacking
- insider net abuse
- unauthorised insider access
- system penetration
- sabotage.

The statistics in figure 7.2 indicate a common problem with viruses, denial of service, theft of information and hacking in both the USA and Australia. It appears that either these attacks are not being experienced in Hong Kong or, much more likely, that they are not being reported. In fact the HKCert report suggests that 69.1 per cent of attacks in Hong Kong are not reported to senior management. This figure seems very high and quite noteworthy, but if most attacks are from a virus, Trojan or worm, this might not seem worth reporting within an SME unless the attack is responsible for major disruption or financial loss.

More recent figures from the AusCERT 2004 survey indicate that after a very small decline in figures for physical security, digital IDs, encrypted files, intrusion detection systems, smart cards and access controls, the use of this technology has now returned to their previous levels. A hundred per cent of companies surveyed use antivirus protection. Most significant is the adoption of virtual private

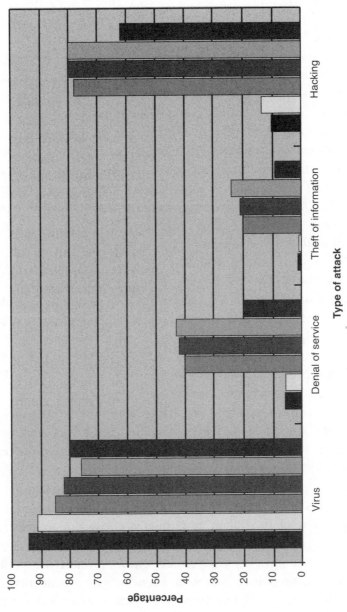

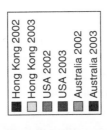

Figure 7.2 **Types of computer attack: Australia, Hong Kong and the USA, 2002–03**

Source: data from HKCERT 2003; AusCERT 2003 and 2004; CSI/FBI 2003.

networks, which has jumped from 0 per cent in 2002 and 2003 to 74 per cent in 2004 (AusCERT 2004, p. 7). Most companies still report between one and five attacks a year, but the percentage of companies affected is rising, although more slowly than in the period 2002–04 (AusCERT 2004, p. 13).

A slight decline in insider abuse, system penetration by outsiders, laptop theft, website defacement, sabotage of data of networks, computer facilitated financial fraud and unauthorised privileged access was visible in 2004, but virus, worm or Trojan infection rose to 71 per cent from 57 per cent (AusCERT 2004, p. 17).

The AusCERT (2004) report cited here shows that Australian companies are maturing in their approach to computer security issues and moving away from a reactive use of technology and plans for what action might be taken after an event. An organisational approach is being taken that considers what security policies and procedures are used, what IT standards are in place and what is necessary to attain an appropriate IT security qualification, training, experience and aware-ness for IT staff and management. Also considered separately are the factors that might have contributed to the attack in terms of the organisation's vulnerability and the nature of the threats and the problems experienced by management in addressing these issues. This represents a shift in focus away from reporting after the event towards anticipating future attacks.

In terms of staffing IT security, only 37 per cent of companies in Hong Kong employed full-time or part-time staff to deal with information security issues. Nearly half (46.8 per cent) do not spend any of their budgets on information security-related issues (HKCERT 2003, p. 26). In contrast virtually all of the Australian respondents have IT staff; however, 49 per cent considered their staff to be inadequately trained. Sixty-seven per cent of the questioned Australians spent money on updating information security in 2003 and employed IT staff (AusCERT 2004, p. 3).

If we examine attitudes to reporting crime we find that in 2003, 50 per cent of US respondents who experienced an attack did not report the incident. Thirty per cent reported the crimes to local authorities, and 21 per cent reported them to legal counsel. The most common reason for not reporting the incidents was negative publicity (70 per cent). Fifty-three per cent of those who did not report did not know they could report such incidents (CSI/FBI 2003, p. 18).

These numbers differ from those reported in Australia and Hong Kong. Sixty-two per cent of Australian respondents chose not to report attacks in 2003 (37 per cent in 2002). In Hong Kong only 1.8 per cent chose to report the crimes to HKCERT, and only 0.3 per cent chose to report them to the police. Incredibly, this means that at least 97 per cent of the respondents who suffered an attack in 2003 chose not to report it. The most striking difference between percentages of expressed reasons is that of 'trivial attack'. Again this could be attributed to the smaller sizes of IT security staff in Hong Kong; hence their in-ability to recognise a serious threat. Figure 7.3 shows the most common reasons for not reporting such incidents to outside organisations.

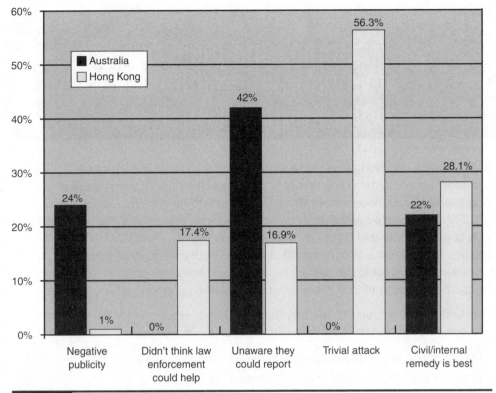

Figure 7.3   Why companies did not report attacks: Australia and Hong Kong 2002–03

Source: data from HKCERT 2003; AusCERT 2003.

Physical security

In chapter 2 we examined issues related to physical security. We saw that 'physical security' refers to the protection of the computer system from natural disasters and from unauthorised intruders.

Natural disasters include a range of threats, including fire, floods, earthquakes, volcanic activity, tidal waves, cyclones, tornadoes and typhoons, snow storms and lightning strikes. Although the issue of physical security is one that might seem of limited importance to an IT security manager, a disruption to the AARNET (university Internet) that disrupted the Internet connection to three universities in Adelaide, South Australia, over a two-week period in March 2005 was caused by a 'natural' disaster. It occurred when a water main burst flooding a university's server rooms, which housed both the AARNET servers and all the back-up machines. This incident was complex since the server rooms are situated in the basement of a building located on a steep slope. In fact the water main flooded the servers from the top down, an unexpected event that could have been predicted owing to the sloping nature of the whole site. Poor planning of physical security caused considerable damage, expense and inconvenience.

So an IT security manager has to have due consideration for the possibility of the events described below.

IT risk 7.1

Comparing the risk of working internationally: Hong Kong and Australia

Both Australia and Hong Kong have experienced the chaos and loss that accompanies computer crime in recent years, and they are fighting back with increased security measures. Both regions appear to be implementing individualistic security measures to combat their own computer crime problems. Recent statistics in Australia indicate that computer attacks are on the rise (AusCERT 2004, p. 3), and this reinforces the importance of utilising computer security policies and procedures. Each computer system is unique, and therefore customised security measures are recommended to suit the individual requirements of any business.

The Australian Computer Crime and Security Survey recommends the use of all, or a combination of, any of the following defence mechanisms:

- implementing physical security measures
- antivirus software in conjunction with regular updates
- encryption
- firewalls
- biometric devices
- callback systems
- intrusion detection systems
- digital certificates
- passwords
- employee monitoring
- access control.

In Australia, unpatched or unprotected software vulnerability and inadequate staff training and education in security practices were identified as the two most common factors that contributed to harmful electronic attacks (AusCERT 2004, p. 3).

In contrast, computer crime attacks have decreased in Hong Kong. This trend has been attributed to improved security technology deployed (HKCERT 2003, p. 11). Ninety per cent of companies surveyed in Hong Kong had deployed security technology. Trends in Hong Kong indicate that large companies are more proactive in implementing a more comprehensive security management strategy as compared to their smaller counterparts. Overall security has improved in the past few years, but security among small companies is still at a concerning low. Antivirus software, passwords, physical security and firewalls were the four most common security measures in place (HKCERT 2003, p. 25).

Information Technology Security & Risk Management

Floods

Floods can result from rising water, such as burst water pipes, rivers, dams, tides and waves, as well as from falling water caused by rain or a leaking roof and burst overhead pipes. With rising water the equipment could be damaged by the water or mud, but if it is detected early there is normally sufficient time to protect all or part of the equipment and particularly the organisation's data. The location of computers, storage media, modem banks and other important hardware as well as back-up tapes and disks must be carefully considered in the design of the organisation's IT capability. It would be inappropriate, for example, to create an area of vulnerability by locating such resources in underground levels of a building that might be prone to flooding or close to sewerage and other pipe work that might damage the equipment should it burst.

Fire

Fire is a far more serious threat than floods as there is far less time to react and the consequences can be catastrophic. Again location of the site is important; so too is the choice of materials, both in the building construction and its furnishings. When choosing where to locate the organisation's buildings, fire-prone sites should be avoided. Fire extinguishing equipment is mandatory whether the building is located in a fire-prone area or otherwise. These protection measures are generally covered by the occupational health and safety standards enacted by law in different countries; yet these need to be validated while ensuring the security of the information system's infrastructure. It is important to ensure that the building is equipped with adequate smoke detectors, smoke alarm systems and fire extinguishers and that they are tested periodically. Microprocessor-based fire detection systems that help in early detection of fire are also available. They allow early reaction.

It is important to select the best possible location for such equipment as fire or smoke detectors and fire extinguishers. The fire or smoke detectors should be placed in fire-prone areas after careful examination of the building, electrical wiring system and the electronic infrastructure in the building. The fire extinguishers should be placed conveniently so that they are easily approachable in case of a fire. However, while putting out fires, it should be noted that there are different fire extinguishing mechanisms for different fires; for example, electrical fires cannot be extinguished by extinguishers containing water or other liquids. Electrical wiring is the most common cause of fire; therefore wiring needs to be checked periodically to assess whether the power load is within safe limits. Circuit breakers or fuses usually cater for power overloads and sparks; however, they disconnect the electricity supply only from specific points and cannot help to contain the fire erupted by the sparks. When extinguishing fires resulting from electrical equipment or fires that include equipment connected to electricity, the use of carbon dioxide (CO_2) fire extinguishers is recommended. Carbon dioxide is an inert gas that does not react with other chemicals, and therefore there is no danger of increasing the toxic fumes and smoke during the process of extinguishing the fire. It discharges a white vapour and freezes the items it is applied to. In addition, it is a clean gas that leaves no residue, which means that it does not damage electrical equipment. Therefore, it provides maximum salvage value for the equipment. Some of the other commonly used fire extinguishing systems include fireproof cable coating and sealing system; FM-200 gas-based extinguishing systems; automatic fire hydrants that include sprinklers and spray systems; and dry chemical powder extinguishing systems.

In case of fire it is also important to ensure employees' health and safety. Businesses generally have certain procedures that they enact in case of fire, which include safe evacuation from the building and ensuring that nobody is exposed to smoke and other toxic gases for a longer period. In case the emergency services are not located at a convenient distance, it is important to have ample supply of breathing apparatus, gas masks and fire-fighting suits.

Lightning strikes

Lightning is a form of natural disaster, and there is no hard and fast rule that defines which areas are prone to lightening strikes. Lightning occurs because of the negative and positive charge in the clouds. This charge keeps increasing until the voltage difference between the base of the clouds and the ground becomes so much that it breaks resistance from air, which creates lightning discharge. This discharge is very powerful and usually measures several thousands of volts. It is highly attractive to a favourable path, such as electrical circuits, as it provides it with a path to flow through to the ground. This high voltage obviously destroys the path, and therefore all electrical and electronic systems are at high risk of being damaged by lightning strikes. Direct lightning strikes on the building or power surges that result from the strikes in power transmission lines, transformers and substations are equally disastrous to computer equipment.

A typical defence mechanism against lightning strikes is surge suppressors. However, this is a very basic form of defence against such a powerful catastrophe. Other common measures include storing back-ups in grounded storage media or installation of uninterruptible power supply (UPS) units on all critical IT resources. Nonetheless, two main measures can be taken to protect an organisation from lightning disasters:

1. Switching off and unplugging computer equipment and other associated resources in case of thunder or prediction of lightning strikes. This is usually an impracticable option for businesses.
2. Installation of a lightning protection system. Many types of lightning protection systems are available commercially, and each is designed to protect specific types of application. Some protect only outdoor equipment, some indoor equipment and some protect both types. These protection systems work on the simple principle of having surge protectors at several points on the IT infrastructure. Ideally, these protectors are installed to

safeguard power lines and load cells used by the IT equipment. These surge protectors are properly earthed, which increases the efficiency of the protection mechanism.

Developing network security policies

As we have seen in earlier chapters, a sound information security policy is the most important method of protecting any system, but also unfortunately it is one of the most neglected areas.

Research proves that there are three main problem areas in information security management that need to be dealt with by means of proper policy development. The first is external attack; that is, non-authorised users trying to access the company's computer network to perform malicious acts. This also includes the most recent form of attack known as distributed denial of service or DDOS. The second and probably biggest issue is that of authorised users — that is, company employees — unintentionally causing harm to the company's network because they are uninformed or there are just too few mechanisms controlling their actions. The last problem, and the hardest to manage, is that of authorised users intentionally abusing the company's network because they are either disgruntled or in search of external profits to be made by selling or manipulating company data.

A **security policy** should cover four main areas:
1. *people:* define who is an authorised user of the system
2. *policies:* defining what can be done, to what and when
3. *procedures:* set steps for doing tasks
4. *technology:* products and services available.

Companies can be easily rated by how well they deal with security in the above four areas. Companies may be categorised according to the following five categories: insecure, partially secure, semi-secure, reasonably secure and secure, which are described below.

Insecure

An insecure company has no security at all. There is no security or risk management, no auditing process, no documentation and no accountability. The company is 100 per cent open to attack.

Partially secure

In a partially secure company, the barest of minimum precautions are in place. Usually this situation arises when an insecure company attempts to stop or prevent attacks, but the company does not possess the knowledge or resources to develop a security policy. The security will most likely consist of basic unauthorised access prevention in the order of low-tech firewalls and/or hardware.

There would be some sort of virus protection that might not cover the entire system and is unlikely to be updated. Users remain uninformed of the dangers of opening unknown emails or downloading malware and the importance of data integrity. Users have basic computer security policies, usually consisting of just a username and simple password. The policy still allows them to accidentally or purposely manipulate or corrupt sensitive data. Procedures are non-existent.

Semi-secure

In a semi-secure company, there is a medium level of computer and information security. Physical security is taken into account, and hardware assets do have some type of physical boundary, whether they are stored in a locked case or a secure room. The internal network has a medium-level combination of software and hardware devices that protect it from external networks. Computer security policies prevent users from manipulating critical data and accessing data that they do not have the correct security clearance to use. Critical business data has some minimal protection and is backed up. There are procedures in place that deal with looking for vulnerability and reacting to disasters after they happen.

Reasonably secure

In a reasonably secure company, security systems are becoming technical. Most if not all hardware assets have some type of physical security. Servers are in sealed, air-conditioned, locked rooms only accessible to administrators and maintenance engineers. User terminals have security cables to prevent hardware being stolen. The network is protected by a series of hardware and software devices and is constantly monitored by an intrusion detection system (IDS). The IDS also monitors the internal network for unusual behaviour that might suggest an authorised user is up to no good. Users have strict computer user policies allowing them access only to data and processes that they absolutely require to perform their duties. Users have to authenticate themselves properly before accessing the system and are required to use more complex passwords and change them on a regular basis. Critical business data is protected and backed up regularly; access to it is restricted and possibly logged. Information is provided to users on the dangers they could be placing the company in and the steps they need to take to prevent attack. Procedures dealing with vulnerability detection and mitigation and disaster prevention and reaction are in place. Auditing of the security system might or might not take place.

Secure

In a secure company, all hardware assets have physical security. Servers are in sealed, air-conditioned, EMI-shielded, fireproof, security card–accessible rooms. User terminals have security cables to prevent hardware being stolen and possibly have motion detectors inside to prevent hardware being tampered with.

The network is protected by a multi-series of hardware and software devices and is constantly monitored by an intrusion detection system. There is a possibility of dummy networks and servers (called 'honey pots') being set up to lure attackers from critical systems and actively attempt to trace attackers. IDS plus other internal network monitors scan the network for unusual behaviour that might suggest an authorised user is up to no good. Users have strict computer user policies allowing them to access only data and processes that they absolutely require to perform their duties. Each user's action and data or process usage is logged and monitored. Users have to authenticate themselves properly before accessing the system and are required to make more complex passwords and change them on a regular basis. Critical business data is protected and backed up periodically, at an off-site location. Access to this business critical data requires authentication; access times and length of time using the data are logged. Proper training sessions are provided to users on the dangers they could be placing the company in and the steps they need to take to prevent attack. Training is a continuous process, which could consist of online knowledge quizzes, appended training sessions and emails informing users of new dangers. There are procedures in place that deal with vulnerability detection and mitigation and disaster prevention and reaction. All security breaches are dealt with offensively; systems are constantly tested, monitored and updated. Auditing of the security system by an external party takes place on a regular basis.

Companies become secure by developing, implementing and maintaining an enterprise-wide security policy; the key issue then is that the company must have an adequate network security policy. The group of policies in IT Risk 7.2 is an example of that which might be applied to the network infrastructure of a typical organisation requiring a reasonably secure network. Policies relating to network traffic between computers can be the most variable of all, because a company's network is a unique component of its computing infrastructure and because companies use their networks in different ways.

Securing databases

Data security is paramount to the successful operation of a business, so steps must be taken to protect sensitive data in the context of a company's activities. Databases are an integral part of any business network. They offer a wide variety of advantages to the company, including shared and controlled access, minimal redundancy, and data consistency and integrity. Database systems need to be designed to provide the best protection possible from all types of human, physical and logical attacks. This design should be coupled with a comprehensive security policy that covers all personnel in the company.

The major need for security in the database management system (DBMS) is to protect sensitive data while revealing non-sensitive data. Enquirers gain

An example of network security policies

- *Blocking of unauthorised Internet access.* All users must be automatically blocked from accessing Internet sites identified as inappropriate for company use. This access restriction must be enforced by automated software that is updated frequently.

- *Segmentation of extranet connection network.* All extranet connections must be limited to separate network segments not directly connected to the corporate network.

- *Control of extranet connection access.* All extranet connections (connections to and from other companies' networks outside the corporation, either originating from the external company's remote network into the internal network or originating from the internal network going out to the external company's remote network) must limit external access to only those services authorised for the remote company. This access control must be enforced by IP addresses and TCP/UDP (i.e. Transmission Control Protocol/User Datagram Protocol) port filtering on the network equipment used to establish the connection.

- *System communication ports.* Systems communicating with other systems on the local network must be restricted to authorised communication ports. Communication ports for services not in use by operational software must be blocked by firewalls or router filters.

- *Inbound Internet communication ports.* Systems communication from the Internet to internal systems must be restricted to use by only authorised communication ports. Firewall filters must block communication ports for services not in use by operational system software. The default must be to block all ports and to make exceptions to allow specific ports required by system software.

- *Outbound Internet communication ports.* Systems communicating with the Internet must be restricted to use only authorised communication ports. Firewall filters must block communication ports for services not in use by operational system software. The default must be to block all ports and to make exceptions to allow specific ports required by system software.

access to data only with precise accurate information, in response from legitimate enquiries. Security control in databases can minimise and curb seemingly illegitimate queries, such as in the inference problem. Security controls also can diminish or restrict performance and manage access with authorised users permitted only to view or modify data.

Some DBMSs also allow certain types of data lock to be used, such as the integrity and sensitivity locks, which both help protect or maintain the sensitivity levels of elements in the database so that they cannot be changed by end users. Trusted front ends (a guard between the user and the DBMS) and commutative filter (an interface between the user and the DBMS) are also useful security controls.

There is a need to ensure differentiated security in databases to permit different levels of access to data, at differing levels of sensitivity. Multilevelled security management is based on partitioning the database and encryption of data using encryption modes or methods, such as block chaining and integrity locks. Partitioning involves the complete categorisation of data, ranking the sensitivity of data according to its security level.

Access decisions are founded on an access policy that consists of such factors as the need for availability of the data, acceptability of the access and legitimacy of the user. In security versus precision, the goal of security is to protect all sensitive data, whereas precision is to reveal as much non-sensitive data as possible. Overall the database should give specific answers to legitimate queries without interference from security requirements. The need to secure the database against the inference problem tends to shift the balances towards security, however.

The integrity of a database can be compromised when there is physical damage in the event of a disk crash, fire or power failure or when data is unreadable or corrupted. Back-up routines on systems as well as log files of transactions should be implemented to avoid the risk of losing data and information. Physical damage can be fixed by restoring the entire systems from back-ups, and logical damage can be repaired using the information in the log files to help restore the system to correct operation.

Two different types of database attack can be made by a user who can get inside the organisation with authorisation, username and password or who can access a database remotely using legitimate or illegitimate means. **Direct attack** is when an attacker directly tries to find the information from the database by using a specific query to obtain sensitive data and information directly from the database. **Indirect** or **inference attack** uses statistical measures to seek information from the database to infer the desired secured information or data.

A direct attack simply involves the attacker querying the database in an attempt to extract the sensitive data, whereas indirect attacks involve the attacker using several separate queries, then piecing them together to derive the sensitive data (Pfleeger 1997). These types of attacks make it difficult to secure the database without restricting the usefulness of the database. Suppressing sensitive data will make the database more secure but will obviously restrict its usefulness. Tracking the user's movements and disguising data will both help to prevent these attacks. But these too will also affect the efficiency of the database and data consistency.

The susceptibility of a company to inference attacks varies according to the amount and type of data that is made publicly accessible. As long as an enterprise allows external access to a database only through a web-based service, the threat of inference attack to a company is relatively low. This kind of control would allow no external access to sensitive information such as, for example, credit details or the orders of customers, so the amount of useful data that could be gleaned from any inference attack on a database would be minimal. Access control and user authentication can be used to stop unauthorised users from accessing restricted data when they are on-site as a contractor, visitor or employee.

The most important thing to remember when suppressing sensitive infor-mation is that the usefulness of the database might be restricted. When using many com-plementary security measures, performance can be negatively affected as well. It is important to try to find the right combination of security measures that allow the right type of access to data. If data misuse is suspected, additional security methods can be implemented, such as user tracking or multilevel security.

In addition to the protection of the network from active human interference, it is vital to utilise a strong form of virus protection on databases and to maintain this protection by keeping the virus definitions up to date.

The best approach to database protection is layered security. Combining several techniques will give the database the best protection; if one layer is breached there are other layers to prevent access. Such techniques as access restriction through views, query analysis, encryption, passwords, physical separation, monitoring, locks and access protocols should be combined to achieve the layered security. This layered defence design will lead to a more secure database management system, allowing the company to utilise the benefits that databases offer without com-promising the security of the enterprise data (Pfleeger & Pfleeger 2003, p. 357).

The network architecture within an organisation can also serve to act as extra security. If we assume the network architecture shown in figure 6.1, it can be seen that measures can been taken to secure a company's databases against attacks. External access to the web server (and to the underlying database) is controlled using firewalls, coupled with an intrusion detection system (IDS). The installed IDS will enable logging of all activity through this path, which will help to alert the company's IT department to any unusual activity — as well as gathering digital evidence for use in a forensic investigation after a suspected attack.

Backing up each database in the company is essential as information loss can be devastating. Back-ups should be automated to occur nightly, with a compre-hensive back-up at the end of the week. This comprehensive back-up should be securely stored off-site, carefully following the standard operating procedure for this task, which will be detailed in the company's security policy. Back-ups should be written to an appropriate storage system, preferably one that can offer high-volume secure storage.

IT Risk 7.3 details the consequences for a New Zealand firm after its database security was breached.

Firm faces ruin after database break-in

Aria Farm, a food company in Waikato, faces potential ruin following industrial sabotage, says director Erik Arndt.

Computer hackers have broken into the database and emailed 3000 of the company's customers, saying a company product — lamb chips — is being recalled due to an infectious agent.

The warning has since been posted on Internet message boards.

Arndt said the full product recall was emailed to his customers at the weekend as coming from his own company's computers, and had the potential to destroy a business.

The attacker also announced free chips were available at a Takapuna coffee bar, but they tasted awful.

The first Arndt and wife Anna knew about the fake recall notice was on Monday morning through replies to the email message.

'We got in touch with supermarkets straight away and let them know it was all a hoax,' he said. Arndt also reported the incident to police, who have said they are investigating.

Aria Farm employs 14 people at its Hamilton factory and has an annual turnover of $3 million.

The company was formed in 1997 after Mr and Mrs Arndt became frustrated by low returns from their 526ha dry stock farm at Aria in the King Country.

They now produce beef, lamb and chicken chips; lamb strips with basil and mint; and easy-flow mince.

Last year they launched some of the products in Britain through supermarket chain Sainsburys. Their UK company was reported to have invested $NZ3 million in a processing plant in Blaenavon, near Pontypool in Wales, where it received a grant of over $NZ1 million from the Welsh Development Agency towards establishment costs and for marketing.

In New Zealand, the company has also received a Government 'enterprise award' to help it develop export markets in Australia and South America.

Arndt said computer hacking was not something a small family business in Hamilton would expect.

'We're busy going for export licences. We were busy focusing on food safety … We weren't focused at all on anything like a computer hacker.

(continued)

Chapter 7 Securing network operations, databases and applications

Security of software and applications

Every organisation uses software of a proprietary or specialised nature, and some organisations develop software in-house or customise it for their own use, which puts the organisation at risk from any kind of insecurity in the software. Therefore software security is an important issue for all organisations and another risk that needs to be managed.

Although, as we observed in chapter 3, the need to develop a culture of security has been recognised since the 1990s, and even with the widespread use of software quality systems, it is recognised that software has not always been and, in some cases, still is not part of the software development lifecycle. Security is often still added to software as a plug-in or an after-thought. It is often not specified as part of the functional requirements for a user and has not appeared as part of the process models incorporated in common lifecycle models. Therefore it is important for the software developer to begin to incorporate security into the process model so that at each step of the software development process security then becomes an important and integral part. It is also necessary to use some kind of secure coding or programming methodology to ensure that secure code is the result of every project.

Good software engineering

Typically most programmers and software engineers have learned one of the two major software engineering process models. The **waterfall software engineering process model** is characterised by a multistep process whereby steps follow each other in a linear, one-way fashion. The **spiral model** has steps in phases that execute in a spiral fashion, repeating at different levels with each revolution of the model.

However, security can be embedded in all aspects of the process, from requirements to system architecture, to coding to testing, and is not dependent on the software engineering process model being used. If the organisation or software developer has not embedded security issues in their software process model, the user requirements should define the specific security needs, if they are to be designed into the project.

Significant issues that need to be dealt with during the design process are:
• The system architecture must reflect the user requirements, and these

requirements should be mapped to subsystems and components. Security components must be part of this process.

- The coding process for each component can have a significant effect on the security response of a system, and security components must be part of this process, too.
- The testing phase of a project is the opportunity to determine compliance with requirements and even discover unexpected behaviour that results in unexpected security issues that did not arise earlier in the design process.

This implies a level of testing that is distributed throughout the development process and must have an accompanying set of requirements to stipulate stepwise security testing.

Sound coding

Insecurities can enter code if either of the following errors occurs: desired functionality is not included, or unknown and undesired behaviour is inadvertently programmed into the code. The first of these is easy to detect by rigorous testing, but the second flaw is more obscure and to some extent undetectable since the behaviour will be unknown until it occurs.

Buffer overflows are seen as a major problem, and many common breaches are caused in this way. The basic fault is that a buffer, a storage space, of fixed size is allocated, then it is overwritten, in some way, with more data than it is designed to hold. This usually happens because of poor programming and can be caused by strings of the wrong length; that is, buffer size mismatches. It can be attributed to poor programming skills and practice or known weaknesses of a programming language or both.

Other errors arise from incomplete mediation within coding, which allows parameters to be out of range or tampered with. Another common error is the 'time of check to time of use' error whereby, for the sake of ease of programming, the time of use of (for example) a file lags behind the time of access and checking of the file — the file could be substituted or damaged in the intervening period.

It is therefore most important to deal properly with input to programs and validate it in such a way that one presumes the code is hostile, intent on causing a buffer overflow, then code cautiously, ensuring that such a buffer overflow cannot take place. Strings should be handled properly, and string length should be determined beforehand to ensure security.

All processes should be designed to run with least privilege. The programmer needs to design and plan with an understanding of the desired nature of the software's interaction with the operating system and system resources. Whenever the software accesses a file, a system component or another program, the issue of appropriate access control needs to be addressed.

In summary, then, it will be seen that secure practice includes building security into the software development process from requirements to testing. A large software development company could have a default set of security requirements attached to all projects providing a security baseline. A code review should also be part of the process so that another programmer from a separate team walks through the code to make sure all requirements have been met. Testing, then, should be carried out with the same emphasis on security as part of the requirements.

Fundamentally new security models, methods needed

We urgently need to expand our focus on short-term patching to also include longer-term development of new methods for designing and engineering secure systems. Addressing cyber security for the longer term requires a vigorous ongoing program of fundamental research to explore the science and develop the technologies necessary to design security into computing and networking systems and software from the ground up. Fundamental research is characterized by its potential for broad, rather than specific, application and includes farsighted, high-payoff research that provides the basis for technological progress.

The vast majority of cyber security research conducted to date has been based on the concept of perimeter defense. In this model, what is 'inside' an information system or network is protected from an 'outside' attacker who tries to penetrate it to gain access to or control its data and system resources. However, once the perimeter is breached (whether by virtue of a technical weakness such as a software vulnerability or an operational weakness such as an employee being bribed or tricked to reveal a password), the attacker has entirely free rein and can compromise every system connected in a network with not much more effort than is required to compromise only one.

This weakness of the perimeter defense strategy has become painfully clear. But it is not the only problem with the model. The distinction between 'outside' and 'inside' breaks down amid the proliferation of wireless and embedded technologies connected to networks and the increasing complexity of networked 'systems of systems'.

One element of a more realistic model for cyber security may be a principle of mutual suspicion: Every component of a system or network is always suspicious of every other component, and access to data and other resources must be constantly reauthorized. More generally, cyber security would be an integral part of the design process for any large, complex system or network. Security add-ons will always be necessary to fix some security problems, but ultimately there is no substitute for systemwide end-to-end security that is minimally intrusive.

Source: PITAC 2005, pp. 12–13.

Information Technology Security & Risk Management

Summary

Network security is a significant challenge. A breach is potentially an enormous problem with major consequences for an organisation. Threats can be unstructured, in the form of viruses, Trojans, worms and other malware, or targeted and structured attacks in the form of distributed or localised denial of service attacks. The motives of attackers vary greatly, but can be broadly seen as: satisfaction, profit, dissatisfaction, business competition, policy-making and price-setting, information warfare and terrorism. Most attacks use a common set of steps: probing, scanning, compromise of a user account and the use of a packet-sniffing program.

The approaches to security differ between countries, perhaps owing to different business needs, cultural differences and different perceived threats. The AusCERT 2004 survey suggests that Australian companies' approach to IT security is maturing. Australian businesses are increasingly adopting security measures based on policies and procedures, standards and training, qualifications and awareness of staff.

Networks must be secured from physical threats, both natural or environmental disasters (fire, flood, lightning and so on) and unauthorised intruders. A sound information security policy is the most important method of protecting any system. The policy should cover external attack, accidental damage from authorised users and intentional damage from authorised users. A security policy should cover people, policies, procedures and technology. Data security is crucial for protecting a company's sensitive data. The challenge is to prevent unauthorised access while not impeding legitimate users. Insecure software also presents a security issue for organisations. Software is often developed without due regard to security. Security is provided as an afterthought or as a patch after the software has been released. Software developers should implement secure code from the ground up.

In chapter 8, we examine the security of e-business in which we see the convergence of some of the technology we have already examined with traditional business models to enable potentially complete solutions to customers through technology and services.

back door, p. 192

compromise, p. 191

direct attack, p. 205

hacker, p. 188

indirect or inference attack, p. 205

key logger, p. 191

probing, p. 191

root, p. 191

scanning, p. 191

security policy, p. 201

sniffer, p. 189

spiral model, p. 208

waterfall software engineering
    process model, p. 208

Questions

1. Compile a list of the possible motives of hackers, and rank them according to what you consider to be the biggest threats.
2. Briefly describe the steps common to most hacking attacks.
3. In your opinion, how important is it to have trained and qualified IT security staff? What role should they play in the organisation's IT security and risk management?
4. Discuss the need to achieve database security and efficient access for legitimate users. Is a trade-off necessary, or can both requirements be fully met?
5. Why should an organisation adopt secure coding?
6. What is the involvement of a user in the software development process?

Case study
7: Network security

In this chapter we again deal with some of the security issues raised by Elisabeth Chan in the last chapter.

To recap: Elisabeth has improved her organisational and technical skills, and her company is growing. She has gained a new awareness of the IT security environment in which she is trading, and has decided to go back to basics and have a look at her network architecture and its security. Elisabeth now also has a good understanding that a secure network is founded on a sound security policy. She is using e-commerce effectively, and her network has grown and resembles the one in figure 5.7 (p. 156).

Questions

1. Prepare a network security policy for Elisabeth's network.
2. Given the organisation chart supplied in chapter 5 and the network architecture in chapter 6, prepare brief reports to Elisabeth on the risk to her network from internal attack or of an inference attack on her databases (i.e. who might attack, and how would they do it?).

3. Prepare a brief overview to Elisabeth (who is not an experienced software engineer) of the pros and cons of starting developing software for the control system of her new micro mini widgets.

Suggested reading

AusCERT 2003 and 2004, *Australian Computer Crime and Security Survey*, www.auscert.org.au/crimesurvey.

President's Information Technology Advisory Committee (PITAC) 2005, Report to the President February 2005, *Cyber Security: A Crisis of Prioritization*, National Coordination Office for Information Technology Research and Development, Arlington, VA.

References

Australian Computer Emergency Response Team (AusCERT) 2003, *2003 Australian Computer Crime and Security Survey*, www.auscert.org.au/crimesurvey.

—— 2004, *2004 Australian Computer Crime and Security Survey*, www.auscert.org.au/crimesurvey.

Computer Security Institute/FBI 2003, *2003 Computer Crime and Security Survey*, www.gocsi.com/awareness/fbj.html;jsessionid=JRSJPVOAGXROQSNDBCSKHY.

Cyberpunk 2004, 'The hacker's ethics', accessed 2 September 2004, http://project.cyberpunk.ru/idb/hacker_ethics.html.

Foltz, B 2004, 'Cyber terrorism, computer crime and reality', *Information Management and Computer Security*, vol. 12, no. 2, p. 154.

HKCERT, HKPF & Information Technology Services Department 2003, *Information Security Survey 2003*, www.hkcert.org.

Pfleeger, CP 1997, *Security in Computing*, 2nd edn, Prentice Hall, Englewood Cliffs, NJ.

Pfleeger, CP & Pfleeger, SL 2003, *Security in Computing*, 3rd edn, Prentice Hall, Upper Saddle River, NJ.

President's Information Technology Advisory Committee (PITAC) 2005, Report to the President February 2005, *Cyber Security: A Crisis of Prioritization*, National Coordination Office for Information Technology Research and Development, Arlington, VA, pp. 12–13.

Chapter 8

Strategies for e-business security

Learning objectives

After studying this chapter, you should be able to:

- describe e-business infrastructure

- explain the requirements for a secure e-business transaction

- describe electronic payment systems security

- describe the types of security technology available to preserve the security of an electronic financial transaction

- discuss m-commerce security

- explain smart card and biometric security technology

- describe legal issues in e-business.

Chapter overview

E-business in general and e-commerce in particular are commercial activities that deal with the exchange of goods and services in which the electronic communication medium plays a central role. It includes communication of information associated with the exchange of goods and services, management of payments relating to this exchange, negotiation and trading of financial instruments and management of information. However, the most important contribution of communication media, especially the Internet, is the creation of a marketplace in cyberspace. This electronic marketplace has been constantly evolving through innovative business models. These new business models have challenged the logic and assumptions of traditional business models. In certain cases these models enable complete customer solutions through the convergence of technology and services, and in others they allow for tighter integration in the organisation as well as in business partners.

By definition, e-business involves the exchange of confidential information. This chapter examines the security issues surrounding e-business, looking as always at confidentiality, integrity and availability.

E-business fundamentals

Although **e-commerce** refers to the actual electronic financial exchanges of value and **e-business** refers to the wider spectrum of activities, such as the facilitation and support of business transactions, the two terms have in most cases been used interchangeably. E-business via the Internet operates globally, 24 hours a day, throughout the year. Having its roots in simple electronic data interchange (EDI), it has transformed into various paradigms and models, such as the well-known business-to-consumer (B2C) and business-to-business (B2B) models, as well as consumer-to-business (C2B) and consumer-to-consumer (C2C) and other initiatives, such as e-government.

The most prevalent e-business models in the contemporary business paradigm are summarised in figure 8.1. The first category represents businesses with a web presence, in which sellers use their websites for a variety of purposes, such as advertisement and information. This category often represents sole business proprietors, whose objective in having a website is to create awareness about certain services, objects or trends. The second category represents the sell-side solutions, which also constitutes the major portion of web-based businesses. In this category, businesses allow customers to make purchases of their offerings online. In the third category, it is actually the buyer that brings different vendors together, such as that the buyer takes advantage of the services offered by different solution providers on the Internet, such as those provided by Commerce One and SAP. The fourth category represents creation of value networks around certain products or services. The creation of networks between organisations is becoming increasingly prevalent and often tends to yield enormous power; that is, the power to create new markets (i.e. common e-marketplaces and e-procurement) and dominate old ones, change structures of communication and collaboration, and mobilise coalitions in a short period. From a buyer point of view, they get a complete solution, and from the vendor point of view, individual companies become involved in many complementary e-markets, ranging from a few transaction-oriented exchanges to numerous partnership-driven value networks.

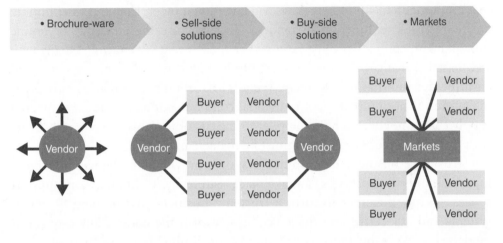

| Figure 8.1 | E-business models |

A fundamental driver of these trends is the quest for adding value to the goods and services offered to customers. However, generated value frequently transcends industry sectors as companies from different fields collaborate to create value for the customer. As a result, boundaries between industry sectors disappear and traditional industry sectors overlap in new organisational models (Tapscott 1999). Globalisation plays an important role in influencing change in the structure of value chains, as many markets are 'born global' and hence require fast actions from companies acting in them (Timmers 2000).

Another major force of change is the shifting of customer preference towards personal customisation and quick gratification, which encourages chain members to surround their joint customers in new ways. The continuously changing roles of the chain members result in power shifts in the traditional chains and redefine the chains (Andrews & Hahn 1998). In addition to the power shifts some nodes in the traditional value chain are totally removed (disintermediation) whereas others are added (infomediation). Linear value chains can no longer respond to the requirements of the turbulent environment. The linear model might have suited value creation in the industrial economy, but it is insufficient in several ways for defining the much more complex value creation of today. The new value chain, on the other hand, resembles an interwoven web of enterprises that behave like amoeba-type organisms: constantly changing their shape, expanding, shrinking, multiplying, dividing, shifting and mutating.

A fundamental objective driving business towards these horizontal partnerships is the concern for cost reduction and efficiency in the overall business, and modern information and communication technology via the Internet allows these partnerships to come to fruition. Isolated business activities, such as marketing, material procurement and stock management, manufacturing and distribution, are reorganised to function in tandem. To maximise the efficiency of online procurement, companies must tie together their inventory control systems with web-based exchanges. Online sales need to be linked to order entry systems and customer relationship management. What is important here is that the process of integration is not limited to an individual company but applies to all firms in a supply chain, moving from the supplier to the customer. This will naturally bring with it distinct security risks that must be managed.

A trusted e-business environment is one in which exchanges of information, money and services can take place seamlessly. Technology and support processes come together to form a trusted e-business environment. Payment systems and associated security mechanisms form the core of any e-business model. However, e-business security in not just limited to the security of information exchange between the customer or business partners and the selling organisation or host organisation; it is also focused inwardly such that there is no intrusion from within the organisational information systems. Although intra-organisational security has been discussed in other chapters, it is briefly touched upon here.

IT risk 8.1

An end to electronic commerce?

E-business and e-commerce both depend on customers' willingness to take part in electronic payment via their banks. The recent combined growth in phishing via Trojans and banking scams has been undermining confidence in Internet banking and e-business, as the following extract shows.

> Trojans, which are almost impossible for banks to detect, could undermine confidence in electronic commerce and force the banks to act, a confidential industry-funded report has concluded.

> Banks have rejected card readers and other forms of secure authentication based on smart tokens because of their high cost compared to passwords.

But the Association of Payment Clearing Services (APACS), the trade body for banks, said it was only a matter of time before online banks rolled out two-factor authentication.

'There is quite a debate going on in the industry about two-factor authentication. I do not think it is a question of if banks are going to use it, but when,' said an APACS spokeswoman.

The report, by the Information Security Forum, a security group funded by 270 banks and businesses, concluded that the appearance of phishing Trojans could tip the economic balance in favour of two-factor authentication.

The banks have been working with Barclaycard on a trial to test user reaction to two-factor technology. Customers insert chip and PIN cards into a portable card reader to generate a one-time eight-digit passnumber to access banking and retail sites.

The Anti-Phishing Working Group, a coalition of banks, businesses and IT suppliers, reported a 42 per cent increase in phishing e-mails between December and January, equivalent to a 30 per cent average monthly growth in its latest update at the end of February.

'There is no business case to introduce two-factor authentication for consumers yet. But Trojans may change the cost equation. We may see them in the next year for business accounts. The problem is we do not know how bad it is going to be,' said Colin Dixon, author of the Information Security Forum report.

Although the cost of fraud caused by phishing is minimal compared to credit card fraud, banks are concerned Trojans could damage confidence in e-banking, the report said.

'With traditional e-mail phishing you know you are under attack because you get e-mail bounce-back. This allows the banks to prepare and put in a number of restrictions. With Trojans you are not going to be prepared,' said Dixon.

Phishing Trojans, which can infect users through websites or e-mail, first started to appear on the Internet towards the end of last year. The most sophisticated wait until users visit their online bank then create false screens asking for users' log-in details and passwords.

Source: Goodwin 2005.

▪ Electronic business security

Figure 8.2 (p. 220) illustrates a typical network security model that most web-based businesses follow to project their information resources from within the company. A typical network in contemporary business is based on a firewall, which is a configuration of hardware and a set of programs that reside in a network server and protect the network resources from outside access. The network that the firewall protects is called DMZ (demilitarised zone).

Usually a firewall works closely with routers. A router is a network traffic manager that acts as a liaison between sub-networks and manages data to and from the segments to which it is attached. Together with a firewall, it acts as a filter and determines which network packets are worth forwarding to their destination. Generally a firewall is installed at the edges of a network such that no incoming request could get direct access to network resources. Firewalls utilise a number of screening techniques. The most commonly used involves the screening of requests to ensure that they come from an acceptable IP address and domain name. In the case of mobile users, it uses secure logon procedures and authentication certificates to verify access. However, despite all these measures, it is not uncommon for intrusion to occur, for which a typical defensive measure used is an IDS (intrusion detection system). An IDS detects break-ins or attempts made to break in by observation of security logs or audit information.

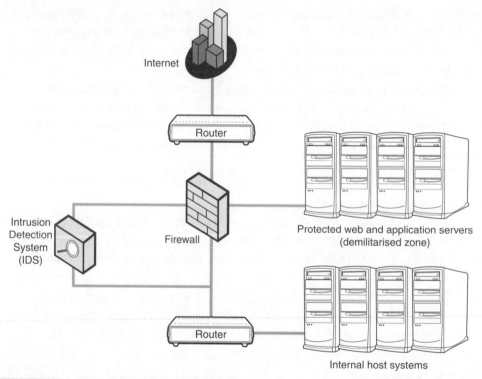

Figure 8.2   A typical network security model

In case of a web-based commercial organisation, motivation of an attack increases owing to the monetary exchanges with business partners and customers. Therefore, quite like the conventional business environment, monetary exchanges in cyberspace are also at the peril of pilferages, fraudulent behaviour and open theft. Disparity in base technology employed by businesses and customers, inconsistency in business processes and differences in security infrastructures employed by businesses make the creation of a trusted and safe environment even more cumbersome. That is why numerous payment systems exist and likewise a range of security techniques that make up for the secure transaction in the contemporary e-business environment. The following sections discuss the payment systems and their security requirements.

Electronic payment systems security

An **electronic payment system** comprises the process and components that make up the electronic exchange of money in return for goods or services. The foremost objectives of an electronic payment system are twofold: first, to create an environment of honesty in which a payer is confident in the process of making a payment for the goods and services being purchased; and second, to prevent an unauthorised party becoming involved in the process. This process, on the whole, further requires elements of trust, honesty and privacy.

The e-business environment is, however, different from the conventional business environment, and the creation of an environment of trust, honesty and privacy is different and much more difficult. In conventional business, face-to-face conversation or first-hand knowledge of goods and services makes up for a lot of misconceptions; however, in e-business it is largely dependent on textual information. In general, the e-business environment is affected by the following factors:

- The Internet is an open system without established security architecture.
- The seller is not physically present in an online transaction.
- The buyer is not physically present in an online transaction.
- Only a virtual representation of the goods is available.
- Payment and delivery of goods are not synchronised.

In addition, an electronic payment system needs to cater for the needs of a global market and has to be cost-effective, technologically interoperable and strong enough to prevent any unauthorised interference. However, in spite of these relatively straightforward requirements, which have been recognised for a long time, there is no standardised payment system. More than two dozen electronic payment standards are being used in e-business. Among these are AIMP (Anonymous Internet Mercantile Protocol) by AT&T Bell Labs, CAFE (Conditional Access for Europe) for the European Union, and SET (Secure Electronic Transaction) promoted by MasterCard and Visa. Subsequently, many software and hardware systems are based on these open standards, including CyberCash, Digicash, Mondex, NetBill and NetCheque.

Although the variety of these products indicates the fierce competition among the electronic payment solution providers, it makes it extremely difficult for ordinary users to pick an appropriate payment mechanism. At the same time, financial transactions in cyberspace are carried out through intermediaries, EFT (electronic funds transfer) and electronic currencies. This complexity further complicates the security of an electronic transaction, as it is not easy to address the security needs of all the systems and processes involved in a transaction.

Types of electronic payment system

Before examining the types of electronic payment system, it is appropriate to discuss the working of the conventional process of payment, to ensure that an understanding of the necessary underpinnings for a payment system exists. In a conventional purchasing process that involves modes of payment other than cash, settlement of the payment takes place in a financial network, as shown in figure 8.3.

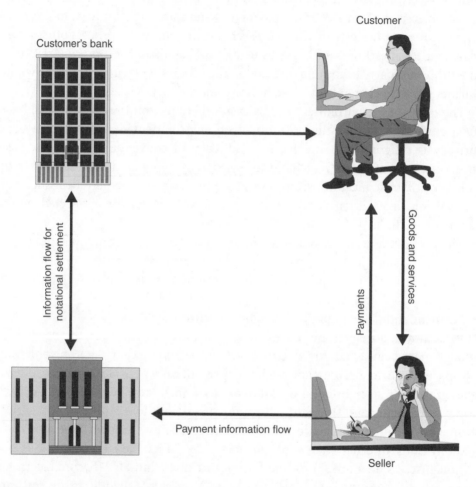

Figure 8.3 **Conventional model for payment**

The medium of exchange of money is either a credit card or a cheque, and the payment flows from the buyer to the seller. Cash payments require withdrawal from a customer's account and its transfer to the merchant's or seller's account, whereas the non-cash payments — that is, credit payments — are settled through information flows rather than cash flows between banks. In the case of credit payments, payments are settled between the bank of the payer and that of the payee through notational means. That means there is no cash flow; however,

the respective banks update debit and credit accounts by the information associated with the purchase. Nonetheless, these two modes of payment involve certain intermediaries, which are involved in the process of clearance of payments and perform such tasks as credit card services and cheque clearance. The information associated with the purchases, therefore, comprises some or all of the following:
- information on customer and seller identity and directions and instructions about the settlement of payments, which happens without either party having to reveal their financial information
- information concerning credit cards and/or bank accounts, such as account number and credit card number
- monetary value to be transferred.

In the electronic paradigm, there are three major ways of settling payments: payment clearing services, electronic funds transfer and electronic currency.

Payment clearing services

A typical purchase in cyberspace involves locating and selecting products, asking for a quotation on price, negotiating or accepting the price, and finally an agreement between the buyer and seller on payment. These activities are followed by establishing the validity and identity of the payment mechanism, shipment of products and receipts. However, in the absence of face-to-face interaction it is not possible for either party — that is, seller or buyer — to develop the environment of trust and therefore they look for a trusted third party — a **payment clearing service** — to provide for security, identification and authentication, as well as payment support.

Figure 8.4 (p. 224) illustrates an online transaction using an intermediary. In this situation the role of the intermediary is not just that of settling the payments but also that of confirmation of the order by establishing the authenticity and identity of the buyer and the payment information. In figure 8.4, the ordering and confirmation are two activities that occur online; the settlement of payment occurs offline by the intermediary. The payment here is based on the concept of traditional funds transfer and utilises private value networks.

The intermediary in this figure adds to the efficiency of the market. It resolves uncertainties about security and identity and relieves the sellers of the requirement to set up hardware and software constraints to facilitate online payment clearing processes. In this case the intermediary maintains membership and payment information for both sellers and buyers. A customer sends the seller only the customer identification number assigned by the intermediary. When the order is received, the intermediary authenticates and validates it with both the customer and the seller, and takes care of sensitive information, such as payment information, on behalf of the customer as well as the seller.

The advantage of using this type of payment system is the separation of sensitive information from non-sensitive, which eases the concerns with security in cyberspace. Such a system does not necessarily require elaborate security systems and works on the trust that its processes develop with sellers and customers. However, a major disadvantage of this type of system is that only registered members can make purchases, and consequently one-off customers are unable to make purchases.

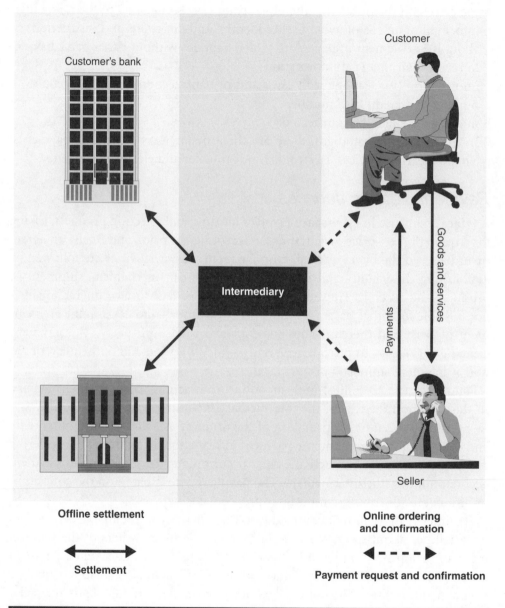

Figure 8.4   An online transaction using an intermediary

Payment by electronic funds transfer

The majority of electronic systems rely on electronic funds transfer (EFT). In this kind of payment system no intermediary is involved; however, the credit card information of the customer is sent along with the order. In simple terms, it is an application of the traditional EDI (electronic data interchange); in this case it's the financial EDI (see figure 8.5). In **electronic funds transfer**, credit card numbers or electronic cheques are exchanged on secured private networks between banks and sellers. It utilises an online payment service to add capabilities to process orders, accounts and receipts, and EFT to clear payments and settle accounts.

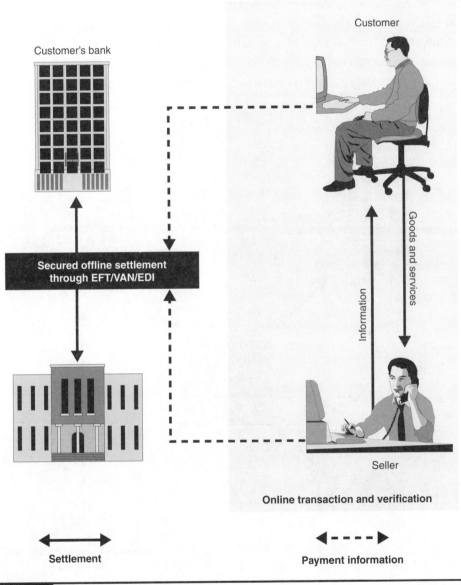

| Figure 8.5 | Electronic funds transfer |

This type of payment system makes use of **SET (Secure Electronic Transaction)**, which is a protocol that ensures security of financial transactions in cyberspace. SET has been supported by MasterCard, Visa and Microsoft among others. It works on the principle that the customer is allocated a digital certificate, and the transaction is executed and authenticated by using a combination of digital certificates and digital signatures among the buyer, seller and the buyer's bank such that the privacy and confidentiality of the transaction is protected. SET utilises SSL (Secure Sockets Layer), Microsoft's STT (Secure Transaction Technology) and Secure Hypertext Transfer Protocol (S-HTTP) of Terisa System.

Although these payment systems use EFT, the funds transferred are notational. At the same time the information associated with the notational transfer is sensitive and consequently at the peril of being intercepted and misused. The advantages of this type of payment system is the ready purchasing facility; however, the major challenge is to ensure interoperability between different protocols and the integrity and security of the payment messages being transmitted.

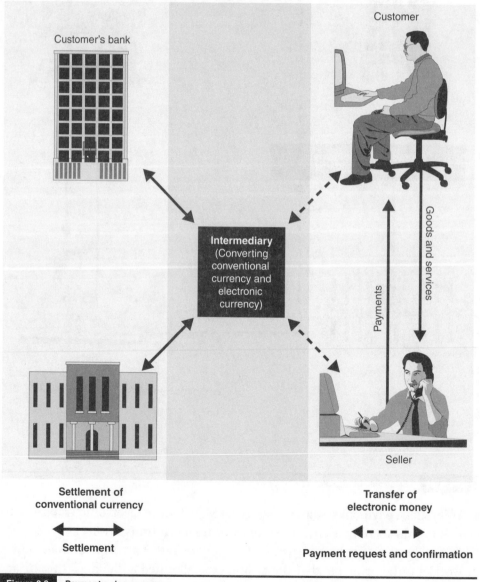

Figure 8.6   **Payment using currency**

Payment by electronic currency

This type of payment system uses an alternative to conventional currency in cyberspace, which is in the form of electronic currency. Payment by **electronic currency** does not transmit the payment information; instead it transmits a digital product that represents the value. The obvious advantages that these types of payment systems present are anonymity and convenience.

This kind of payment scenario (see figure 8.6) also utilises an intermediary, but this intermediary only acts as a digital bank and converts the conventional money, such as dollars, into tokens or e-cash. However, for electronic cash the customer requires e-cash software, which stores digital money signed by the intermediary (i.e. the bank). This money is signed by the bank and stored on the customer's local computer and could be spent at any web shopfront that accepts e-cash. The way it works illustrates that the customer needs to open an account with an e-cash accepting bank using the e-cash software. Money deposited by the customer is converted into electronic money, and when the customer runs the e-cash software for the first time a pair of RSA keys is generated. RSA is a public key cipher used to encrypt messages and to make digital signatures. It allows secure transactions between the customer and the bank. Once the customers have obtained e-cash, they can spend it on any website that accepts e-cash. However, the sellers have to pay a nominal fee to redeem e-cash.

As with other electronic payment systems, security is also an issue in this kind of payment system. With electronic currency, the security concerns are related to counterfeiting, liability and double spending.

Electronic payment systems security requirements

There is no standardised set of requirements to establish the security of an electronic transaction, for security of a transaction depends on the type of payment system and its features and trust assumptions. Nevertheless, the last section identifies a set of generic requirements that a payment system must embody to ensure transaction security. These are: integrity and authorisation, confidentiality, authentication, availability and non-repudiation, which are discussed in more detail below.

Integrity and authorisation

Integrity of a transaction illustrates that there is no unauthorised modification to the information exchanged between the buyer, seller, intermediaries and the banks involved in the transaction. A payment system must not allow any money to be taken out of a customer's or seller's account without their explicit consent and authorisation.

Authorisation of payment is an important aspect of an electronic transaction. There should therefore be a mechanism to obtain unequivocal consent, which should also disallow payments without an explicit consent. Electronic transactions could be authorised in three major ways: out-band authorisation, password authorisation and signature authorisation.

Out-band authorisation

In this type of authorisation, the bank advises the payer of a transaction carried out on the payer's behalf. The payer is required to verify the payment, by accepting or rejecting the payment by using a secured out-band medium, such as through mail or telephone. This is important to reduce the possibility of misuse in case of credit card number theft; otherwise anyone with the knowledge of someone else's credit card number could make purchases fraudulently. Legitimate users must know their account status; therefore the bank verifies the statement with the payer so that the payer knows about the transactions. However, if the customer or payer does not respond within a specified time limit, the transaction is approved automatically.

Password authorisation

A password-protected transaction requires a cryptographic check value to be included in every piece of information that emanates from the authoriser of payment. This value is worked out using the secret that is known to the authorising or verifying parties involved in a transaction. Generally this secret is a personal identification number, a password or a shared secret code.

Signature authorisation

A signature-based authorisation requires a digital signature of the authorising party. This method of transaction requires signing the messaging by using a secret signing key such that anybody who knows the corresponding public key could verify the authenticity of the signatures. This form of authorisation also provides for non-repudiation.

Confidentiality

Confidentiality of transaction is not just limited to the current transaction; it also means the previous history of transactions between the parties involved in the current transaction. This is sought to stop unauthorised profiling of customers and their behaviour. A payment system has to ensure that information is not made available to any party other than the ones involved in the transaction and that the information provided remains within the legal bounds of transaction stakeholders.

Authentication

Authentication deals with ensuring that stakeholders involved in the transaction are actually who they claim to be. It is process of associating a unique identity with each stakeholder, such as the order number, customer identification numbers and password. Using these unique forms of identification, customers and sellers can track orders and order stock and banks can settle payments.

Availability

Parties involved in a business transaction always require the safety of their money. A transaction therefore either has to be undertaken in full, or it should not take place at all; there are no two ways about it. None of the stakeholders in the transaction would like to lose their money at any cost. That is why features like the **availability** of the hardware and software systems and reliability of the process as well as the equipment involved in the process are of utmost importance. These features assume that the networking services and all other hardware and software components are fully tested and dependable and that appropriate measures have been taken to secure the transaction from within the system as well as when it is in transit. These features also require appropriate recovery and back-up strategies and the availability of resynchronisation protocols. At the same time the onus of availability and reliability also falls on the buyer or customers, for it is their duty to keep their systems free of viruses and malicious code and to insulate their systems from intrusion.

Non-repudiation

In simple terms **non-repudiation** is the process that establishes or makes known the sender to the receiver. It works as an accountability mechanism, so that the identity of the imitator of a message can be established or the sender would know that a message intended for a particular user has actually been delivered. This control ensures denial of information to unauthorised users and is generally applied at the sender and receiver ends. A digital certificate is an example of this control. A digital certificate uses encryption technology and works as a digital stamp.

The following section describes the technological solutions available for taking care of these requirements.

Security techniques for electronic payment systems

The underpinning objectives of the electronic payment system's security are to provide confidentiality, integrity, authentication, identification, availability and non-repudiation of the business transactions. Technology available to address these dimensions of security is discussed below.

Cryptography

Cryptography (see chapter 5) is used mainly to maintain the confidentiality of a message. A range of cryptographic methods is available for user authentication, secret communication and non-repudiation. The Internet is an open system, and these methods or techniques work as essential tools for providing a secure platform for secure payment systems. **Cryptography** is a process by which plaintext is scrambled into ciphered text and then changed back or deciphered. The fundamental objectives of cryptography are to maintain:

- *confidentiality*, such that the information cannot be comprehended by unauthorised users, even if they somehow gain access to the information
- *integrity*, such that the information cannot be altered and, if there is an alteration, it could be detected
- *non-repudiation*, such that the creator or sender of the information cannot deny the creation or transmission of the information
- *authentication*, such that the sender and receiver of information can identify each other and their respective destiny.

The systems that embody some or all of these are called **cryptosystems**. The sections below describe some of the commonly available cryptography techniques.

Symmetric cryptography

As described in chapter 5, symmetric cryptography is also called private key cryptography. In this technique, the parties involved in communication have a common secret, hence the name 'symmetric'. This secret is called the key, which encrypts and decrypts the message. The message authentication follows a cryptographic check value, which is a function of both the key and the message. The check value is called message authentication code (MAC). This type of cryptography is important to the SSL (Secure Sockets Layer) protocol that is used for authentication, detection of alteration and encryption over TCP/IP networks. SSL uses Data Encryption Standard (DES), which uses a 40-bit and 56-bit key to encrypt and decrypt information.

Asymmetric cryptography

This type of cryptography, unlike symmetric cryptography, does not require the keys to be transmitted. In this technique the keys are not keys; in fact they are numbers. It involves a pair of keys, that is, a public and a private key, which are related to an entity involved in the transaction process that needs to authenticate their identity electronically or to sign or encrypt data. Each public key is published; however, the related private key is kept secret. Information encrypted with a public key is decrypted only by the corresponding private key. In simple terms, the information communicated to a person could be encrypted by using the public key of that person, whereas it could be decrypted only with the private key. Public key encryption requires much more computation than the private key and is therefore not appropriate for large amounts of data. Common examples of this kind of cryptography are RSA (Rivest-Shamir-Adleman) cryptography and ECC (Elliptic Curve Cryptography).

Hybrid cryptography

A hybrid cryptosystem combines the best of the two worlds; that is, public and private key cryptography (see figure 8.7). When a message is encrypted the information is also compressed. This compression saves transmission time and storage space. Patterns in plaintext are an important source of deciphering a message. The compressed information reduces the chances of pattern recognition. A hybrid cryptosystem creates a session key, which is a one-time-only secret key. This key is actually a random number that has been generated, and it works with a secure and fast encryption algorithm that ciphers the plaintext. Once the information is ciphered or encrypted, the session key is encrypted to the receiver's public key and is transmitted along with the encrypted text to the receiver. At the receiver's end, the receiver's cryptosystem uses their private key to obtain the session key that is then used to decrypt the encrypted text. A common example of hybrid cryptosystem is PGP (Pretty Good Privacy).

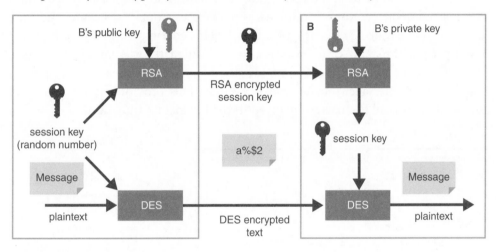

Figure 8.7   **Hybrid cryptosystem**

Message digest

A **message digest** is a technique used to maintain the integrity of a message. This is similar in operation to symmetric key encryption, as in this case the sender of a message computes a message digest by computing a one-way hash function using a secret key only known to the sender and receiver. The receiver needs to perform the same one-way hash function, using the secret key, which creates a new message digest. When the two digests are compared, they have to be identical for the sake of the message's integrity. If the digests are not identical, it means that their contents have been tampered with or corrupted in some way.

Digital certificates

Digital certificates are used to establish the authentication of the message and identification of the parties involved in a transaction. The testimonials of parties involved in a web-based transaction are established by means of a certificate that includes the name, serial number, expiration dates, a copy of the certificate holder's public key and the digital signature of the authority that issues the certificate. By means of this certificate the receiver verifies the genuineness of the certificate. This digital certificate is a data structure that is used in a public key system to bind an authenticated individual to a particular public key. The key is used for encryption and decryption of messages and digital signatures.

Digital signatures

Digital signatures are used for non-repudiation, such that the origin and destination of the message could be authenticated and substantiated. As mentioned earlier, in public key encryption, a private key could be used for encryption and a public key could be used for decryption. The signing software uses this method and, instead of encrypting the information, it creates a one-way hash of the data, then uses the private key to encrypt the hash. This encrypted hash, together with hashing algorithm and other information, is called the digital signature (see figure 8.8). It is as important as a handwritten signature because, once a person has signed the message, they cannot deny that. This provides non-repudiation and legally binds all the parties involved in the business transaction.

We accept your order and will deliver 1,000 cases of cheese at $500 each on 1/12/2004.

Bob

Robert Food (Messages@foods.com.au)
Foods, 44 Main Street, Adelaide, SA 5000
Phone (08) 8888 7777

Message

iQCVAwUBMARo7vgyLN8bw6ZVAQF6ygP/fDnuvdAhGID
WsSMXUIRMuNHYzdZ00cqkDb/Tc2+DuhuEa6GU03AgZY8
K9t5r9iua34E68pCxogUz009b1OcjNt6+o+704Z3j1YY9ijYM8
BWNaSp9L2W4nUuWBdlylWyoI/2PjjRVNZEtqtSRQnPEpJ2
IHtz9iGovHf0SqhSZKZs==+Q3l

Digital Signature

Figure 8.8   Digital signature

Electronic payment framework

Insecure transactions, or the fear of them, have been a major cause of the relative lack of popularity of business-to-consumer (B2C) electronic commerce. Much research and development is taking place to devise a secure and authentic payment system that includes technical as well as procedural controls. One such initiative is **IOTP (Internet Open Trading Protocol)**, which as the name implies is an open standard and is being developed as a standardised payment framework.

IOTP is a set of standards for electronic purchases. It is being developed by the Internet Engineering Task Force. IOTP introduces consistency into the process of electronic purchasing by providing the buyers, sellers and other stakeholders with a platform- and application-independent trading environment, regardless of the technology or payment system that they use. As an interoperable framework for e-commerce, IOTP classifies five roles in a web-based transaction: customer, seller, payment handler, delivery handler and customer support.

IOTP embodies a variety of payment systems, such as the SET (Secure Electronic Transaction), Mondex, DigiCash, CyperCash, credit and debit cards, and electronic cheques. IOTP takes care of a variety of activities involved in a purchase through the web: it facilitates placing an order, receiving an order, credit checking, and certification and handling of payment and delivery. It embodies customer support, which deals with customer dispute negotiation and resolution on behalf of the seller, and the delivery-handling feature delivers the purchased products and services.

As previously stated, it is an open systems standard. It utilises XML (Extensible Markup Language) to define information and data that cover every aspect of a transaction. In conventional purchases, the buyer is at liberty to negotiate the price, choice of payment mode and medium, provision of purchase receipt and delivery of goods. IOTP is intended to allow for all these facilities in e-business while ensuring transaction security and success. It is in the evolution stage, but it is aggressively supported by Hewlett Packard, IBM, JCP, MasterCard International, Smart Card Integrations, Sun Microsystems and Wells Fargo Bank.

The IOTP framework supports eight basic types of transaction:
1. authentication
2. deposit
3. purchase
4. refund
5. withdrawal
6. value exchange
7. ping
8. transaction status inquiry.

These activities are referred to as baseline transactions, and they are further classified into three areas: (1) authentication transaction, (2) payment-related transaction and (3) checking transaction.

The authentication transaction utilises a range of authentication mechanisms and provides for the parties involved in the transaction to identify themselves to others. On the other hand, the payment-related transaction facilitates deposit, purchase, refund, withdrawal and value exchange. A checking transaction verifies the correctness of the transaction and identifies the active status of the server involved in the transaction.

IOTP could be employed in business-to-business (B2B) as well as business-to-consumer business models. The baseline transactions provide support for the business logistics in cyberspace, such as purchases and refunds. Baseline transactions identify four major scenarios of data exchange among different roles in an e-business transaction (described below), and each scenario is termed a trading exchange in the baseline transaction.

1. *Offer trading exchange.* This is the base scenario, where the seller makes an offer to the buyer and the buyer must accept the offer in order for the purchase process to continue.
2. *Payment trading exchange.* A payment trading exchange is a payment from a buyer to the payment handler. However, in the case of a refund it will be from the payment handler to the buyer; therefore the exchange happens in both directions.
3. *Delivery trading exchange.* This exchange delivers the online goods and services purchased, or transmits the information associated with their delivery, to the buyer.
4. *Authentication trading exchange.* This exchange of information is aimed at establishing the identity of a stakeholder involved in the transaction by other stakeholders in the transaction.

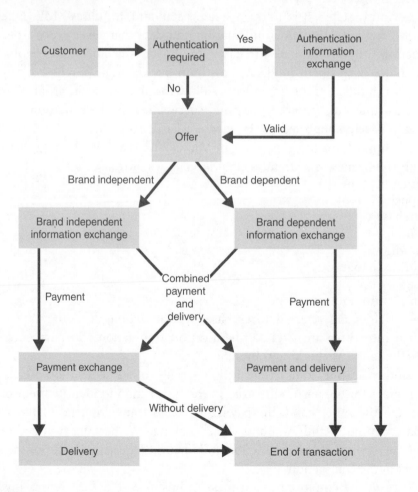

Figure 8.9   A typical web purchase using IOTP

IOTP transactions consist of combinations of these exchanges; for example an IOTP purchase transaction could include offer, payment and delivery trading exchanges. In another example, an IOTP value exchange transaction could include an offer exchange and payment trading exchange.

The typical web purchase that uses IOTP is illustrated in figure 8.9. A consumer who wishes to make a purchase sends a username and password through baseline authentication transaction. The authentication mechanism establishes the validity and authenticity of the customer and, if authenticated, the buyer is then allowed to choose a payment method through the purchase transaction. The two payment methods offered by the purchase transaction are brand-independent payment and brand-dependent payment. Brand-independent payment allows buyers to select from a payment brand and protocol, whereas brand-dependent payment makes the buyers stick to a particular payment brand and protocol. In brand-dependent payment, buyers can select from payment methods, such as Visa or MasterCard credit cards, before making a purchase, while in brand-independent mode the seller has already selected a payment method. Once the payment is made, the payment handler generates a payment receipt to the buyer, which is forwarded to the delivery handler by the buyer. The delivery handler then delivers the goods or provides the services.

Mobile commerce security

Mobile commerce or **m-commerce** is an increasingly popular means of transacting business using mobile phones. M-commerce involves the purchase of intangible digital products delivered to the mobile phone, as well as tangible products that are delivered to the customer's address. M-commerce transactions could be carried out remotely using a digital mobile network or locally through a point of sale. Although, in the contemporary paradigm, digital products like ring tones, screen savers and wallpaper are purchased more often, games, music and video clips are also becoming popular. Nonetheless, m-commerce technology is still in its infancy, and it will be some time before its real capabilities are realised.

M-commerce technology potentially boasts significant advantages in value adding, as it provides instant access and delivery, convenience, flexibility, personalisation and better customer support and service. M-commerce, like e-commerce, is also fraught with security issues, and the concerns for security are much the same: confidentiality, authenticity, identification, availability and non-repudiation. However, since the infrastructure involves wireless communication, these security problems crop up differently. Therefore it is important to understand m-commerce technology before the security issues are discussed. Wireless and mobile security issues will be discussed in more detail in chapter 9.

Fundamentals of a GSM

In mobile commerce the most essential ingredient is a mobile phone. Most of today's mobile phones are based on GSM (Global System for Mobile Communications), which is a technology based on TDMA (Time Division Multiple Access). GSM was first deployed in 1992, mainly in European countries. It operates in the 900 MHz to 1.8 GHz bands in Australia and Europe and the 1.9 GHz band in the USA. A GSM phone uses a Subscriber Identity Module (SIM) card that keeps subscriber account information and could be programmed as soon as the SIM card is plugged in. This makes the phone easy to use, and the programmability of the SIM card means users can program their phones for personalised services. Figure 8.10 presents an illustration of GSM architecture.

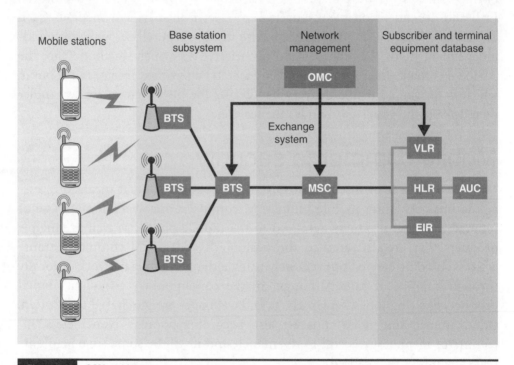

Figure 8.10   GSM architecture

Mobile station

Mobile stations are referred to as mobile phones. The SIM card forms the most important component of a mobile station. A SIM card keeps the IMSI (International Mobile Subscriber Identity), which is the subscriber's identity. Every mobile station also has a specific IMEI international device recognition called IMEI (International Mobile Equipment Identity). Newer applications, particularly the data communications applications, allow mobile stations to work as GSM interfaces.

Base Transceiver Station

In order to make a connection with mobile stations in the cellular network, the GSM system utilises radio stations that are called BTS (Base Transceiver Station). It comprises radio emitters and receivers, antennae and PCM interface. BTS takes care of the channel encoding and decoding and data encryption and decryption. Several transceivers used in a BTS handle performance and liability issues. These allow a BTS to be set as many-directional or selective, which covers a particular area.

Base Station Controller

Radio resources are administered by a BSC (Base Station Controller), whereby several BTS are connected to a BSC. However, technological advances now allow smarter BTS, which perform tasks that were previously meant for a BSC. However, the essential function of a BSC is to maintain a stable connection. Generally, all mobile stations report their receiving field strength to the BSC every 480 metres and, on the basis of this information, the BSC takes a decision on handing over a change to the neighbouring cell, for a change in the strength of the signal.

Mobile Switching Centre

An MSC (Mobile Switching Centre) works like an operator in a conventional wire-based telephone network. It performs such functions as registration, authentication, updating whereabouts registration, handovers to neighbouring cells and roaming.

Home Location Register

HLR (Home Location Register) is a subscriber management database. It keeps the international phone number of the subscriber, ISDN number of the mobile station and the present address of the VLR (Visitor Location Register). The data stored in the database contains the whereabouts of the mobile station so that calls to subscribers could be forwarded. A single HLR is capable of handling several MSCs.

Visitor Location Register

A VLR (Visitor Location Register) contains information about the current location of the mobile stations and the selected administrative information of the HLR. This information is used for controlling calls and for the provision of booked or reserved services for mobile stations within the zone controlled by the VLR. However, a VLR is attached to an MSC and generally integrated with the MSC hardware.

Equipment Identity Register

EIR (Equipment Identity Register) is a collection of databases that keeps a record of the valid mobile stations in the network. This database coud be used to uniquely identify every mobile station through its IMEI (International Mobile

Equipment Identity). There are essentially three databases in EIR, which contains all known and valid IMEIs, defected or stolen mobile devices, and all devices or IMEIs of dubious status.

Authentication Centre

AUC (Authentication Centre) is a protected database that keeps a copy of the subscriber's SIM card's secret key. AUC is used for authentication and encryption within the radio channel and therefore offers security against unauthorised usage of the mobile station. Usually it is installed with HLR in the GSM network.

Operation and Maintenance Centre

Operation and Maintenance Centre (OMC) is the system that manages and supervises GSM functions and aids in maintaining the proper functioning of the GSM network. OMC takes care of the control and maintenance of MSC, BSC and BTS.

How GSM works

The GSM mobile phones connect the user to a telephone network. The phone number is associated with the SIM card, which also stores the user's address book. When a call is made, the speech is converted into a stream of data and is transmitted to and from the base station, while the handset and the base station keep track if there is a better cell to transfer to. A base station provides coverage in a series of cells, which are organised like checks or boxes, such that each cell can be from 50 metres across to tens of kilometres across. When a mobile is switched on, it looks for a network and chooses the best signal strength to log on to. When it moves to another area, it reports its location and repeats the same process to transfer to a network with a better signal strength. When the phone is in idle state, the mobile keeps monitoring which base station it can reach and the network monitors where the mobile phone is. All this is done in a way that uses as little battery power, radio transmission and computing overhead as possible.

In order to make purchases using a mobile phone, the customer needs a phone that is WAP enabled. A WAP (Wireless Application Protocol) application is formatted using WML (Wireless Markup language), and WMLScript adds interactivity to wireless applications. The following section describes how WAP works.

Wireless Application Protocol

Wireless Application Protocol (WAP) is a specification for a set of communication protocols in order to standardise the access of wireless devices, such as mobile phones, pagers and personal digital assistants to the Internet and its contents.

It is based on such standards as HTML, XML and TCP/IP and comprises a WML language specification, WMLScript specification and a WTAI (Wireless Telephony Application Interface) specification.

When customers want to place an order using the mobile phone, they access the WAP browser from their mobile phone and open the particular website they want to visit. The customer thus initiates a connection and transmits data from their mobile through the GSM (see figure 8.11). The transmitted information leaves the wireless network and moves along a PSTN network. The phone is assigned an IP address and communicates to the seller's web server through a WAP gateway.

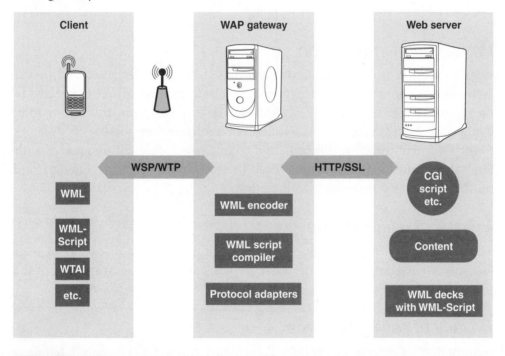

| Figure 8.11 | WAP model |

The gateway behaves like an intermediary between the Internet and the mobile network by converting the WAP requests into HTTP requests. The gateway uses HTTP for requests and receives WML-based information in return from the web server. This information is compiled into WBXML (WAP Binary Extensible Markup Language) before it is sent back to the phone from which the purchase inquiry was made. WAP gateways are generally owned by wireless service providers for individual users, whereas banks and other institutions would rather like to have their own gateways. Nevertheless, the WTSL (Wireless Transport Security Layer) in the WAP model takes care of the security of the information transmission and embodies the same security features that are found in the TLS (Transport Layer Security) component of TCP/IP. This layer checks information integrity and client server authentication as well as providing encryption.

Mobile commerce security

M-commerce architecture needs protection against misuse and deliberate attacks. Apart from the fundamental security concerns, a mobile commerce system needs to be protected against the following areas.

Protection of call-setup information

While setting up a call process, the mobile terminal communicates information regarding call setting up to the network. This information includes the number of the caller, calling card number, service requested and so on. This information needs to be protected from eavesdroppers.

Protection of information

Communication from a mobile device needs to be properly encrypted by the cryptographic system, such that it cannot be intercepted by anyone connected to the radio interface and other interfaces of the system. Protecting this information is not easy in a mobile phone, as different protocols are popular in different countries and at the same time different countries use different frequency bands for military and security reasons. Lack of standardisation in technology and control leaves open many ways of intrusion.

Privacy of user location

The subscribers of mobile phones need to be protected from disclosure of their location. An attacker can find the location of a subscriber by getting hold of the signalling information on the network.

Privacy of calling patterns

Information relating to outgoing and incoming traffic from a mobile phone is kept in the subscribers' databases by the network operators. This information could be tapped by hackers for illicit use.

Integrity protection of data

In addition to securing traffic data, there needs to be a verification provision for detection at the device and network levels to detect whether the information has been altered or otherwise.

Requirements for preventing theft of service or equipment

This provision directly relates to the availability dimension of security and calls for safeguards against theft. It is an important issue as the network is not able to detect whether the calls made are from a legitimate user or from a stolen phone. However, two types of theft could occur: first, equipment theft and, second, theft of the services offered by the service provider. A robust cryptographic protection could minimise the reuse of stolen terminals, and effective anti-cloning techniques could block the theft of services. In systems like GSM, where the account information is logically and physically separated from the mobile phone, stolen equipment poses a lucrative incentive for those with an ill intent. Unique identification of equipment reduces the potential reusability of stolen equipment.

Cloning is the ability to determine information about a mobile phone stored in the SIM card and make a perfect copy of it, that is clone it, using the collected information. The seriousness of this type of fraud is enormous, as legitimate users can also do this to enable multiple users to use a single account.

Virus protection

Current mobile devices are not extensively programmable; therefore from that perspective mobile devices are relatively safe from the threat of traditional viruses. Nevertheless, with an elevated ability to program mobile phone or mobile-enabled PDAs, the threat of viruses and malicious code will increase.

Smart card security

A **smart card** is a plastic card like a bank card or a credit card; however, it also has an embedded microprocessor. The ability to process information makes it 'smarter' than other cards. When a smart card is inserted into a reader, the microprocessor on the card is powered and consequently is able to store and process information. In particular, this processing generates cryptographic keys and algorithms for digital signatures and other encryption. It has a variety of applications, such as a conventional bank card and a credit card; nevertheless, it also works as an electronic wallet to keep electronic cash and to act as a secured identity card for access control to premises and software applications. The different types of smart card are memory cards, processor cards, electronic purse cards, security cards and Java Cards. All of these applications demand availability of some information, such as biometrical information of the holder of the card, history of the usage of the card and cryptographic keys, for identification and authentication.

Similar to the other technology in use, smart cards face challenges of security and widespread use. However, these issues originate in a vast variety of cards that do not conform to a particular standard and consequently lack interoperability of software and hardware. Other associated issues have arisen from this issue.

Smart card architecture

Conventional smart cards have an 8-bit microcontroller, but these days 16- and even 32-bit microcontrollers are in common use. They do not have multi-threading and other capabilities that modern computers possess. The CPU of the cards can perform instructions at 1 MIPS of speed; however, for encryptions often a coprocessor is required. A smart card utilises three types of memory and their sizes are also relatively small; for instance, RAM is 1 K, Electrically Erasable PROM (EEPROM) could be up to 24 K and ROM could also be up to 24 K. The inputs and outputs are managed by a single port that ensures standardisation in information communication through APDU (Application Protocol Data Unit).

Smart cards require power to operate, but they are passive cards and do not possess any boardpower provision. The solution is the interface device or the card reader device, which provides the card's power when it is in contact with the reader. The reader is also responsible for clock signals and opens a communication channel between the operating system in the card and the application running in the computer that is attached to the reader, which allows for the reading and writing of the card. This communication channel is half duplex, which means that information can be either read or written at one time, but it cannot flow in both directions at the same time. There are many vendors of smart cards and they use different operating systems, but a card's operating system generally embodies the following:

- read operation, which retrieves information from the memory area
- write operation, which writes information to the memory area
- search operations, which look for given patterns of inquiry
- erase operations, which delete selected memory contents
- operational security and information protection, although key checking and card lifecycle management are done through the following instructions:
  — write locks, which set the lock bits in the manufacturing area to zero
  — key or code submission, so as to facilitate the authentication of the smart card owner for such operations as reading, writing, updating and erasing of protected memory contents
- implementation of cryptographic algorithms, which constitute the important elements of the smart card security
- certificate calculation, which triggers cryptographic algorithm execution maintained by the smart card.

Security issues

As mentioned earlier, a smart card and a card reader communicate with each other through data packets known as APDU, which also provides a few security features that make it hard to attack the system. Although they are not completely attack-proof, it still provides a credible defence. These features are: the small bit rate making use of a serial bi-directional transmission line and based on ISO standard 7816/3, and the half duplex information transmission, which does not permit information communication in both directions.

The smart card and the reader use an authentication protocol to identify each other. The card generates a random number, which is sent to the reader that encrypts the number using a shared key and returns it to the card. The card compares the encrypted message with its own encryption, and the process can be carried out in the reverse direction. Nevertheless, after having established the communication each subsequent piece of communication between the card and the reader is validated and verified using an authentication code. The authentication code is computed through information, a random number and the encryption key. In this way, if information has been tampered with by a third party or by the communication process itself, the message has to be retransmitted. However, if the card supports adequate memory and processing capability, digital signatures can be used for information communication. The most common encryption methods used are symmetric DES, triple DES and public key RSA.

Hardware security issues

Information stored in the EEPROM is at the peril of environmental as well as voltage hazards. For example, information could be erased owing to a voltage surge. Some cards and readers use sensors to keep track of any voltage supply and other critical environmental variables, such as temperature and light; nevertheless, sensors have not yielded a confident level of creditability. In other ways of deliberate tampering with the card, ultraviolet light is used on the EEPROM to remove the security locks. Other intentional attacks include removing the processor from the card.

Operating systems security

In smart cards, information or data is arranged using a tree hierarchy. Its organisation illustrates that there is one master or root file that consists of many elementary and dedicated files. Dedicated files correspond to directories, whereas elementary files correspond to files, which is similar to the hierarchy of the operating systems for personal computers. The difference lies in the fact that dedicated files can also hold data. However, a header of dedicated, elementary and master files holds security features similar to the access rights of a common operating system. Information from any application can pass through the file tree; however, it can move only to a node with appropriate rights. There are five fundamentals of access rights; however, some operating systems might have more. These are:
- always (ALW), which means there is no restriction to the file access
- card holder verification 1 (CHV1), which means access is granted only when a valid CHV1 value is there
- card holder verification 2 (CHV2), which means access is granted only when a valid CHV2 value is there
- administrative (ADM), which means the access provision is the responsibility of the administrative authority
- never (NEV), which means access to the file is not allowed.

CHV1 and CHV2 correspond to the two security personal identification numbers that are held in the card. One is a user identification number and the other is a particular unblocking personal identification number that is stored in the card.

Software programs and routines also add to the security threats, since the loopholes in applications can lead to intrusion from a third party. Advanced cryptographic algorithms supported by hardware and operating system-based instructions are the most credible form of defence for such security hazards.

Biometric security

In the wake of growing social and political turbulence, newer forms of threat to security are emerging. A basic issue with any form of information technology is the relative ease with which it could be emulated. This not only shows us how ill-equipped and even defenceless we are in the face of unforeseen challenges but also highlights the need for continued safeguarding against any untoward attack on what constitutes the most important asset of a business: its information resources. For this reason, another form of secured authentication is increasingly gaining attention, and that is biometrics. **Biometrics** is the science of analysing the measurable biological characteristics of an individual so as to establish their identity to allow them access to information and the resources that keep and process them. Generally a biometric measure is a twofold security mechanism employed in conjunction with an intangible information-based form of identification, such as a password. Biometric measures include physical characteristics, such as fingerprints, hand or palm geometry, retina, iris, facial characteristics and even the chemical composition of an individual's DNA. Behavioural characteristics comprise signatures, voice patterns and way of walking.

Selecting the right biometric largely depends on the type of information system and applications in place in a business. It also requires taking stock of future developments in the business as well as in technology. It is not easy to predict technological changes, yet it is not difficult to assess the level of biometric automation. The driving principle needs to be that of taking a closer look at the security requirements of a business and making a decision according to the financial, capacity and expertise constraints of the business.

Legal issues with e-business security

A distinguishing feature of an information society is how the abundance of information is changing human activities and human relations. As a global and easily accessible mass medium, the Internet provides information on almost every aspect of life, for example news, entertainment, medicine, merchandising and religion. However, abundance of information does not necessarily mean that people become informed. It is important to ascertain the right information quickly and easily, in order to distinguish between what information a user needs and what information appears nice to the user, so that the user doesn't sink in electronic junk information.

Authenticity, reliability and validity of Internet-based information are therefore more important than just being able to access information. The Internet's self-regulating and open structure makes it an easy platform on which publish, access, retrieve, manipulate and distribute information, and hence the problem of authenticity of information arises as does that of the potential beneficial or harmful effects of cyber information on society. These problems have increased with the increasing flow of information resources being distributed in cyberspace without editors and fact checkers (traditional gatekeepers for print publications) monitoring them. Hence, the very nature and growing importance of the Internet calls for a fundamental re-examination of the institutional structure in which rule-making takes place.

Since web-based business mainly involves money, we will examine three pertinent legal issues here. The first two, trade marks and copyright, have been discussed in chapter 3. The third relates to the ability to enforce agreements that cross legal jurisdictions.

Trade marks

A **trade mark** can be a word, a sentence or a symbol that relates to particular products. Businesses that register their trade marks can assert their right to exclusive use of the trade mark to sell goods. It must be remembered, however, that different countries have different trade mark processes and, given the global nature of e-business, trade marks might need to be registered in multiple countries. Trade mark laws are directed at ensuring that customers are able to identify the sources of goods and services correctly. Using marks that are the same as, similar or closely related to registered trade marks is misleading and could trap customers into believing that the products on sale are from one company when in fact they are being offered by another.

Copyright

A business's website can be an important marketing tool, as it can provide potential customers with information about products and services and indeed enable them to make a purchase. A business is likely to place a substantial amount of its intellectual property on its website, including graphics files of logos, slogans, photos and specifications of products. It is very simple for another party to copy these.

It is a common practice to copy the contents and layout of a website, so as to lure customers into believing that the website they are visiting is either related to the business whose website has been copied or that the customers are actually visiting the same website. The law of **copyright** entitles the creator of intellectual property to exclusive use of it and so provides a legal protection against copying of this type.

Sales agreements

Sales agreements constitute an important aspect of web-based trading. Since e-business is a global business, there is no way to resolve or protect implied legal warranties in sales of products of goods, customers' identities, legal use of the site, trading disputes and limits of liability.

Existing legal frameworks are insufficient to control the Internet; therefore, governments are ill-equipped to handle the legal issues of e-business. A range of solutions have been proposed, which include virtual courts and virtual governments within cyberspace; international law, with particular emphasis on political and social aspects; and cyber norms as a substitute to legal legislation, especially considering the fact that the Internet population is not homogeneous and many countries lack a legal system that deals appropriately with violations in cyberspace.

Summary

The operation of electronic business and electronic commerce depends on the security of exchanged data and in particular the security of electronic payment systems. E-commerce is a particularly attractive target for attackers because it involves money. The lack of standardisation of technology and processes have combined to create customer mistrust and consequently have hampered the growth of e-business.

Electronic payment system security is aimed at creating an environment of trust between buyer and seller and preventing an unauthorised party being involved in the process. At present, more than two dozen electronic payment standards are being used in e-business. This complicates the security of electronic transactions. There are three approaches to online payment: payment clearing services, electronic funds transfer and electronic currency. A secure payment system must provide: integrity and authorisation; confidentiality; authentication; availability and reliability; and non-repudiation.

Forms of technology to support electronic payment system security include cryptography, message digest, digital certificates and digital signatures. The Internet Open Trading Protocol is being developed to provide a standardised secure payment framework to meet the technological and business aspects of e-business.

Mobile commerce is increasingly popular. It involves e-commerce conducted via mobile phones. M-commerce is subject to the same security issues as e-commerce, as well as the additional security threats introduced by the use of wireless communication. Smart cards and biometrics offer relatively new approaches to security but are facing impediments, such as a lack of standards.

A number of specific legal issues relating to e-business are complicated by the existence of a global marketplace and the absence of a global legal system.

These issues include the use and protection of trade marks, copyright of intel-lectual property and the enforcement of legal warranties.

~~~~~~

Key terms

authentication, p. 228	electronic payment system, p. 221
authorisation, p. 227	integrity, p. 227
availability, p. 229	Internet Open
biometrics, p. 244	Trading Protocol (IOTP), p. 232
confidentiality, p. 228	message digest, p. 231
copyright, p. 245	mobile commerce
cryptography, p. 230	(m-commerce), p. 235
cryptosystem, p. 230	non-repudiation, p. 229
digital certificates, p. 231	payment clearing service, p. 223
digital signatures, p. 232	Secure Electronic
e-business, p. 216	Transaction (SET), p. 225
e-commerce, p. 216	smart card, p. 241
electronic currency, p. 227	trade mark, p. 245
electronic funds transfer, p. 225	

~~~~~~

Questions

1. What are the major electronic business models in practice?
2. Briefly describe the minimum infrastructure required to operate a web-based business.
3. What is the purpose of an electronic payment system? Briefly describe each type and its security requirements.
4. How does the IOTP work?
5. What is the difference between symmetric, asymmetric and hybrid cryptosystems?
6. How does a WAP model work, and what are its security limitations?
7. How does a smart card operate, and why is it a relatively safe medium?

Case study ~~~~~~
8: Securing money online

A large multinational corporation operating in Australia was positioned at the high end of the competitive mass market. It was continually striving for better efficiency in its business transactions.

Before 2003, its Australian and Asia–Pacific stores used an MS-DOS-based point-of-sale system that required each individual store to initiate a dial-up session twice a day to download new product details and upload sales data. This system also initiated a session each time a customer used an ATM card. The dial-up tended to be secure because of its dynamic IP-address characteristics, but the whole network was slow and inefficient.

At this time the company was continuing to grow at a fast pace, and its systems were no longer able to cope with the number of transactions made or data stored, and staff error in small branches was causing huge delays in central data processing at head office. Both IT training and support were becoming increasingly problematic to the company.

The company implemented a modern POS (point-of-sale) system with a new EFTPOS (electronic funds transfer at point of sale) interface. It also wanted to connect its EFTPOS network over the Internet to a central bank.

Questions

1. Analyse the organisational changes made to the company's business processes and their ability to affect IT risk.
2. Create a logical and physical solution to manage the risks to the newly implemented e-business solution.
3. Create an outline of a training program for the staff who would be expected to implement this new e-business solution in a range of large and small retail outlets in the Asia–Pacific region.

Suggested reading

Quirk, P & Forder, J 2003, *Electronic Commerce and the Law*, 2nd edn, John Wiley & Sons Australia, Brisbane.

References

Andrews, PP & Hahn, J 1998, 'Transforming supply chains into value webs', *Strategy & Leadership*, vol. 26, no. 3, pp. 7–11.

Goodwin, B 2005, 'New wave of Trojan attacks could force banks to adopt two-factor authentication', *Computer Weekly*, 22 March, www.computerweekly.com/articles.

Tapscott, D 1999, *Creating Value in the Network Economy*, Harvard Business School Press, Boston.

Timmers, P 2000, *Electronic Commerce: Strategies and Models for Business-to-Business Trading*, John Wiley & Sons, New York, chapter 2, 'Key features of Internet electronic commerce'.

Chapter 9

Mobile and wireless security

Learning objectives

After studying this chapter, you should be able to:

- describe the foundations of wireless networking
- discuss the IT security risks arising in wireless networking
- explain how to secure a wireless local area network
- explain why businesses protect transactions with virtual private networks
- describe the security risks associated with Bluetooth-enabled devices
- discuss the IT security risks arising from new trends in mobile commerce.

Chapter overview

More and more companies (and households) are turning to wireless networking and the convenience of mobile e-commerce solutions. This exposes them to new and major IT security risks. As we shall see in this chapter, wireless networks and mobile and wireless devices are relatively new technology.

We first examine the principles of wireless communications to understand the basic threats faced in the use of mobile devices and wireless local area networks. We then examine the technology of wireless networks and mobile devices to understand the major areas of risk and how these risks can be managed. We look at virtual private networks as a growing method of managing IT security risk. We end by looking at trends in the use of wireless and mobile communications and how we can manage the security risks associated with these developments.

Wireless networking and mobile communications

Several forms of technology are aimed at wireless networking:

- Satellite, a form of wireless networking, has been used for providing data communication capabilities over long distances for wide area networks for many years. Because of the enormous costs, it is typically limited to large organisations or Internet backbones.
- Third-generation (3G) mobile networks have been hyped by telecommunication carriers since the spectrum was sold off by governments several years ago. They promise data rates of between 144 Kbps and 5 Mbps across entire metropolitan areas, although coverage is still limited.
- Bluetooth is a standard for low-power, short-range wireless networks with a coverage area of less than 10 metres. It is commonly used for connecting peripherals without wires, such as connecting a mobile phone to a hands-free headset, or a keyboard and mouse to a PC.
- IEEE 802.11 wireless LANs are another form of wireless networking. They are sometimes also known as Wi-Fi or WLANs. IEEE 802.11 is the most popular method for wirelessly networking computers. It is widely used in business settings and in the home (Edney & Arbaugh 2004).

Wireless and mobile technology is now widely available, and many companies are encouraged by the financial advantages of sharing electronic resources without having to roll out cable. Taking advantage of the ease with which wireless access points can be purchased, simple wireless area networks are increasingly being set up in companies, schools, offices and homes. Wireless and mobile devices are commonplace, and PDAs and mobile phone functionality are more and more integrated to give ubiquitous wireless communication with some (still limited) computing power for emailing and Internet browsing.

In our studies so far, we have discovered that our networks and systems are vulnerable to intrusion, and we have learned some of the issues we need to deal with as we struggle to provide *confidentiality, availability* and *integrity* of data and *non-repudiation* within business transactions. Wired networking provides the security advantage of a physical closed architecture that wireless does not possess. In a **wireless area network**, data is broadcast through the air rather than travelling along wires and cables and, just like the radio transmission that provides the music we hear on our local radio stations, anyone within range can receive the transmission.

However, when wireless technology is involved, there are other more complex issues that we must face:

- Wireless communications are far easier to interfere with since wireless networks and devices cannot be physically protected in the same way as wired networks and static devices.
- Large enterprises, such as the Department of Defence, are able to use high-tech methods to safeguard wireless communications, but this is at far greater expense than small commercial enterprises can afford.
- Personal and corporate privacy is at risk since communications are difficult to secure, and solutions involving encryption often offer a reduced quality of service (QoS).
- Wireless security issues are affecting business practices, enterprise security policies and national and international legislation (Nichols & Lekkas 2002).
- Wireless communication regulatory issues are continually under review, and legislation has to evolve with the development of wireless protocols and technology and their accompanying security threats and risks.
- The take-up of wireless technologies is proving challenging to the telecommunications and media industries as they seek to gain their share of the market.

Trust in wireless security networks and devices is mediated through protocols that have often been developed too quickly to meet market demand for new wireless devices and so are continually under development.

How wireless communications work

Wireless or radio waves, television waves and microwaves are all types of electromagnetic waves. They differ from each other only in wavelength. (Wavelength is the distance from one crest or trough of a wave to the next. The measurement of the number of crests or troughs that move past a point in one second is the frequency.)

Radio or wireless is simply a means of communication from a distance by sending a signal that carries a message. This is accomplished by means of a transmitter and a receiver. Many different signals can be sent and received if we use electromagnetic waves in different frequency bands; in wireless, these vary from 10 kHz to 3000 GHz.

Wireless security and user acceptance

In investigating the most important research topics in wireless security the recent report by Christian Guenther of the European Union's Sixth Framework Programme PAMPAS project (PAMPAS 2003) provides this comment on the link between wireless device take-up, user acceptance and wireless security. He makes the point that the growth of wireless networking is largely dependent on user opinion and perspectives on its effect on their everyday lives. 'The successful evolution of new *wireless* into the default communications medium will depend essentially on user acceptance.' He goes on to state:

> There are some very basic user uncertainties:
> - What control can the user maintain over what happens to personal or commercially sensitive data?
> - Will the user be under constant attack from latter-day mobile viruses and unsolicited intrusion into privacy?
> - Can charging and billing be trusted and how can costs be kept under control?
>
> Security lies at the heart of all these matters. (PAMPAS 2003, p. 20)

Basic IT security risks in mobile and wireless networking

Wireless networking has all the accompanying flaws of early radio technology, and currently it still evokes the early days of amateur or citizen band radio. As with early radio, anyone listening on a specific channel can monitor or even reply to a conversation since this communication methodology is designed to encourage dialogue and is not designed with any kind of security in mind.

The inherent dangers of wireless communications

Since there is no need for wires, network connection sockets and physical barriers, many traditional network security concepts cannot be applied when wireless networks and devices are being deployed. Just like tuning into a local FM radio station, a user with a wireless-enabled device need only be close to a transmitting base station that sends data digitally across a network — **a wireless access point** — to sense a network's presence. Some versions of the Windows operating system will alert the user to the presence of a wireless network and even give a report on its state of protection; this is all useful information for an intelligent hacker and one that network administrators and IT managers need to guard against.

Even without the threat of hackers, 802.11b and 802.11g wireless LANs (see later for definitions) have to contend with microwave ovens, baby monitors and cordless telephones, which also operate on the unregulated 2.4 GHz radio frequency. Some interference of this nature is accidental, but common household devices can be used to make widespread attacks on wireless networks.

How wireless communications can be intercepted or interfered with

In a traditional wired network, data communication is physically separated and confined by the wire within a building. In wireless communications, this wired encapsulation does not exist, and eavesdroppers who monitor, even at distances as great as several kilometres, with the right equipment (metallic food packaging and baked bean cans!) can view and capture the transmitted data. This is particularly true when cryptographic technology has not been employed.

Once an unprotected wireless signal has been detected, and depending on the motivation of the hacker, a company's resources (typically its Internet connection) could be used or its files could be accessed and copied or modified.

The IEEE 802.11 standard for wireless LANs

In 1997, IEEE ratified **802.11**, making it the first international wireless LAN standard (WildPackets 2003). 802.11 included an infrared (IR) layer and two radio frequency (RF) signalling layers. However, at 2 Mbps, speeds supported by the 1997 standard were limited. In an effort to increase throughput, IEEE established two task groups. Task Group A explored the 5 GHz band, while Task Group B explored the 2.4 GHz band. In 1999, 802.11a and 802.11b, which operated at 54 Mbps and 11 Mbps respectively, were standardised. Later, Task Group G improved speed in the 2.4 GHz band to operate at 54 Mbps, releasing the 802.11g standard, which was backwards compatible with 802.11b.

Wireless LAN topology

A group of wireless clients that communicate with each other on an 802.11 network is known as a basic service set (BSS). BSSs can be arranged in two topologies: an independent BSS or an infrastructure BSS. Wireless clients in an independent BSS communicate directly with each other, creating a peer-to-peer network (see figure 9.1 on p. 254). These networks are sometimes referred to as ad hoc networks.

Infrastructure networks allow for more complex topology. They include an access point through which all communication must be relayed. To access the network,

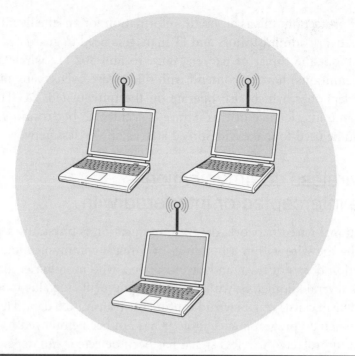

| Figure 9.1 | Independent BSS |

a wireless client must associate with an access point. Access points can also be used as a bridge to a wired network. This allows wired networks to be 'extended' so that wireless clients can access them (see figure 9.2). In an infrastructure network, multiple BSSs can be linked together as an extended service set to create a larger coverage area.

Since it is easier to work with names instead of numbers, a service set identifier (SSID) can be used to assign a friendly name to a particular BSS. A SSID can be any string up to 32 bytes (IEEE 1999).

Wireless LAN security

Wireless LANs operate in a similar manner to wired LANs, except that data is transmitted over a wireless medium instead of cables. The result is that wireless LANs are susceptible to many of the same areas of vulnerability as wired LANs. However, the wireless medium results in further vulnerabilities that are absent from wired LANs (Nichols & Lekkas 2002, p. 334).

As we have seen, AS/NZS ISO/IEC 17799:2001, the Code of Practice for Information Security Management, defines three main goals of information security: confidentiality, integrity and availability. Together these three goals, with another important goal: authentication, which underpins any security strategy because part of the reliability of data is based on its origin (Menezes, van Oorschot & Vanstone 1996, p. 4; Gast 2002, p. 89), achieve security (Pfleeger & Pfleeger 2003, p. 11). Collectively, these goals form the necessary framework for the security of wireless LANs.

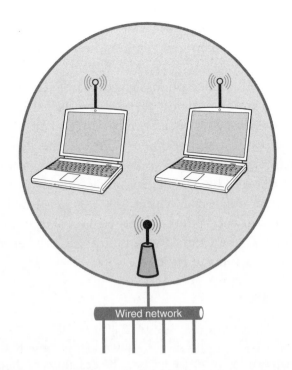

Figure 9.2   Infrastructure BSS

Confidentiality in WLANs

Confidentiality means the restriction of information from people who are not authorised to access it. It is sometimes called secrecy or privacy (Pfleeger & Pfleeger 2003, p. 10). Confidentiality can be achieved through encryption, to prevent unauthorised parties from eavesdropping.

As we have seen in chapter 5, there are two types of encryption: symmetric and asymmetric encryption. With symmetric encryption (sometimes called secret key encryption or shared key encryption), both parties require the same key to encrypt and decrypt the message. On the other hand, asymmetric encryption (or public key encryption) uses one key for encryption and a different one for decryption. Each type of encryption has various advantages and disadvantages.

Symmetric encryption is particularly favourable for wireless networks where bandwidth is a precious commodity. Symmetric encryption schemes can be designed to support high rates of data throughput while using relatively short keys. According to Menezes, van Oorschot and Vanstone (1996, pp. 31–2), throughput rates for asymmetric cryptography are several orders of magnitude slower than the best known symmetric schemes, and key sizes are typically much larger. Furthermore, Pfleeger and Pfleeger (2003, p. 59) state that symmetric schemes also provide authentication. Symmetric encryption ensures that a message received was not modified by someone other than the declared sender.

Only the legitimate sender can produce a message that will decrypt properly with the shared key. However, symmetric encryption schemes suffer from the problem of key security.

IEEE 802.11 specifies an encryption algorithm to encrypt data between the wireless access point and the wireless clients connected to it. Wired Equivalent Privacy (WEP; discussed below) is a symmetric algorithm in which the same key is used for encryption and decryption. WEP was intended to prevent eavesdropping on authorised users of a wireless LAN and to provide functionality equivalent to that provided by the inherent physical security of a wired medium (IEEE 1999). However, Allen and Wilson (2002) argue that the worst fault of wireless LANs is lack of encryption. Despite its inclusion in the standard, they maintain that WEP was not designed with business security encryption in mind and has been widely cracked and criticised.

Integrity in WLANs

Integrity means safeguarding the accuracy and completeness of information. Pfleeger and Pfleeger (2003, p. 10) add that information should be modified only by authorised parties or in authorised ways. The designers of the 802.11 standard addressed integrity by including a cyclic redundancy check (CRC) integrity check value (ICV) in the payload of data frames.

Availability in WLANs

Availability is about ensuring that authorised users have access to information when required. Availability is particularly problematic with wireless LANs, which are susceptible to interference and jamming. Interruption of availability can be quite difficult, if not impossible, to defeat in wireless LANs.

Authentication in WLANs

Authentication is the process of proving one's identity to another individual or system (Rawat & Massiha 2003). In the context of wireless LANs, authentication is required to prevent unauthorised users from gaining access to the network. An intruder who enters a wireless LAN without authorisation or disguised as an authorised user can violate the confidentiality and integrity once inside (Nichols & Lekkas 2002, pp. 335–6).

The more secure the method of authentication, the more confident you can be that individuals who interact with the system are who they claim to be. Authentication comprises one of the following: something you know, something you are or something you have.

Allen and Wilson (2002) state that authentication strength is determined on a sliding scale. They say that using one category of authentication alone results in a low level of authentication and that its strength depends on its implementation.

Something you have is probably the weakest method of security, while *something you know* is only as strong as the uniqueness of information used and the confidentiality of that information. The username/password challenge, a common method of authentication, is an example. *Something you are* is a bit more secure, but recent studies have shown that it can be foiled. For stronger authentication, at least two categories should be combined. This is known as **two-factor authentication**. For example, a password (something you know) and a smart card (something you have) could be considered to provide a relatively strong form of authentication — much stronger than using one factor on its own.

To realise the importance of authentication, consider what an unauthorised user could achieve on a corporate LAN: everything from free Internet access through to theft, modification or deletion of data. The 802.11 standard includes mechanisms to provide for authentication but, like WEP, these are also flawed.

802.11 security mechanisms

IEEE 802.11 designers recognised the inherent differences between the wired and wireless environments (Petroni & Arbaugh 2003) in meeting the fundamental security goals. Since the transport medium is RF signals instead of cables, anyone within range of the signal with a capable receiver can intercept transmissions between an access point and a wireless client. Accordingly the 802.11 standard includes mechanisms for data confidentiality and authentication to bring it 'in line with wired LAN assumptions' (IEEE 1999). However, a number of well-documented flaws in both mechanisms have been discovered.

Wired Equivalent Privacy

The goal of **Wired Equivalent Privacy (WEP)** was to provide encryption to protect against 'casual eavesdropping' and to provide functionality equivalent to that provided by the physical nature of a wired network (IEEE 1999).

WEP was designed to encrypt data at the link layer between the access point and the wireless client to prevent unauthorised access to 802.11 data frames. It uses the well-regarded RC4 symmetric stream cipher (Petroni & Arbaugh 2003). As well as its goal of data confidentiality, Borisov, Goldberg and Wagner (2001a) add that WEP can also be used to prevent unauthorised access to a wireless LAN. Although not considered an explicit goal in the 802.11 standard, it is recognised as a secondary feature of WEP.

WEP also incorporates an integrity check in the form of a CRC-32 checksum. The checksum is appended to the data frame, which is encrypted (along with the plaintext data) using the WEP algorithm (IEEE 1999). However, Borisov, Goldberg and Wagner (2001b) argue that the CRC checksum is not cryptographically secure and does not ensure that an attacker cannot tamper with a message. This is just one of a long list of flaws that have been exposed in WEP.

An obvious limitation of WEP is that its use is optional (IEEE 1999). To promote 'user friendliness', wireless hardware vendors mostly do not enable WEP encryption by default. As a result, according to Cam-Winget et al. (2003), many installations never even turn on encryption.

Another limitation of WEP is that it uses static, shared keys common to all users of a wireless LAN. Since the standard does not specify a key distribution mechanism, keys must be manually entered on every wireless client. The key is stored in software-accessible storage on the client (and usually in clear text), so anyone with access to it also has access to the key. Clearly, this is undesirable and does not scale well. Furthermore, if a wireless client is stolen or misplaced, the key has been compromised, and the only recourse is to change the shared key in all of the remaining wireless clients (Cam-Winget et al. 2003). The other effect of using a single shared key is that one party's traffic can be decrypted by everyone else on the network since they have the same key.

However, the most serious problem with WEP is that its encryption keys can be recovered through cryptanalysis, rendering it completely incapable of meeting its objectives. Walker (2000) identified the first flaws in WEP. He observed that the small IV size could be exhausted in a matter of hours on a relatively busy network, guaranteeing IV reuse and therefore key stream reuse that rendered it ineffective. Walker concluded that since this attack was a result of the IV, 'increasing the key size does nothing to increase WEP's resistance to attack' and that 'WEP's design attempted to adapt RC4 to an environment for which it was poorly suited'.

Borisov, Goldberg and Wagner (2001b) published several other attacks. They described methods attackers could use to eavesdrop or modify encrypted messages without fear of detection and showed that the shared key authentication mechanism is easily defeated. Their findings meant that WEP was not able to enforce any of the security objectives: data confidentiality, integrity or authentication. Arbaugh (2001) extended their findings into a practical attack against WEP that could decrypt any chosen packet in a few hours.

In August 2001, Fluhrer, Mantin and Shamir (2001) published a paper in which they showed that 'RC4 is completely insecure in a common mode of operation which is used in the widely deployed Wired Equivalent Privacy protocol'. This was devastating news for the already flawed protocol since it meant that WEP encryption keys could be recovered in around 30 minutes when combined with an active attack to generate enough traffic. Several freely available tools have since been released that automate recovery of WEP keys using off-the-shelf hardware. Because of these flaws, WEP falls short of its fundamental objectives of wired-equivalent confidentiality. It also fails to meet the expected goals of integrity and authentication (Cam-Winget et al. 2003).

Authentication services

The other security mechanism specified in the 802.11 standard is that of authentication. The standard facilitates two different approaches: open system authentication and shared key authentication.

For open system authentication, the wireless client sends an authentication success request message, and the access point responds with an authentication response. This is essentially a null authentication algorithm (IEEE 1999), providing no security at all. Sadly, this is the default configuration offered by most access points.

Shared key authentication is the other type of authentication defined by 802.11. To authenticate, the wireless client sends the same authentication request message to the access point as per shared key authentication. However, instead of automatically responding with an authentication success response, the access point sends a 128-bit nonce (the challenge). The wireless client encrypts the nonce with the secret key using WEP and sends it back to the access point (the response). The access point decrypts the returned message using the shared key and verifies that it is the same nonce that was transmitted to the client. If the two match, the access point transmits an authentication success response. However, shared key authentication also exhibits problems.

First, 802.11 assumes the access points are in a privileged position because they are typically controlled by network administrators (Gast 2002, p. 120). In other words, authentication is not mutually performed. The client has no way to verify that the access point knows the shared key, since the access point and the wireless client do not reverse roles and repeat the challenge–response process.

Second, the key used for authentication is the same as the shared key used by WEP. This is problematic for many reasons. For one, it suffers the same key distribution problems as WEP and it is not capable of authenticating an individual user — it only proves that the client knows the shared key. In addition, Arbaugh, Shankar and Wan (2001) show that the protocol is vulnerable to a passive attack. It provides an attacker eavesdropping during the authentication phase with both cipher text and matching clear text. Knowledge of this information can be used by an attacker to join the network without demonstrating knowledge of the shared key.

802.1x port-based authentication has been proposed as a better authentication. Originally intended for wired networks, it can also be used on wireless LANs. However, it operates at the lower levels of the OSI 7 layer model for networks. Consequently, specific support for the protocol is required within the access point.

Attacking wireless LANs

As we read in chapter 1, most security professionals agree that attackers generally fall into one of two broad categories: targeted attackers and attackers of opportunity.

In recent research (Billard & Janezic 2003) a number of issues were raised regarding the dichotomy between the known security risks arising with the use of wireless and mobile technology and the Australian Department of Defence's desire to use pervasive computing techniques for administrative and defensive purposes.

Much of the Australian Defence Force's (ADF) operations are by their very nature geographically dispersed and mobile. Wireless and mobile technology clearly have great potential for use in this context and, indeed, defence technology experts and the ADF are excited about the possibilities of the huge number of wireless technology innovations being developed in the commercial arena. However, businesses that design wireless technology for commercial use simply do not design their products to meet the military's strict information security standards. This is a major barrier to the ADF's adoption of this technology and poses the dilemma of how Defence can take advantage of wireless and mobile technology without compromising security. Another major barrier is the lengthy and detailed evaluation process Defence must conduct on a product before it can be adopted for defence use.

A possible solution that could be investigated is to create the ability to 'retro-fit' other hardware to safeguard commercial mobile devices in defence use. This approach offers significant practical advantages, and Billard and Janezic (2003) recommended that future research investigate technical solutions to this effect.

Source: information from Billard & Janezic 2003.

Targeted attackers are relatively few in number, but they present the most dangerous threat. They deliberately target, attack and compromise systems of high value or high interest (Spitzner 2003, p. 25). It is not worth the effort to attack a wireless LAN that operates in a home or a small office (Potter 2003), but a network containing valuable information, such as financial information or trade secrets, is an attractive target. The risk of being targeted by an attacker is small, even remote, but Potter (2003) argues that it warrants a more secure solution than WEP is able to provide.

Attackers of opportunity aim to intrude into as many systems as possible with the least effort (Spitzner 2003, p. 14). Potter (2003) remarks that a wireless LAN is more likely to be attacked because it is a target of opportunity. Many wireless LANs are installed with the default security settings disabled and can therefore be easily compromised.

Attackers are motivated by numerous goals, which can be summarised as MEECES (Money, Ego, Entertainment, Cause, Entrance to a social group, and Status) (Kilger, Ofir & Stutzman 2004).

Attackers' skills and tools vary widely. Most have relatively weak tools and relatively little expertise. If they encounter any security measures, they will often move on. Some, however, have sophisticated tools, and their expertise in attacking systems is a match for those defending the systems. Further, they are often driven by ego, challenge and social status. They are attracted to high-value systems and will not be deterred by security measures. In the middle are often attackers driven by profit or revenge, seeking to steal information, damage systems or alter data. They have specific objectives and targets and are often prepared to spend time and money achieving them.

Threats

So far, we have shown how wireless LANs suffer from a security problem. Areas of vulnerability exist for each of the security goals of confidentiality, integrity, availability and authentication. This section discusses common threats facing wireless LANs with little or no security.

The principle security threat is a compromise of confidentiality through eavesdropping (Nichols & Lekkas 2002, pp. 334–5). Anyone within range of the wireless signal that has a capable receiver can potentially eavesdrop on transmissions between an access point and a wireless client. The result is that an attacker could capture passwords, financial information and other private data using readily available technology (Vollbrecht, Rago & Moskowitz 2001). Furthermore, they could capture the information that is required to gain unauthorised access to the wireless LAN. Using WEP does not protect against eavesdropping since it can be compromised in a number of different ways (Intel 2003).

Without strong authentication, a second threat to wireless LAN security is the potential for an intruder to enter a wireless LAN without authorisation or disguised as an authorised user. The intruder can violate the confidentiality and integrity of network traffic (Nichols & Lekkas 2002, p. 335). Defeating violations of this sort is challenging because authentication credentials are obtainable through eavesdropping, and tracing and locating an intruder is difficult. Rawat and Massiha (2003) note that sometimes employees decide to set up their own access point without proper security, providing an easy route in for intruders. Gartner (cited in Townsend n.d.) believes that at least 20 per cent of enterprises already have rogue wireless LANs attached to their corporate networks.

In practice, most wireless LAN intrusions are an attempt to gain free Internet access (Potter 2003). However, intruders can use that access for more malicious purposes, including using the LAN as a platform from which to launch attacks against external resources. Such attacks could range from sending spam to making a denial of service attack (Phifer 2002). Owners could be liable for attacks launched from intruders gaining Internet access through unprotected access points, creating the possibility of both civil and criminal litigation. An attacker using a wireless LAN for external attacks is virtually anonymous as their connection cannot be traced to a phone line.

Integrity is also at risk in a wireless LAN. Vollbrecht, Rago and Moskowitz (2001) argue that an attacker who gains unauthorised access to a wireless LAN could potentially poison ARP tables or spoof MAC addresses, so that traffic from the wired network is routed to the attacker's system. The attacker could capture the packets before forwarding them to the destination system, or attempt a man-in-the-middle attack. Another risk is that an attacker could set up a rogue wireless LAN near a legitimate network, with the same network ID. Unbeknown to users, they could be connecting to the rogue network instead of the legitimate network, while the attacker is capturing network packets.

Wireless LANs employing shared key authentication are particularly vulnerable to both attacks, because the authentication scheme performs only one-way authentication, not mutual authentication. Furthermore, although 802.11 appends an integrity check value to each packet, it is not cryptographically secure, so it can easily be altered by an attacker.

Wireless is especially susceptible to attacks on availability in the form of denial of service attacks. Such attacks can take many forms, such as radio interference, flooding access points or replaying captured disassociate messages (Intel 2003). A low-cost attack was recently discovered by Wullems et al. (2004), whereby an attacker can cause disruption by transmitting certain packets so that transmission devices behave as if the channel is always busy. This prevents any data from being transmitted over the wireless network.

In a survey developed by Phifer (2002), companies were asked to identify security incidents that had been experienced on their wireless LANs. Only half of those participating were willing to divulge such sensitive information. However, of those who responded, approximately one in six reported at least one incident of rogue access points, wireless clients associating with the wrong access point, war driving and active intrusions on the wireless LAN.

Attack methods

In trying to achieve their goal, an attacker typically follows a process (although perhaps unknowingly). This process consists of reconnaissance, planning and collection, analysis and finally execution (Edney & Arbaugh 2004, p. 338).

Reconnaissance is one of the most important aspects of any attack since the purpose is to identify a target. In April 2001 Peter Shipley demonstrated how easy it was to discover insecure wireless LANs. By driving around with $150 worth of technology, Shipley discovered more than 80 networks in an hour (Poulsen 2001).

An unpublished study by one of the authors on wireless network security in an Australian city discovered 63 wireless networks, 55 of which were situated in the CBD and eight of which were found in residential areas. Of these, 51 were operating in infrastructure mode and two were operating as a peer-to-peer network.

An analysis of the security on these wireless networks uncovered some disturbing facts. Data accumulation was achieved from public areas, and at no time was private property entered. This indicates that businesses are not considering the perimeter of wireless networks, which extends far beyond their building or office.

Of the 63 networks discovered, only nine had WEP enabled, representing approximately 14 per cent of all networks. Although WEP does not guarantee a secure wireless network, it serves as a basic security mechanism. Although many of the wireless networks that did not have WEP have undoubtedly been secured using a different security mechanism, this is not apparent without accessing the network. However, it is highly probable that many of the wireless access points discovered were completely vulnerable to attack.

The reasons behind these unsecured networks are hard to determine; wireless networking is still a relatively new and cutting-edge field, the range from access points is underestimated by information security officers and home users; and the technical information required for the construction of an effective solution is beyond most users.

However, such reasons might explain the situation, but the fact remains that there are a large number of vulnerable networks, many of which are connected to commercial enterprises. Although it is understandable that this creates vulnerability, implementing technology that is not understood can be potentially dangerous for a company.

The practice of driving around looking for wireless LANs is so popular that the term 'war driving' was coined for it. A search on war driving using popular Internet search engine Google returns about a quarter of a million results. War driving derives its name from 'war dialling', the technique by which hackers found networks by dialling random numbers until a modem answered in the movie *WarGames* (Poulsen 2001). War driving has spawned another activity: 'war chalking', in which buildings and footpaths are marked to indicate the presence of wireless LANs and whether or not they are secure (Wi-Fi Alliance 2003).

In the case of wireless LANs, planning and collection is where an attacker determines whether a wireless LAN has security enabled (such as WEP). If it does, enough data must be collected to crack the WEP keys. Once a target has been identified and, if necessary, enough data has been collected to recover WEP keys, the key must be recovered and the network parameters are identified (analysis). Finally, the attacker is ready for execution and can join the network.

Edney and Arbaugh (2004, pp. 340–53) identify the tools most commonly used by an attacker during each stage of the process:

- NetStumbler (www.netstumbler.com) is one of the most popular programs for war driving because it runs on Windows and is easy to install and use. The information it displays includes the SSID of each access point discovered, whether or not it has encryption enabled, the channel on which it operates and so on. It even estimates the GPS coordinates of the access point if the user has a GPS device plugged in. MiniStumbler is also available for handheld PCs, allowing an attacker to walk around without needing to carry a bulky laptop that could draw attention.
- Kismet (www.kismetwireless.net) is another popular war-driving tool that runs under UNIX-based operating systems. However, unlike NetStumbler, it is completely passive, and its use is therefore undetectable. It is capable of gathering the same sort of information as NetStumbler and more. Furthermore, it can collect all received packets for later analysis.
- bsd-airtools (www.dachb0den.com/projects/bsd-airtools.html) is a suite of utilities for scanning and cracking WEP networks.
- Airsnort (http://airsnort.shmoo.com) is one of the original tools for implementing the FMS attack against WEP. It is easy to use, and runs under Windows and UNIX-based operating systems.
- Airjack is a series of tools that gives an attacker the ability to perform a DoS attack against an access point, actively determine the SSID for a closed network, establish a man-in-the-middle and set the MAC address of the wireless card. It runs only under Linux.

Securing wireless communications with virtual private networks

As we have seen previously, virtual private networks (VPNs) have been developed for and used in many applications over wired networks and have proved more than adequate for protecting privacy. Defence and commercial institutions have readily adopted this technology to expand the potential use and scalability of their intranets.

Wireless communications require a protocol that can authenticate an entity and guarantee private, secure interaction, as offered by the wired counterpart. Virtual private networks were previously developed to meet these criteria; they have developed continuously and are implemented widely throughout industry; and they have proved to be an effective means of implementing a secure channel for communications. VPNs have been used on wired networks for creating a secure channel through the public telecommunications infrastructure to extend local area networks. VPN implementations have been adopted and tested by defence, commercial and private parties, with adequate results. This tunnelling technology should be applied to wireless communications, in addition to the packet-based encryption, WEP, to maximise the security.

Security threats to current mobile technology

Before examining the security issues in 3G mobile systems, it is necessary to describe the security issues that threaten existing mobile systems. It is not until the known issues are defeated that the threats arising in newer technology can be explored.

Before digital handsets were introduced in the early 1990s, analogue systems offered little privacy from eavesdropping. Although electronic devices such as radios do not pick up mobile phone calls, it is possible to receive them with scanners that can intercept signals at the frequencies reserved for mobile phone communication. Most countries have enacted laws prohibiting the use of such scanners, but this would not impede the determined. Nichols and Lekkas (2002, p. 119) reveal that a radio scanner available from electronic stores can be easily modified to intercept the cellular telephone signal for only a few hundred dollars. 2G cellular networks such as GSM introduced some countermeasures to prevent the interception issues that plagued the original analogue networks. However, it was soon discovered that these were vulnerable to attack. Furthermore, some of the other features, like short message service (SMS) and the subscriber identity module (SIM), contained serious flaws that were exploitable by eavesdroppers or those trying to commit fraud.

GSM was the first public telephone system to introduce integrated crypto-graphic mechanisms. These mechanisms have been effective in reducing fraud and providing protection against eavesdropping (Howard, Walker & Wright 2001). Encryption occurs between the mobile station (MS) and the base transceiver station (BTS). It relies on a symmetrical encryption algorithm called A5. The secret key is shared between the MS and the operator and is stored on the SIM and at the authentication centre (AuC), respectively. Since the key is stored on the SIM, which was designed to be tamper-resistant, it cannot be easily exposed or dupli-cated (although duplication has been shown to be possible through SIM cloning, explained below). The SIM can be protected by an optional PIN in the case of theft (Gindraux 2002). There are three flavours of the A5 encryption algorithm, but they are all considered to be flawed.

In addition to encryption between the MS and the BTS, GSM enforces a challenge–response mechanism to identify users to the network and to protect against fraud. This is implemented through A3 and A8. The network oper-ators can choose their own algorithm to implement with A3/A8, although most choose the COMP128 algorithm. Unfortunately, COMP128 was a reference algorithm that was never intended to be used. It was broken by David Wagner and Ian Goldberg, although it takes a significant amount of time to achieve. The result of this meant that it was possible to clone SIM cards (Gindraux 2002; Lord 2003).

It has already been mentioned that the SIM card was originally designed to be difficult to tamper with or duplicate. The realisation that SIM cards can be cloned is a real threat to both the user and the telecommunications operator. For instance, a cloned SIM card could be used by somebody to commit fraud. Calls made using the duplicated SIM would be billed to the legitimate owner of the original SIM from which it was cloned. Furthermore, the user of the cloned SIM would be able to make calls with complete anonymity, since their identity might not be known to the telecommunications operator. COMP128-2, a new version of the COMP128 algorithm, has resolved many of the issues and, as such, requires much more exotic methods of attack (Lord 2003).

Since the opening up of SMS between the three major cellular carriers in Australia, it has become a huge source of revenue. SMS is enormously popular among young people and is now also becoming a critical tool for business communications, as SMS messages are perceived to be secure. For example, some banks are now providing SMS banking facilities for account management.

CNN (2000) and Lord (2003) cite certain Nokia phones were found to be susceptible to an availability attack by which a specifically crafted message could cause the phone to crash. The attack involved using a broken user data header within an SMS message. The only way to recover from an attack was to put the SIM card into a phone that was not affected by the attack and delete the offending message. Although not as severe, it is also possible to flood an MS with a mass of SMS messages. The result would be that the memory on the MS would eventually fill up, thereby denying access to further messages.

A number of attacks on the integrity and non-repudiation of SMS messages are possible, which are based on forging the originating address (OA) in the SMS-DELIVER header. The OA can be arbitrarily set to anything (including alphanumeric characters) using a variety of methods. This makes it possible for a spammer to send messages that appear to come from an invalid number. It could also be used to mount a social engineering attack, whereby an SMS could appear to come from a trusted source. Tools are readily available to exploit such attacks.

Security threats to third-generation technology

The principles of 3G security build on the security of 2G systems. The security elements from GSM and other 2G systems that have proved to be needed and robust were adopted for 3G security. Furthermore, 3G security improves on 2G systems. It addresses and corrects weaknesses in 2G systems. Finally, 3G security offers new security features and aims to secure the new services offered by 3G.

One of the major advantages of the development of 3G security is that it was a completely open and transparent process. The algorithms and standards have been analysed and scrutinised by interested researchers or developers (or anyone, for that matter). This is a contrast to 2G systems, where most of the algorithms went unpublished. The consequence of this was that 2G security systems did not undergo peer evaluation and subsequently were eventually reverse engineered to reveal massive weaknesses. As a result of the transparency in the development of 3G security, it is hoped that 3G will prove to be much more robust than its ancestors.

Confidentiality

Attacks on confidentiality probably result in the most severe consequences and are what concern users of mobile telephones the most. They can occur in one of several ways: eavesdropping, theft, masquerading, external attacks or at application level.

Availability

Attacks on availability either degrade performance or deny service completely. The benefit of an availability attack (if there is such a thing) as opposed to an attack on confidentiality or integrity is that it is relatively easy to identify that an attack has occurred, and hence it is possible to take appropriate action. Some of the more common examples of attacks on availability include jamming, physical attack and natural hazards.

Integrity

One of the security objectives is integrity, which is a requirement that data and information can be modified only by an authorised person or in authorised ways (Pfleeger & Pfleeger 2003). In the context of mobile phone technology, information and data integrity can be affected by such attacks as impersonation. Impersonation is performed when an unauthorised person poses as a service subscriber, takes advantage of the service and uses the service being charged to the legitimate subscriber.

Enhancing mobile phone security

Despite its security improvements compared with the previous mobile technology, 3G is still vulnerable owing to its over-the-air transmission, increased flexibility, and mobile and compact nature. The effect of these attacks is more severe because of the nature of applications and services that 3G provides.

Biometrics

The biometrics industry is currently developing solutions to secure mobile phone and device technology. The use of biometrics in small mobile devices is not a breakthrough. It has been implemented for the iPAQ Pocket PC h5400 series, which combines the FingerChip technology with the BioSwipe software (Smart Handheld Group 2003). The PDA provides a combination of authentication mechanisms, such as a PIN and/or a fingerprint, or a password and/or a fingerprint.

Voice biometrics is an alternative to the fingerprint biometrics. It should be considered because it makes use of the existing properties of a mobile phone device, such as voice processing.

The real advantage of biometric-based authentication is the elimination of passwords. Most people set their passwords to something easy they can remember readily, or something long and complex but hard to remember. These passwords can be easily cracked by a persistent cracker, who can use brute force attack to try out every combination in the dictionary or watch people's behaviour when they enter their passwords (Prabhakar, Pankanti & Jain 2003). Biometrics, on the other hand, cannot be lost or forgotten. They are hard for attackers to forge or repudiate. Biometrics offer users the convenience of not having to remember passwords. Prabhakar, Pankanti and Jain (2003) state that biometric systems can be protected against Trojan horse attacks using the building blocks of standard cryptographic techniques.

A combination of one or more biometrics systems with password or ID authentication will provide more reliable security.

Digital signatures

In current 3G mobile technology, security is mainly implemented at the application level. Using WTLS, user identification and authentication are carried out through the Wireless Identity Model (WIM). Despite these capabilities, WTLS does not provide persistent authentication for transactions that might occur during the established and client-authenticated connection. The current WAP WMLScript specification provides a standardised solution for digital signatures, whereby a digital signature will be associated with data generated as the result of a transaction.

To support this requirement, a WAP browser provides a WMLScript function that asks a user to sign a piece of information to be sent over the network. By doing so, the user confirms that they have sent this piece of information. Finally, both the signed and encrypted data and the signature are sent across the network (WAP Forum 2002).

Digital signatures, however, are not the perfect solution for proving the validity of transmitted data. They prove that the data was signed with a particular key that belongs to a particular person. However, they do not prove that the data was signed by that particular person. This is because the key used for signing is stored on the actual device, not with its owner.

One solution to this problem is the use of a smartcard. Smartcards are used as a secure and tamper-proof device to 'carry' passwords and certificates for identification purposes (both locally and within the Internet) and secret keys for encryption and digital signatures. No other devices can read the information stored on a smartcard. The smartcard identifies its authorised owner by checking a PIN or a user password. Once the user has been identified to the smartcard, the card generates a digital signature for the user (Aufreiter 2001).

Of the countermeasures available, biometric-based authentication mechanisms have yet to be used to their full potential. Recent implementations on other small devices have been demonstrated to reduce the effect of theft by protecting the integrity and confidentiality of sensitive user data. Stronger cryptographic mechanisms, digital signatures and improved security for IP services would all help in minimising and preventing the potential threats.

As the wireless generations evolve, such attacks as eavesdropping, impersonation, theft and jamming — whether intentional or not — have the potential to cause more damage than ever before. Consequently, security will also need to continue to develop to keep up with evolving technology in future.

Mobile devices and Bluetooth security

Bluetooth wireless technology is a standard for low-cost, short-range radio links between mobile PCs, mobile phones and other portable devices (Zomaya 2002). It is named after Harald Blåtand, a Viking king nicknamed Bluetooth who lived in the early Middle Ages (Wesolowski 2002). Bluetooth began as a university project in Lund, Sweden. The aim was to make a wireless connection between an earpiece or cordless handset and a mobile phone. When the students discovered they could tap into a low radio frequency freely available to anyone in the world, they started experimenting with microchips. In 1988 Ericsson, Nokia, IBM, Toshiba and Intel came together to form the Special Interest Group (SIG), a voluntary organisation that created the Bluetooth specifications. Motorola, 3com, Lucent and Microsoft all eventually joined SIG. On 20 May 1998 Bluetooth was publicly announced, and on 26 July 1999 specifications for Bluetooth 1.0 were released.

Bluetooth technology

Overall, Bluetooth technology aims to be low-cost, available universally, power-effective, mobile and interference-free. Bluetooth differs from other wireless standards, such as the 802.11. In most cases, having many wireless computer accessories in the same vicinity will cause these to interfere with each other. Most of these devices operate on only one or two frequencies. Bluetooth provides a way for these devices to share the RF spectrum and not interfere (Truelove 2002). Wireless devices using Bluetooth to transmit information have the ability to search for and recognise other such devices operating close by. Then, one device can instantiate a spontaneous network (or **piconet**) with the other device. Devices using the same frequency in different piconets cannot interfere with each other.

Bluetooth networks

A Bluetooth network is created spontaneously when an enabled device finds other wireless devices to interact with. This is done using SDAP, the technology that provides the capability for a device to discover which services are available (Morrow 2002). The first device establishes the piconet and initialises transmission to another device. This becomes the master device and the second becomes the slave. A piconet composed of one slave and one master is known as 'point-to-point'. This is the simplest piconet. A piconet with one master and more than one slave is known as 'point-to-multipoint' (Truelove 2002). There can be up to seven such slave devices active within a piconet at one time and around 256 parked devices. Although parked slaves can become active without much trouble, the limitation is one disadvantage of Bluetooth piconets (Wesolowski 2002). It is possible to have two piconets in the same space. In such a case, the two will communicate with one another. This entire set of piconets is referred to as a scatternet (Blankenbeckler 2000).

Bluetooth aims to make everything possible. Beyond the basics, it is impossible to contain all scenarios in which Bluetooth could be implemented. It is left to any individual's imagination. Motorola imagined one such scenario. In 2001 Motorola dreamed of releasing a car with Bluetooth wireless applications, including a phone that controls the vehicle's air, heat and radio (Hattori 2000). The car could use Bluetooth technology to retrieve information about specials at shops it was approaching. Another scenario that has been envisaged is an airport with Bluetooth devices embedded into the parking lot (Hattori 2000). It could tell travellers which gate their flight leaves from or what time it departs even before they get out of the car. As previously mentioned, hundreds of organisations have contributed in one way or another to this developing technology. All of them have examined how Bluetooth could fit into their product. VCRs, washer-dryers, stoves, microwaves and CD players could all be controlled by Bluetooth.

All Bluetooth's aims have been achievable on a small scale, but not a large scale. Its main limitation in achieving these goals has proved to be its short-range operability. Bluetooth has come a long way in achieving its goals. A wireless office has been created. However, most Bluetooth equipment is designed for the lowest Class 3 output power (Truelove 2002).

Security risks of Bluetooth

Owing to the mobile nature of all wireless devices, security measures have to be taken to prevent eavesdropping and falsifying the message originator (Kitsos, Sklavos et al. 2003). Authentication is used to prove the origin of data and to ensure that the data has not been altered. Interception is prevented by the use of encryption.

Bluetooth reduces eavesdropping by the use of frequency hopping spread spectrum (FHSS). It provides an encryption layer that can be used by the applications of the Bluetooth device (Kitsos, Sklavos et al. 2003). This multilayered approach is considered to reduce interference, although several security holes have been reported for Bluetooth.

Its known areas of vulnerability are spoofing through keys, spoofing through a Bluetooth address and PIN length. Spoofing through keys can be explained as a man-in-the-middle attack whereby the identification and encryption keys are stolen before the start of the session. The Bluetooth device will then talk to a false third party rather than the real second party. Spoofing through a Bluetooth address occurs when an intruder obtains the unique address of a device. The intruder can then pretend to be someone other than who he is. The PIN code is a major problem as it can be extremely short and cannot be controlled. It has been claimed that the ability to change the password adds security (Träskbäck 2003). However, this is not a very good argument as no-one forces the user to change the password. Neither are there any other password requirements; the PIN code is usually as short as four digits.

Managing Bluetooth security risks

It is possible to secure current Bluetooth implementations by using additional software (Träskbäck 2003). But to fully secure Bluetooth we will have to provide additional security measures, both in the application layer and in the link layer, ensuring usage protection and data confidentiality (Davies 2002). A better solution would be enforcement of hardware implementation with strict configuration management in compliance with redesign of the Bluetooth protocol.

A problem with securing Bluetooth devices is that they are low in power, and this is where a hardware solution appears. A hardware implementation is advantageous for time-critical systems and is well suited for the processing and power constraints of mobile phones and their applications (Kitsos, Sklavos et al. 2003). The hardware implementation offers methods for authentication, key generation and encryption. Both private key and public key encryption generate large code size and have high power requirements, and consequently the level of security often has to be compromised because of the constraints of the device. Having key generation and authentication implemented in hardware, as opposed to software, will result in faster connection times and lower power consumption. Furthermore, it is possible to reduce power consumption by putting inactive system portions into standby mode (Kitsos, Sklavos et al. 2003).

The spread of Bluetooth has been slower than predicted despite promising future applications (Davies 2002). Lack of security and privacy are the main reasons for the slow spread of Bluetooth as well as other wireless technology. A further issue is that in many countries the government is controlling the highest level of encryption. Governments keep the strongest encryption to themselves to allow interception by security agencies (Davies 2002).

For Bluetooth to have a long-term future, more security is required. Research has shown that Bluetooth is an improvement on IEEE 802.11 with respect to security (Hager & Midkiff 2003). Bluetooth has also inherited some of the weaknesses present in most wireless systems. A future solution would have enforcement of hardware implementation with strict configuration management in compliance with a redesign of the Bluetooth protocol. A hardware implementation is advantageous for time-critical systems and is well suited to the processing and power constraints of mobile phone applications (Kitsos, Sklavos et al. 2003).

Hardware implementation using the SAFER+ algorithm has been successfully carried out at a research level, as mentioned in earlier sections. The implementation is working on a low frequency and has much higher throughput than other implementations. As hardware implementations are dropping in price, it will be viable to build high-performance circuits with low power consumption (Kitsos, Sklavos et al. 2003). It is believed that hardware implementations for low-power microprocessors will play a significant role in securing Bluetooth devices.

Summary

Wireless and mobile technology is widely available, and many businesses are attracted to the financial advantages and flexibility of sharing electronic resources without having to roll out cable. Mobile and wireless networking, however, lacks the security inherent in the physical nature of wired networks. Wireless access points are easily identifiable and provide a relatively easy way for attackers to enter a network. The major areas of security risk in the use of common forms of mobile and wireless networking include the extension of commercial local area networks with wireless access points and mobile devices, such as PDAs and wireless laptops, to form complex enterprise-wide, wireless local area networks. There are security flaws in the use of common protocols, especially IEEE 802.11b, but these could be mitigated by the use of virtual private networks.

The evolving generations of mobile phones and other mobile devices also have security flaws. The Bluetooth wireless protocol offers much potential, but take-up has so far been limited. Bluetooth also has security vulnerability, including spoofing through keys, spoofing through a Bluetooth address, and the limited size and complexity of the PIN codes used.

802.11, p. 253
Bluetooth, p. 269
piconet, p. 269
two-factor authentication, p. 257

Wired Equivalent Privacy (WEP),
    p. 257
wireless access point, p. 252
wireless area network, p. 251

Questions

1. Describe how a start-up SME would need to plan for an IEEE 802.11b wireless network in terms of confidentiality, availability and integrity. How would you express this risk within your company security policy?
2. Explain how you would begin to define acceptable risk in the context of an SME and its wireless network.
3. Identify some of the IT security risks that might be involved in a large enterprise using SMS as a marketing tool.
4. Examine the latest mobile phones from two major manufacturers. Compare and contrast their security strengths and weaknesses.
5. Look at the current information available to you on WAP, and map out the development of this protocol. Has it, in your opinion, become totally superseded?
6. Research the latest protocols used in voice-over IP security, and determine whether a consistent standard has been established.

Case study
9: Optus and the development
of wireless hotspots in Australia

Optus has invested more than $7 billion in its Australian operations, building an infrastructure that now makes up Australia's second-largest telecommunications provider. Its current network consists of fixed, mobile and satellite networks, its own optical fibre national trunk providing telephony and high-speed data and pay television.

Optus Wireless Connect offers a subscription to a service that allows wireless-enabled laptops or PDAs to connect to the Optus Wireless Connect network from certain enabled areas across a city and then access their office machines or Internet at a high speed. The limitation of the product is that you must be in an area that has the ability to connect you to the wireless network. 'Zones' or 'hotspots' are the common terms used to refer to these areas. To provide these hotspots, Optus negotiates with third parties to allow access so that it can install and erect antennas to offer its wireless service in areas likely to attract potential customers for its wireless product.

Optus's decision to enter the wireless market was based on detailed research into Australia's emerging markets and Internet figures. Market research had consistently shown major growth in the number of Internet users, their use of the Internet and the use of Internet-related solutions in the workplace. The Internet ratings report for June 2003 revealed that web usage in the workplace grew a massive 35 per cent in the previous year. Optus realised that with such a growth rate the idea of ubiquitous connection to the office would appeal to any employer as it could improve productivity at little expense.

At the time of the introduction of Optus Wireless Connect, three other major telecommunications companies were planning and negotiating hotspot agreements in a race to be the first to market. Reports from Australian IT (2003a, 2003b) detailed three separate telecommunication companies. Telstra was negotiating with major fast-food franchise McDonald's, and iPrimus was conducting trials with companies in one of Melbourne's fashionable shopping and dining areas.

Hotspots and security risks

The primary security risks in the use of hotspots are:
- *Eavesdropping:* a passive attack whereby the eavesdropper can listen to the message without altering the data; hence the receiver and sender might not even be aware of the intrusion.
- *Identity theft:* a user enters the wireless network disguised as an authorised user, gaining unauthorised access to the network. The unauthorised user can violate the confidentiality and integrity of the network by sending, receiving, altering or forging messages. This can be carried out using a wireless adapter compatible with the targeted network or by using a compromised (e.g. stolen) device linked to the network.
- *Interference and jamming:* either this interference is accidental and caused by users on unlicensed channels or it might be intentional. An attacker who has a powerful enough transmitter could create radio signals strong enough to overwhelm weaker signals, thus disrupting communications. This type of attack is known as jamming and is a denial of service attack.
- *Man-in-the-middle attack:* when a user initiates a connection to a wireless network, the attacker will intercept the connection and complete it to the intended resource. The attacker will then proxy all communications to the resource, allowing them to modify, eavesdrop on and inject data into a session.
- *Physical threats:* damage to or destruction of the underlying physical infrastructure of a wireless network can also compromise security. Such factors as weather, accidents and vandalism can cause the damage.

Optus hotspot security solution

Remote Authentication Dial-In Service (RADIUS) is a widely deployed protocol that enables authentication, authorisation and accounting for wireless network access. The RADIUS client sends their user credentials and connection parameter information to a RADIUS server in the form of a RADIUS message. The RADIUS server then authenticates and authorises the RADIUS client's request, following which it will then send back a RADIUS message response. The RADIUS client will also send a RADIUS accounting message to the RADIUS server. RADIUS standards also support the use of RADIUS proxies, which is a computer that forwards RADIUS messages between RADIUS clients, RADIUS servers and other RADIUS proxies. Something to note is that RADIUS messages are never sent between the access client and the access server.

To protect Wireless Connect, Optus uses RADIUS authentication layered over the top of 802.11b and not WEP because of the known security flaws.

RADIUS is not seen as totally secure. The first issue in RADIUS security is that access-request messages are not authenticated and there is no cryptographic verification of the incoming access-requesting message by the RADIUS server. The RADIUS server does verify that the message originated from an IP address from a configured RADIUS client, but source IP addresses for RADIUS messages can easily be spoofed.

Another issue is that the RADIUS secret key can be weak owing to poor configuration and limited size. In many RADIUS instillations, the same shared secret is used to protect many RADIUS client/server pairs. Also, the shared secret does not have sufficient randomness to prevent a successful brute force attack. This situation is made worse by the RADIUS client/server implementations that limit the size of the shared secret and require that it comprise only characters that can be typed on a keyboard. This means that it can use only 94 out of the possible 256 ASCII characters.

A third issue of RADIUS security is that the cryptographic method used to encrypt passwords and other data is not considered strong enough and allows a dictionary-based attack.

The future of hotspots

The wireless market in Australia is growing phenomenally. The number of worldwide hotspots for 802.11b is expected to grow to 260 000 in 2007; that is, a sixfold increase in under three years. North America has the highest population of wireless users and density of hotspots access, closely followed by the Asia–Pacific with 2.7 million people currently utilising the technology on a regular basis.

Questions

1. Research the growth of hotspots from 2002, when Optus Connect first became active, until now. Has this market developed in Australia as had been predicted?
2. Investigate how many and what kinds of security breaches have occurred through this type of wireless networking. Have any major companies suffered damage to their networks or their reputation through breaches to hotspot security?

3. Investigate the development of RADIUS technology and its application in all kinds of Internet service provision. Are there other more sophisticated and less cumbersome methods of providing hotspot security?

Suggested reading

Drymalik, D, Wilsdon, T & Slay, J 2003, 'The vulnerabilities of 3G wireless systems with respect to proposed Australian implementations: A literature review', Fourth Information Warfare and Security Conference, Adelaide, November.

Nichols, R & Lekkas, P 2002, *Wireless Security: Models, Threats and Solutions*, McGraw-Hill Telecom, New York.

Turnbull, B, Nicholson, D & Slay, J 2003, 'Wireless networking security: A practical summary of 802.11b in Adelaide, Australia', Fourth Information Warfare and Security Conference, Adelaide, November.

Wilsdon, T & Slay, J 2004, 'A review of the security and performance issues in the use of voice-over ip for rural telecommunication provision', EICAR (European Institute for Computer Anti-Virus Research) 2004 Conference, Luxembourg, May.

References

Allen, J & Wilson, J 2002, 'Securing a wireless network', User Services Conference, ACM Press, New York, pp. 213–15.

Arbaugh, W 2001, 'An inductive chosen plaintext attack against WEP/WEP2', IEEE Document 802.11-02/230, May 2001, http://grouper.ieee.org/groups/802/11.

Arbaugh, WA, Shankar, N & Wan, YCJ 2001, 'Your 802.11 wireless network has no clothes', www.cs.umd.edu/~waa/wireless.pdf

Aufreiter, R 2001, 'Biometrics and cryptography: Match on card paves the way to convenient security', accessed 24 July 2003, www.itpapers.com/cgi/PSummaryIT.pl?paperid=26696&scid=442.

Billard, A & Janezic, K 2003, 'Evaluating security in emerging wireless technologies', Fourth Australian Information Warfare and Security Conference, Adelaide.

Blankenbeckler, D 2000 'An introduction to Bluetooth', Wireless Developer Network, www.wirelessdevnet.com/channels/bluetooth/features/bluetooth.html

Borisov, N, Goldberg, I & Wagner, D 2001a, '(In) Security of the WEP algorithm', accessed 13 January 2005, www.isaac.cs.berkeley.edu/isaac/wep-faq.html.

—— 2001b, 'Intercepting mobile communications: The insecurity of 802.11', in *Proceedings of Seventh Annual International Conference on Mobile Computing and Networking*, Rome, Italy.

Cam-Winget, N, Housley, R, Wagner, D & Walker, JR 2003, 'Security flaws in 802.11 data link protocols', *Communications of the ACM*, vol. 46, no. 5, pp. 35–9.

CNN 2000, 'Messages can freeze popular Nokia phones', accessed 24 July 2003, www.cnn.com/2000/TECH/computing/09/01/nokia.freeze.idg.

Davies, AC 2002, 'An overview of Bluetooth Wireless Technology/sup TM/ and some competing LAN standards', *Proceedings of ICCSC '02,* First IEEE International Conference on Circuits and Systems for Communications 2002, St Petersburg, Russia.

Department of the Attorney-General 1979, *Telecommunications (Interception) Act,* accessed 14 July 2003, http://scaleplus.law.gov.au/html/pasteact/0/464/top.htm.

—— 1992, *Radio Communications Act,* accessed 17 July 2003, http://scaleplus.law.gov. au/html/pasteact/0/300/top.htm.

—— 2001, *Cybercrime Act,* accessed 14 July 2003, http://scaleplus.law.gov.au/html/ ems/0/2001/rtf/2001072001.rtf.

Edney, J & Arbaugh, WA 2004, *Real 802.11 Security: Wi-Fi Protected Access and 802.11i,* Addison-Wesley Professional, Boston.

Fluhrer, SR, Mantin, I & Shamir, A 2001, 'Weaknesses in the key scheduling algorithm of RC4', in *Proceedings of Eighth Annual International Workshop on Selected Areas in Cryptography (SAC 2001),* S Vaudenay & AM Youssef, eds, *Lecture Notes in Computer Science,* vol. 2259, pp. 1–24, Springer-Verlag, Berlin.

Gast, MS 2002, *802.11 Wireless Networks: The Definitive Guide,* O'Reilly, CA.

Gindraux, S 2002, 'From 2G to 3G: A guide to mobile security', in *Proceedings of the Third International Conference on 3G Mobile Communication Technologies,* IEEE, pp. 308–11.

Hager, CT & Midkiff, SF 2003, 'An analysis of Bluetooth security vulnerabilities', *IEEE Wireless Communications and Networking Conference (WCNC),* March, Vol. 3, New Orleans, LA, pp. 1825–31.

Hattori, J 2000, 'Bluetooth developers aim to usher in a wireless era', accessed 15 July 2005, http://archives.cnn.com/2000/TECH/computing/09/01/bluetooth/index.html#2.

Honeynet Project 2003, *Know Your Enemy: Learning with VMware,* accessed 19 January 2005, www.honeynet.org/papers/vmware.

Howard, P, Walker, M & Wright, T 2001, 'Towards a coherent approach to third generation system security' in *Proceedings of the Second International Conference on G Mobile Communication Technologies,* IEEE, pp. 21–7.

IEEE 1999, *IEEE Std 802-1990,* Technical Committee on Computer Communications of the IEEE Computer Society, USA.

Intel 2003, 'Deploying secure wireless networks: Intel's strategies to minimize WLAN risk', accessed 26 June 2005, www.intel.com/ebusiness/pdf/it/wp032201.pdf.

Kilger, M, Ofir, A & Stutzman, J 2004, 'Profiling', in Honeynet Project, *Know Your Enemy,* 2nd edn, Addison-Wesley Professional, Boston.

Kitsos, P, Sklavos, N, Papadomanolakis, K & Koufopavlou, O 2003, 'Hardware implementation of Bluetooth security', *IEEE Pervasive Computing,* vol. 2, no. 1, January–March, pp. 21–9.

Lord, S 2003, *Modern GSM Insecurities,* Internet Security Systems, ISS, accessed 24 July 2003, www.itsecurity.com/papers/iss8.htm.

Menezes, A, van Oorschot, P & Vanstone, S 1996, *Handbook of Applied Cryptography,* CRC Press, Boca Raton, FL.

Morrow, R 2002, *Bluetooth Operations and Use,* McGraw-Hill Telecom, New York.

Nichols, R & Lekkas, P 2002, *Wireless Security: Models, Threats and Solutions,* McGraw-Hill Telecom, New York.

Petroni, NL & Arbaugh, WA 2003, 'The dangers of mitigating security design flaws: A wireless case study', *IEEE Security & Privacy,* vol. 1, no. 1, pp. 28–36.

Pfleeger, C & Pfleeger, C 2003, *Security in Computing,* 3rd edn, Prentice Hall, Upper Saddle River, NJ.

Phifer, L 2002, 'Understanding wireless LAN vulnerabilities', *Business Communications Review,* September, pp. 26–32.

Pioneering Advanced Mobile Privacy and Security (PAMPAS) 2003, 'Final roadmap (extended version)', accessed 1 July 2003, www.pampas.eu.org.

Potter, B 2003, 'Wireless security's future', *IEEE Security & Privacy,* vol. 1, no. 4, pp. 68–72.

Poulsen, K 2001, 'War driving by the Bay', *Security Focus,* accessed 18 January 2005, www.securityfocus.com/news/192.

Prabhakar, S, Pankanti, P & Jain, AK 2003, 'Biometric recognition: Security and privacy concerns', *IEEE Security & Privacy,* vol. 1, no. 2, pp. 33–42.

Rawat, KS & Massiha, GH 2003, 'Secure data transmission over wireless networks: Issues and challenges', IEEE Region 5, 2003 Annual Technical Conference, 11 April, pp. 65–8.

Smart Handheld Group 2003, 'Biometric security with the iPAQ Pocket PC h5400 series', Hewlett-Packard, accessed 24 July 2003, http://au.itpapers.zdnet.com/abstract.aspx?scid=442&kw=&dtid=0&docid=42551.

South Australian Consolidated Acts 1953, *Summary Offences,* accessed 14 July 2003, www.austlii.edu.au/au/legis/sa/consol_act/soa1953189.

Spitzner, L 2003, *Honeypots: Tracking Hackers,* Addison-Wesley Professional, Boston.

Townsend, K, n.d., 'Management guide to securing your wireless LAN', *BlueSocket,* accessed 29 August 2005, www.bluesocket.com/guide/m_guide.pdf.

Träskbäck, M, 2003, *Security of Bluetooth: An Overview of Bluetooth Security,* accessed 11 July 2003, http://opensource.nus.edu.sg/projects/bluetooth/noosphere/Bluetooth_Security.pdf.

Truelove, J 2002, *Build Your Own Wireless LAN,* McGraw-Hill, New York.

Vollbrecht, J, Rago, D & Moskowitz, R 2001, 'Wireless LAN access control and authentication', Interlink Networks, www.bsgu.edu/offices/its/noindex/wireless/InterlinkWirelessACandAuth.pdf.

Walker, JR 2000, 'Unsafe at any key size: An analysis of the WEP encapsulation', IEEE, http://grouper.ieee.org/groups/802/11/Documents/DocumentHolder/0-362.zip.

WAP Forum 2002, Wap 2.0 Technical White paper, www.wapforum.org/what/WAPWhite_Paper1.pdf,p. 5.

Wesolowski, K. 2002, *Mobile Communication Systems,* John Wiley & Sons, Chichester, West Sussex.

Wi-Fi Alliance 2003, 'Securing Wi-Fi wireless networks with today's technologies', accessed 26 June 2005, Wi-Fi Alliance, www.weca.net/OpenSection/pdf/Whitepaper_Wi-Fi_Networks2-6-03.pdf.

WildPackets 2003, 'WildPackets' guide to wireless LAN analysis', WildPackets Inc, accessed 31 July 2003, www.wildpackets.com/elements/whitepapers/Wireless_LAN_Analysis.pdf.

Wullems, C, Tham, K, Smith, J & Looi, M 2004, 'A trivial denial of service attack on IEEE 802.11 direct sequence spread spectrum wireless LANs', in *Proceedings of 2004 Wireless Telecommunications Symposium*, 14–15 May, Pomona, CA.

Zomaya, A 2002, *Handbook of Wireless Networks and Mobile Computing*, John Wiley & Sons, New York.

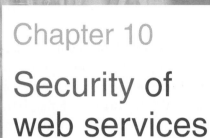

Chapter 10

Security of
web services

Learning objectives

After studying this chapter, you should be able to:

- define and explain the purpose of web services

- explain how web services work

- describe the security requirements of web services

- describe the security threats to web services

- explain the different ways of enhancing web service security.

Chapter overview

Advances in information and communication technology hold great promise for contemporary businesses. This promise comes in the shape of massive information storage, processing and communication. These advances on the one hand allow for the automation of inter-organisational and intra-organisational business processes and on the other hand provide for the realisation of new business models.

Nevertheless, a fundamental issue in this regard is the integration and interoperability of information. It is easy to imagine an organisation as a complete entity of information and knowledge that could be used to answer any question relating to making the business function properly. This sum total of information and knowledge actually consists of a range of applications, systems, databases and repositories, many of which have been developed years ago and have stayed the same, since changing these legacy items could prove too disruptive to the smooth functioning of the business. Not only is changing these systems expensive but also making the business adapt to a new system can be even more cumbersome. When businesses adopt newer, faster technology and develop new systems to address their emergent needs, the technological diversity of the entire business is increased. At the same time, when the same business participates in intra-organisational business processes, this multiplicity increases manifold.

In these circumstances, the fundamental issue for any business is to make these 'islands of information' talk to each other. Indeed information interoperability and integration means better process integration, and business process integration means overall business efficiency. Electronic data interchange (EDI) methodologies aimed at enterprise application integration (EAI) have tried to address this issue of information interoperability and integration. However, EAI solutions tend to be costly and highly complex, as they rely mainly on proprietary technology that is itself expensive to acquire, operate and maintain. EAI solutions at best make systems communicate with each other under stable conditions, and any change to these systems also requires changes to the EAI solutions.

The advent of e-business requires enterprises to interact and exchange information continuously. The focus is shifting towards reducing human involvement in information exchange as much as possible. As the e-business landscape is gaining stability, more and more businesses are tapping the potential of web-based technology to enhance their operational efficiency. Therefore there is a need for technology that could provide generic, flexible interfaces for application integration that could be reused, rather than being changed every time there was a change in application, systems or their configuration. Web services (WS) have emerged as a response to such needs. WS allow easy, efficient and secure business-to-business communication, so that disparate systems and applications can connect with each other as part of the business process.

What are web services?

A **web service** is a software component that is built on an open standard and is accessible via a network. Web services are independent of systems, platforms, programming model and language restrictions, so they allow otherwise separate applications to communicate with each other. Web services can be used as modules to create an application. In this way they are relatively simple building blocks for potentially complex and powerful applications.

Web services are the next step forward in distributed computing. They build on and expand the client/server architecture. Web services leverage loose coupling: technologically incompatible systems and applications combine to create more powerful services and applications. Web services primarily utilise **Extensible Markup Language (XML)** to provide interfaces across participating disparate systems, thereby allowing the services to be accessed as distinct components of a business process, implemented as stand-alone services or joined with other services to form composite applications. An obvious advantage of making up services in this manner is the creation of a service-oriented architecture (SOA), which means that resources in a network are available to participating members in a standardised way and without any restrictions. Such a flexible coupling of systems provides for the different components of the network to be executed in a context that the participant or component owner had not envisaged before. Traditionally, the participants in a business process can exchange information only if their systems have an appropriate application programming interface (API). A major shortcoming of this approach is the need to upgrade the API every time a new application or system is added to the business process or the process is re-engineered. SOA provides a way to move forward, from the existing approach of tightly coupled systems and API-oriented application integration to a more flexible way of integration that does not require any upgrading or any API, as web services are open standards–based and platform independent.

The seamless flow of information between applications and systems not only has advantages for the realisation of businesses processes but also contributes to the reshaping of the business strategy and direction. Contemporary businesses are moving away from the strategy of vertical integration in which they have tried to bring the vital building blocks of the business value chain under their own control. Owing to fierce competition and changing markets, businesses are now looking for horizontal integration, whereby the aim is to create a network of businesses around specific products and services so as to provide for total solutions. This network consists of related businesses, and the dominant business draws upon the core competencies of the other businesses to provide an enhanced product or service. This setting is especially significant for Australia, since 95 per cent of businesses in Australia are considered small to medium-sized enterprises (SMEs). SMEs often have limited financial and other resources, and therefore partnerships seem a logical solution to the emerging business landscape.

In such partnerships, a major impediment is the lack of standardised technology, which hinders the ability to form efficient business processes. Web services overcome the barriers created by different hardware and software platforms, providing for the easy linking of trading partners' applications and systems, thus enabling a greater degree of flexibility and new business opportunities.

A key objective of any business is to maintain its competitive position cost-effectively and at the same time expand the channels of suppliers, distributors, partners and customers. Web services are built on open standards and therefore provide an easy solution to integrate business applications for smooth facilitation of transactions relating to supply chain management, customer relationship management (CRM) and even collaborative manufacturing and design. This reduces the need for costly middleware and allows improved levels of process automation while saving costs and optimum utilisation of existing resources. Web services also open the doors for application service providers (ASPs), whereby a specific element of an application or complete applications relating to CRM or ERP (enterprise resource planning) could be made available to small businesses that could benefit from those applications but otherwise might not have the resources to own them.

The foremost advantage of web services is the freedom that they provide to businesses regarding the choice between developing in-house custom-made systems and procuring off-the-shelf systems. Furthermore, web services themselves are available as off-the-shelf packages or can be custom-made. This flexibility allows businesses to choose the solution that best fits their business requirements rather than having to stick to what is available to them. However, since web services are based on open standards and developed in open source language, they can easily be altered to meet the changing needs of the business. This also means that businesses do not necessarily have to redo or upgrade their legacy systems to address the current demands of business, as web services are backwards compatible and therefore allow for conversion and sharing of data from old applications and systems.

The platform independence of web services allows for sharing of information between different sources, such as online forms, databases, electronic correspondences, wireless and mobile applications. By linking this technology together, web services realise greater personalised customer relationship management. At the same time, this linking provides for the ability to collate and analyse data about a business process, or phenomenon in its entirety, for informed decision support. This is an important hurdle that many businesses have traditionally struggled to overcome. A consolidated case history of such activities as inventory movement or sales allows for detection of trends that might have significant consequences for the choice of suppliers, customers, and leakages and losses in production and manufacturing. At the same time, this consolidation of information allows for trust of customers and business partners in business processes. For example, at Amazon.com customers are able to access the website of the business and check stock levels before placing an online order, and after ordering they can track the movement of their orders. All of this happens seamlessly, regardless of which platform Amazon's inventory system and that of the customer is based on.

Nonetheless, seamless flow of information and the associated acceleration in data sharing creates opportunities for unauthorised hacking and infringements of information. This issue has further been amplified by the proliferation of web-based solutions, as the Internet itself is not a secure system by any means and provides for several access points for intrusion. Web services, as they are run on the Internet as well as intranets, are therefore also vulnerable to these security threats. However, before delving into security issues relating to web services, it is important to understand the technology and architecture involved in the development of web services.

Web services model

Web services are based on exchanges between three components: a service provider, a service registry and a service requestor. The exchange of information involves finding, binding and publishing operations. Together, these operations and components constitute the web services software module. In a typical scenario, a **service provider** hosts a software module that implements the web services on a network. The service provider delineates the description for the web services and makes available, or **publishes**, the web services to the service requestor and service registry. On the other hand, the **service requestor** uses a **find** operation to retrieve a description of the service from the **service registry**, then **binds** with the service provider and interrelates it with the implementation of web services. Figure 10.1 describes these components, operations and their interrelations, which are discussed in detail below.

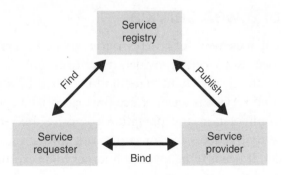

| Figure 10.1 | Web services model |

Source: based on W3C web services architecture description (W3C 2004).

Service provider

Service providers, speaking in terms of business, are the owners of the service. This does not necessarily mean that they represent the developers of the service, as 'service provider' here means the business that owns the process that the service is destined to realise. However, from a structural point of view, a service provider is the system or the application server that provides access to the service.

Service requestor

In terms of business a service requestor is the entity that requires certain functionality to fulfil the obligations of a process and therefore needs to find interested parties or other entities that could help. On the other hand, from an architectural perspective, a service requestor is an application that wants to initiate a contact with a service. It could be done by a user interface through which a user requests information, or it could be an application program without a user interface, which also means that it could even be another web service.

Service registry

A service registry is a searchable repository of service descriptions published by service providers. Service requestors perform a find operation to locate services and obtain binding information. Binding can be static or dynamic. Static binding is initiated during the web service development phase, and for static-bound service requestors the service registry has an optional role, as the service provider can send it directly to the service requestor. At the same time service requestors can obtain a service description from sources other than the service registry, such as local files, an FTP (File Transfer Protocol) site, website, Advertisement and Discovery of Services (ADS) or Discovery of Web Services (DISCO). Dynamic binding, however, occurs during execution.

Essentials of a web service

There are two essential elements of a web service: service and service description.

A *service* is realised by a service provider. It performs one or more tasks, has a service description and a service interface, and is owned by a person or organisation. Where a web service is an interface prescribed by a service description, its execution, implementation and operation comprise the service. However, a service is software that is accessible on a network through a host provided by the service provider. It needs to be invoked in order to be executed and can itself work as a requestor for another service.

The *service description* contains details of the interface and implementation regarding the service. It comprises data types, operations, binding information and network location of the web service. It could also include metadata that facilitates service requestors in discovery and onward utilisation of the service.

However, the service description needs to be published to a service requestor or to a service registry for it to be discovered.

Operations in a web service

In order for an application to take advantage of a web service, three activities need to take place: publishing service description, finding service descriptions and binding or invoking services on the basis of descriptions. These activities could occur at once or in a loop:

- *Publish.* In order for the service description to be accessible, it needs to be published so that the service requestor can find it with ease. It is the role of the service provider to publish the service and its functional descriptions, such that the interested parties can collect them without having to seek permission from the service provider.
- *Find.* The service requestor can retrieve the service description directly or query the service registry for the type of service required. In order to do that the service requestor is required to perform a find operation. This find operation is performed at two stages, at the design time to retrieve the service's interface description for developing the program and at execution, in order to retrieve the service's location, invocation and binding.
- *Binding.* The service requestor, through the binding operation, initiates the service at runtime using the service description's details to locate, contact and invoke the service.

Web services technology

The web services architecture (see figure 10.2, p. 288) illustrates a layered approach and involves different forms of technology, which fulfil the roles that have been described above and therefore are deemed to be critical for WS. This architecture provides a bottom-up perspective of the WS tools used in the design, development and deployment of WS. In order to perform the operations of publishing, finding and binding, in an interoperable manner, the WS layer needs to be based on some standards for information interoperability. These standards are shown on the left-hand side of the WS stack. The concept of this architecture model illustrates that the upper layers build on the foundations provided by the lower layers. Nonetheless, there are three requirements (shown on the right-hand side) associated with each layer to work steadily and efficiently.

The first layer is the **network layer**. As mentioned earlier, web services work on the Internet or intranet, and therefore an essential requirement of web services is that they be network accessible so they can be published by the service providers and invoked by the service requestors. Web services that are publicly available, such as the ones used by search engines on the Internet, use common network protocols. HTTP (Hypertext Transfer Protocol), owing to its wide adoption,

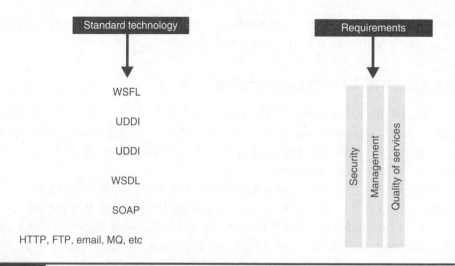

Figure 10.2 Web services architecture

Source: based on W3C web services architecture description (W3C 2004).

has become a universal mechanism for information exchange at the application level between web-based systems. That is why it is also the de facto standard network protocol for web services; however, other Internet protocols, such as SMTP and FTP, can also be used.

The next layer, **XML-based messaging**, stresses the use of XML (eXtensible Markup Language) as the basis for the messaging protocol and is a data-tagging language of web services. XML is flexible and provides a standardised set of rules for adding structure to any form of data using a system of mark-up tags. Using XML, anybody could create their own vocabulary (commonly known as XML schema) to ensure that the structure is intelligent enough to be understood by anybody who confers with the XML schema document. At the same time an important feature is the fact that XML schema allow XML-based or XML-aware software to work with data without having any advanced knowledge of the structure. **SOAP** (**Simple Object Access Protocol**) is the standard for web services messages and is based on XML. It describes an envelope format and a set of rules for defining its contents. It is the preferred messaging protocol as it provides standardised enveloping means for communicating document-centric messages and RPCs (remote procedure calls) using XML. It is basically an HTTP POST with an XML envelope as payload. SOAP messages help in publishing, finding and binding operations in the web services architecture. SOAP, together with **WSDL (Web Services Description Language)** and **UDDI (Universal Description, Discovery and Integration protocol)**, provides for the three foundation standards of web services.

The next layer, **service description**, is based on WSDL, which is an XML-based standardised format for describing a web service. A WSDL layer is actually a stack of description documents, and it provides description for the ways to access a web service and the operations that the web service is designed to perform. WSDL is the de facto standard for XML-based service description and is a minimum standard service description necessary to support interoperable web services. It delineates the interface and interactions of the web services, such as quality of service and service-to-service relationships. The business context or the process context is described using UDDI data structures in the WSDL document. UDDI is a directory model for web services, and it provides for maintaining standardised directories of web services information, such as location and requirements. The composition of the web service and its flow are, however, described in a **WSFL (Web Services Flow Language)** document.

Web services in operation

Systems integration for an enhanced level of information integration and interoperability has been a dream of businesses for many years. To this end business process automation with a reduced level of human interaction has been an important objective. Although human interaction is required at various levels in a business process, research has revealed that the issues relating to information quality crop up owing to human intervention, and at the same time interactions between various functions and departments of a business could be carried out more reliably and efficiently if the systems facilitating those processes could interact with each other seamlessly. Traditionally, businesses have employed numerous EAI tools, such as to integrate plant sites, sales and marketing and financials; however, they have not yielded required levels of information interoperability and integration. The ways web services help in achieving this is illustrated in the example below.

Let's consider the example of an Australian automobile manufacturer in Melbourne that relies heavily on a particular supplier in Adelaide for major assembly of its product. These assemblies are large products but are not manufactured in large quantities. This means that the stock is not readily available. For manufacturing and sales planning, the automobile manufacturer in Melbourne shares a forecast planner with the supplier in Adelaide. Therefore, when an overseas customer places an order and asks for a shipping date, it is important to know the availability of supplies in stock from the supplier before a shipping date could be submitted to the customer. Ideally the manufacturer's sales order system on receiving the purchase request and its confirmation generates a demand for assembly of the products, which is communicated to production planning for scheduling of production. The production planning system sends a message to the supplier's system, asking the date by which the supplies could be delivered, or whether a certain quantity of supplies could be made available by a specific date. The supplier's system then checks for existing inventory levels and planned production status and responds to the manufacturer with an appropriate reply. The manufacturer's system is then able to confirm the order and provide the shipment date to the overseas customer.

This seems quite simple, but in reality it is much more difficult to achieve. In this situation the manufacturer's system needs to know what information is required and how much of it is coming from outside sources so as to satisfy the customer query. It must construct questions like 'when' or 'is it possible' along with supporting data, such as item number, quantity and date required, and send all of it to the supplier's Internet address. This is what SOAP defines; that is, the format and contents of the message. On the other hand, definition of what the supplier's system can do and needs to do is described by WSDL. The SOAP message is developed according to the receiving or supplier's system's characterisation; that is, how it works and what it expects to be given as prerequisites for it to work. The receiving system also needs to interpret the message and recognise the request for what it means, know what information is required and where to look for the information in the internal systems. The supplier's system then starts a service to process the request, determines the response and sends the response to the manufacturer's systems according to SOAP and WSDL definitions. The manufacturer's system recognises the message, interprets the response and sends the same to the application that started this entire exchange. In this case the supplier's system is providing a service to the manufacturer's system, as that service was requested and initiated by a requesting system at the manufacturer's end. This approach allows for technologically incompatible environments to interact and exchange information seamlessly, as long as the systems conform to SOAP and WSDL and both understand the common language of XML.

In a more familiar example, Amazon web services offer a variety of applications to its customers, ranging from registering as customers to retrieval of information about products to adding items to their shopping cart and finally making a purchase. A customer is able to access these web services from a browser client from anywhere in the world, through XML over HTTP or a SOAP interface. XML and SOAP allow customers and web developers to process information directly from Amazon's servers and present it in any way on their own websites. To illustrate how Amazon's web services are used, consider the following five steps involved in the registration of customers.

1. The customer's web browser client, through the web-based registration form, packages account registration information into a SOAP message.
2. The SOAP message is transmitted to the web service through a HTTP POST request.
3. On receiving the message, the web service unbundles the SOAP request and changes it into commands understood by the registration application running on Amazon's server. The application processes the information provided and generates a unique account number for the customer.
4. The web service bundles the response into a SOAP message and sends it to the customer's client as a reply to the HTTP request.
5. Finally, the browser client unpacks the message and displays its contents; that is, the account registration number.

To explain this more fully, consider another example. Suppose that you are looking for a restaurant. You might want to access the web and use a search engine such as Google to search for a restaurant. Once you have found the restaurant that suits your taste, price and location, you can then download its details, including the directions for getting there. This means that you have used a protocol to access the search engine, you used the search engine to search the web for the required restaurant and finally used some kind of interface to download the details of the resulting search. In web services similar activities take place. SOAP enables the WS connection to take place, UDDI is the look-up for locating the service and WSDL retrieves the selected WS. However, while searching for information using Google itself, software developers can use the Google Web API services to query more than three billion web documents directly from their own programs. Since Google uses SOAP and WSDL standards, developers can develop their programs in the preferred platform, such as Java, Visual Studio or .NET, while still being able to use Google web service.

Web services security

The major issue with the utilisation of web services is the vulnerability of this technology to security breaches, owing mainly to the non-availability of broadly adopted specifications for web services security and the susceptibility of the Internet as a secure medium. Ratnasingam (2002) identifies a number of security concerns and barriers in the development of web services:

- *Lack of established standards.* The current standards used in web services lack interoperability, quality, security and performance, which pose a challenge for early adopters.
- *Discovery.* 'Discovery' refers to the way a web service advertises itself so that it can be noticed by other services. Although WSDL and UDDI currently address this issue, no support is given to the way the discovery issue caters for changes made after it had advertised. This can cause conflicts, dissatisfaction and mistrust among trading partners.
- *Reliability.* 'Reliability' refers to the accuracy and integrity of business transactions.
- *Availability.* What happens when a web service host goes off line temporarily? What will be the effect on real-time transactions? Is the requester responsible for finding an alternative service, or should they wait for the original provider?
- *Integrity.* 'Integrity' refers to the quality of the way web services maintain correct transactions.
- *Transactions.* Traditional transaction systems use a two-phase approach as all of the participating resources are gathered and locked until the entire transaction can take place, at which point the resources are released. This approach works fine in a closed environment where transactions can span hours and even days. But with web services, the demand for real-time transactions, security risks such as spoofing, masquerading, repudiation and a lack of access control can cause blockage of transactions.

- *Data ownership.* Web services architecture does not guarantee real-time transactions all the time. Compatibility problems complicate connections between .Net and non-.Net based web services. In addition, web services pose barriers owing to a lack of bandwidth, trust issues and questions about who owns the data.
- *Manageability.* What kind of mechanisms are required for managing a highly distributed system? Since the properties of the system are a function of the properties of its parts, do the managers of each of the various web services need to coordinate in a particular way? Is it possible to outsource the management of a few web services to an application server?
- *Accountability.* How do you define how long a user can access and execute a web service? How do you charge for web services? Will the dominant model be subscription-based or pay as you go? If you sell a web service, how do you designate that the ownership has changed? Can a web service be totally consumed on use, or can you reuse the service multiple times as part of your purchase agreement?
- *Testing.* How do you achieve predictable response times? How do you debug web services that come from different operating systems? A system comprising many web services whose locations and qualities are potentially dynamic might mean that testing and debugging could take much longer.

Security challenges posed to web services

A fundamental issue with the use of web services is that the applications which are otherwise internal to the business are exposed to the outside world. Since the application is closer to information than to the network, it opens up security threats not only to the web service hosting system and the network but also to the entire information and communication infrastructure of the business. Traditionally, point-to-point technological solutions, such as Secure Sockets Layer (SSL), Transport Layer Security (TLS), Virtual Private Networks (VPNs) and Internet Protocol Security (IPSec), have been used to secure the contents of the message exchanged. Along with these protocols for providing a secured passage, encryption techniques are used, such as Secure Multipurpose Internet Mail Exchange (S/MIME) protocol through which information can be communicated digitally signed and encrypted through the Internet, which is an insecure medium. However, these protocols do not constitute a complete solution as these security fences could be breached in many ways, such as denial of service attacks; intrusion attacks; Trojans and viruses through electronic mail; improperly configured web, email servers and client browsers; replay attacks; and domain name server (DNS) attacks. Although traditional security technology is commonly used to provide security for web services, it is also known that these measures are insufficient for providing an end-to-end security environment for web services, which are message-based.

Are web services an extra risk to manage?

A literature review covering the past few years shows the IT industry swinging from pessimism through to optimism and now, apparently, back to pessimism again when the IT security risks brought about by the adoption of web services are considered.

In a recent review the Gartner group (which supplies statistical market reports to industry) saw web services potentially importing yet another wave of vulnerability.

Web services are likely to create the next generation of vulnerabilities, according to Victor Wheatman, Gartner managing vice-president for security.

The introduction of new technologies and business practices will mean that organisations with their IT security battened down today will have to work hard to keep it that way, he said.

'Whenever new technology is introduced or business fundamentals change, management's focus in terms of funding and resource allocation shifts from the old to the new, creating a security gap,' said Wheatman.

In recent years, each major development in technology has left businesses with new security gaps.

Network PCs eroded the gains companies had won securing individual desktops. The introduction of distributed applications, external networks and wireless networks created further waves of vulnerabilities.

'Each new wave of technology obliterates the security architecture appropriate to its predecessor, opening the enterprise up to an ever-increasing raft of security risks,' said Wheatman.

The next threat will come from the emergence of web services, which allow data to bypass firewalls, Wheatman said.

At the same time, IT departments will have to contend with a steady stream of new threats, including viruses on personal digital assistants, spyware, vulnerabilities introduced by instant messaging and hybrid worms.

But loss of business confidence from cyberterrorism has peaked and, barring new physical attacks, will remain at current levels, according to Wheatman. Cyberterrorism hype causes more loss of confidence than actual attacks, he said.

'Continual scanning for new vulnerabilities and monitoring for new threats are critical and a much better investment than to passively sit back and wait to detect attacks. In security, the best defence is a good offence,' said Wheatman.

Source: Goodwin 2004.

As mentioned earlier, web services security does not involve just transport-level security aimed at providing an end-to-end safe passage for information transmission. At the same time, the number of intermediaries involved in message transmission and information exchange illustrates that for web services security, message-level security is equally important. A number of threats are associated with message-level security, such as:

- *Message alteration.* These are also known as semantic attacks, as they affect the authenticity and integrity of the message, whereby the attackers aim to modify part or all of the message. For example, an attacker could modify the header and/or body of the message by deleting or inserting information. Another form of attacking the message is by manipulating its attachments or adding wrong attachments to it.

- *Confidentiality.* This threat is becoming more serious in cyberspace, as unauthorised entities obtain classified information from within the message. Common examples of threats to confidentiality are stolen identities and credit card numbers from customer databases.

- *Man-in-the-middle.* These attacks are also referred to as bucket brigade attacks. In this kind of attack, the attacker conciliates a SOAP intermediary and intercepts messages between the web services requestor and its intended destination, while the actual parties think that no intrusion has occurred and that they are actually communicating with each other. However, authentication techniques to reduce the occurrence of attacks of this type are becoming increasingly important.

- *Spoofing.* Spoofing is a multifaceted attack aimed at exploitation of the trust relationship between two parties. The attacker assumes the identity of one of the parties to affect the other party and the trust relationship. If remote applications can connect to the back end of an organisation, they can also do a lot of damage to the organisation's databases. Applications can be modified to allow actions that their designers never intended, for example snooping by an employee who is already inside the firewall and has access to the servers, databases and information. Common forms of these attacks are forged messages and leaking of confidential information that is critical to the business.

- *Denial of service.* These attacks are aimed at preventing the legitimate user of a service from using it. These can be synchronised attacks, whereby more than one machine on an intranet is paralysed and consequently the whole network loses access to the service. Denial of service attacks could bombard websites with an overwhelming amount of traffic, creating an effective logjam that denies service to legitimate users. A more powerful form of this attack is the distributed denial of service, whereby a Trojan distributed to unsuspecting servers erases its tracks and awaits the order to start the attack. These attacks are easy to implement and, quite ironically, they exploit the inherent weaknesses in the security mechanisms themselves.

- *Replay attacks.* In this type of attack, the attacker replays the same message over and over again to its target, thereby causing overload and confusion. However, attacks of this type could be minimised by sequencing and time-based authentication of messages.
- *Viruses.* These are pretty common attacks, whereby the attacker aims to spread malicious code to paralyse a host or the participating systems in a process.

These attacks depend on the location, access level and expertise of the attacker and could be launched at network, host system or application level. It is important to note that it might be impossible and financially draining to counter every type of attack; hence prudence dictates a focus on containing the risk and stopping it from spreading to the entire infrastructure.

Managing web services security

Web services offer benefits for business and are rapidly being adopted for inter-organisational transactions. As Internet protocols are primarily unsecured it is imperative that for business-to-business activity to occur safely security issues of web services need to be addressed. Many of the types of threat discussed in this book so far also apply to web services; threats such as authentication, confidentiality of transmission, integrity of data and denial of service are real security concerns in the deployment of web services. Web services, through their ability to connect corporate resources through the Internet, can create greater exposure of such resources to security threats with possibly disastrous consequences.

It is critical for organisations to be proactive in protecting their business as well as the businesses of their customers, suppliers and partners from both intentional and unintentional attacks. Figure 10.3 (p. 296) illustrates a comprehensive model of web services security management. An important aspect of this model is the emphasis on management of security issues rather than controlling the security issues, as well as stressing the necessity to approach the problems from technical, process and management viewpoints.

At this time, there are no broadly accepted specifications for web services security; consequently, web services implementation might require point-to-point or end-to-end security mechanisms or both, as demanded by the degree of threat or risk posed. However, security measures necessarily are the balance between risk assessment and the costs incurred on offsetting measures. Some of the security measures are discussed below in the light of the web services security management model presented above. According to the model, the security measures must be aimed at three levels: information and data resources, mechanisms to enforce security, and management policies enacted to secure the information resources.

Policies can be logically divided into two categories: permission policies and obligatory policies. A permission policy deals with the actions that entities are 'permitted' to carry out, whereas obligatory policies deal with the actions that

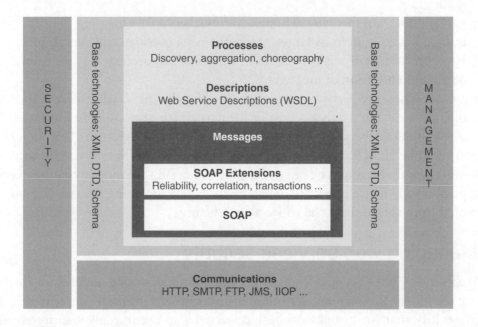

| Figure 10.3 | Web services security management model |

Source: http://www.w3.org/TR/2004/NOTE-ws-arch-20040211/

the entities are 'required' to perform. These policies are interrelated and inter-dependent, with one complementing the other; therefore a policy document could contain a combination of obligation and permission policy assertions. Enforcement of these policies follows different strategies; however, a widely projected technique is enacting guards. These guards are agents, which could be a set of techniques, humans or software that could be used for verification of actions and obligations. In a well-developed system it would be possible to enact guards that do not make themselves visible to the service requestor or provider; for example, the threat of unauthorised access could be defended by mechanisms for validating the identity of potential participants who attempt to access controlled resources. These mechanisms are, however, controlled by the policy that contains the substantiation process of the proof offered by the participant before access. For example, an important role of SOAP intermediaries is to restrict or grant access to resources or actions, which it carries out by not forwarding a message if the policy has been violated. However, not all guards are active. For example, encryption is used as a technique for maintaining the confidentiality of a message. At the same time, it is also important to conceal the identity of the sender and receiver. Here the guard is the 'encryption', which needs to be backed up by other guards that affect the policy.

At the highest level in using web services is the fundamental objective of creating an environment in which message-level transactions and business processes could be carried out in an end-to-end secure manner. Secure messaging is essential to maintain privacy, confidentiality and integrity of business transactions. There is therefore the need to secure messages during transfer, whether there are intermediaries or otherwise. A corollary to this initiative is securing data storage. The initiatives for providing end-to-end web services are summarised below.

Authentication mechanisms

Appropriate authentication mechanisms must be enforced to verify the identities of requesters and providers of the web service. In certain cases, shared or mutual authentication could be required as the participating members might not be bound directly by a single step. For example, they could be requesters and intermediaries. However, depending on the security policies, it might be possible to authenticate the requester or receiver, or to authorise the use of mutual authentication.

There are different ways of enforcing authorisation mechanisms, such as passwords and certificates. However, password-based techniques might prove insufficient, and it might be necessary to combine password authentication with another authentication and authorisation process, such as certificates, Lightweight Directory Access Protocol (LDAP), Remote Authentication Dial-in User Service (RADIUS), Kerberos and Public Key Infrastructure (PKI).

Authorisation

This technique is foremost in controlling access to resources. It works in conjunction with the authentication mechanisms, whereby the authorisation mechanisms control the requester's access to appropriate system resources. Access rights are, however, determined by the access control policy. As a rule of thumb, the principle of least privilege access should be used in granting access rights to a service requester.

Integrity and confidentiality of data

In order to maintain the authenticity, privacy and credibility of messages and their contents, it needs to be ensured that the data is accessible only by the authorised users. Digital signatures techniques and data encryption techniques are important facilitators in this regard.

Integrity of transactions and communications

An accountability mechanism is required to ensure that the business process was carried out appropriately and the associated flow of information occurred accordingly. This audit of the process could help to uncover any irregularities in the pattern of process output and events.

Non-repudiation

Non-repudiation is itself a security service that protects a party from false denial of service. Non-repudiation technology, such as digital signatures, provides evidence on the incidence of transactions, which can be used by third parties to determine disagreement.

Audit trails

Audit trails must be used to trace user access and behaviour. Audit trails could be performed by software agents, acting as guards to monitor resources and validating whether the established procedures are being respected. In practice, audit trails are used to trace how a security breach occurred, and they are seldom used to enact policies. Therefore, it is stressed that businesses need to take a proactive stance to security and used it as a security enforcing mechanism rather than as a disaster management tool.

Distributed enforcement of security policies

Businesses must enforce security across various platforms with standardised privileges.

Web services security specification

As mentioned earlier, there are no standardised specifications for web services security. However, standards bodies such as the World Wide Web Consortium (W3C), the Organization for the Advancement of Structured Information Standards (OASIS) and the Liberty Alliance, along with others, are in the process of developing web services infrastructure standards and specifications so that businesses can overcome the challenges posed by conventional security technology. To this end, a variety of technology and protocols have been developed (Sun Microsystems 2003), some of which are discussed below.

XML Signature

XML Signature is one of the most common XML-based security standards. It is a specification designed for using digital signatures with XML documents, and it provides XML-compliant syntax for the signatures of Internet-based resources and sections of protocol messages. The capability to sign individual elements within an XML-based message rather than the whole message is deemed to be significant for multistage workflow process support where the message is modified at every step. This technique therefore provides for granular security implementation at message level.

XML Encryption

XML Encryption is a process of jumbling up the contents of information in such a way that only the intended recipient knows how to put all the pieces together to make sense of the message. When sensitive data, such as personal or financial information, is exchanged on the web, secure communication is a must. That is why different technology is employed by senders and receivers of information to ensure the safe passage of data and information. However, these mechanisms address only point-to-point safe passage and are not of much help at the content level. Together with XML Signature, XML Encryption allows for encryption of the whole or portions of communicated information. This encryption of information results in an encrypted XML element containing the information that points to ciphered data.

SOAP Message Security

Simple Object Access Protocol (SOAP) is a standard that supports security mechanisms that use XML formats defined by XML schema. These mechanisms include using XML Signatures for SOAP message integrity; using XML Encryption for SOAP message confidentiality; security tokens in the headers of SOAP messages, carrying security information for intermediaries; and matching signatures with security tokens.

XML Key Management Specification

An XML protocol allows a simple client to obtain key information (value, certificate, management or trust data) from a web service. It also describes protocols for distributing and registering public keys, suitable for use in conjunction with the standards for XML Signature and XML Encryption. XML Key Management Specification (XKMS) helps overcome PKI complexity by allowing web services to become clients of a key management service.

Extensible Access Control Mark-up Language

Extensible Access Control Mark-up Language (XACML) describes both an access control policy language and a request/response language. The policy language is used to express access control policies (who can do what and when). The request/response language expresses queries about whether a particular access should be allowed (request) and describes answers to those queries (responses). A new specification called the Web Services Policy Language (WSPL) is being developed as a generic language to express policy information. It is based on the XACML work.

XML Key Management Specification

XML Key Management Secification (XKMS) allows for a normal client to retrieve such information as certificate, management or trust data from a web service. It prescribes protocols for distribution and registration of public keys that could be used in combination with other standards like XML Signature and XML Encryption. However, a significant feature of XKMS is that it eases the complexities of Public Key Infrastructure (PKI) by permitting web services be clients of a key management service.

Extensible Rights Mark-up Language

Extensible Rights Mark-up Language (XrML) allows for secure specification and management of managing rights and limitations related with digital content and services.

Security Assertion Mark-up Language

Security Assertion Mark-up Language (SAML) is a protocol that specifies a structure for exchange of security information. The security information is defined as assertions about entities, such as humans or computers, and these entities belong to a security domain, for example a user who could be identified by their email address in a particular DNS. Assertions convey information about the entity's authentication acts, attributes and decisions regarding authorisation to access certain resources. These assertions are, however, defined in XML and contain statements about authentication, authorisation and attributes.

Digital Signature Standard

Digital Signature Standard is a developing specification, which aims to provide support for the processing of digital signatures as web services and specification of a protocol for centralised verification of digital signature and cryptographic time stamping, according to set policies.

Electronic Business XML

Electronic Business XML (ebXML) provides a landscape that enables XML to be used for electronic businesses and the associated information in electronic business. ebXML Messaging Service (ebMS), which is an extension of ebXML, addresses the security requirements of information transfer over the Internet.

Many other specifications have also been proposed for web services security, including WS-Trust, WS-Federation, WS-SecurityPolicy and WS-SecureConversation.

Summary

Web services have enormous potential for the emerging business landscape. Web services, while making two systems exchange information, actually realise many innovative business models, and as more and more businesses move to take advantage of cyberspace, there will be a manifold increase in the use of web services. More often than not web service security is taken for the security of SOAP; however, securing web services involves not just the security of the infrastructure but also that of the information being exchanged. It requires provisions of secure information transport mechanisms and security of information content embedded with the information, which needs to be backed up by security policies. Therefore, web services security must be aimed at information and data resources, mechanisms to enforce security and management policies enacted to secure information resources.

Key terms

binds, p. 285

Extensible Markup
    Language (XML), p. 283

find, p. 285

network layer, p. 287

publish, p. 285

service description, p. 288

service provider, p. 285

service registry, p. 285

service requestor, p. 285

Simple Object Access
    Protocol (SOAP), p. 288

Universal Description,
    Discovery and Integration
    protocol (UDDI), p. 288

web service, p. 283

Web Services Description Language
    (WDSL), p. 288

Web Services Flow Language
    (WSFL), p. 289

XML-based messaging, p. 288

Questions

1. Why would a business want to use web services, and what advantages would they provide to help manage changing business needs?
2. How can the current or future web services security model and technology address the security risks of calling a web service from a mobile device (i.e. a mobile client)?
3. What additional software or services should be installed on an existing or traditional network infrastructure in order to support the web services security model and its implementation?
4. How can users add the auditing function to the current web services security model, and how could they determine whether a security failure has occurred?
5. It is possible for a sender to sign only certain parts of a document using XML Encryption. How can this be done?
6. A number of tools and strategies for web services security are available on the market. However, is there a measurement standard, criterion or guideline to assess the secure level of the current web services?

Case study

10: Northern Trust

Web services you can bank on

With $2.3 trillion in assets under its management in 97 financial markets, multi-bank holding company Northern Trust treats business processes such as auditing, logging and security with the utmost seriousness.

Take Northern Trust's approach to Web services. While Audra Lind, manager of the company's architecture division, loves the idea of a service-orientated architecture (SOA), she doesn't want application developers creating Web services willy-nilly. Instead, she wants all application teams to follow the same set of best practices.

Until recently, what little work had been done on Web services related to a few 'one-off' Java-based applications, says Lind, who also is a vice president within Northern Trust's Worldwide Operations and Technology business unit in Chicago. 'These weren't something you could support at an enterprise level, only within one line of business. There wasn't a repository to catalogue services. There wasn't a common way to do authentication and security. They were done in a very secure way, but they just weren't enterprise solutions,' she says.

To get beyond this limited scope, Northern Trust would have to adopt an enterprise management framework, Lind realized. A framework would allow a Web-services–based trading application to use the same sign-on and authentication procedures as a Web-services-based reporting application, for instance. The framework also would deliver performance information to ensure Web-services-based applications meet specified service levels, and provide data for auditing and logging purposes.

'Our framework opens the door for application teams to develop Web services based on business logic without having to worry about or support the underlying security, auditing or logging functions,' Lind says. 'With the old way, they would have been completely on their own … Now they can use what we have in place. We have all sorts of documents — best practices, road maps — for building a Web service.'

The result is a robust SOA that promises to drastically reduce the complexity, development time and cost of building applications while giving Northern Trust a testing ground for how to use Web services with external clients.

A new world

The framework, created using Management Foundation from AmberPoint, allows for the first time interoperability between development environments that Northern Trust uses for online applications. 'This nestles right into the Java space and right into the [Microsoft] .Net space, with very little custom coding required,' Lind says.

Northern Trust has used BEA Systems' WebLogic application server, which supports the Java 2 Platform Enterprise Edition platform, for about five years. In late 2003, it upgraded to the latest version — 8.1, aimed at SOA development — coincident with bringing .Net in house. Lind says .Net appealed to the architecture division for a number of reasons: the component-oriented Visual C# programming language, the rapid development environment, ease of integration with other Microsoft applications, and availability of .Net applications from independent software vendors.

Today, Northern Trust has about 100 Java-based applications across its various lines of business and five to 10 core .Net-based business applications, with hundreds of smaller applications across the company. The AmberPoint management framework opens a new world for the developers for two reasons: its agents run natively in the WebLogic and .Net servers, and it provides service brokering between applications, Lind says. The framework supports the World Wide Web Consortium's Simple Object Access Protocol for communications.

'The framework opens the ability to talk between those two environments, which is great because a lot of our applications can share code and call each other to get certain functions. Now people who want to build the applications in. Net to take advantage of the rapid development environment can do that while leveraging Java code for some of the business logic,' she explains.

Under the framework

The first application produced using the Web services management framework features a .Net front end and Java in the back end, Lind says.

Via the management framework, developers enabled the application to collate data from multiple disparate sources and then present the information for use by Northern Trust traders, Lind says. Developers relied on the framework for the security and management functions, needing only to focus on the business logic and thus reduce the project's complexity, duration and cost, she notes. Traders will begin using this investment application as part of their daily jobs starting in 2005.

With one successful Web service on its way to deployment, Lind says she now expects developers to make those one-off, Java-based Web services-based applications enterprise-class by moving them on to the prescribed management platform. She also anticipates that developers will look to the management framework as they consider how to update existing applications with new features and functions.

'We hope to always have the Web services hook in there to say, "We have this framework in place. We have this new way of sharing data between the platforms. This could simplify your application in this 15 ways, let's do it,"' Lind says. 'This will be an iterative, continuously moving effort.'

Of course, she adds, any brand-new application that needs to share data, talk across platforms or expose functions as Web services definitely would go under the framework.

'Everyone is very excited about this potential,' Lind says, although she wouldn't venture a guess as to how many Web services Northern Trust eventually will have in its framework. 'Our [AmberPoint] contract says that next year I can have up to 50, and then I'll have to pay for more, but I have absolutely no idea ... I would expect that the first few applications will get in there, and with their success stories, a lot of other application managers will jump on the bandwagon.'

On the safe side

Still, until the company's Worldwide Operations and Technology group is 100 per cent comfortable with security and performance, Web services will be for internal use only. For now, any Web applications used by clients must remain in the Java realm. 'Sharing data with other organizations would be an excellent use of Web services, but we need more due diligence before we go down that path,' Lind says.

Tim Theriault, president of Worldwide Operations and Technology, elaborates: 'We haven't just said, "Web services for everything and everybody." For technology, that sounds elegant. But for business reasons, that doesn't make sense.'

Getting comfortable with security and management issues internally first makes far more sense, Lind adds. Her team initially focused its framework efforts on supporting Web services for transport over HTTP.

Next year, she says, the team will work on three framework initiatives: supporting Web services over the company's MQ Series messaging infrastructure, providing a catalogue for Web services (most likely using the UDDI specifications), and nailing down additional security functionality.

'But what we have done so far, focusing on fixing the biggest problems of security, auditing and logging, has been a good first step for us, to begin solving these issues for Northern Trust,' Lind says. 'And just as the management framework is opening doors for us internally, I'm hoping that it will open doors externally over time, too.'

Source: Schultz 2004.

Questions

1. What advantages have the use of web services brought to Northern Trust?
2. Describe the security processes and mechanisms that Northern Trust has implemented to secure its web services.
3. Northern Trust has detailed the further work it intends to carry out within its web services framework. Consider the security implications of this work, and comment on any additional security functionality that might be required.

Suggested reading

Clark, KG 2003, 'The Architecture of Service and A Tour of Web Services Architecture', XML.com, available at www.xml.com/pub/a/2003/06/18/ws-arch.html.

Fairchild, AM 2003, 'Value positions for financial institutions in Electronic Bill Presentment and Payment', in *Proceedings of the 36th Hawaii International Conference on System Science (HICSS '03)*, IEEE, 6–9 January, Big Island, HI.

IBM developerWorks: Web Services: New to Web services.

Prescord, P 2002, Second Generation Web Services, Webservices.xml.com, accessed 1 July 2005, www.webservices.xml.com/pub/a/ws/2002/02/06rest.html.

Siddiqui, B 2004, 'Web services security', parts 1 and 4, http://webservices.xml.com/pub/au/140.

Web Services-Interoperability Organization (WS-I) 2004, 'ws-i security scenarios', February, www.ws-i.org/Profiles/BasicSecurity/2004-02/SecurityScenarios-0.15-WGD.pdf.

Webservices.xml.com: A Web Services Primer.

References

Goodwin, B 2004, 'Web services look set to be the next big risk', *Computer Weekly*, accessed 23 March 2005, www.computerweekly.com/article133508.htm.

Ratnasingam, P 2002, 'The importance of technology trust in web services security', *Information Management and Computer Security*, vol. 10, no. 5, pp. 255–60.

Schultz, B 2004, 'Web services you can bank on', *Network World Fusion*, accessed 29 April 2005, www.nwfusion.com/power/2004/122704northerntrust.html.

Sun Microsystems 2003, *Securing Web Services: Concepts, Standards and Requirements*, Sun Microsystems White Paper, accessed 25 August 2004, www.sun.com/software/whitepapers/webservices/securing_webservices.pdf.

World Wide Web Consortium (W3C) 2004, 'Web services architecture', accessed 25 August 2004, www.w3.org/TR/2004/NOTE-ws-arch-20040211.

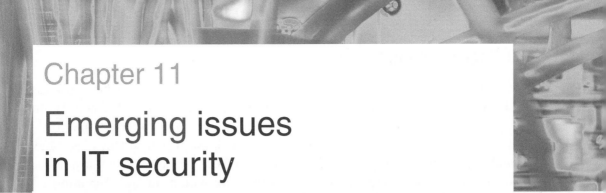

Chapter 11

Emerging issues in IT security

Learning objectives

After studying this chapter, you should be able to:

- discuss the concept of trustworthy computing

- describe the operation of RFID technology

- explain data at rest and data in motion encryption

- describe quantum encryption

- explain the privacy issues arising from the Internet

- appreciate the need for establishing credibility and authenticity of information on the Internet.

Chapter overview

Computers have penetrated every walk of life. There would hardly be a business that does not use information technology. Nevertheless, as the cyber population is increasing with every passing moment, the requirement for a reliable and trustworthy computing environment cannot be underestimated. At the same time, with increased business automation, there has also been an increase in the number of attempts to access, manipulate or destroy information through unauthorised access. It is for the same reason that people are reluctant to trust contemporary computer systems with personal information: they are increasingly concerned about the security and reliability of these systems. Simultaneously, other concerns about cyberspace have emerged, such as cyber terrorism, the proliferation of child pornography and the credibility of information. This has only increased the scope of information security, which demands not only secure information systems but also that certain procedures and processes be in place to minimise the threat of misuse of information. Innovations in information technology suggest that security of information systems is not a one-time measure; it is a continuous exercise and in fact will only increase with time. This chapter discusses some of the important advances in information and communication technology and the associated security risks. It also discusses the various privacy issues that are emerging owing to the increased dependence all over the world on the Internet and related technology.

Trustworthy computing

In the contemporary business paradigm, it is important for businesses to provide their customers with a trustworthy environment: one in which the customers feel safe to transact business, without having the fear of losing their personal and financial information to unauthorised third parties. Software vendors and service providers are striving to provide security mechanisms embedded in their products in order to facilitate business and create a safe business environment. 'Trustworthy computing' is a term coined by Microsoft in its attempt to enhance computer security and reliability to the same levels as modern telephones. This means that as people are able to use the telephone system and have the confidence that they will, on most occasions, receive a dial tone in order to initiate a call, then be assured that the call will not be abruptly interrupted by a technical problem or that its security will be compromised by an eavesdropper, so access to the computer should be trusted as secure, private and reliable. The telephone has taken several decades to reach a level of maturity to qualify as trustworthy on the criteria above. Although the computer is not yet at the same level of maturity, it is likely that it will reach it much faster than the telephone did. Hardware, software and process advances will need to be achieved in order for the vision of trustworthy computing to be achieved.

Businesses can take maximum advantage of computing devices and related information services only when they are dependable and trustworthy. A fundamental problem with technology is the ease with which it can be emulated. That is why security infrastructure needs to be updated and upgraded as technology changes.

Trustworthy computing framework

The term 'trustworthy' is perhaps more complex than providing a trustworthy computing environment. The subjectivity and relativity of this term suggests that there could be millions of ways of defining this term. However, in terms of computer security, **trustworthy computing** could be termed as an environment in which computer systems, software and information resources are insulated from unintentional and intentional unauthorised access, manipulation and destruction. For example, there are 'trusted' systems in electronic commerce transactions and 'trust' between the systems that authenticate the transactions. Even this example illustrates that the trustworthy environment created for an electronic commerce transaction requires integration of systems, engineering, policy, procedures and processes and attitudes of the users of the systems.

The first and foremost requirement of this integration is reliable computer systems, which could be used with the other systems and would not fail for a definite period of time. Next are the software considerations, such that it is equally reliable in terms of operations, viruses and malfunctioning. Next comes the fact that the processes have been mapped onto the application software properly and that there are no loopholes which could be exploited. Last but not least, the entire computing environment must conform to the policies laid down by the business, and there must be no threat from the employees or users of the systems. It might look simple on paper, but it is complicated to induce end-to-end dependability and reliability in today's highly interconnected corporate world. In the following paragraphs, some of the objectives, resources and execution of a trustworthy computing environment are described, based on Microsoft's 'Trustworthy Computing' white paper (Mundie et al. 2002).

Objectives of trustworthy computing

Table 11.1 (p. 310) considers the objectives of a trustworthy computing environment from a user's perspective. It examines the problem from the user's end and tries to answer questions such as: is the technology available when needed? Does it have the requisite provisions for safeguarding my information? Is the technology doing what it is supposed to do? Do the people who run the business do what they say?

These objectives encompass performance as well as behavioural matters. A trustworthy computing environment is one that exhibits the following qualities and inspires trust in the customer in the following areas:

- *Security.* Viruses and other malicious code will not enter the customer's system via the business system. There will be no unauthorised access to the customer's system or unauthorised alterations to information stored on the customer's system.
- *Privacy.* Personal information that the business collects on behalf of the customer will not be disclosed to an unauthorised third party. The customers are informed of what will happen to that information.
- *Reliability.* On installation of new software the customer does not have to worry about whether it will work properly with the existing applications. At the same time, the customer does not have to worry about the system of the business with which it interacts.
- *Business integrity.* The service provider responds rapidly and effectively to queries from the customer.

Table 11.1   Customer trust

Goals	The basis for a customer's decision to trust a system
Security	The customer can expect that systems are resilient [against] attack, and that the confidentiality, integrity and availability of the system and its data are protected.
Privacy	The customer is able to control data about themselves, and those using such data adhere to fair information principles.
Reliability	The customer can depend on the product to fulfil its functions when required to do so.
Business integrity	The vendor of a product behaves in a responsive and responsible manner.
Source: Mundie et al. 2002.	

Resources for trustworthy computing

After having specified the objectives, the next task is to identify resources to be employed for creating a trustworthy computing environment. These resources are the business considerations, process considerations and technological solutions that ought to be employed to meet the objectives. However, since the objectives are focused outwardly towards the customer, these resources are inwardly focused and are internal to the business. In other words, the objectives specify what is to be delivered and the resources specify how it is going to be delivered. Table 11.2 summarises the business considerations and the resources.

These resources and considerations provide for security measures to be taken at the system level as well as at the process level, so as to complement the objectives specified in the earlier section. Some practical examples are as follows:
- *Secure by design.* Secure design architecture could use encryption for sensitive data such as passwords before sending it in databases and could use SSL

protocol to transfer data across multiple locations. Software could be designed according to built-in threat modelling methods and all code cross-checked for any vulnerability.

- *Secure by default.* This means securing the software with appropriate security measures and disabling the vulnerable models or parts of the software before shipping the software, such that the customers are provided with instructions to sort of assemble the product before use.
- *Secure by deployment.* In large organisations, security updates (for example virus shield updates and so on) could be installed automatically after every new release or after a specified period of time. Making these security tools, software, patches and updates easily available helps in managing security risks across large organisations.
- *Privacy.* This entails giving customers and users appropriate notices about how their personal information would be collected used, disseminated and destroyed. It also includes providing them with a facility to correct their information online. Nevertheless, most companies already conform to privacy legislation, which stipulates that they do not disclose customer information to a third party and that they ensure privacy of customers' information by having appropriate external and internal auditing procedures.
- *Availability.* This entails maximising mean time between failures, by communicating performance objectives, policies and standards for system availability throughout the organisation.

Table 11.2   Business considerations

Means	The business and engineering considerations that enable a system supplier to deliver on the goals
Secure by design, secure by default, secure in deployment	Steps have been taken to protect the confidentiality, integrity, and availability of data and systems at every phase of the software development process — from design, to delivery, to maintenance.
Privacy	End-user data is never collected and shared with people or organisations without the consent of the individual. Privacy is respected when information is collected, stored and used consistent with privacy legislation.
Availability	The system is present and ready for use as required.
Manageability	The system is easy to install and manage, relative to its size and complexity. (Scalability, efficiency and cost-effectiveness are considered to be part of manageability.)
Accuracy	The system performs its functions correctly. Results of calculations are free from error, and data is protected from loss or corruption.
Usability	The software is easy to use and suitable to the user's needs.

Source: Mundie et al. 2002.

Chapter 11 Emerging issues in IT security

- *Manageability.* The computer systems are designed to manage themselves, such as being able to install software updates with minimal user intervention.
- *Accuracy.* The design of systems should consist of such measures as RAID arrays to minimise data loss or corruption as much as possible.
- *Usability.* The software applications that run on the systems are user friendly and appropriate help should be available to users in simple language.
- *Responsiveness.* This deals with the commitment by senior management to the principle that credibility, availability, reliability and security take precedence over any other process. This commitment must be made clear throughout an organisation. At the same time, systems are continuously monitored and action is taken when performance does not meet the accepted levels.
- *Transparency.* Transparency and integrity of the business transactions are maintained at all costs. The organisation and its employees are required to communicate honestly with its stakeholders.

Execution of trustworthy computing

Execution reflects the way an organisation carries out its business operations in order to deliver the building blocks of trustworthy computing. There are three constituents of execution: intents, implementation and evidence. Intents are the organisational policies and procedures that provide the specifications for design, implementation and support of the computer and information resources; whereas implementation is the process that realises the intents. Evidence is the means for verification of whether the implementation has delivered the desired results. Table 11.3 provides some examples of these three constituents.

Creating a trustworthy computing environment is not a one-time activity; it is a continuous activity. The task of a business is to continuously monitor the changing perceptions of its customers about security in order to assess these perceptions. This allows the organisation to gain an appreciation of the known problems and take appropriate measures to handle those threats. At the same time, not every issue will be resolved; therefore it also allows the business to know what could be fixed and what could be managed in the constraints of the current systems.

There is a lot of work still to be done in securing the computing environment; yet these efforts will not resolve all the problems. Eventually, it is the systems and software vendors who are best placed to identify and resolve these challenges and incrementally provide built-in security measures in legacy systems. Obviously, it is a long-term technological replacement cycle, during which time businesses would need to identify critical infrastructure and systems weaknesses and take appropriate measures on a high-priority basis. Business also need to ensure that new infrastructure is built on sound security principles.

Table 11.3	Constituents of execution
Intents	Company policies, directives, benchmarks, and guidelines
	Contracts and undertakings with customers, including service level agreements (SLAs)
	Corporate, industry and regulatory standards
	Government legislation, policies and regulations
Implementation	Risk analysis
	Development practices, including architecture, coding, documentation and testing
	Training and education
	Terms of business
	Marketing and sales practices
	Operations practices, including deployment, maintenance, sales and support, and risk management
	Enforcement of intents and dispute resolution
Evidence	Self-assessment
	Accreditation by third parties
	External audit

Source: Mundie et al. 2002.

RFID technology

Radio frequency identification (RFID) systems are fast becoming popular for identification and a variety of supply chain applications. An RFID system comprises transponders (commonly referred to as tags), readers and application systems for further processing of the acquired data. There are varieties of RFID systems, which operate on low, high or ultra-high frequencies. Furthermore, different varieties of tags are being used. These can be divided into two categories: active and passive. Passive tags do not have an onboard power supply and consequently have limited memory. On the other hand, active tags support onboard memory and are capable of storing several megabytes of information. Applications of RFID tags are varied and range from logistics, point-of-sale checkouts, access control, animal identification and books management in libraries to baggage handling at airports. However, RFID also has the potential to be used in industrial environments for sophisticated uses, such as configuration management and environmental condition monitoring.

How RFID systems work

A typical RFID system consists of a tag, a reader and an application host that not only governs the systems but also acquires information from the tags and processes it. An RFID tag could be as small as a grain of rice. However, the more commonly used passive RFID tags are about the size of a 50-cent coin.

An RFID tag consists of a microchip or memory, capacitors and an antenna coil. All of these are embedded in an encapsulated material, for example a plastic substrate or a smart label. The tag holds a unique identifier in its memory, the electronic product code (EPC), which provides a unique number for each item throughout its lifecycle. An EPC works just like a bar code; however, with a bar code it is possible to identify a class of items but it is not possible to identify a particular item. An EPC provides for this facility. EPC is Auto-ID Centre's coding scheme that identifies an item's manufacturer, product category and unique serial number. (The Auto-ID Centre is a consortium of universities.) This standardisation guarantees interoperability and security as well as allowing millions of items to be identified uniquely. At the moment 64- and 96-bit tags are in common use. A 96-bit EPC provides unique identifiers for 268 million objects.

A reader in an RFID system can be fixed as well as mobile, which means it could be a peripheral or a handheld device. An RFID system works on one of two principles: inductive coupling or backscatter coupling. In inductive coupling, the reader's antenna coil generates a magnetic field and by so doing induces voltage in the coil of the tag. Using the amplitude shift keying (ASK) method, data is transferred from the reader to the tag; whereas from the tag to the reader the data is transferred using load modulation. This type of system works below the 30 MHz frequency. The other method, backscatter coupling, is used with frequencies in excess of 100 MHz. In this system the tag receives energy from the electromagnetic field that is emitted by the reader. Data is transferred to a reader through reflection of modulated power by the transponder. The reader then sends the collected data to the application program that runs in the background for further manipulation. In this case the readers are directly attached to the system, using RS 232 or USB interface. In the case of mobile readers, connectivity to the host is provided through standard network protocols, such as TCP/IP, through a wireless link or ethernet. The range of transmission, however, depends on different parameters, and ranges from a few centimetres to several metres in different applications.

In a typical supply chain environment, each item might be fitted with an RFID tag. The unique EPC for each item could be electronically programmed into the tag, which could be read from a distance of up to 100 metres. Tags attached to each item are read by an antenna, which passes the EPC information to the middleware or a 'savant'. A savant acts as a buffer between the reader and other organisational information systems, and it consists of various modules or subprograms, each of which performs specific functions. The savant remains connected to the readers and behaves as a router of the RFID network; its primary functions being data smoothing, data forwarding and data storage, along with reader coordination and task and event management. These savants use algorithms that take care of the reader collision, such that each tag is identified uniquely and is read each time it is attempted to be read. The middleware or savants needs to be based on open standards so as to provide for easy information interoperability.

Since the EPC is the only information stored on the tag, it has to be used in such a way that it provides additional information about the item to which the EPC is attached. Data exclusive to the item could be stored on a server located on a connected local area network or the Internet. However, access to this information is made possible by an application of the concept of domain name system (DNS). The EPC stored in the savant is interpreted into a unique address of an object naming service (ONS), which points to a physical mark-up language (PML) server. PML is a version of the popular XML metadata language.

The server stores PML files that contain information about the item to which the RFID tag is attached. Ideally, the manufacturer of an item maintains a PML server for its products. This server contains such information as item name, description, manufacturer, date of manufacturing, quantity, safety instructions, location of the item, carrier's description, and shipping and receiving person. As this information is common, it resides in standard databases. Instance information, however, is specific and unique for each instance. Once the stock is issued from the manufacturer's warehouse, different supply chain points and stakeholders are able to access this information and update their own PML files. On receiving the inventory, this information resides on the PML server of that organisation, where it is updated according to the usage and utilisation of the item.

Security of RFID systems

RFID technology is increasingly being embraced by businesses around the globe; however, like other wireless technology, RFID technology has a number of security problems. Even the basic security goals — for example confidentiality, availability, integrity, authentication, authorisation, non-repudiation and anonymity — are difficult to achieve, and special security mechanisms need to be integrated into the system if these goals are to be attained. At the same time, the privacy aspect has gained special attention because customers carrying tagged items could be identified anywhere by anybody. In this case the technology itself provides assistance to hackers, as passive tags do not have a mechanism of authentication or verification when they are powered by the readers. So many different standards are being developed that it is difficult to conform to one standard. Considering the potential of this technology, businesses are concerned about the privacy issues, which are discussed below.

Confidentiality

Most of the tags do not have an access control mechanism, and therefore the communication between reader and tag could be intercepted in the immediate vicinity. It is easy to tap into communication that occurs between the reader and the tags, owing to the longer range. In a fully implemented system, all a hacker needs is the EPC or the unique identifier and the rest of the information becomes easy to find, as it will point to the relevant ONS and the PML server.

Integrity

With the exception of ISO 14443-based systems that utilise the message authentication codes, there is no way of preserving the integrity of the data being transmitted. In the absence of access control, it is also easy to manipulate the tag memory.

Availability

Frequency jamming devices could be used to disturb the frequency of the RFID system. Research reveals that denial of service attacks, such as the 'RFID blocker', are easy to implement as they utilise tag anti-collision mechanisms to interrupt the communication of a reader with tags.

Authenticity

The authenticity of a tag is at risk because the unique identifier of the tag could be spoofed or manipulated. Furthermore, generally these tags are not tamper-resistant and might malfunction in areas with a high magnetic field.

Anonymity

As mentioned before, it is not difficult to read a tag carried by a consumer on an item that they purchased. Not only is the privacy of the consumer being infringed but also at the same time their movement or that of the item could be traced and tracked.

Security safeguards for RFID systems

Considering the fact that the primary objective of RFID technology is to provide cheap automated identification, it is not easy to embed security measures in the front-end RFID system. Nevertheless, a couple of security measures could be employed to enhance the security of an RFID system:

- *Access control and authentication.* It is not difficult to incorporate access control mechanisms in the tags for read and write operations on memory. For example, some tags based on ISO 14443 and MIFARE® tags have a provision of authentication before allowing for the memory to be read and written. Standards in the development stage, such as part 4 of ISO 15693, would allow an authentication protocol with DES or 3DES.

- *Destroying the tag after use.* Another option that has been proposed is the destruction of the tag after use or, in other words, killing of the tag. However, that might work only for the individual customer because businesses would want to keep the valuable information stored in the tag for later use.

RFID technology is in its developmental stage, and that is why there are many problems relating to its security. At the same time most of the efforts made are in terms of standards development, which ironically means that there would not be a single standard to conform to. Nevertheless, at this stage the viable options are to isolate the sites with RFID systems from unauthorised intrusion.

Data-at-rest encryption appliance technology

As has been said before, there is no single solution that totally protects a system. Encryption makes it difficult to breach security, although it doesn't stop anyone from deleting information. However, before implementing encryption techniques an important aspect is to ensure access control, such that only authorised persons are able to view and manipulate information. It is just like having ciphered text in a drawer and keeping a key to the drawer. In other words, encryption provides a second line of defence in situations where someone has already broken through the first line of defence. It should be noted that access control is not easy to implement, as for example, with the widely used Windows operating system there are several ways of gaining access, such as:

- There is no provision in NTFS permissions, which could restrict the system administrator from accessing the files.
- A hacker who gains access to the operating system can easily use system administrator privileges to manipulate information.
- Even permission checking could be bypassed by booting the server to a different operating system to get around any access control that might be in place. For example, if a hacker knows the buffer overflow in Microsoft Windows 2000, which allows shell commands to be run on the server, then the hacker can reset the administrator's password.

That is why Windows provides an encrypted file system (EFS), which is capable of encrypting the file on the user's password. However, it is important to keep two facts in consideration, which are:

1. Encryption cannot and does not restrict anyone from deleting the files.
2. Encryption cannot provide protection against changes to the file contents; however, it can tell whether changes have been made.

Nevertheless, encryption is done at two levels; that is, data in motion encryption and data at rest encryption. As the names suggest, **data in motion encryption** is carried out on the data in motion, whereas **data at rest encryption** is carried out at the data that resides in the corporate databases.

Data in motion encryption

Data in motion encryption is a way of safeguarding data when it is in motion; that is, when it is being transmitted from the client to the server on a network, or when it is being transmitted from the server to a client. The network involved in this transmission does not necessarily have to be a local area network; it could be a wireless network or even the Internet. Secure Sockets Layer (SSL), Transport Layer Security (TLS) and Secure Internet Protocol (IPSEC) are some of the security mechanisms used during data in motion encryption. Data in motion encryption is implemented at the session level; that is, the network layer higher than the encryption of the protocol. Data transmission is encrypted as it is transmitted over the network and decrypted when it is received at the other end. While accessing a database each command is encrypted and decrypted at the client and server end.

Data at rest encryption

Since data in motion encryption helps in encrypting only data that is in motion, data at rest encryption safeguards data that is at rest, whereby it helps in encrypting information that resides in corporate databases. This encryption is extremely important as most attacks are aimed at the databases, where data resides for long periods. However, quite ironically, data in motion encryption is more widely adopted than data at rest encryption.

Encrypting data at rest

Data at rest can be encrypted at several levels. We could encrypt the whole database or selected columns of a database, which means it could be encrypted at three levels. However, encrypting the entire database also introduces certain limitations, such as:

- *Performance problems.* When the entire database is encrypted, every time data is to be read, the whole database is encrypted and decrypted, which hampers the speed and efficiency of any action performed on the data in the database.
- *Different encryption keys.* Encrypting the whole database causes problems when more than one department uses the same data or when the database contains data regarding two business functions; for example, when the database contains information regarding sales that needs to be accessed by the sales department to estimate revenue and the human resource department for giving commission on sales. In this situation the file-level encryption cannot be used, as in that situation the whole file is encrypted and not just sections of the file.

- *Unauthorised access.* File-level encryption protects information from the attacks that are made at the operating system level. However, if someone breaks into the database access is allowed as the user is considered to be legitimate in that way circumventing encryption.

Nevertheless, a more efficient way of encrypting data is to encrypt sections of a database. This not only takes care of all the above problems but also enhances the security of the database. For example, consider a table with the following information: customer ID, customer name, customer address and customer credit card number. It has been explained above that it is not feasible to encrypt the entire table. However, you can see from these data files which data might be of more value to hackers. It is obviously the credit card number; therefore encrypting the credit card number file would suffice. An obvious advantage is that of enhancing performance by encrypting the sensitive information only. In this case the encryption system utilises a single key to encrypt and decrypt information in each column. A copy of this column key is stored with the user's password, such that every time the encrypted data is to be accessed it uses the same key. A user who wants to change their password must first log in using the old password, decrypt each column key, then encrypt each column with the new password and replace the old key, such that at their next logon, the user can access information using the new password. The biggest advantage of this technique is that it restricts the system administrators from accessing the database. With this technique encryption depends on a secret that only the user knows.

However, it is important to know what data to encrypt and whether encrypted data will hamper the database's performance. Considering the performance problems, it should be noted that a database cannot afford to have every bit of information it contains encrypted and decrypted each time an action is performed on it.

Quantum encryption

Although quantum cryptography has only recently gained popularity in computer security, it has been known since 1970, when Stephen Weisner proposed it and coined the term 'conjugate coding'. **Quantum encryption** applies the laws of quantum physics to improve modern cryptographic techniques. Using quantum cryptography Bell Labs has recently developed techniques for quickly cracking seemingly 'secure' encryption codes. Public key encryption provides significantly higher security than other methods because of the difficulty in performing complex computations to factor extremely large prime numbers. This means that potential eavesdropping can be extremely difficult unless the perpetrator possesses extremely high processing power.

However, the process of public key encryption requires significant processing, and for this reason it is mostly used for the secure distribution of private encryption keys. Bell Lab researchers demonstrated that a 129-digit number could be factored in only a few seconds using quantum methods that related factorisation to the problem of finding the period of a function. Using non-quantum computing methods, the same factoring had previously taken a thousand networked computers eight months to achieve. For organisations whose data must be securely transferred between two devices in separate locations, quantum cryptography offers the only known secure and efficient communication transmission scheme. Confidentiality of data transmission is the main reason for an investment in quantum security.

One of the most difficult problems of modern cryptographic systems has been the 'key distribution problem', which requires a robust way to generate, store and distribute encryption keys. Although a 'big brother' trusted key server is often set up for this purpose, a secret key can also be agreed without necessarily having to set up a key distribution server. One such mechanism is the Diffie-Hellman key exchange protocol. However, this relies very much on the limitations of complex mathematical operations, such as clever techniques for factoring large numbers. Quantum encryption relies on techniques that keep data secret through the application of the laws of physics.

The most common application of quantum encryption is as a replacement of existing protocols for the secure and fast distribution of encryption keys.

How it works

Quantum cryptography uses the physical phenomenon of light called polarisation. Polarisation occurs when light waves are passed through a polarised filter, which allows only light waves with the same orientation as the filter to pass. A photon detector will identify information about the polarisation of the photons. These polarisation states can therefore be used to encode data as 'zeros' and 'ones'. This single quantum information is usually referred to as a 'qubit' and is detected by the recipient by passing it through a polarisation filter of the same orientation as its transmission.

Pairs of perpendicular polarisation states are called 'bases'. A basis can be a horizontal or vertical basis or a pair of polarisations at a particular pair of angles, for example '45deg 135deg basis'. When the measurement of the polarised light from one basis completely randomises the measurement of the polarised light from another base, we have what is called 'conjugate' bases. This property can be used in quantum encryption to transmit secret encryption keys.

If, for example, user A transmits a photon using 0deg/90deg basis and user B uses the 45deg/90deg basis to detect the transmitted photon, user B will detect no information whereas, if user B had used the same basis (0deg/90deg) as user A, user B would have detected this photon. So can the eavesdropper intercept this? Certainly. In the same way as user B, if the eavesdropper uses the correct basis, he will detect the photon; however, if he uses the wrong basis he will not detect the photon, as this would have destroyed the photon and it would not therefore reach user B. If user A is smart enough and quick enough to fabricate another photon to send to user B, the eavesdropper would not know what was the original basis on which to reconstruct the originally transmitted photon and would therefore have interrupted the transmission. In the transmission of a string of photons this tampering would easily be detected, and hence the eavesdropper's presence would be revealed.

However, the principle of quantum encryption does not operate on securing the message as it is transmitted but on the retrospective realisation of whether it has been tampered with along the way. This means that eavesdroppers can access all the transmitted information, but by doing so cannot they cannot avoid revealing to the recipient of the message that they have done so; thus the sender and the receiver ignore the intercepted information and retransmit new information. Clearly, then, this means that quantum encryption is not suitable for keeping the message secret but for transmitting the encryption keys that could then be used with traditional encryption schemes to protect the message itself.

Quantum key distribution can be achieved by sending a string of photons that have random polarisations, which are converted to a series of binary numbers. If this string of numbers representing the encryption key is intercepted by an eavesdropper, this is detected by the sender and the receiver. The key is discarded and a new one is requested until a key that has not been intercepted is received.

Quantum encryption protocols

A number of protocols have been developed for the secure distribution of encryption keys using quantum encryption techniques. The most popular of these is the BB84 protocol named after its developers, Bennett and Brassard, who developed it in 1984.

In the BB84 protocol, the sender and the receiver must have two polarisers, one 0deg/90deg basis and the other 45deg/135deg basis. The sender and receiver also need two communications channels: one will be the quantum channel and the other a traditional public communication channel used to discuss the communication process. The sender polarises each photon that it sends to the receiver with one of four random polarisations. When the receiver receives each photon it measures its polarisation with a random polariser. Given that neither of them know which polariser the other used, in the case of the sender, to send the photon and, in the case of the receiver, to measure the received photon, some of the polarisations will match and others will not. As mentioned earlier, those photons that do not match their polarisation will also be destroyed.

After the sequence of the polarised photons designated as an encryption key has been transmitted, the sender and receiver can discuss the sequence used for this string of photons. Using this discussion, they are able to reject the non-matching bits and keep those that matched, thus achieving the distribution of an encryption key without any possibility that such a key has been intercepted by an eavesdropper.

Some of the issues in quantum cryptography are achieving and detecting single photons, degradation of photons over a significant distance, and denial attack.

Privacy on the Internet

The last two decades of the twentieth century saw enormous political, social, economic and technological changes that tested the social, political and economic structure of nation states in such a way that they were confronted with unprecedented challenges and issues. On the political front, the emergence of a unipolar world and globalisation pushed the international system into a new phase in which the notion of balance of power seems to be losing relevance. After almost 90 years, we are again witnessing the globalisation of economy, although this time the facilitator is not colonialism but information. Businesses around the globe now have capacity to reach the remotest parts of the world without needing a physical presence there. This world of unlimited flows of information and images is punctuated by uncontrolled and confusing change; global society is going through a transitional period in which there is a propensity for people to rearrange themselves around such identities as religion, ethnicity, territory and nationality.

Information and communication technology, especially the Internet, is at the core of these political, economic and social transformations. The Internet is unregulated, and the laws and legislation of any one country do not apply to Internet activities that originate in a different country. For the same reason the cyber public needs to be extra careful about giving away personal information, as there is always a chance of its being misused. When people are surfing the Internet, they usually believe that what they are doing is not known to anybody. However, that is not the case, as there are many ways of knowing who is doing what. Furthermore, anyone with appropriate skills could gather as much information about a person using the Internet as possible, without the knowledge or consent of that person. The following sections provide some of the ways privacy could be infringed on the Internet.

Cookies

Cookies contain information that a website sends to the browser of a user when the user accesses information from that website. These cookies reside on the user's computer, and each time the user accesses the same website, the cookies pertaining to that website are updated. Cookies actually represent a mechanism that allows website operators to assign a unique identifier to a computer that requests information from the website. Consequently, businesses use these cookies to profile customers who visit their website as well as for other marketing purposes. Cookies themselves do not pose any harm to the individual. However, if the website asks for personal information from the customer, and the customer provides that information to buy a product and so on, then cookies could be used by a hacker to profile the buying trends and habits of the customer.

Nevertheless, many browsers allow for turning the status of the cookie file to Read-only, which means that cookies last only for the time that the browser is active. This, however, does not mean that if a computer is hacked during that time, these cookies could not be hacked. Another way of handling this problem is deleting the cookies whenever the browser is shut down. Many software programs are available that manage cookies for an individual user, such as Cookie Crusher and Cookie Cruncher.

Surfing history

HyperText Transfer Protocol (HTTP) provides the set of rules for communication between the website and the browser, and the browser locates a website's page through a Uniform Resource Locator (URL). However, HTTP has certain provisions that allow for tracking the surfing history. Other information that could be sent through the HTTP are email address and the last website visited. This, however, depends on whether the browser is configured with the individual's email address and whether the browser supports the provisions described above.

Information gathered by agencies

Many agencies such as universities, businesses such as telephone services and government departments such as the Australian Electoral Commission sometimes publish the collected information on their websites. They do so in order to provide their users with an option of online searching. This information is gathered by different web-based companies, which then sell it to businesses and other agencies. This information could be used to create a rough profile of a person. There is no apparent defence to this infringement, as the information is collected by different agencies, which might not be geographically present in a particular country. Nevertheless, being cautious about providing information that could be published on the Internet might prove useful.

Freeware software

Lots of free software is available on the Internet, and the high price of licensed software makes it lucrative to download free software. However, some of this software might contain spy programs (spyware) that relay usage data to the originator of the software. This is extremely dangerous, as free software might also contain viruses or malicious code. Ghost applications are even capable of sending screen shots of the computer screen along with other critical data about the machine and the user.

Electronic commerce

Electronic commerce provides a lucrative option to hackers in the shape of credit card numbers. Although, when the data is being transferred, most of businesses use Secure Sockets Layer and other security measures, there is no particular fool-proof security mechanism when data is stored in databases. In some instances data from the ISPs or websites has been hacked and credit card numbers used to make purchases over the Internet. The only defensive measure could be ensuring that the business is genuine and has appropriate security mechanisms in place.

Email

An email address bears lots of information about a person. For example, abc@xyz.com means that person's name is abc and that he or she works at the organisation xyz. Most organisations use the family name and at least one letter of the first name in the email ID, which further helps in locating a person. At the same time other extensions, such as .gov, .org, .edu, .net, .au., .uk. and so on, further help in determining where a person lives or the type of business a person works in. At the same time, in most organisations the email ID is also the user ID for logging on to the organisation's computers. The email ID also provides potential hackers with a starting point for hacking into a system.

Spam

Spamming is sending junk emails. It starts when people give out their email addresses at websites where they buy something or register online and so on. Different companies keep track of these addresses, then sell them to businesses that operate on the Internet. Some ISPs also sell their customer lists to different businesses. These are, however, chargeable offences in Australia as they violate the confidentiality as well as the privacy of customers.

Chatrooms

Chatrooms and groups are quite popular. However, at such places it is easy for someone to conceal their identity and lie about who they actually are. In a chatroom it is easy to get carried away and start thinking the other person is really who they say they are. In such circumstances people might give out personal details, such as their address, real name or phone number.

Capitalising on the potential of information and communication technology, communities, groups, nations and businesses are striving to outclass their adversaries. Conflicts of knowledge economy are not restricted to battlefields; in fact there is a constant war in pursuit of economic, social, cultural and political agendas, ironically without tangible weapons, as the major weapon used is information and the major mode is the 'infringement of privacy'. Therefore fast acceptance of Internet and other e-commerce technology on the one hand is playing an important role in the intellectual rise of global population and on the other hand, owing to their open structure, is rendering the security and privacy of their users vulnerable. All it takes is a small computer terminal and an individual with requisite hacking skills, and the whole security of a nation could be at risk. Information security and assurance are indeed the foremost challenges facing nation states and businesses, and in fact organisations of all types, in the new economy.

Information security and civil liberties in cyberspace

Controlling the flow of information on the Internet is extremely difficult, if not impossible. Owing to the subjective nature of authenticity and the openness and self-regulation of the Internet, the problems associated with information in the information society are enormous. The Internet is not only becoming a part of our lives but is also fostering new types of behaviour. Perhaps the most important construct that derives from information dissemination by the Internet is the perceived attributes of the Internet; that is, the attitudes, beliefs and information received by the user from their social environment about the Internet. There is much information available in electronic form on which we rely and believe to be what it appears to be, for example Internet-based news sources, business and academic documents and images, most of which has its own intention and purpose. The Internet on the one hand fosters critical thinking and on the other could also prove to be a tool for cultural and cognitive invasion. Pluralism of information is leading us to suspect that what we see is not what it actually is.

The availability of information in cyberspace can be likened to an almost limitless library where anyone can upload any information for the public to read. To live up to our belief in freedom of expression, such openness should be defended as long as the material is not aimed at fermenting communal hatred, inciting violence or affecting public opinion. Lack of control and ease of publication signifies that a fair proportion of cyber information is unauthentic. The Internet is a self-regulated system and inhibits semantic, pragmatic and social barriers, which have the ability to create swings in the cognitive styles and beliefs of its users. Cyberspace represents a diverse community, which consists of libertarians, communitarians, communists, socialists, rich, poor, nerds and literati. It is very unlikely that they will reach consensus on any subject. Therefore, the fundamental problem is are establishing not just the authenticity and security of the available information but also its intent.

A distinguishing feature of the information society is the abundance of information that is changing human activities and human relations. As a global and easily accessible library, the Internet provides information on almost every aspect of life; for example, news, entertainment, medicine, merchandising, religion and so on. However, having an abundance of information does not necessarily mean that people become informed. It is important to ascertain the right information quickly and easily, in order to distinguish between what information a user needs and what information appears nice to the user, so that the user doesn't sink in electronic junk information. Popular websites, for example Yahoo, AltaVista, Google and so on, belong to search engines that enable people to find information they value. However, the real value produced by the information provider comes in locating and communicating what is going to be beneficial to society. It is expected that more than 20 per cent of all future jobs will require the employees to have the skills to locate pertinent information, assess data and make decisions on the basis of their analysis. Information serves as the foundation for our thinking, judgement, belief system, choices and understanding of our world. Utopians argue that the Internet offers novel and enhanced modes of information dissemination, whereas dystopians contend that the information potential of the Internet can take people away from their communities. The authenticity, reliability and validity of Internet-based information is therefore more important than just access to information.

Nevertheless, the Internet's self-regulating and open structure makes it an easy platform to publish, access, retrieve, manipulate and distribute information, and hence raises the problem of authenticity of information as well as of the potential beneficial or harmful effects of cyber information on society. These problems have grown with the increasing flow of information resources in cyberspace without monitoring by editors and fact checkers (traditional gatekeepers for print publications). As information moves from an established paper-based reality to electronic existence, its physical characteristics, which are vital for establishing the authenticity and reliability of the evidence they contain, are threatened. Traditionally a variety of different criteria, such as authorship, purpose, authority, origin, scope, paper quality and print, have been used to evaluate the authenticity of a document; however, these criteria cannot be applied in an electronic paradigm because it is often difficult to find these traditional authority indicators. The Internet is also changing our traditional faith in visual documentation, and as we move into virtual reality, more digital manipulation is expected. In fact new digital works have already started to affect our concepts of authentic representations; for example, digital imaging or photography, in which digital manipulation moved beyond the practice of retouching photographic prints to create something misleading.

Information generally has bias; therefore, authenticity is not limited to verifying authorship and attributes of a document. In fact it includes such attributes as completeness, accuracy, trustworthiness, correctness, validity, integrity, faithfulness, originality, meaningfulness and suitability for an intended purpose. Trust in information is generated through beliefs or levels of confidence derived from general assumptions and stereotypes existing within one's own culture. It is, therefore, the context from which authenticity is derived, and it is from within that context that an endeavour to establish it has to be made. Human behaviour, beliefs, cultural attitudes, familiarity with and trust in technology are some of the aspects that render authenticity and believability of information subjective. People have distinct approaches when they evaluate information. On these bases, they could be divided into two cultures (Hall 1989):

- *Low-context cultures*, comprising indigenous English- and German-speaking cultures and Scandinavian cultures. People from these backgrounds look for depth and detail of information and like to receive important information in a simple and uncomplicated way.
- *High-context cultures*, which refers to the rest. People in these cultures are concerned about the source of the information, the status or position of the information source and the method chosen to deliver the message.

Considering the multiplicity of beliefs and viewpoints of the cyber population, it is unlikely that one set of criteria for authenticity could be arrived at. Authenticity of information in cyberspace depends largely on the affiliation of the website, any endorsements that it enjoys from professional and non-professional bodies and opinion leaders, the context from within which the information originates, the content's trustworthiness and public perception about the contents. The intensity of this issue is further amplified as people with varying degrees of knowledge, different ethnicities, variety of beliefs and values use the Internet for an assortment of reasons. It also raises a few questions about the influence of the Internet, whether it will contribute towards the decline of social interaction and assimilation, community involvement, political participation and integration, or whether it will foster new forms of identity and social interaction.

Authenticity

In order for information to be useful, it must have an essential purpose, which could be attributed to its originator and its interpreter. This highlights an important relationship between information, the behaviour of its users and the social context from which the information originates.

Search engines on the Internet assist users in finding information but also contribute towards pluralism or multiplicity. These engines are mostly used for keyword searches; consequently the information that they find is often irrelevant to what the user intends to find. Because of this diversity, a variety of new ideas emerges, each with its own perspectives, set of laws, contents and modes of admission. The user is exposed not only to a differing and often conflicting set of ideas but also to a variety of new social settings, each of which carries within itself its own embedded standards for judging the authenticity and suitability of the opinion. Reading the information through the associated links for a search string makes the user conscious of the pliability of authentic knowledge or truth.

For example, a simple search for 'depression' will give a variety of different responses, including information on metal depression, economic depression, mental depression and so on. A further exploration of mental depression reveals different approaches to handling anxiety and stress. Some of these sites also support euthanasia. Now the question arises: which information is authentic and trustworthy? For some it might be fine to commit suicide, whereas for some it might be totally unthinkable or a grave sin. However, at the same time the credibility, genuineness and truthfulness of the information provided on these websites cannot be questioned, as they represent particular social groups. It can be argued that although the Internet facilitates critical thinking skills, it also points in another direction: that there is no ultimate truth available on the Internet; therefore, the authenticity of information is subject to doubt if it is taken in isolation from the environment in which the information originated.

One of the vital issues in the information society is that postmodern institutions are being controlled by those laws, regulations and norms that came into existence as a by-product of industrial revolution. With the wide presence of misinformation or spurious information, beliefs in the accepted wisdom of knowledge society and common economic and cultural spaces cannot be realised. Instead we face predicaments of ideology, identity and social integration.

Literacy in the form of the printed word encouraged the development of abstract thinking, concern with literal meanings and search for universal truths. This helped to shape the foundations of a single rational and logical worldview; that is, modernism. The basic idea of modernism implies that there is always a truth to be revealed. It is concerned with the search for universal principles through linear, hierarchical and logical means. Postmodernism as opposed to modernism advocates the bias inherent in truth owing to the context in which meaning is fashioned and the plurality of perspectives that emerge as a result. The postmodern ideas of perspectivism and multiplicity on the Internet are relevant not only to the illustration of information or knowledge but also to the self. All the way through the period of growth in literacy in human civilisation, the written word symbolised a trustworthy voice for both literate and illiterate alike. Interpretation as it is understood now, as a subjective course of action, was not what was derived from text. A manuscript was expected to have unique connotations: those of the intent of the author. This uniqueness of understanding was a prerequisite for endowing the text with ultimate authority. It can be argued that just as these ideologies are rooted in the technology of print on paper, new thought patterns are being fashioned in the electronic paradigm in response to a new set of forces acting on it, such as the interactivity of the Internet.

The issue of authenticity is embedded in the architecture of the Internet, through its emergent self-regulation, openness, decentralisation and self-stabilising tendencies. As an emergent self-organising system, it is far from equilibrium but rather in a non-linear and chaotic state, and possesses vast amounts of information. The characteristics of openness and decentralisation are essential to the Internet, as they provide it with its fuel; that is, information. Consequently the system is bound to accept different kinds and levels of information for its operation and growth, and inevitably there will be information that could be termed as unauthentic, manipulated and unqualified.

IT risk 11.1

What is true?

In 2000 a press release was distributed by major financial media companies stating that server and storage provider Emulex had revised its earnings downward from $0.25 per share to a loss of $0.15 per share and had lowered its reported net earnings from the previous quarter as well. Within minutes, Emulex shares had fallen from their previous day's close of about $104 per share to just $43. Shareholders who sold their shares while they were falling faced losses.

The company had not authorised the press release; in fact the details of it were completely untrue. The release was actually initiated by a former employee of a Los Angeles firm that distributes press releases on behalf of other organisations. The former employee launched the release from the company's server. He didn't hack into the computer systems nor did he develop any complex algorithm to do that, he just manipulated the perception of people. All he did was to write a convincing press release, use a believable distribution medium and sit back to watch events unfold. This shows how easy it is to manipulate information on the Internet and influence public judgement.

Source: based on Cybenko, Giani & Thompson 2002.

Role of institutions in establishing authenticity on the Internet

Establishing the authenticity of Internet resources is a phenomenon that is too broad to be addressed by any legislation or standard, mainly because the actors in cyberspace have power to make their own rules. This poses a problem because these entities do not have to adhere to any laws or ethical principles that would allow for the legitimate interests of all stakeholders.

Some scholars have proposed international law, with particular emphasis on political and social aspects, as the appropriate way of governing the Internet. Others suggest norms as a substitute for legal legislation, especially considering the fact that the Internet population is not homogeneous and that in many countries the legal system does not address cyberspace issues adequately. Existing legal frameworks are insufficient to control the Internet; therefore, national governments are ill-equipped to handle the issue. They argue that the solution to this problem is creating virtual courts and virtual governments within cyberspace.

The Internet and its apparatus function as a global unit, and any national government embarking to control information on the Internet cannot succeed. The solution to the issue of authenticity of information in cyberspace lies in cooperation between communities, nations, commercial and non-commercial organisations, and supranational organisations. There needs to be a mechanism for authentication of Internet content that could certify the origin of the content. This needs to be supplemented with legislation in each country that would regulate the publishing of content. At a broader level there needs to be a global convention for Internet content, to which every country needs to conform.

Summary

As the level of business automation is increasing, so are the threats to information and information resources. Instant information is no longer a request; in fact it is the fundamental requirement of individuals as well as businesses. Initiatives like trustworthy computing are just a step towards the journey of a secure business world. However, even this step is difficult to take as the rate at which technology is changing is enormous. Computer security is at a crossroads with technology like RFID, whose major attraction is its cheapness. Cheap also means, however, that less security mechanism is embedded in the technology. It will be some time before the same technology is available at the same cost with enhanced security. However, issues relating to privacy are just coming to the forefront. Ironically it's the technology that is allowing unauthorised usage of information, in terms of infringing the privacy of people. At the same time, a relentless war of words is being waged in cyberspace that is further complicating the already complicated world. In the absence of global legislation for information security, technological solutions will not prove to be of much help. As has been said many times in this book, the issue needs to be tackled at the functional, business and strategic levels, and information and information systems security safeguards need to be employed at both the system and process levels.

Key terms

data in motion encryption, p. 317
data at rest encryption, p. 318
quantum encryption, p. 319

radio frequency identification (RFID), p. 313
trustworthy computing, p. 309

1. What are the constituents of a trustworthy computing environment?
2. How does RFID technology work?
3. List the two methods that RFID systems use to read a tag.
4. What are the security threats faced by RFID systems?
5. How does data at rest encryption work?
6. How does data in motion encryption work?
7. What is quantum encryption?
8. Describe the threats to privacy on the Internet.

Case study

11: RFID security risks

Risks rise as factory nets go wireless

Wireless technologies for harvesting real-time data off factory networks — and strategies for putting such information to use — were hot topics at [the] National Manufacturing Week conference.

However, some manufacturing IT professionals highlighted the risks involved in deploying wireless technology in factories, or converging plant control networks with IT systems and back-office data centers. Others voiced concerns that gleaning too much data from manufacturing processes could complicate rather than streamline a manufacturing operation.

'Manufacturers are getting closer to where demand and supply are more synchronous,' says Bob Parker, an analyst with IDC. 'We're seeing the emergence of RFID and sensor networks as the means for collecting the kind of data that is needed to make this synchronization happen.'

Among those moving in this direction is General Motors, which has deployed RFID, 802.11 and sensor networks in several plants.

'The goal isn't just to merge manufacturing plants with IT [infrastructure],' says Pulak Bandyopadhyay, group manager for plant floor systems and control group in General Motors' Manufacturing Systems Research Lab in Warren, Michigan. 'It's the collection of real-time data and what you do with that data you've collected.'

Part of General Motors' move toward IT/shop floor integration has been the deployment of standard ethernet and IP as a backbone technology for connecting most factory equipment and assembly line systems.

'We've been trying to get rid of separate control networks for everything,' Bandyopadhyay says. 'Everything now is connected to an ethernet backbone.'

Now the automaker is looking toward 802.11 technology in factories to support technicians using wireless PCs and PDAs on the shop floor. GM is also deploying sensor networks, which use tiny nodes that can monitor a process or device and send data to a computer via a wireless mesh — in which each sensor point is also a mini switch that can send data to and receive it from any point on the plant floor. Deploying sensors on machinery could help GM technicians get more data on why a machine broke down and to repair equipment faster. Tying these sensor networks to back-end systems also could help predict when a machine is likely to fail.

'We spend over $1 billion a year in maintenance on our factories,' Bandyopadhyay says. 'If we have real-time systems that can track mean time to failure on a piece of equipment, that can help us.'

GM is also using a mix of wired ethernet, 802.11 access points and RFID to track parts in some plants — all the way from suppliers to each stage of manufacturing. This gives the company a more exact picture of how far along a car is in the production cycle.

For GM, the ultimate business driver for integrating real-time data from plants, logistics and other areas of the supply chain is a bit more radical. Bandyopadhyay says he wants GM's networks to be integrated to the point where communications with dealerships, logistics and manufacturing can turn the traditional model of manufacturing on its head; instead of making cars based on forecasts of what buyers want, GM will make cars based on what auto consumers want now. But this is still a way off.

'Getting information on what people want out of the dealerships and making changes to the manufacturing process on the fly is still a work in progress,' Bandyopadhyay says. 'When you connect all of this together, that's where the big payoff is.'

Other manufacturing IT pros question how far a plant should go in putting critical processes on the same network, or cutting the cord and going wireless.

The efficiencies of a single IP network and wireless are attractive, says Scott Buettner, project manager of information services for Honda of America Manufacturing, in Anna, Ohio. But there are concerns, such as a failure of an IP switch or router causing stoppages on an assembly line.

And with wireless, things might get even scarier.

'If an application is mission critical and relies on a wireless connection that is susceptible to interference, then that is a safety issue,' he says. In a scenario where a piece of heavy equipment is being operated via a wireless control, 'maybe a 1,000-pound die is being moved by a crane ... then someone comes along, working on a spreadsheet on their wireless laptop, and the signals interfere with each other. Best-case scenario, the person with the laptop loses their work ... worst case, maybe the [crane controls] fail and the die falls on that person's head.'

The collection of real-time data — whether through wired or wireless network infrastructure — poses another dilemma for manufacturers; the sheer amount of data collected from factories, warehouses, suppliers and distribution facilities can become unwieldy and difficult to parse.

'You've got massive amounts of data coming into management these days,' says Gary Matula, CIO at Molex, a manufacturer of electrical plugs, cabling and electronics components. Beyond the challenges of collecting factory data are the issues of making sense of it and putting the information to use.

'We're pushing them to make more decisions based on data,' Matula says. 'But when you deal with people who have been in the industry a long time, they think they have all the experience in the world.'

Even smaller companies are becoming more efficient with integrating back-end IT systems with plant floor operations. Weil-McLain, a maker of home heating systems, recently moved its plant from Michigan City, Indiana, to Eden, North Carolina. The company moved from a plant with older, inflexible production lines to a modernized factory. At the same time, it rolled out software from J. D. Edwards (now owned by Oracle) to revamp its back-end processes.

'We're basically moving from the dark ages of technology on the plant floor and spreadsheets to manage everything, to demand-flow manufacturing,' says Tony Bauschka, director of IT.

Instead of building boilers based on forecasts computed in spreadsheets, the software ties the company's sales order system into the factory production schedule; the only boilers that are built are ones that have been sold already. The software also streamlines how bills of materials and assembly instructions are passed from the design applications to the plant floor. For example, Weil-McLain has gone from text-based work instructions to visual-based assembly guides for workers. All of these improvements have allowed the company to reduce lead times from three weeks to eight days, Bauschka says.

Source: Hochmuth 2005.

Questions

1. Identify the efficiencies brought about within the manufacturing and operational environments of the companies discussed in this case study by the adoption of new technology.
2. Discuss the accompanying areas of IT risk that will need to be managed and mitigated alongside the implementation of the new technology.
3. Consider the privacy and other ethical implications of the implementation of the new technology under discussion.

References

Cybenko, G, Giani, A & Thompson, P 2002, 'Cognitive hacking: A battle of the mind', *Computer*, August, vol. 35, no. 8, pp. 50–6.

Hall, ET 1989, *Beyond Culture*, Arrow Books, Garden City, NY.

Hochmuth, P 2005, 'Risks rise as factory nets go wireless', *NetworkWorld Fusion*, 14 March, accessed 29 April 2005, www.nwfusion.com/news/2005/031405-factory-networks.html.

Mundie, C, de Vries, P, Haynes, P & Corwine, M 2002, 'Trustworthy computing', Microsoft White Paper, Microsoft Corporation, accessed 29 April 2005, www.microsoft.com/mscorp/twc/twc_whitepaper.mspx.

Glossary

802.11 The first international wireless LAN standard. *253*

access control A control that limits the user to accessing and using only those IT resources necessary to performing their tasks. *47*

access control matrix A matrix that defines a set of subjects (S) or requesting e ntities (e.g. users), a set of objects (O) or requested entities (e.g. data, programs or devices), and a set of access types (T) (e.g. read, write, append, execute) that are used to control access. *49*

access list A list of source and destination addresses that are and are not accepted by the firewall. *165*

accountability model A security model aimed at the prevention of fraud and losses by employing the principle of separation of duties and clear documentation of all the activities associated with a transaction. *54*

algorithm A mathematical formula or set of functions. *131*

anomaly-based IDS An intrusion detection system that contains a database of 'normal' patterns of network behaviour and looks for behaviour or activity that does not match this collection of signatures. *168*

application gateway A type of firewall gateway that uses specially written code for each specific application to examine and interpret the data within the packet, not just the packet header, as in the case of a circuit-level gateway. *166*

asymmetric encryption Encryption based on the use of two different keys; one key is used for encryption and another for decryption. *143*

audit trail A record of activity that enables the identification of specific patterns and behaviour and the origin of a problem, be it internal or external. *23*

Australian Computer Society (ACS) The professional body for IT professionals in Australia. *69*

authentication A process that guarantees correctness and verification of information, such as verifying the identity of stakeholders in a transaction. *48, 228*

authorisation Unequivocal consent. *227*

availability The characteristic that information assets or a service and the components that make it up can be accessed and used when needed. *28, 229*

awareness Part of the IS security principles in which every enterprise, large or small, is aware of the need for security within their own organisation and the measures they need to take to ensure the security of their organisation's information systems. *83*

back door An alternative entry point in a system that can be used by a hacker in future. *192*

Bell–La Padula model A security model that classifies subjects and data into precise sets according to confidentiality levels (e.g. secret and top secret). *52*

Biba model A security model that classifies data into levels of integrity. *52*

bind Initiation of a web service at runtime using the service description's details to locate, contact and invoke the service. *285*

biometrics The science of analysing the measurable biological characteristics of an individual so as to establish their identity. *244*

block cipher A cipher that processes bits in blocks of predetermined size. *133*

Bluetooth A wireless technology standard for low-cost, short-range, radio links between mobile PCs, mobile phones and other portable devices. *269*

boot sector virus Virus found in the boot sector of hard disks. *113*

brute force attack An attack in which an exhaustive search for the secret key is made using every known key combination. *133*

business continuity management (BCM) An approach that identifies risks with the potential to interrupt normal business operations, implements preventive controls to prevent such risks eventuating, and develops corrective controls to cope should the preventive controls fail and the risk eventuate. *4*

business continuity plan A clearly defined and documented strategy and set of processes, designed to ensure the recovery of key business processes when an event threatens business continuity. *5*

centralised security An approach to security in which an administrator provides access to information, software applications and the network. *7*

certificate The part of a PKI that contains the public key linked to the personal ID of the certificate holder. The signed combination of personal data and public key becomes the certificate. *149*

certificate authority A trusted third party that issues and manages certificates. *150*

cipher text *see* code

cipher text-only attack An attack in which a cryptanalyst is able to identify a portion of ciphertext but has no access to the associated plaintext. *132*

circuit-level gateways A type of firewall gateway that examines and interprets the data within a packet header. *165*

civil law Legal matters between individuals or organisations. *72*

code, cipher text, encoded text Secret text produced by encoding plaintext. *131*

code of ethics A set of rules to govern the behaviour of professionals, detailing expectations of morality and conduct, and an ethical rationale behind professional decision-making. *69*

common law Judge-made law derived from court judgements handed down throughout the history of the legal system. *71*

compromise The point at which a user account becomes insecure. *191*

computer forensics The search and analysis of stand-alone computers or single hard disk drives to determine what the machine has been used for and what the machine has done. *115*

confidentiality A characteristic of information such that it is available only to those authorised to view and use it. *28, 228*

copyright Law that entitles the creator of intellectual property to exclusive use of it and so provides a legal protection against such copying. *79, 245*

corporate governance The responsibility to ensure that the decisions made in an organisation align with its vision, values and strategy. *6*

corporate security policy A set of rules, regulations and practices that comprise the ways in which the IT assets, including data, of the organisation are to be protected. *84*

criminal law Law that applies to those actions that the state considers significant enough to warrant taking action against. *72*

cryptanalysis The deciphering of hidden messages or codes. *131*

cryptography A process by which plaintext is coded into ciphered text, then changed back or deciphered. *130, 230*

cryptology The study of both writing and deciphering hidden messages or codes. *130*

cryptosystem A combination of algorithm, keys and cryptographic standards and protocols that enable encryption and decryption in a particular context. *131, 230*

cyber terrorism Terrorist activity that uses or targets a computer or other electronic device. *103*

data flow model *see* multilevel model

data in motion encryption Encryption carried out on data in motion. *317*

data at rest encryption Encryption carried out on data residing in corporate databases. *318*

decipher, decode, decrypt The process of turning code into plaintext so that it is readable in the language in which it was written. *131*

decode *see* decipher

decrypt *see* decipher

defence in depth A security strategy that provides overlapping layers of control. *161*

Demilitarised Zone An intermediate network placed between the protected internal network and any untrusted part of the network, such as the Internet. The DMZ allows external sources to access permitted information, such as company web pages, while not having access to its internal network. *161*

democracy Negotiation, where there is any dissension or disagreement, in a consultative fashion. *83*

denial of service (DOS) attack The sending of so many requests for service to a given server that it becomes overloaded and thus unavailable. *114*

digital certificate A certificate that includes the name, serial number, expiration dates, a copy of the certificate holder's public key, and digital signature of the authority, which is used to establish the authentication of the message and identification of the parties involved in a transaction. *231*

digital signature An encrypted hash together with the hashing algorithm and other information used for non-repudiation, such that the origin and destination of the message can be authenticated and substantiated. *146, 232*

direct attack When an attacker directly tries to find the information from a database by using a specific query to directly obtain sensitive data and information from the database. *205*

direct observation The interception of data by simply looking at it at the source. *45*

discretionary access control A control that limits access to information and information systems by restricting a user's access to an information source, such as a file, server or workstation. *48*

distributed denial of service (DDoS) attack The use of many different computers simultaneously to launch a denial of service attack. *114*

distributed security An approach to security in which team leaders or supervisors grant access to information, software applications and the network. *7*

e-business A broad range of electronic activities that facilitate and support business transactions. *216*

e-commerce Electronic financial exchanges of value. *216*

electromagnetic interception The interception of data by accessing and reading data using a radio receiver to intercept electromagnetic energy radiated by the computer. *45*

electronic crime; e-crime Offences that use or target a computer or other electronic device. *103*

electronic currency Payment that transmits a digital product that represents the value. It does not transmit payment information. *227*

electronic funds transfer The exchange of money using credit card numbers or electronic cheques on secured private networks between banks and sellers. *225*

electronic payment system The process and components that make up the electronic exchange of money in return for goods or services. *221*

elliptical curve cryptography (ECC) A public key encryption technique that generates keys through the properties of the elliptic curve equation, creating faster, smaller and more efficient cryptographic keys than the traditional method of generation — the product of very large prime numbers. *144*

encipher, encode, encrypt The process of disguising plaintext so that it cannot be understood without a secret key. *131*

encode *see* encipher

encoded text *see* code

encrypt *see* encipher

ethics Impartially defined principles and values that pertain to an individual or group in society. *68*

evaluation criteria A set of predetermined features that can be used as metrics to determine system security. *84*

Extensible Markup Language (XML) A standard language that allows the context and function of data to be specified. *283*

external firewall A security mechanism that determines which internal services can be accessed from outside. *161*

fabrication The creation or manipulation of information and information resources so that the information appears correct but is not. *46*

find The process of retrieving a description of a web service from a service registry. *285*

forensic computing The process of identifying, preserving, analysing and presenting digital evidence in a legally acceptable manner. *114*

forensic readiness Preparing in such a way as to maximise the potential to use digital evidence and minimise the cost of a forensic investigation. *121*

fraud Criminal deception. *111*

guidelines Publications designed to help organisations implement sound practices. *82*

hacker Any person with the desire and technical knowledge needed to attempt to gain unauthorised access to a computer system. *188*

hardware interruptions Interruptions that occur because of a hardware-related issue, such as damage from natural disasters, advertent or inadvertent misuse of equipment, crashed servers, unwarranted additions to computer equipment, and theft. *47*

hash algorithm A mathematical expression containing one or more hash functions. *145*

hash function A mathematical function that is easy to calculate but difficult to reverse engineer so as obtain the inverse. *145*

hash value The result of applying a hash function. *145*

hashing A technique to provide assurance that a message has not been altered or modified in transmission; it determines whether the number of bits of text received are the same in length and nature as those transmitted. *145*

header An area of a packet that contains information about the packet. *164*

identification The process of establishing the identity of users and other entities involved in the operation and maintenance of IT systems. *48*

identifier A number by which an individual supplying information may be identified. It is used for indexing the data. *78*

identity crime Offence in which a perpetrator uses a false identity, or a real identity other than their own, in order to commit a crime. *113*

identity fraud The use of a false identity to gain illegal benefit. *113*

identity theft The use of another's identity to commit a crime. *113*

indirect or inference attack The use of statistical measures to seek information from a database to infer the desired secured information or data. *205*

information warfare (IW) War-like activities that use or target information or information assets. *103*

integrity A characteristic of information such that the information and any changes to it are accurate and complete. *28, 227*

intellectual property Literary, artistic and scientific works, performances, inventions, scientific discoveries, industrial designs, trade marks and protection against unfair competition and all other rights resulting from intellectual activity in the scientific, literary and artistic fields. *79*

interception An attack on the confidentiality of information and associated resources. *44*

internal firewall A security mechanism that protects the internal network from the Demilitarised Zone. *162*

internal network That part of the network that should not be accessible by outsiders. *161*

International Information Systems Security Certification Consortium (ISC)[2] A non-profit organisation that oversees professional IT security certifications. *69*

international law The body of international treaties or conventions that some countries have agreed to observe. *72*

Internet forensics *see* network forensics   *232*

Internet Open Trading Protocol (IOTP) An open standard being developed as a standardised payment framework.   *232*

interruption A stoppage in the flow of information, or IT services that realise the flow of such information.   *46*

intrusion detection system (IDS) A security mechanism that alerts the administrator should an intruder breach the firewall.   *161*

intrusion detection system sensors Intrusion detection system components that are placed at various points on the network and act to monitor only the most sensitive areas of the network.   *161*

IP address A network address for each device on a network, which enables them to be located on the network.   *164*

irreversible modification A change made to the information or data that cannot be undone.   *46*

IT governance The responsibility of IT managers to deliver value to business through IT and mitigate the IT risks that might be faced.   *6*

IT security risk The chance that an IT asset could be adversely affected by some event.   *7*

key *see* secret key

key clustering A fault in an algorithm that results in two different values of a key producing the same cipher text from the plaintext.   *132*

key logger Code or hardware that records all keystrokes, allowing an attacker to retrieve this data remotely, then hack into the system with the employee's credentials in their own time.   *191*

key space A range of numbers from which an algorithm can choose the key in any given act of encoding a message.   *132*

lattice model A security model that works on the need-to-know basis; the information is classified into certain levels of security and the user must have security clearance in the form of a codeword to access information. In this model, a lattice is formed of the flow and relationship of information.   *54*

law Expresses particular behaviour that is deemed acceptable to a given society or culture and then seeks to enforce this behaviour.   *68*

local area network A network that exists in just one location.   *163*

logical security Security measures that protect the confidentiality, integrity and availability of the information.   *41*

MAC address An exclusive and specific hardware address of a device on a network.   *164*

macro viruses Viruses visible within Microsoft Office macros.   *113*

mandatory access control A control that imposes universal security conditions that apply to all the users, information systems and information resources.   *49*

message digest A technique used to maintain the integrity of a message by comparison of message digests created using a hash function and secret key at both the receiver's and sender's ends.   *231*

message integrity The property of completeness or wholeness of transmitted data.   *145*

misuse-based IDS An intrusion detection system that contains a database of suspicious or malicious patterns, which it matches to current network behaviour. *168*

mobile commerce, m-commerce A means of transacting business using mobile phones. *235*

modification Changing the nature of data. *46*

multi-homed host A firewall that prevents hosts inside and outside it communicating directly with each other. Packets can go from one network to another only after being inspected, authenticated, authorised and proxied. *168*

multilevel model (data flow model) A security model in which information is categorised by sensitivity and users are provided with access on the basis of their level of responsibility. *51*

Network Address Translation A method that determines the route of a packet which was created outside the company network. *165*

network architecture The design of IT networks. *163*

network forensics (Internet forensics) The analysis of network traffic to examine an entire sequence of events or intrusion on a network. *115*

network interception The interception of data by accessing and reading data as it moves through the data transmission channel. *45*

network layer The first layer of web services architecture that makes the web service accessible via a network. *287*

non-repudiation The process by which the identity of the sender is known

to the receiver and the sender is acknowledged on the delivery of information at receiver end. *229*

one-time pad A non-mathematical means of producing cipher text. *133*

operating procedures Detailed security arrangements, staff responsibilities and staff duties. *85*

organised crime Criminal activities by well-organised, large and networked organisations. *103*

packet The smaller pieces into which data is broken for broadcast over a network. *164*

padding The use of blank characters in a coded message to hide the real length of the message. *134*

payment clearing service A trusted third party to provide for security, identification and authentication, and payment support. *223*

personnel security policy A set of rules, regulations and practices to ensure that staff operate IT equipment in such a way as to ensure the safety and security of data. *84*

phishing Seeking personal, confidential information through social engineering and technical means. *112*

physical security Security measures that protect IT assets from physical damage, such as fire or flood. *41*

piconet A spontaneous network between Bluetooth devices. *269*

plaintext A simple message readable in normal language. *131*

plaintext attack An attack in which the cryptanalyst is able to access some plaintext and the parallel encoded ciphertext. *132*

polyalphabetic cipher A cipher that uses two or more simple alphabetical substitutions. *134*

probing Trying to find simple system weaknesses or information about a system that can then be used to gain access to the system. *191*

product cipher A strong cipher formed by combining two other kinds of cipher. *135*

protocol An established technical format for exchanging or transmitting data between systems, enabling computers and other devices to communicate. *164*

proxy servers Code that represents both clients and servers. *166*

Public Key Infrastructure (PKI) A complete cryptographic framework of software, hardware, algorithms, standards and protocols to protect an organisation's data and electronic transactions. *149*

publish The process of making a web service available to the service requestor and service registry. *285*

quantum encryption Encryption based on the laws of quantum physics to improve modern cryptographic techniques. *319*

Radio Frequency Identification (RFID) Systems comprising transponders (tags), readers and application systems for processing of the acquired data. *313*

reassessment Regular reassessment of security management of an organisation as its systems change or grow. *83*

recovery The process whereby the business restores its processes and operations. *22*

response Action taken if a computer or network is breached. *83*

responsibility Knowledge that users are personally accountable for system security. *83*

reversible modification A change made to the information or data that can be undone. *46*

risk assessment Regular assessment of systems to ascertain whether there are new security risks to be understood and dealt with. *83*

risk management A continuous process designed to assess the likelihood that an adverse event will occur, implement measures to reduce the risk that such an event will occur, and ensure that the organisation can respond in such a way as to minimise the consequences of the event. *2*

risk management framework A framework to structure the risk management process. *87*

role-based access control A control that allows or restricts access to information systems and resources on the basis of the individual's role in the organisation. *49*

root Control targeted by hackers that gives the privileges of administrator and allows them to control all of the system resources of an organisation. *191*

router A device that provides the mechanism by which routing is carried out. *164*

routing The route by which packets are transported from one network location to another. *164*

running key ciphers A non-mathematical means of producing cipher text. *133*

scanning An automated probing process. *191*

secret key, key A number that depends on an algorithm that allows a code to be broken. *131*

Secure Electronic Transaction (SET)
A protocol that ensures security of financial transactions in cyberspace. It works on the principle that the customer is allocated a digital certificate, and the transaction is executed and authenticated by using a combination of digital certificates and digital signatures between the buyer, seller and the buyer's bank. *225*

security design and implementation
Security controls and processes embedded during the initial system design and implementation stage to aid in the process of risk management. *83*

security level A security model that applies different levels of security to groups of people and data objects rather than controlling access at the individual subject or object level. *51*

security management The act of managing the security of data and systems within an organisation. *83*

security policy The people who are authorised to use the system; the policies defining what can be done to what and when; the procedures outlining how tasks are done; and the technology (products and services) available. *201*

segmentation The separation of departmental networks to prevent staff having access to information assets beyond those required for their work role. *162*

service description A description of a web service and how to access it; based on WSDL (Web Services Description Language). *288*

service provider The component of the web services model that hosts a software module on a network. *285*

service registry A searchable repository of service descriptions published by service providers. *285*

service requestor The component of the web services model that seeks a software module on a network. *285*

signature database A collection of patterns and definitions of known suspicious or malicious activity that enables the intrusion detection system to identify new instances of such activity. *161*

Simple Object Access Protocol (SOAP)
The standard for web services messages; based on XML. *288*

smart card A plastic card on which a microprocessor is embedded. *241*

sniffer Code that enables a hacker to gather information being sent via network cabling to external cables. *189*

software interruptions Interruptions that occur because of a software-related problem, such as modification and fabrication of data, bugs in application software, illegal copies of software, programming code alteration, Trojans, viruses, and the destruction of original and back-up data. *46*

software piracy The copying of software, usually by a licence holder, for distribution and resale to others who do not hold licences to the product. *81*

spam Unsolicited email. *75*

spiral model A software development process in which software is engineered in steps that execute in a spiral fashion, repeating at different levels with each revolution of the model. *208*

staff interruption An interruption caused by the actions of employees. *47*

standards Publications by international and national standards organisations that establish practices for organisations. *82*

statute law Legislation enacted by parliaments. *71*

steganography A non-mathematical means of producing cipher text. *133*

stream cipher A cipher that encrypts data one bit at a time. *133*

subsidiary security policies A set of rules, regulations and practices for each specific major system or network within the company. *84*

substitution cipher A cipher in which one character is replaced in a logical manner with another. *133*

symmetric encryption Encryption that relies on the receiver of an encrypted message having the same secret key as used by the sender. *139*

TCP/IP A reliable Internet protocol requiring a three-way connection (known as the three-way handshake) to initiate and sustain a connection. *164*

technical security policy A set of rules, regulations and practices that specifies hardware and software security matters in detail. *84*

trade mark A word, sentence or symbol that relates to particular products and which a business has registered in order to assert its right to exclusive use of the mark. *245*

transposition cipher A cipher in which the characters in the message are forced into swapping places by writing the lines in the message over a specified number of columns, then writing each column of letters as a row. *133*

Trojan A type of malicious code that appears to have one function but actually has another. *114*

trustworthy computing An environment in which computer systems, software and information resources are insulated from unintentional and intentional unauthorised access, manipulation and destruction. *309*

two-factor authentication Authentication that uses two different types of identification. *257*

UDP An alternative Internet protocol that is less reliable than TCP/IP. *164*

Universal Description, Discovery and Integration (UDDI) protocol A protocol that describes the business context or the process context of data structures in the WSDL document. *288*

Virtual Private Network (VPN) A network that operates on the public telecommunication infrastructure, using a tunnelling protocol and security procedures to maintain its privacy. *169*

virus A type of malicious code that attempts to infect other programs by attaching a copy of itself to them. *113*

waterfall software engineering process model A multistep software development process in which steps follow each other in a linear, one-way fashion. *208*

web service A software component built on an open standard and that is accessible via a network. *283*

Web Services Description Language (WSDL) An XML-based standardised format for describing a web service. *288*

Web Services Flow Language (WSFL) A document that describes the composition of the web service and its flow. *289*

wide area network (WAN)
A large, dispersed network. *163*

Wired Equivalent Privacy (WEP)
Encryption of data at the link layer between the access point and the wireless client in a bid to protect against casual eavesdropping and to provide functionality equivalent to that provided by the physical nature of a wired network. *257*

wireless access point A transmitting base station that sends data digitally across a wireless network. *252*

wireless area network Data is broadcast through the air rather than along wires and cables. Anyone within range can receive the transmission. *251*

worms A type of malicious code that can multiply and spread without becoming attached to a piece of existing code. *114*

XML-based messaging The use of XML (eXtensible Markup Language) as the basis for the messaging protocol and as the data-tagging language of web services. *288*

Index